'This is a courageous book that outlines a vision for an international order that welcomes diversity but responds much more firmly to the abuse of fundamental rights'
Gita Sen, Professor of Economics and Social Sciences, Indian Institute of Management and Founding Member, DAWN

'*Future Positive* grapples with a central dilemma of our times: the growing mismatch between a globalising economy and national political decisions, arguing persuasively for new forms of global governance that are as flexible and decentralised as the new economy itself. This book's emphasis on NGO transparency and accountability will be especially valuable'
Will Marshall, President, Progressive Policy Institute

'At a time when aid fatigue threatens global co-operation and debates on the global order have become increasingly acrimonious, this well-informed and compassionate book states the case for human solidarity with unusual lucidity and grounded optimism'
Thandika Mkandawire, Executive Director, United Nations Research Institute for Social Development

'Mike Edwards' vision of the importance of co-operation and its enormous potential is powerful and persuasive. It is particularly refreshing to read a book which sets out how such changes might be achieved, and which is fundamentally optimistic that they can be'
David Bryer, Director, Oxfam

'*Future Positive* is an optimistic vision of how to get to a future where people co-operate universally to end injustice, poverty and conflict. Michael Edwards has a passion for finding practical ways to make the world a better place. He deserves to be widely read'
Tim Garden, *Times Higher Education Supplement*

'Michael Edwards' refreshingly optimistic and readable book calls for widespread reform of an international system which interferes too much in the detail of other people's lives and not enough when it really matters. His approach is wholehearted and convincing. Edwards combines his breadth of vision with a realistic focus on building constituencies for change'
Natasha Franklin, *Foreign Policy Review*

D1241972

'What a joy! Each chapter is interesting, observant and sometimes violent in its opinions. I urge you to read this book because you will need to take a position yourself, whether you are donor or recipient, from the rich or poor world'
Michael Brophy, *Alliance Magazine*

'This comprehensive and profound work presents a new perspective on how to deal with the emerging problems and challenges for the global community. Michael Edwards' optimistic vision for the future gives inspiration as well as alternative means of resolving humanitarian crises, inequality, poverty and violence'
Connections Magazine

'This book belongs to a small minority of analyses of world politics that are inspired yet modest, deep yet readable. Edwards' rich combinations of personal resources generates powerful insights and compelling prescriptions. However, Edwards does not preach down; he shares his ideas in ways that leave the reader feeling enabled and enthusiastic'
Jan Art Scholte, *International Journal of Urban and Regional Research*

'In addition to making the links between theory and practice, self-interest and social conscience, this book offers concrete proposals for change in a globalising world and contributes to the much-needed repoliticisation of the discipline of development studies'
Helen Yanacopulos, *Millennium*

Future Positive
International Co-operation in the 21st Century

by

Michael Edwards

Earthscan Publications Ltd, London

For my parents, David and Millicent Edwards,
who did so much to help me escape

First published in the UK in 1999 by
Earthscan Publications Ltd

Reprinted 2000

A catalogue record for this book is available from the British Library

ISBN: 1 85383 631 1 hardback
       1 85383 740 7 paperback

Typesetting by PCS Mapping and DTP, Newcastle upon Tyne
Printed and bound by Creative Print and Design (Wales), Ebbw Vale
Cover design by Andrew Corbett

For a full list of publications please contact:
Earthscan Publications Ltd
120 Pentonville Road
London, N1 9JN, UK
Tel: +44 (020) 7278 0433
Fax: +44 (020) 7278 1142
Email: earthinfo@earthscan.co.uk
http://www.earthscan.co.uk

Earthscan is an editorially independent subsidiary of Kogan Page Ltd and
publishes in association with WWF-UK and the International Institute for
Environment and Development.

This book is printed on elemental chlorine-free paper

Contents

List of Figures and Tables

FIGURES

TABLES

Preface

In 1978 I left London to work in the slums of Latin America. In the 18 years that followed, I worked for Oxfam, Save the Children and other organisations across three continents, yet still I was perplexed by the question that had set me off on my original journey: how can we help each other to lead more fulfilling lives, both on the small scale of family and community and the grand scale of international relations? My experience left me disillusioned with a system that interferes too much in the detail of other people's lives and not enough when it really matters – like the recent genocide in Rwanda. Is this really the best we can do? After two years of intensive research, my conclusion is clear: a world that manages its affairs to mutual benefit is well within our reach, and this book attempts to shows how we can get there. The story that unfolds in these pages touches all our lives, since in an increasingly interdependent world no one has a future unless we learn to work together. However, there is nothing in the bookshops that deals with these issues in an accessible way, without jargon and without lapsing into simplistic judgements.

Future Positive aims to fill this gap. Can we abolish global poverty? Should we do away with foreign aid? Is the United Nations redundant? Why should I bother, and how can I help? If you have ever wondered aloud about these questions, then I hope this is the book for you.

These are big subjects, and the sheer diversity of contexts and cultures makes generalisation hazardous, especially when there is so much experience and scholarly work to draw on. The basic message of this book is simple: we must chart a new path at the global level between heavy-handed intervention and complete laissez-faire that gives people the opportunity to solve their problems without imposing unfair costs on anyone else. This path must be defined democratically, so that everyone has a say in the solutions and a stake in the outcomes – otherwise it will not work. And that requires action in three further areas: the first is the need to equip everyone with enough voice and security to participate in shaping alternatives; the second is the need to regulate – and ultimately transform – all exclusionary systems of power; and the third is the need for solutions that are not dependent on action by recalcitrant governments. The result is a radically different framework for international co-operation that breaks free from the failures of the past. Readers who want a quick summary of what this means in practice should turn to Chapter 12.

Globalisation is often seen as a threat, but this book sees the changing world context as an opportunity to do things differently. The Introduction (Chapter 1) shows why global trends make international co-operation both more necessary and more possible. The next five chapters look back in time to assess the record of international co-operation to date. Chapter 2 provides an overview of foreign aid and global institutions, and traces the ideas that formed them back to their historical roots. Chapters 3,4 and 5 re-evaluate progress at the national level, the local level, and in humanitarian emergencies. In each case, success comes not from universal solutions, but from people's capacity to solve their problems and the freedom to use it creatively, against certain boundaries they set for themselves. This is not a surprising conclusion: our experience as parents tells us that we must give our children space to develop in their own ways, so long as their lives are not endangered and they do not endanger the lives of others. We give them both freedom and support knowing that they – and we as members of the same family – will benefit from a community of responsible and independent individuals. *'There is no need to think alike,'* says the historian Theodore Zeldin, *'if friendship is seen as an exploration rather than a search for security'.*[1] This is just as true at the global level, but its implications are revolutionary: an international system that welcomes diversity but responds much more firmly to the abuse of fundamental rights.

The second part of the book shows how this system can work. Chapter 7 explores the role of foreign aid in nurturing national creativity and 'room to manoeuvre'. This is especially important in tackling the costs and inequalities of the global market economy, a challenge that Chapter 8 calls 'humanising capitalism'. There are many ways that this could be done, but they all require co-operation to prevent one country's sacrifices being exploited by others – an international system in which all countries can be stakeholders and whose rules are seen as fair. Chapter 9 explores what it might look like, but who would support such radical changes in politics, professional life and the general public? As Chapters 10 and 11 explain, building constituencies for international co-operation is the hardest task of all, but it is possible through strategies that combine moral force with legitimate self-interest. It is this challenge – finding ways to balance the competitive and co-operative forces that motivate each one of us – that provides the key to *Future Positive*.

Acknowledgements

Most of the research for this book was carried out at Manchester University, to whom I am grateful for a Simon Industrial and Professional Fellowship during the academic year 1996/97. Manchester's Institute for Development Policy and Management provided a happy and challenging environment in which to work. I am also indebted to the Leverhulme Trust in London for a Personal Research Fellowship in 1995/96, and to the Save the Children Fund-UK for granting me a sabbatical. Many people have offered help and encouragement along the way: my agent David Grossman, who took me on out of the blue and stayed with the manuscript from start to finish; my colleagues at Oxfam and Save the Children; the staff of aid agencies around the world who took part in interviews and suggested ideas; Gu Dehong and T Miyoshi, my research assistants at Manchester; and the following individuals: Louk Box, Peter Burnell, Lincoln Chen, Alan Fowler, Ann Grant, David Hulme, Kamal Malhotra, Robert Molteno, Sally Morphet, Peter Nyoni, Gita Sen, Ian Smillie, Frances Stewart and John Toye. Four other people deserve special mention: my spiritual teacher Gurumayi Chidvilasananda, for opening my heart and focusing my mind; my wife Cora, constant companion and gentle critic, who lived and breathed the book as I did; and my parents David and Millicent Edwards, to whom the book is dedicated. None of them bear any responsibility for what has ended up here, but all of them had a hand in making it possible.

Michael Edwards
London, August 1998

Acronyms and Abbreviations

ACP	African, Caribbean and Pacific Countries
ACFOA	Australian Council for Overseas Aid
ANC	African National Congress
APEC	Asia Pacific Economic Council
ASEAN	Association of South East Asian Nations
BBC	British Broadcasting Corporation
BRAC	Bangladesh Rural Advancement Committee
CAP	Common Agricultural Policy
CCIC	Canadian Council for International Co-operation
CFVS	Commission on the Future of the Voluntary Sector
CIIR	Catholic Institute for International Relations
CNN	Cable News Network
DAC	Development Assistance Committee (of the OECD)
DANIDA	Danish International Development Agency
DFID	Department for International Development (UK)
ECA	Economic Commission for Africa
ECDPM	European Centre for Development Policy and Management
ECOMOG	Economic Community (of West African States) Monitoring Group
EU	European Union
FAO	The Food and Agriculture Organisation (UN)
FFHC	Freedom from Hunger Campaign
GATT	General Agreement on Tariffs and Trade
GDP	Gross Domestic Product
GNP	Gross National Product
HIV	Human immunodeficiency virus
ICG	International Crisis Group
ICRC	International Committee of the Red Cross
IDA	International Development Association
IDPM	Institute for Development Policy and Management (Manchester)

IDS	Institute of Development Studies (Sussex)
ILEIA	International Livestock Extension Association
IMF	International Monetary Fund
INTRAC	International NGO Research and Training Centre (Oxford)
IRDP	Integrated Rural Development Programme
ITDG	Intermediate Technology Development Group
MAI	Multilateral Agreement on Investment
MBA	Master of Business Administration
MERCOSUR	Southern Cone Common Market (Latin America)
MONDEP	Moneragala Rural Development Project
MPLA	Popular Movement for the Liberation of Angola
NAFTA	North American Free Trade Association
NATO	North Atlantic Treaty Organisation
NEF	New Economics Foundation
NGO	Non-governmental organisation
NORAD	Norwegian Agency for International Development
OAU	Organisation of African Unity
OECD	Organisation for Economic Co-operation and Development
OPEC	Organisation of Petroleum Exporting Countries
PLA	Participatory learning and action (or sometimes PRA)
PREM	People's Rural Education Movement
SAARC	South Asian Agricultural Research Consortium
SAPES	Southern Africa Political and Economic Studies
SCF	Save the Children Fund
SEWA	Self-Employed Women's Association (in India)
SLORC	State Law and Order Committee (Burma)
UNCTAD	United Nations Conference on Trade and Development
UNDP	United Nations Development Programme
UNHCR	United Nations High Commissioner for Refugees
UNICEF	United Nations Children's Fund
UNIDO	United Nations Industrial Development Organisation
UNITA	Union for the Total Independence of Angola
UNITAR	United Nations Training and Research Institute (Singapore)
UNPROFOR	United Nations Protection Force
UNRISD	United Nations Research Institute for Social Development
USAID	United States Agency for International Development
WTO	World Trade Organisation

Chapter 1

Introduction: the Co-operative Imperative

'I have seen a man on the bank of a river buried up to his knees in mud, and some men came to give him a hand and help him out, but they pushed him further in up to his neck'

Abba Paphnutius, Hermit of Egypt,
Fourth Century AD

'The golden rule is to help those we love to escape from us, and never to try to begin to help people, or influence them, till they ask'

Friedrich von Hugel, *Letters to my Niece*, 1852

Money, power and sex. The history of the world can be told in three words, yet a fourth word – co-operation – has an important history of its own. People's desire to help each other and work together for the common good is a characteristic of human beings, though so, of course, is competition for supremacy. According to science writer Matt Ridley, co-operation is literally *'in our nature'*, carried along through evolution by selfish genes but making us – for our own long-term welfare – social and trustworthy creatures.[1] In reality, our co-operative instincts are always muddled, because helping others raises questions of personal identity and motivation. Deep down, we know von Hugel is correct, but few of us can resist the temptation to interfere. After all, we know best. In a broader sense, helping raises complex questions about policy and tactics that are inextricably entangled with institutional self-interests. Hidden agendas, inappropriate interventions and imposed ideas are commonplace. '*Good advice is rarer than rubies,'* says Salman Rushdie.[2] This is especially true for the subject of this book: international co-operation for peace and prosperity.

When world leaders gathered together in the aftermath of World War II they had many different agendas, but they also had an overarching self-confidence that co-ordinated action would be able to engineer a world without conflict or poverty. Thus began an unprecedented period of co-operation around monetary systems, aid and trade, conflict-mediation and humanitarian intervention, what Robert Heilbroner called *'the first real act of world history'*.[3] The Marshall Plan was worth over $200 billion in today's prices, almost four times the total amount of foreign aid provided by rich nations in 1996.[4] However, the new mood was soon corrupted by cold-war interests, turning 'international co-operation' into a battleground for superpower politics and commercial gain. As the cold war progressed, the ideal of co-operation in the new United Nations took second place to intervention in the affairs of others.

Fifty years on, consensus and confidence have all but evaporated. Half a century is enough for the system to have proved itself, and while there are a few well-publicised success stories, there has been no general gain in prosperity or security. We still live in a world scarred by absolute poverty (with 1.3 billion people living on less than $1 a day[5]), rising inequality both within and between countries, and continuing ethnic conflict. Foreign aid is declining almost everywhere, assailed by critics from across the ideological spectrum.[6] The end of the cold war has not revitalised international co-operation as many had hoped, and support for military intervention in conflict zones has fallen away since the debacles in Somalia and the Balkans. The United Nations and other international bureaucracies are under constant threat; and even support for non-governmental organisations (NGOs) – the darlings of the development world – seems to have peaked. The international business of helping is in serious trouble.

Doubts about the value of well-meaning outsiders are not new. Seven hundred years before the Hermit issued his warning in the desert, the Chinese sage Lao Tzu was even blunter. *'Act for the people's benefit,'* he said, *'leave them alone.'* His modern counterparts are no less critical, but much more prone to purple prose. Third World charity is the 'Road to Hell' according to Michael Maren[7] – paved with good intentions but uniformly disastrous in its effects. Robert Kaplan[8] sees only 'The Coming Anarchy', a nightmarish vision of war, disease and corruption which outsiders can do little to influence. Why waste money on foreign aid when, as US Senator Jesse Helms famously remarked, it all disappears *'down the rathole'* anyway, all $878 billion of it donated since 1950?[9] Such views are popular but sloppy. Kaplan's assessment is based on fleeting visits to a small number of global trouble spots, as though one could capture the underlying condition of the USA by reference to south-central Los Angeles and the Bronx. Maren takes a few examples of failure and turns them into a seductive orthodoxy. Helms and his allies ignore the lessons of history even in their own society, which show how important external resources can be. Perhaps these books capture our attention because their prognoses have yet to be overtaken by events.[10] They confirm what many want to hear about developing world corruption, and relieve us of the duty to keep on caring. And their tone chimes with the nervous spirit of the age – 'pre-millennium tension'.

It is true that the record has been mixed, but there is another side to this story which shows that international co-operation can work, and work well. Each of us needs help at some point in our lives, and no society has prospered by cutting itself off from the resources and ideas of others. This is especially true in an interdependent world, where individual welfare is increasingly affected by collective choices about how we use our resources and shape our environment; what rights we claim and which obligations we agree to share. In this context we co-operate because our own well-being depends on it, not just because others need our help. Poverty in the developing world has never had enough political purchase to make international co-operation a reality, but the perceived threats to the West posed by rising prosperity in some parts of the developing world and the continued instability of others will eventually create the necessary will. Helping others to grow and develop with fewer costs to themselves and more benefits for the rest of the world is crucial to the peace and prosperity we all seek. Why help people in other countries to 'escape', as Friedrich von Hugel advised his niece? Because no one wants to live in a dysfunctional family (it hurts too much), and everyone benefits from being part of a community of responsible, independent, developed individuals. That is as true at the global level as it is within a single family. However, if it is hard to 'let go' among people we love, it is much more difficult when political and commercial interests are at stake.

Co-operation implies reciprocity (not complete equality), a willingness to give as well as take, the voluntary acceptance of limits, and action on all sides rather than one. That is what marks it out from intervention, the approach which has characterised our attempts to help on the international stage over the last 200 years. Co-operation means creating opportunities for others to develop themselves, not just giving them things directly. It is a much more advanced form of helping, which accepts that the best way to support others may simply be to put our own house in order. Moving from intervention to co-operation is the key to helping more effectively.

Defining 'development' is much more difficult, and poses questions that have sparked intense controversy in recent years.[11] The problem is a long-standing tendency to see development as a linear transition from tradition to modernity, defined in universal terms. As this book makes clear, this is ignorant of history, divisive, and incapable of generating the results we say we want to see. There is no such thing as a universally accepted definition of the good life (still less how to get there), but people everywhere aspire to have more as well as to be more – to be free from poverty and violence and the servitude these bring in their wake; to be loved and enjoy a sense of belonging; to feel more in control and less vulnerable to the vagaries of unaccountable power; and to be subjects of their own destiny rather than objects of the intentions of others. It is development in this sense that forms the subject of this book: the reduction of material want and the enhancement of people's ability to live a life they consider good across the broadest range possible in a population.

As will be seen, markets, science and other aspects of modernity have played a major role, at least in bringing about the material conditions in which people have more choices about the kind of life they want to lead. These choices are central to most people's conception of the good life. We do want material prosperity, but we don't want our wider sense of fulfilment to be frustrated by economic systems dictated by profit and cost. What to do? There are many signs that, after a period during the 1980s when individualistic, competitive values held sway, opinion is turning once more to the potential of co-operation. Co-operation means different things to different people; some favour the light hand of voluntary agreements, and others a more interventionist approach involving the enforcement of rules and standards. These differences are explored later in this Introduction, but all solutions to the dilemmas of the 21st century will involve more co-operation of one sort or another, a shift from 'I' to 'we', and the balancing of economic imperatives with the demands of democracy and a wider sense of well-being.

After the victory of the British Labour Party in the General Election of 1997, incoming Foreign Secretary Robin Cook introduced an 'ethical dimension' to UK foreign policy. Clare Short, the Minister for International Development, declared that Labour's victory marked a decisive break with the selfish individualism of the 1980s, and a rebirth of public commitment to issues of international justice. The 'giving age' had arrived, said Prime Minister Tony Blair. In a poll conducted by the Henley Centre for Forecasting, 70 per cent of respondents seemed to agree, stating that society does best when people act collectively instead of looking after their own interests first.[12] Positive government, civic values, and international co-operation are back on the political agenda. Foreign ministries and aid agencies accept that old ways of doing things are increasingly outmoded, but there is little clarity on what should replace them, save a rhetorical commitment to 'co-operate more'. Turning rhetoric into reality requires a revolution in the quality of international co-operation, as well as the quantity. This book shows what that means in practice.

A NEW CONTEXT

One of the characteristics of pre-millennium tension is a sense of foreboding, captured in a growing series of books entitled *The End of...* (history, the nation state, work, capitalism, economics and so on – though fortunately not the writing or buying of books about these things). This is the literature of collapsing states,[13] clashing civilisations,[14] and corporations ruling the world,[15] not to mention the apocalyptic visions of social and environmental catastrophe unleashed on unsuspecting readers by John Gray, Tom Athanasiou and the ever-gloomy WorldWatch Institute.[16] It is true that the changing global context poses serious threats which make co-operation imperative, but the same context offers opportunities to help co-operation flourish as never before.

Globalisation and its discontents

Nowhere is this more true than globalisation, the defining theme of current times and the mantra of the moment. There are widely divergent interpretations of what globalisation actually is, never mind whether it is a 'good or a bad thing', but all of them make 'business as usual' redundant. Globalisation challenges the authority of nation states and international institutions to influence events, while the scale of private flows of capital, technology, information and ideas makes official transfers look increasingly marginal. The emergence of 'newly-industrialising countries' and new patterns of economic and social exclusion in rich nations makes traditional 'donor-recipient', 'North-South' thinking increasingly unconvincing, but the case for international co-operation in a globalising world grows ever stronger.

A first interpretation focuses on globalisation as technology-driven fact: increased flows of money, people, goods and services are crossing national frontiers at ever greater speeds. This is not new, though what is happening now is on a much larger scale than in any other period in history, made possible by the power of information technology to process millions of transactions and communicate across the world in an instant, declining transport costs, the rise of more flexible forms of organisation, and the growing importance of knowledge – that most mobile of assets – to economic success.

It is true that private capital is much more footloose nowadays. The volume of foreign exchange trading increased from $640 billion a day in 1989 to $1.2 trillion in 1994, though these flows are concentrated in the industrialised world together with a few big emerging markets in East Asia and Latin America.[17] Seventy-five per cent of countries in the world see little sign of globalisation in this sense since they receive less than ten per cent of total foreign direct investment. Although the world's 500 largest corporations control 25 per cent of global output, they employ only a tiny fraction of the planet's population.[18] Most corporations trade internationally but are based in a particular country, so they can still be regulated. International trade is growing, but not as a proportion of world output: most jobs, in the aggregate, stay local.[19] A truly global economy would have open borders, integrated infrastructure, the same domestic economic policies worldwide, and universal access to the knowledge required for entry.[20] Despite freer trade and migration, we are a long way from any of these conditions. Globalisation is still at an early stage in its history.

Underlying these facts is a more controversial process – a global homogenising of values, cultures, and aspirations; the penetration of market processes into every sphere of life; and the destruction of non-capitalist norms of reciprocity and sharing: the arrival of 'McWorld' as Barber calls it.[21] This is dismissed by others who claim that different worlds are adapting to each other, rather than fighting a battle in which all the spoils of victory go to one side. '*Christians and Muslims may worship different Gods, but they still have to wash their hair, and want the best product to do the job*'.[22] Whether one can have the benefits of globalisation as fact without the costs of globalisation as culture is a vital question which occupies much of the rest of this book. But short of disinventing the computer and the telephone, placing a ban on air travel and rebuilding the Berlin Wall along every national boundary, there is not much that can be done to reverse the underlying dynamics of this process. Technology and science establish an increasingly uniform horizon of production possibilities, integrating markets around the world and internationalising decisions about jobs and investment. Domestic actions which are out of step with the demands of international markets will be punished. A memorandum from Chase Manhattan Bank provides a graphic illustration of what this means: *'while Chiapas, in our opinion, does not pose a fundamental threat to Mexican political stability, it is perceived to be so by the investment community. The government will need to eliminate the Zapatistas'*.[23] Citizenship and national autonomy are both threatened when a sudden withdrawal of capital by international investors can destabilise a whole country (as happened in the Mexican peso crisis of late 1994 and early 1995); when tax revenue disappears as corporations shift operations to low or no-tax locations; when free-trade agreements like NAFTA and the World Trade Organisation protect corporations but abandon workers; when private capital is used for speculation instead of productive investment (one trillion dollars a day in foreign exchange trading for whose benefit?); and when the ownership of key resources becomes increasingly concentrated in the hands of unaccountable institutions. In 1992 the Agracetus Corporation applied for patents covering 60 per cent of the world cotton crop.[24] What price democracy in a globalising economy like this?

All countries must adapt to global markets, but integration rewards those with more skills and other technologies that make for international competitiveness. Since these endowments vary greatly between individuals and countries, globalisation rewards some more than others, and that increases inequality. If countries are not competitive at high levels of skill they must capture jobs by reducing labour costs, cutting environmental standards (the so-called 'race to the bottom') and promoting 'flexibility' among workers above all else. The impact of this process is dramatic – the disappearance of a 'job for life', the erosion of trade union and other forms of protection, and long working hours in poor conditions, especially for women. All these things eat away at personal security and social cohesion. Doubt permeates everyday life, and risk and uncertainty grow.[25] That is what makes us feel increasingly vulnerable to forces out of our control. Ironically, in an era when location is not supposed to matter, judgements about globalisation depend most of all on who and where you are, though less and less does this divide into solid blocs of 'rich' and 'poor' countries.

Are you struggling to survive in the 'global South' of low-paid, low-skill, insecure jobs, or growing ever richer (though with less time off work to enjoy it) in the 'global North' of knowledge-based occupations? The king of the global North is Bill Gates of Microsoft, whose net worth is greater than the poorest 40 per cent of the US population put together.[26] Although GNP per capita in the USA grew by 82 per cent between 1956 and 1986, the Index of Sustainable Economic Welfare (which measures the quality of life) grew by only eight per cent.[27] Despite the economic advantages of integrated markets, globalisation is not leading to a generalised growth in incomes, still less in wider well-being. According to United Nations figures, at least 100 countries are worse off now than they were 15 years ago.[28] The combined income of three billion people in the developing world is less than the assets of 358 multibillionaires.[29]

However, *'since the onset of the industrial revolution…no economic system other than capitalism has been made to work anywhere'*.[30] The market is the only proven mechanism of economic integration since no other can respond to the constant signalling that complex systems demand.[31] Sustained growth in incomes and employment requires a continuous shift from declining to expanding industries, and the removal of those things (like communal property rights and kin affiliations) that get in the way of market efficiency – the famous process of 'creative destruction' christened by the economist Joseph Schumpeter. Are the costs of globalisation anything more than the latest, transient illustration of the same thing? Technology-driven globalisation is good news because, like all other technologies (such as steam power in the 18th century, railways in the 19th and electric power and cheap oil in the 20th), it will produce more and better-paid jobs in the long term. Back in the Stone Age there must have been plenty of conferences fretting about the impact of the wheel on jobs and family life. There is little evidence that jobs are relocating en masse from the industrialised world to lower-income countries; the unemployment problem in North America and Western Europe is caused by technology and rigid domestic labour markets, not competition from Asia and Latin America.[32] As Hamish McRae illustrates, the second half of the 20th century has turned out economically far better than anyone had hoped in 1945.[33] More people have moved out of poverty in the last 50 years than in the previous 500, and health and education standards have improved enormously.[34] South Korea, Botswana and other high-growth countries in the developing world show that the benefits of economic globalisation can be harnessed through the right combination of hard work, sensible policies and luck. Capitalism has triumphed, not because it is the best economic system we can think of, but because it has been more successful than anything else we have tried in satisfying the material incentives that matter to people across the world. In the absence of political support for self-reliance or redistribution, capitalism creates the material conditions under which alternative economic systems might eventually be feasible – a basic level of security which gives people more opportunity to limit their consumption, reduce the number of children they have, and help others as well as themselves. This is the paradox of globalisation: although it carries severe long-term costs, it also offers the prospect of material advancement to enough of the world's population to make future conservation and solidarity a viable proposition. 'Sustainability' has little meaning in a world marked by poverty and inequality. Growth – suitably shaped to redirect its costs and benefits – is the only way forward, yet it will be costly and unequal unless we can find better ways of blending market processes with social and environmental objectives.

It is here that international co-operation has a vital role to play, by developing minimum standards in global markets, improving the endowments of poor people so that they can compete more effectively in an integrated world economy, and altering patterns of consumption and production, especially in the global North.[35] Globalisation makes this easier, because consumers have more power even though workers have less; they have more choices and more information in an expanding marketplace. That is what underpins the rise of 'ethical' consumption, trading and investment – coffee produced by people who get a higher share of the proceeds, or footballs which are not stitched by children working as slave-labourers. In turn, this stimulates corporations to abide by codes of conduct and demonstrate greater social and environmental responsibility in their businesses. They would have to be terminally foolish not to build long-term shareholder value by reorganising around a 'triple bottom line' that promotes sustainability.[36] Some are already modifying the rules of the market by engaging in strategic co-operation. In an increasingly interconnected global economy, this makes good business sense, just as individual sites on the Internet link with each other to promote its use as a whole. The use of information technology makes resistance more effective too, as for example in the international campaigns against giant oil companies like Shell and BP, and the way in which supporters of Aung San Suu Kyi in Burma are using the Internet to get their message across in support of an economic boycott.

The real debate is not whether globalisation exists and will continue (it does and it will), but about how its costs and benefits are distributed, and on this question there is little that is preordained by technology or impervious to politics. Although couched in new terms, this is an age-old debate: how to retain the growth-producing potential of capitalism while reducing its social and environmental costs. By itself, competition cannot answer this question. If there are problems with what globalisation is already doing, they are unlikely to be solved by doing more of the same. We cannot compete ourselves into a co-operative future – that would be like asking a man to pull himself out of a swamp by his own hair. The tension between individualism and social benefit has been the subject of heated debate since the 17th century. As thinkers from Adam Smith onwards have pointed out, capitalist society depends on the non-capitalist values of trust, honesty and co-operation to hold together, prosper and continue evolving into something better. As a means to improve productivity, competition is crucial, but the ideology of competition excludes other, better ways of organising to meet social and political objectives. Capitalism produces inequality, but democracy insists on equality. When duties and obligations are subsumed by market transactions, the common good suffers. As economist Lester Thurow points out, markets cannot represent the needs of the future to the present, nor can they satisfy feelings unless they are revealed in decisions about buying and selling.[37] That makes them a poor guide to the long-term and non-economic questions which occupy so much of our search for the good life. As societies move from the communal and co-operative to the individualistic and competitive, people gain in self-awareness and freedom, but at the cost of their own security. Robert Archer puts it in a nutshell: *'we must run with economic and technological change because it gives us the means to solve material problems, and we must stand against it because if we do not we will lose essential features of ourselves'*.[38] Even the 'man that broke the Bank of England', George Soros, now thinks that the *'arch enemy of the open society is no longer the communist threat but the capitalist one'*.[39] We know we have to find a better balance – a 'third way' – between economic liberalism and social democracy, individual freedom and collective obligations, shareholder returns and stakeholder interests, efficiency and love.

The question is, how? This is difficult to answer in the context of one society, but globalisation internationalises both the dilemma and the response. Unilateral action in a globalising economy will either hurt people elsewhere, be undermined by international markets, or

erode the global commons on which all our futures depend (like the
atmosphere and water reserves). We cannot build a decent society in
a single country, because the necessary sacrifices (like environmental
taxation or higher labour market standards) will be exploited by
others unless there is wider agreement for all to move in step.
Although co-operation cannot supply all the answers to the problems
we face, no solution will work without it. Either we pursue our own
self-interest against a background of growing inequality, insecurity
and degradation, or we embark on a new era of collective action. *'The
supreme difficulty of our generation is that our achievements on the
economic plane have outstripped our progress on the political plane.'*[40]
Thus said *The Economist*, not in 1998, but in 1930. International co-
operation is the only way to harness the power of globalisation to a
vision of the good life for all.

Calling for more co-operation is uncontroversial, but what does it
mean in practice? There are at least three schools of thought. The
first includes those who believe that economic growth is the problem,
so if we are to co-operate it should be to reduce consumption in the
global North and encourage everyone to become self-reliant. In this
vision, co-operation implies a harmonious patchwork quilt of self-
governing, self-provisioning communities interacting with each other
through consensus, in order to call higher-level institutions to account.
Their slogan is *'globalise consciousness, localise economies'.*[41] Since
our problems are built into the current model, recommending more
growth to deal with them is like suggesting promiscuity as a contra-
ceptive. In view of the social and biophysical limits to world
population and consumption levels, economic celibacy is the only
answer. We need a vision of the good life that does not require physical expansion, rather than growing more to raise the money to deal
with the problems created by that very growth! What have we got to
lose – only two brands of milk in the supermarket instead of thirty?

Those of a less-developed global consciousness find this unper-
suasive. *'Putting up barriers to technology and capital means you end
up like towns in Victorian England that were not connected to the
railway.'*[42] The story of how countries grow is not as simple as that,
and some Victorians preferred the quiet life anyway. But the critics
have a point. At higher levels of income, self-reliance has always been
an attractive proposition (even if most people get bored with it after
a while), but for poor people it sounds like a recipe for stagnation.
Apart from a small number of indigenous communities, *'the rest of
the globe aspires to live as well as we do and is unlikely to be deterred
by gloomy prognoses of the consequences',*[43] especially when the

technological frontiers of resource-efficient production and transport are constantly advancing. According to the new Club of Rome report,[44] we can double wealth and halve resource use using existing technologies alone. It would be a curious form of empowerment to deny others the choice of their own trade-offs, and there seems no obvious political constituency for the material sacrifices the no-growth scenario requires. As the economist Joan Robinson once remarked (paraphrasing Oscar Wilde), *'the only thing worse than being exploited by capitalism...is not being exploited by it'*. In addition, who in this decentralised world will produce the things that require economies of scale or are best traded internationally (or won't we need computers?). Who will level up opportunities between communities in resource-rich and resource-poor areas? How would any community stand against the realities of international competition, factor movements and the shifting division of labour? In short, this is not a credible alternative. As we shall see later in this book, localisation does have a role in securing development goals, but as a means to an end, not an end in itself.

A second school of thought wants to 'humanise' capitalism rather than replace it, but this school covers a wide range of positions: economic liberals see virtue rising up through civil society to correct the 20 per cent or so of market economics that do not work;[45] advocates of 'stakeholding'[46] and social market theorists stress the need to widen corporate accountability and incorporate *'human values into the core of market processes'* to promote 'inclusion'; communitarians[47] emphasise the role of small groups in teaching people moral values and responsibility at a scale where they can see that the welfare of the whole depends on the actions of individuals; and further to the Left are those who advocate more government intervention and a bigger role for the 'third sector' in doing what markets don't or won't do.[48]

This is a tempting smorgasbord, but what do these ideas have in common? First, these writers believe that the problems capitalism creates can be mitigated by more 'social capital' – trust, reciprocity and a sense of obligation – to underpin voluntary co-operation and caring.[49] Second, this won't always be enough to secure a healthy society, so there is still a need for formal regulation enforced by states. When combined, so the theory goes, market mechanisms, citizen action and government activism can each address the failings of the others. Active citizenship and partnerships of this kind require a re-energising of democracy and a basic level of material security for everyone (otherwise they are unlikely to participate), so writers and politicians in this group place a lot of emphasis on lifetime learning and investment in skills and education to get people off welfare and into work. Other common features include market remedies for market problems (like taxing pollution), making regulatory bodies more transparent, and encouraging performance by giving people the autonomy to manage within a framework of rigorous accountability.[50] The emphasis is on light forms of intervention that do not damage incentives.

These ideas were designed in the industrial democracies, but they also have potential at the international level – rules and standards that halt environmental degradation, for example, and more accountability for multinational corporations. Such things could be done without killing growth, so these ideas are more credible than those in the first school. However, there are many questions. One difference is that 'starting conditions' (the endowments of resources and skills mentioned earlier) vary much more between rich and poor countries than they do within the industrialised world, so the application of rules and standards has to be carefully graduated – otherwise those in the weakest position will not be able to reach them, or will have to sacrifice their own growth in order to do so. One of the weaknesses of communitarian and stakeholder thinking (and a criticism levelled at New Labour in Britain and at the Democratic Administration in the USA), is that their policies are too soft to have much of an impact on hard-core poverty and discrimination. At the international level this is even more important since large-scale intervention and redistribution are needed to mitigate market forces and confront social inequality. A second criticism is that more reliance on voluntary action may leave some groups worse off than others. There has to be a higher authority to guarantee equal access to services and protect basic rights, which are universals.[51] It is not clear what this authority might be at the global level (since the United Nations doesn't work like this), nor what the international equivalent would be of civil society if more functions are devolved away from states. There are campaigning groups with a global reach but they do not, as yet, function as a coherent whole; nor are there many 'global citizens'. The third problem is that these writers still assume there is a model that is valid for different societies at different stages in their history, albeit a different one than the models we've had before.

Blending into these ideas is a third group, which is the most interesting of all because it rejects the validity of all universal models. This group stresses the importance of capacities and mechanisms that enable people to make their own choices about the good life – to decide what sort of 'third way' they want to pursue.[52] Brian Barry calls this *'justice as impartiality'*. It is less about particular policies and more about giving everyone the tools to create a better society. Since that requires equal access to economic resources and political voice, good policies are still important. However, there is no assumption that following a particular recommendation will bring development, only that it will bring solutions closer because all those involved are sharing in decisions. The 'common interest' can only be found through democratic struggle and debate.[53] Solutions are more likely to hold when everyone has a say in the questions and a stake in the outcomes.

Co-operation in this sense has a much deeper meaning – co-determining the future. Not 'either' one model 'or' another, but new syntheses and synergies. Not a choice between tradition and modernity, but a combination of the best in both. Not imposing one set of ideas, but dialogue. Not 'zero sum' (you gain, I lose) but 'positive sum' (we both gain). This is the only approach that can handle radical alternatives to Western orthodoxy (like Islam) and it has obvious attractions at the international level.[54] It offers a way to accommodate diversity without entertaining the abuse of fundamental rights and freedoms, because *'the right to have rights'*, as Hannah Arendt puts it, is non-negotiable.[55] Which rights are agreed on and how they are implemented is left to dialogue, but that itself is the subject of rights, principally an equal voice for everyone. So it is not a case of 'anything goes'. It is this equality of voice – real voice – that is endangered by globalisation in its homogenising aspect.

With a dialogic approach like this, maybe others can avoid some of the costs of Western-style industrialisation, and invent better models of their own. Many scholars and activists from Asia, Africa and Latin America are trying to do just this.[56] Their efforts are a healthy antidote to those who insist there are 'no shortcuts to progress' – no gain without pain; we suffered in our industrial revolution, and so will you. In accepting that there are no grand answers, no 'magic bullets', no ready-made tool kits to resolve complex dilemmas, this approach is much closer to the mess of real life. As Chapter 3 points out, a capacity to make choices about policies, and the support base to see them through, are just as important as the policies themselves, because they provide the room to manoeuvre that countries need in order to learn and adapt in a fast-moving world. With commendable honesty, Inge Kaul, director of a United Nations think-tank charged with finding out how to implement 'sustainable human development', concludes that *'we simply do not know.*

Development theories tell us little about how to reconcile economic, social and environmental concerns; markets and states; the local, the national and the global'.[57] We are all engaged in *'drawing a line while new strategies for ensuring the cohesion of our societies are developed and tested. Modesty is enjoined, but with limits and principles'.*[58]

International co-operation is a necessary part of this search because one person's right to pursue his or her goals must not be bought at the cost of the equal rights of others to do the same. Since people's endowments do differ so much, the ability to participate in finding solutions is much more constrained in Mali, say, than it is in Manchester. So a truly dialogic approach must level up these endowments and regulate all systems of power that prejudice equal participation, whether they originate in social differences such as gender, economic institutions such as multinational corporations, or political systems such as unrepresentative global governance.[59] We must also ensure that future generations have the same opportunities as those living in the present. This has revolutionary implications. Instead of a 'third way' obsessed by political spin, here is something that really engages with questions of poverty and justice. It is non-ideological in recognising that there are different ways of achieving social and economic goals, but principled in insisting on some basic rights that govern them all. This theme forms the core of this book.

New forms of governance

Globalisation poses the most important challenge to international co-operation in the 21st century, but it is not the only significant factor. The great wave of democracy that swept across the world in the years after 1989 was a period of true global significance – the largest enfranchisement of citizens in human history and the death of the ideology of state command and control. However, even a largely peaceful revolution like this had some unforeseen consequences. For one thing, the collapse of communism stoked the fires of the 'neo-liberal' revolution, appearing to confirm what all good ideologues had been saying throughout the 1980s about the worthlessness of government and the virtues of 'free' markets. Letting imperfect markets loose in an already imperfect world simply produces more inequality, pollution, and alienation. There is nothing more damaging to citizenship than social and economic exclusion. It has always been governments that have held these forces in check, and by diluting support for the idea of states (rather than building support for their reform), the value of central authority was forgotten. If that sounds too abstract, imagine conditions under mafia-like rule in Russian cities, ethnic cleansing in the former Yugoslavia, or just a health or education system with no government safety net. Even if their powers are declining (and these claims are greatly exaggerated), it is still only states that can address the threats of the 21st century, since there is no other legitimate authority to which we can turn. When civil society plays a growing role in global governance, who will make sure the 'good guys' win, insofar as big business, gun-toting US militias and neo-Nazi movements are also members? *'Even locally, somebody's got to collect the taxes to pay for the services that no amount of networking will provide.'*[60] Of course, for many people the state never went away – it was Mrs Thatcher who abandoned it. Now, praise be, it has been found again, and it is still alive! The World Bank's flagship *World Development Report* concludes that *'good government is not a luxury – it is a vital necessity for development...an effective state is vital for the provision of the goods and services – and the rules and institutions – that allow markets to flourish and people to lead healthier, happier lives'.*[61] Better late than never, cynics might say, given that the Bank has spent the best part of 20 years dismantling governments on account of their economic inefficiency. The proviso is that this means 'good' government – states that are democratically accountable for their actions, keep their hands clean and don't poke their noses into other people's business unless it is really necessary.

Even more serious are those cases where central authority has collapsed completely (such as Somalia), or where the removal of non-democratic regimes has been replaced by ethno-nationalist movements rather than elected civic governments (as for example in parts of the former Soviet Union and Yugoslavia). Many old conflicts have resurfaced in areas of the world left unpoliced by the great powers after the end of the cold war. There is always a danger that people will return to ethnocentric politics when they are destabilised by what is happening around them. In such circumstances we all tend to look to the familiar for protection.[62] As Michael Ignatieff writes, *'the repressed has returned, and its name is nationalism'*,[63] but this is a nationalism that assumes our deepest attachments are inherited, not chosen – the very opposite of the co-determined future mapped out above. *'Cosmopolitanism is the privilege of those who can take the secure nation state for granted.'*[64] A legitimate central authority may not be a sufficient condition to combat sectarianism and protect minorities, but it is a necessary one. One of the most pressing tasks for a reformed system of international co-operation is to find ways of responding more effectively to cases of state failure and so-called 'complex political emergencies'.

Is this too gloomy? Integration into a globalising economy (if the benefits are fairly distributed) is one way of providing a sense of belonging that is not dependent on ethnicity or religion. Another is membership of a worldwide polity that values human rights – a genuine sense of global citizenship that dilutes attachment to primordial affections. Although the erosion of national sovereignty does leave some groups more vulnerable to the vagaries of unaccountable power, it also opens up greater possibilities for civic organisations to work together across national boundaries in pursuit of new forms of global governance, especially in an era of electronic communication. These organisations include citizens' groups, NGOs of various kinds, campaigners like Greenpeace and Amnesty International, business networks, universities and research institutes, and associations of the media, local government, municipalities, and mayors. There has been an explosive growth in their number, size and reach over the last ten years. The 176 'international NGOs' of 1909 had blossomed into 28,900 by 1993, and the spending of development NGOs registered in the industrialised world grew by over three billion dollars in only 13 years (1980–93). In Nepal the number of NGOs registered with government grew from 220 in 1990 to 1210 in 1993; in Tunisia from 1886 in 1988 to 5186 just three years later.[65]

Some commentators see a fundamental 'power shift' at work here, an 'associational revolution' as profound as the rise of the nation state in the 18th century.[66] Others feel this is greatly exaggerated. It is questionable whether many NGOs form a sustainable part of civil society, since most rely on external funding; nor do many practise what they preach in terms of democratic norms.[67] Romanticising civil society ignores the reality of fundamentalists and anti-democratic groups; just as Western aid agencies imagine there is a 'thing' called civil society that can be manufactured in a couple of years using outside ideas and resources. There is no basis for this in the historical record. Nevertheless, the broad thrust of civil society everywhere is democratic, and civic groups are set to play a greater role in new systems of governance. These are exciting times, when new relationships are developing between unlikely bedfellows – NGOs and businesses, municipalities and banks, international organisations and citizens' groups. Increasingly, international regimes are made up of diverse relationships between different sectors of society, with nation states functioning less as sovereign entities and more as components of an 'international polity', as Hirst and Thompson call it – holding local and global governance mechanisms to account but playing a smaller role in a larger system.[68] If the 21st century is the era of international co-operation, it will not just be co-operation between states.

The return of the state and the diffusion of power through other institutions is good news for the future of international co-operation. It means that, on the one hand, there will be a stronger government authority in most countries to ensure that new systems are not rooted solely in special interest groups; and on the other, that the limitations of state-based regimes in an era of eroding national sovereignty can be addressed by broadening the base of governance. We need global regimes to cope with global problems. However, there are three difficulties with this approach that resurface throughout this book. The first is what an acceptable core of global rules, rights and standards would be, when states and other groups cannot agree on the ones we have already. The second is how a legitimate authority might be constituted at the global level (or reconstituted in the case of the United Nations), and linked in a meaningful way with new patterns of local governance that are emerging around the world. And the third is how to make any global system work to the benefit of its weaker members, when the world is such an unequal place. The answers to these questions lie in new combinations of public, private and civic regulation, and a more democratic way of deciding who does what.

Diversity, Uncertainty and Rational Disagreement

Did the collapse of communism signal the death of the big idea? Many think so. Capitalism's victory leaves no more room for ideological debate, and voters (at least in Britain and the USA) seem to prefer small, achievable and verifiable promises from their politicians. There is no obvious big idea on the agenda for the future, save muddling through as best we can. Even so, there is no shortage of debate across the world, especially on the centre-left which has recaptured the intellectual and political high ground of the late 1990s. Perhaps those who make these judgements don't listen hard enough to post-colonial writing, the feminist movement, or anything that originates outside the Anglo-Saxon intellectual fortress that dominates writing on foreign policy and international affairs. In later chapters of this book, I have tried to incorporate some of the ideas of these writers along with the best of the West.

A second reason for our current scepticism is the 'post-modern' condition. Instead of the comfortable certainties and universal truths of the 'modernist project' we now have complexity (even chaos), uncertainty, diversity and risk. In the social sciences, economic and social phenomena are routinely treated as non-linear, and the belief that complex changes can be engineered (especially by outsiders) looks laughable. Words like 'progress' and 'development', if they are used at all, are seen as terms to be negotiated rather than paths that are prede-termined. *'The idea of development stands today like a ruin in the intellectual landscape,'* says the writer Wolfgang Sachs, though this judgement is too sweeping.[69] It is not the idea of progress that lies in ruins – that remains as a near-universal aspiration – but standardised notions of what it means, how to achieve it, and whether it represents an unstoppable forward march. The philosopher Zygmunt Bauman puts it like this: *'there are problems with no solutions, twisted trajecto-ries that can't be straightened up, ambivalences that are more than linguistic blunders yelling to be corrected, doubts which cannot be legis-lated out of existence, and moral agonies which no reason-dictated recipes can soothe'*.[70] Risk, anxiety and dislocation are characteristic of industrial and scientific development, but under globalisation their causes are more elusive and their effects more mobile. Managing these risks requires international co-operation, though as the writer Ulrich Beck points out, it is increasingly difficult to hold anyone accountable or compensate those who are affected when causes and effects are both diffuse and interconnected.[71]

Others dismiss this as post-modern waffle. There is still a global conspiracy out there, implicating corporations and politicians across the board, and bent on a master plan of world capitalist domination. If this were true it would make things much easier, since we could just find the ringleaders and tie them up. But it sits uneasily with the diversity and ambiguity of real people's motivations. Others ask whether calls to respect difference are not just a shield for traditions that hurt people with less political power, like female genital mutila-tion and child labour. Are there really no universals any more, nothing to hang on to amid the complexity or recommend with any certainty to others? Must we abandon the very idea of 'progress' because it seems politically incorrect? Don't we know anything about the causes of development, nor how we can help? These are important questions, and this book deals with them in two ways: first, it does identify some general conclusions which seem to hold true across different contexts, especially the interlocking power structures that exclude particular groups of people or countries. Second, it searches for principles that are negotiated but not imposed – let's have progress (and more of it please) but defined in all our terms.

Welcoming diversity is a prerequisite for co-operation because no system of collective management can succeed when based on force – it will be incapable of generating the consensus required to make decisions hold firm. Yet collective management is what is needed above all as global problems multiply. The key here is 'rational disagreement' – open, principled debate. That doesn't mean abandoning moral concerns, but it does mean not coercing people to accept the morals of others as if they were absolutes.[72] A core set of universal values does seem to be emerging, cautiously and unevenly. It is coalescing around human rights, non-violent means of resolving disputes, and preservation of the environment, though the expression of these values in current international treaties lacks the democratic mandate that would give them more legitimacy.[73] Despite the problems this causes, the messy emergence of a common core is an historic phenomenon which will be crucial to the success of our collective future.[74] It is certainly a more optimistic vision than the 'clash of civilisations' between West and non-West portrayed by the American academic Samuel Huntington,[75] which exaggerates the differences between 'civilisations' and ignores the diversity inside them. False polarities undermine the conditions for dialogue by strengthening people's self-perception as fundamentally and forever apart, eroding their willingness to identify and negotiate common ground. Long-term material interests will be stronger than any supposed cultural faultline. Iran and Armenia may belong to different civilisations, but they are still building a joint oil and gas pipeline.[76]

Huntington's analysis is attractive because it offers easy answers and – like the conspiracy theorists – a new enemy to fight. In this school of thought, the problem is always with 'them', never with 'us'. In reality, all things are the result of interlocking struggles in which we ourselves are implicated – in markets, politics, culture and social interaction. Their outcome is open to influence, but not control. Throughout this book I have tried to convey a sense of the sheer messiness of development and remain faithful to the diversity of the evidence. The 'big idea' is about means – co-operation – not ends; and the 'solution' is not a model, but a path. The key to this path is dialogue, the basis of all problem-solving in every society. This does not remove the disagreements that arise along the way, but when solutions are negotiated, not imposed, they generate better results in the end.

Trans-boundary Problems and Collective Security

One thing the world is not short of are statistics about impending scarcity. Warnings of ecological disaster abound, and everyone says they are listening. Herman Daly, the pioneer of steady-state economics, points out that *'any subsystem'* (like us) of a *'finite non-growing system'* (like the world) *'must itself at some point become non-growing'*: the party can't go on for ever.[77] There *are* biophysical limits to growth (and social limits too if growth produces too much inequality and saturated consumption). Daly estimates that global resources are sufficient to extend North American levels of consumption to only 18 per cent of the world's population. Therefore rich people should take less and give more; otherwise *'development means colonising the resources of the poor to enable the rich to live beyond their means'*.[78] Leaving aside the difficulty of persuading rich people to do this, it is clear that we are using up the earth's resources at an unsustainable rate. Three billion people face severe water shortages within the next 50 years, oceans are being over-fished, soils eroded, and the atmosphere polluted. According to Sir John Houghton (chairman of the Royal Commission on Environmental Pollution), sea levels would continue to rise even if greenhouse gas emissions from fossil fuels were stabilised according to existing international agreements, forcing millions of people to migrate from coastal lands in southern China, Bangladesh and Egypt.[79] Those who try to rubbish this scenario, he claims, are simply part of the big business lobby. We also know that there is an aggregate shortage of food in the making: food prices rose by 47 per cent between 1993 and 1996 after many years of decline; grain stocks have fallen to an historic low; oil, and phosphate for fertiliser, will eventually run out; and agricultural land will shrink due to rising salt levels and desertification.[80] Food security and control over water will dominate world affairs, and no doubt we will all be vegetarians.

We face other threats too. The World Health Organisation claims that we are on the brink of a global crisis of infectious diseases, with one million potential carriers crossing international borders every day,[81] 30 new infections in the last 20 years, the resurgence of tuberculosis and malaria, and a wave of sexually transmitted diseases invading Western Europe from the former Soviet Union.[82] Other unwanted exports include criminal gangs, drugs, terrorists, illegal immigrants and unregistered armaments, not to mention a super-power arsenal of 100,000 nuclear weapons. As war between states disappears, violence becomes the preserve of terrorist groups and ethno-nationalist factions, often linked together in their own networks across the world.

An increasing awareness of global risks to domestic security is obvious in Western capitals. In the USA, the bipartisan 'Commission on America's National Interests' identified the prevention of a catastrophic collapse of global financial, energy and environmental systems as a top priority.[83] Rich country governments know that mass poverty and spreading civil war will breed insecurity for everyone. However tall the walls we erect around our privileged minorities, it simply isn't good for business. As BP's chief executive, John Browne, said recently, *'big emerging markets are our future'* – the more stability and prosperity there is, the better.[84] Others are more sanguine. Writing in the *New Statesman*, Tom Burke (a former adviser to the British Environment Minister) claims that *'we do not lack the natural resources, technology or capital to deliver a sustainably high quality of life for a population of ten billion'*,[85] which is twice the current total. There is no agreement on the food issue between optimists and pessimists, believers in high and low-technology solutions, and advocates of hugely varying estimates of future yields, production possibilities and environmental implications. Food production has consistently outpaced population growth over the last 40 years (Africa excepted), and India already feeds twice as many people as Africa on 13 per cent of the land.[86] Deforestation is slowing down (at least in rich countries) and global production of the most ozone-depleting substances is down 76 per cent from 1988.[87] Migration has always been a feature of world history, so what's the big deal? What happens in China may well blow the whole thing sky high, but then again, it might not.

Predictions are usually wrong, but even the more optimistic should be nervous about these debates. Different factions will continue the war of words, but there is no reason to wait for the worst-case scenario before starting work to manage these problems through international co-operation – using improved regulatory regimes (to manage refugee flows, and combat crime and terrorism), global financial reform (like taxing polluters), and joint management of natural resources across borders. If rich governments lack the imagination to use aid creatively, the least they can do is to use it as a vaccination against the threats they perceive to their own security, and that means building capacities in poorer countries to find and implement solutions. Two problems remain. The first is the issue of legitimate authority that has surfaced throughout this Introduction: how do we construct political mechanisms that can resolve differences over resource use and retain enough support to make them hold?[88] Second, how do we persuade people in rich countries to limit their consumption so that more is available for expansion elsewhere within known and predictable biophysical limits to growth? This book addresses both these questions.

Although globalisation does expose people to the costs of decisions over which they have no influence, the increasingly clear nature of the transboundary problems that result makes the need for international co-operation evermore obvious. The reality of increasing interconnectedness should make reciprocal relationships more acceptable to a sceptical constituency. We might then have a real shot at turning intervention – the dominant theme of the last 50 years – into co-operation, the dominant theme of the next 50 years. The changing global context makes co-operation both more necessary and more possible. There has never been a better time to pursue the vision of a more co-operative world.

Part 1

Looking Back

Chapter 2

1945 And All That: A Brief History of International Co-operation

'The Hindu, like the eunuch, exceeds in the qualities of the slave'
John Stuart Mill the Elder, 1817[1]

'Their food is inadequate, they are victims of disease, their economic life is primitive and stagnant'
Harry Truman, 1949[2]

'What can someone living alongside a dirt road in Namibia or South Africa do except hope that someone will lift a helping hand to assist them?'
Joan Burton, Minister of State,
Irish Department of Foreign Affairs, 1997[3]

Countries, like people, have always interfered in each other's affairs. For the first 2000 years of history, war and conquest were the driving force. Then came trade, commerce, and control over the raw materials and sea routes that were essential to economic supremacy. The idea that countries might benefit by co-operating surfaced periodically in the 19th century, but had little influence over politics and economics. It took two devastating world wars and the great depression of the 1930s to convince people that there had to be a better way. When it arrived in 1945, the system established by a nascent 'international community' did mark a revolutionary break with the past, but its vision was soon submerged under cold war politics. Only now, with the cold war out of our system and global threats mounting, have we begun to pick up the threads of the post-war agenda in a more concerted fashion. Old habits, however, die hard. The legacies of the past cannot be written out of the present, and to make co-operation work we shall have to confront attitudes and prejudices whose roots lie buried deep in history. What are these attitudes, and from where did they come?

'PROGRESS' AND THE COLONIAL EXPERIENCE

Writers on international development often cite President Harry Truman's inauguration address in 1949 as the beginning of a new era in world affairs. Truman called for the *'vigorous application of modern scientific and technical knowledge'* to improve what he called *'the underdeveloped areas'* of the world. This was not the first time large parts of humanity had been labelled in this way. Karl Marx used the same phrase in *Das Kapital*,[4] and the idea of development as a natural progression to the same end-state goes back to the Christian belief in providence, the continual upward movement toward universal perfection that is God's gift to the world.[5] In the 18th century the philosophers of the European Enlightenment translated providence into its secular equivalent of 'progress', and the hundred years that followed saw progress become 'modernity' – a combination of capitalism, industrialism, science-based culture and the nation state that became for its followers the rational end-point of human evolution.[6] By the beginning of the 20th century, the intellectual framework was already in place for 'development' as a standard set of means to achieve modernity for all.

Central to the Enlightenment (and to thinkers like Bacon, Hobbes and Newton who preceded it) was a core of ideas that were later to prove decisive in shaping approaches to international co-operation.[7] They included the belief that nature placed no limits on human achievement; an abiding faith in scientific knowledge free of moral and ethical constraints; the notion that human evolution, society and economics were all a competitive struggle between self-seeking individuals; a search to impose order on the world through the application of reason; and a consequent denigration of feeling and emotion as criteria for decision making. To the philosophers of the Enlightenment, the world – like the new inventions that proliferated at the time – was a wonderful machine whose actions could be predicted and controlled. Speed, growth and physical expansion were elevated as standards of success. Standardisation and measurement by numbers were characteristic of a culture that became *'precise, punctual, calculable, bureaucratic, rigid, invariant and routine'*.[8] The culture of the Enlightenment laid the foundations for modern government administration and business practice, as well as development planning.

The legacy of the Enlightenment was decidedly mixed: patriarchal, control oriented and aggressively universalist on the one hand; a tradition (though rarely a reality) of individual freedom, justice and equality on the other, plus the scientific advancements and rational thinking that were to prove essential to economic growth everywhere. However, the imperial face of the Enlightenment inheritance was unremittingly destructive. Religion (the mission to 'civilise') and science (racial superiority and the survival of the fittest) provided the perfect rationale for colonisation.[9] There were exceptions, of course, like the Jesuits' attempts to promote self-reliant communities of Indians in 18th century Paraguay, but their failure throws the rest of the colonial experience into sharper relief.[10] Despite a rich history of local resistance and no little collusion by the indigenous elites who benefited, colonialism had a devastating impact on economies and societies. By denying people the opportunity for self-determination and imposing meaningless borders across ethnic divisions (especially in Africa), it also made longer-term political stability much more difficult to secure. Colonialism everywhere was characterised by the exploitation of resources to benefit the metropolitan economies – not just raw materials but human beings too, like the estimated ten million slaves who were forcibly deported from Africa to work on plantations in the New World, the thirty million indentured labourers enticed away from India, and the Indian army which provided a mobile source of support for Britain's imperial adventures.[11] Local industry and commerce were deliberately weakened, peasant initiative stifled, and revenue sucked out of the economy and into colonial exchequers.[12] Infrastructure and industry were oriented to primary exports instead of export-led industrialisation, and the colonies provided markets for goods manufactured in the West (though they proved something of a disappointment in that respect).[13] Cecil Rhodes knew what was wanted: *'we must find new lands from which we can obtain raw materials and exploit the slave labour that is available. The colonies also provide a dumping ground for the surplus goods produced in our factories'*.[14] But the colonial enterprise did not stop at economics. Edmund Spenser wanted the Irish exterminated since they were 'only barbarians'.[15] Smallpox brought over by the Spanish conquistadores wiped out the entire population of Hispaniola and 80 per cent of MesoAmerica and the Andean region.[16] General Von Trotha's 'extermination order' issued in Namibia in 1904 left three-quarters of the Herero tribe dead.[17] If cultural superiority and economics were insufficient, brute force was used to complete the job.

It was the attitudes underlying such actions that made colonisation such a wounding experience, for both host and invader. The rich reality of China, India and the Islamic world which earlier generations of westerners had admired and learned from had to be rejected by the colonisers, because its acceptance would have removed the rationale for their actions – the inferiority of the 'natives' who had to be 'civilised'.[18] That was why the British made the destruction of indigenous education systems in India a priority, and more broadly why local ideas and alternatives had to be subjugated or ignored.[19] *'The totality of Indian knowledge and scholarship did not even equal the contents of a single shelf of a good European library'* was T B MaCauley's verdict.[20] Mill the Elder's three-volume *History of India* suggests that India was entirely populated by lazy natives, liars and cowards.[21] *'It's just wot yer might expect from such a parcel o'dirty black hignorant scoundrels'* seethed a contemporary cartoon after the Indian mutiny of 1857 – how dare they oppose the march of progress?[22] In the colonial world view, difference spelled danger, backwardness and exotica, and often all three together. As late as 1904, the city of Hamburg exhibited Samoan women in the local zoo.[23] By 1917 the USA was the virtual ruler of Haiti, and its Secretary of State William Jennings Bryan was amused at the thought of *'niggers speaking French'*. At least he wasn't forced to *'bow and scrape to the coons'*, as his emissary Colonel Waller put it. It never occurred to him that Haitian farmers at the time were growing cotton more successfully than plantations in his own country, using traditional methods.[24] The Palestinian scholar Edward Said has documented in meticulous detail how writers and others in the West created an image of an incapable 'other' in order to justify their actions and underpin the construction of their own superiority.[25] It was this need to strip people of the right to determine their future that was to prove so destructive to the possibilities of authentic development later in the 20th century.[26]

The horrors of slavery and the destruction wrought by colonisation were not uniquely Western, but in its depth, scale and continuity Western colonialism was uniquely damaging to the potential for co-operation in the post-colonial era.[27] The actions of men like Rhodes strike us now as shameful, even grotesque. But colonialism is long gone. These things are irrelevant to international co-operation today, or are they? Some claim that the conditions imposed on borrowing countries by the International Monetary Fund and the World Bank, or the incursions of Western powers into collapsing states like Somalia, represent 'neo-colonialism' of the most obvious kind.[28] We will hear more about this in later chapters, but my concern is a more subtle legacy – the inequalities of power that still exist between donors and recipients, the insistence on policies and strategies of which 'we' approve, and the continual presentation of the Third World (originally a descriptive term, but now pejorative) as the home of the passive and dependent. Stereotyping other people like this justifies outside intervention, just as the 'backwardness of the natives' provided colonisers with a rationale for their excesses. Behind the mask of raw power, such polarities ward off anxieties about our own competence, assuage our hidden fears, and counsel lingering insecurities.[29] If there is no 'them' to put right, we are forced to confront our own problems, and that is a great deal more painful.

It would be wrong to see the period leading up to 1945 only in terms of colonialism. The first co-operative agreements (such as the International Postal Union and the first Geneva Convention) were already in place by the end of the 19th century, and a growing body of international law exerted at least some influence over politics. The inter-war years were dominated by an unequal struggle between 'Wilsonian internationalism' (expressed in the League of Nations), and the rise of fascist nationalist movements buoyed up by the catastrophic collapse of the world capitalist economy during the 1930s. Woodrow Wilson's fourteen-point 'Program for the Peace of the World' launched in 1918 argued for *'open covenants of peace, openly arrived at'*, but there was little support for his vision even in his own country. Wilson had planned to give 30 speeches in 20 days to rally public support for the League of Nations in 1919, but collapsed early on and later suffered a massive stroke. One year later the League of Nations covenant was signed in Geneva to provide for the peaceful resolution of disputes, and the use of collective force against aggressors. But of the great powers, only France took a leading role; the USA never joined, and Japan, Italy and Germany all left after being censured for 'aggression'.[30] Those who needed to hear its message most ignored the League's disarmament conference in 1932. Deprived of the authority and resources to fulfil its mandate, it was *'completely out of its depth when the major powers of Europe began to unsheath their claws in the late 1930s'*.[31] The result was the Second World War.

Well before the end of the war, voices had been raised about the need to manage the world economy more effectively in order to avoid a repetition of the great depression. The Atlantic Charter signed by

Churchill and Roosevelt in 1941 promised the assurance that *'all the men in all the lands might live out their lives in freedom from fear and want'*.[32] Presumably this applied to all the women too, and it certainly gave added impetus to the movement for international co-operation that took shape a few years later. The Food and Agriculture Organisation (FAO) of the future United Nations had already been formed in 1943. At about the same time, economists in the USA and a group of emigrés from Eastern Europe who had settled in Britain developed the first theories about 'underdeveloped' economies.[33] They were influenced by the practice of wartime planning and the tradition of government interventionism championed by John Maynard Keynes and the Fabian Society which was especially strong at the time. So the new theories were not shy about the potential for planned change. Staley even recommended an *'international invest-ment bank'* to finance global public utilities and the transfer of knowledge and industry across national borders.[34] These currents came together at the end of the war in a momentous series of world gatherings, most famously in the New Hampshire town of Bretton Woods (in 1944), Washington DC (Dumbarton Oaks) and San Francisco (one year later). Although the League of Nations had not prevented the carnage of the 1940s, the trauma of war and economic devastation did create the conditions in which the spirit of Wilsonian internationalism could find the political support it required. The stage was set for the birth of international co-operation.

THE REVOLUTION OF 1945

> *'We the peoples of the United Nations, determined to save succeeding generations from the scourge of war...reaffirm our faith in fundamental human rights...and for these ends agree to employ international machinery for the promotion of the economic and social advancement of all peoples'.*[35]

The opening words of the UN Charter signed on 26 June 1945 in San Francisco still have the power to move us. They seem to herald a radically new spirit in international affairs. Such a high level of agree-ment would not have been possible had it not been for the solidarity engendered by the common sacrifices and huge costs of the war. That, plus the memories of the great depression, made the rationale for international co-operation obvious to all.[36] In retrospect it is tempting to imagine the immediate post-war period as a golden age of ethics and unselfishness, but the motives of the leading players were always mixed. Foreign policy in the USA, as in Britain in an earlier age, wavered between self-centred idealism (a mission to lead the world to a better, American, future) and hard-nosed realism (defending national interests).[37] The UN Charter and subsequent Declaration of Human Rights were never as 'universal' as they claimed to be, a problem which has not gone away in the intervening years. And the institutions born in 1944–45 were shaped to suit the interests of the industrialised economies, especially the one that emerged in the best shape from the war – the USA. Only two of the four 'pillars' envisaged at Bretton Woods actually survived as conceived. The International Monetary Fund (IMF) was intended to oversee currency matters, replacing a counter proposal from Keynes for an 'international clearing union' to regulate global capital movements (something which might have prevented the excess borrowings of the 1970s and the subsequent debt crisis of the 1980s).[38] The World Bank – the second pillar – was given the job of providing funding and technical assistance for reconstruction and development, initially in Europe, and then further afield. The third pillar was the UN, which when formally established a year later was stripped of the authority to supervise the IMF and the World Bank. That meant it could never be the focus for global economic management its architects had envisaged. The decision to give the permanent members of the UN Security Council a power of veto also shifted the focus of decision making away from the General Assembly toward the great powers. The fourth pillar was the International Trade Organisation, but that was replaced by the General Agreement on Tariffs and Trade (GATT), which encouraged, not the structural transformations required for productivity growth in Third World countries, but their integration into global markets using their existing 'comparative advantage' in primary exports (a critical issue which is taken up in Chapter 3).[39] The governance of these institutions reflected the realities of power at the time and put the USA firmly in the driving seat; anyone who wanted to borrow from the new system had to agree to open competition and currency convertibility, favouring the USA as the most competitive nation in the world at the time.[40]

The fundamental objectives of the Bretton Woods system were to promote high levels of employment, enhance world trade (by reducing protectionism and ensuring the convertibility of currencies), and smooth out the fluctuations in markets that had caused such havoc in the 1920s and 1930s.[41] In all of this, the influence of Keynes and Harry White (his American counterpart) was decisive. Faith in the power of wise intervention to redress the imperfections of markets, and the ability of planning to engineer positive social and economic change, was widespread. There was no better illustration than the Marshall Plan, an act of enlightened self-interest on the part of the USA that, in its scale and form, is unique in history. When planners in the USA met in 1947 to discuss the future of the world economy, they forecast that other countries would not be able to buy goods from the USA in sufficient volume to prevent a domestic recession for at least two years.[42] The future wealth of the USA depended in part on its willingness to share what it already had with others. *'The needs and interests of the people of the United States need markets, big markets, in which to buy and sell,'* said Will Clayton, the businessman credited with the original idea for the Plan.[43] Marshall aid was therefore designed to pump-prime rapid economic recovery in Western Europe and so neutralise Soviet influence at a time when Communism was a real political force. The first shipment of aid (900 tonnes of wheat) was shipped from Texas in the spring of 1948.[44] Over the next five years, aid to the value of US$15 billion followed, about US$3 for every person in the USA at the time. Britain, France and Germany took the lion's share. Within three years gross national product (GNP) of all recipients rose by a quarter, industrial production by two-thirds and farm output by 24 per cent.[45] French productivity increased by eight per cent a year between 1955 and 1958, and whole sectors of industry were retooled using state of the art technology. Aid eased import constraints, supplied the capital goods essential to productivity growth, and gave hard-pressed economies and governments the extra breathing space they needed to recover. Japan also received huge amounts of aid from the USA under a separate programme, using 'Special Procurement Dollars' to re-equip Japanese industry at a time when exports were still small in volume.[46]

Critics of foreign aid like to point out that the success of the Marshall Plan cannot be used to justify aid to the developing world.[47] Recovery was already underway before it began; aid would have achieved little without local initiative; and conditions in European economies at the time were very different to those in Africa or Asia at independence.[48] Western Europe provided the ideal setting for the Plan because its economic problems *could* be solved in the short term using external assistance. The governments, infrastructure, skilled labour force, market institutions, entrepreneurial tradition, business acumen, high levels of education and technical competence that were needed to use aid effectively were all present.[49] In other respects however, the Plan does provide some useful lessons which – had they been heeded – might have improved the later record of foreign aid. Although the USA insisted on broad control of the programme (*'we must run this show'* was Clayton's advice), the funds generated by selling Marshall Plan commodities could be spent by recipients more or less as they pleased.[50] Aid was allocated in close consultation with European governments through the Organisation for Economic Co-operation in Europe (later the Organisation for Economic Co-operation and Development – OECD), in which the USA had voting rights equal to those of the recipients. By all accounts there was a genuine sense of partnership, and considerable flexibility in the shape and timing of domestic policies (so long as they were broadly favourable to expanded production and trade).[51] Since aid came in the form of grants, countries were able to cover temporary shortfalls in their balance of payments without incurring more debt.[52] Machinery sent to Europe was at the cutting edge, not the second-hand cast-offs so often provided to Africa in more recent aid programmes. In fact foreign aid to Africa shares almost none of the features of the Marshall Plan that *could* have been replicated despite the different conditions. Why not? Because they were only Africans?

The arrival of 'development planning' as an accepted discipline in the late 1940s built on a combination of Keynesian economic policy, Soviet dirigisme, and the 'scientific management' movement in the USA.[53] Its spirit is captured in the report of the first ever World Bank mission – to Colombia in 1949 – which concluded that *'a great deal can be done to improve the economic environment by shaping economic policies to meet scientifically ascertained social requirements'*.[54] Development planning, and its theoretical underpinnings in development economics, were almost entirely a creation of thinkers in the West (though from the 1950s to the 1970s a healthy, if eventually unsuccessful, alternative tradition grew up, especially in Latin America).[55] The assumption was that growth would accelerate without the long periods of institution building and the 'balanced evolution of private markets and public power' that had been central to the development of the industrialised world.[56] Theorists like Walt Rostow insisted that all countries would have to pass through the same fixed set of stages to reach prosperity. Western experience also permeated the field of social policy, with formalised social work and the welfare state exported wholesale to radically different cultures where traditional social obligations were still in place. Though driven by a different and less destructive philosophy than colonialism, the urge to engineer progress defined in universal terms was just as strong.

SUSPENDED ANIMATION: FROM THE COLD WAR TO SUPPLY-SIDE ECONOMICS

Despite its imperfections, the system established in 1945 did hold out the promise of more co-operative relationships at the international level. The period between 1950 and 1970 was, for those who enjoyed it, the greatest economic boom in history, with world trade increasing fourfold and real incomes up by 300 per cent.[57] In that respect, the post-war recovery stoked up by American aid, and the economic institutions put in place at Bretton Woods, worked better than anyone had hoped. For countries like South Korea and Taiwan that were strategically located in cold war terms and whose governments were able to use aid effectively, these were also times of rapid growth. But while peace and prosperity reigned in the West, the cold war condemned much of Africa, Central America and Asia to continued conflict and instability, with twenty million people killed there between 1945 and 1983.[58] In these circumstances it is not surprising that growth and development were set back significantly. Both the Soviet Union and the USA used aid and other forms of intervention to secure their political objectives and their economic interests.

Cold war motives and developmental objectives were often conflated, with predictable results – witness Arthur Schlesinger's comment in 1954 that US policy toward Vietnam was *'part of our general program of international goodwill'*.[59] Others were more straightforward. With unusual honesty, President Nixon reminded his colleagues *'that the main purpose of American aid is not to help other nations but to help ourselves'*.[60] Domestic interests – and old alliances – overrode any supposed commitment to democracy and human rights. When asked why he refused to authorise military action against the Rhodesian rebellion in 1965, British Prime Minister Harold Wilson replied, *'because we don't do that sort of thing against white ex-colonials'*.[61] Neither West nor East did anything to prevent the killing of half a million people in Indonesia and East Timor by the Suharto regime.[62] Attempts at democratisation were blocked wholesale by the Soviets in the Eastern Bloc, but the USA and Britain were also involved in the overthrow of democratically elected governments, as for example in Iran (where a grateful Shah immediately granted huge concessions to US oil companies) and Guatemala (where Jacobo Arbenz Guzman dared to advocate land reform in a country dominated by the United Fruit Company).[63] Even where successful in narrow cold war terms, intervention often had unintended consequences: the murder of Aung San in 1947 (in which the British were implicated) plunged Burma into a period of instability from which it has yet to recover;[64] US complicity in Guatemala prolonged a civil war that claimed over 200,000 lives between 1960 and 1990;[65] and the British-sponsored Sudanese independence agreement of 1953 institutionalised a conflict between North and South that has led to 40 years of war and famine.

Superpower manoeuvres destroyed one of the founding principles of the UN – that it would act as an impartial judge of its members' misdemeanours. Instead, it became the arena in which these conflicts were played out, with 279 vetoes of Security Council resolutions cast during the cold war by one side or the other.[66] The cold war also diverted resources on a huge scale into military research and expenditure – US$50 billion per annum in the USA alone and $10 trillion for the West as a whole.[67] Imagine what might have been achieved had it been spent on long-term development. Since aid was provided regardless of development performance, there was no incentive for corrupt and incompetent states to reform themselves, and if 'universal' human rights were negotiable according to political criteria, why bother to uphold them? This made a mockery of the principles of the UN Charter, and did enormous damage, not just to the effectiveness and reputation of foreign aid, but to the wider cause of international co-operation. The cold war's perverted interpretation of what co-operation meant made it more difficult for the real thing to gain support later on. Long before the fall of the Berlin Wall, intervention had once again displaced co-operation as the driving force in international affairs.

However, not everyone was obsessed with containing the 'other side'. Behind the scenes of the cold war, the 1950s saw the formation of the Special Fund for Economic Development (later renamed as the United Nations Development Programme – UNDP), the International Development Association (IDA – the soft loan arm of the World Bank), and the Development Assistance Committee (DAC) of rich-country donors. The addition of the International Covenant on Economic, Social and Cultural Rights to the original Universal Declaration (in 1966) was a significant event because it spoke much more to the priorities of newly-independent ex-colonies.[68] They had started to form themselves into organisations like the Group of 77 and the Non-Aligned Movement in order to represent their interests more forcefully in international debates. The Bandung Conference in 1955 was the first ever international gathering which deliberately excluded the Soviet Union, Western Europe and the USA.[69] Co-operation between the members of these organisations increased rapidly and reached its peak during the 1970s, when, for a short time at least, there were serious discussions about the possibility of a new international economic order more favourable to the developing world in which North-South economic relations were to be reformulated on the basis of 'equality and co-operation'.[70] This was a time of fresh thinking about development, much of it generated by scholars and activists in Latin America and Asia. They emphasised the human aspects of development as well as economic growth, and pointed to the structural disadvantages of developing world economies in the international division of labour.[71] 'Popular participation' became a rallying cry for increasing numbers of critics, especially in Latin America where it was popularised by the Brazilian educator Paulo Friere.[72] There was widespread support for international commodity agreements that aimed (not very successfully) to stabilise the prices of primary exports.[73] In stark contrast to later attitudes among donor agencies, there was substantial respect for the independence and sovereignty of recipients. W Arthur Lewis, one of the greatest of the early development economists, said simply, *'give us the money and shut up'*.[74] In 1969, the OECD still had the humility to admit that *'we have only a vague idea of what we are doing'*.[75]

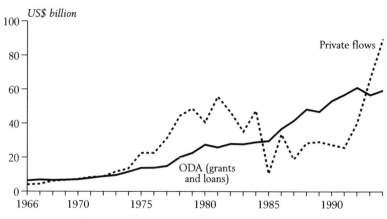

Source: OECD/DAC Annual Reports 1979–92

Figure 2.1 *The Flow of Financial Resources from OECD Countries, 1966–94 (US$billion)*

The volume of foreign aid rose consistently in real terms during this period (Figure 2.1), though the proportion spent on basic needs fell from 38.4 per cent in 1971 to 21.9 per cent ten years later.[76] The increase was partly due to the ready availability of funds from the oil-producing countries after the oil price rises of 1973. In the following decade, the Organisation of Petroleum Exporting Countries (OPEC) provided 22 per cent of total official aid, or US$74 billion, as well as much more in the form of 'petrodollars' recycled to developing world borrowers through a willing global financial system.[77] Many in the West blamed OPEC for the collapse of the post-war economic boom and the dismantling of the framework inspired by Keynes 30 years before. But the world economy had been overheating for some time before 1973 and it was actually President Nixon who pulled the final plug by abolishing dollar convertibility at fixed exchange rates.[78] Rising inflation proved the undoing of the Keynesian consensus, and that in turn prepared the way for the neo-liberal resurgence of the 1980s. It was to be a shift with profound implications for the world's poor.

The free market obsessions of the 1980s affected international co-operation in two ways. First, neo-liberalism deemed economic intervention, management, or even co-operation (in most areas) unnecessary and unhelpful. Markets were assumed to be better at making decisions than states or international institutions, and private initiative was much more important to success than collective action. Domestic policies were the key to results; international structures were irrelevant. Since development was seen as a linear progression to a market economy, getting there meant liberalisation, privatisation, and 'getting the prices right' – a standard set of prescriptions summarised in what came to be known as the 'Washington Consensus'. John Williamson, the originator of this phrase, called it a *'myth driven by a powerful elite'*, but it was a very influential one.[79] Decision makers became obsessed with control over inflation, abandoning the focus on incomes, employment and welfare agreed at Bretton Woods. Interestingly, the Articles of Agreement laid down there for the IMF made no mention of controlling inflation and speci-fied that economic imbalances should be corrected *'without resorting to measures destructive of national or international prosperity'*.[80] Nevertheless, donor agencies focused increasingly on growth rather than distribution, along with social safety nets for those who could not, or would not, be reached by markets. Foreign aid was used to promote the 'right' macro-economic policies. Support to aid-financed projects declined, while programme aid – given on condition that recipients reformed themselves – increased. The proportion of total aid spent on human development priorities fell still further, down to a meagre 19 per cent by 1991.[81]

Second, the deflationary macro-economic policies pursued by the industrialised world during the 1980s triggered a recession of global proportions, accompanied by collapsing commodity prices and rising Third World debt. The absence of Keynesian-style international economic management made decisions taken in rich countries much more damaging in their effects on people in poor countries.[82] A failure to get to grips with the rising budget deficit in the USA stoked the fires of the debt crisis by placing a constant upward pressure on interest rates. With a real risk of large-scale default on the loans that had flown so freely a decade earlier, this was a period of immense risk to the world economy.[83] The result was to reverse the positive net flow of resources to the developing world that had characterised the preceding 25 years. Foreign direct investment declined and aid flows began to stagnate, with the proportion of total aid going to the 'least developed countries' falling to less than a quarter by 1993.[84] These trends made the 1980s a 'lost decade' for many countries, especially in Latin America and sub-Saharan Africa (Figure 2.2). In 1985 poorer countries transferred about US$15 billion more to rich-country donors, banks and corporations than they received in the form of aid, loans and investment – so much for the benefits of international co-operation.

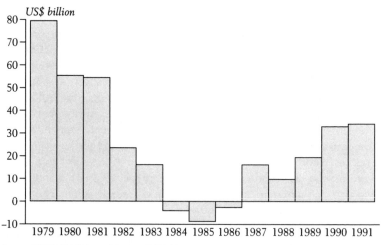

Source: OECD/DAC Annual Reports 1979–92

Figure 2.2 *Net Financial Transfers to all Developing Countries 1979–91 (US$billion)*

THE POST-COLD WAR WORLD

The end of the cold war has not resurrected international co-operation in the way some had anticipated. Nevertheless, there is a new spirit at large, confused and hesitant in its details and still subject to conflicting interests and agendas. This new spirit centres on a fuller vision of development as more than economic growth, and on the right of all people to be included in the fruits of global progress.[85] What reawakened it was the recognition that there were no solutions to the problems generated by free market economics – rising inequality, insecurity and environmental degradation – that did not involve co-operation both within nations and between them. International action is back on the agenda, signified by the joint management of problems such as global warming and deforestation; a succession of global conferences on the environment, population, women, social development, food security and habitat; and the halting acceptance of human rights standards as the bottom line in international affairs. Global jamborees in Rio de Janeiro, Beijing and Copenhagen produced little by way of action, but they did help to raise the profile of global issues in a way which is necessary if politicians are to listen. Huge question marks remain about the shape of international regimes, but the principle of global governance is no longer controversial.

The reactions of the 1990s against crude neo-liberalism have begun to feed through into official practice, but in ways which are incomplete and contradictory. Foreign aid continues to decline (down a further 13 per cent in real terms between 1995 and 1997), but it is now targeted on a smaller selection of countries and a narrower range of priorities.[86] Some donors want to focus the aid that remains on the world's poorest countries in South Asia and sub-Saharan Africa, and others on 'big emerging markets' or 'pivotal states' where short-term returns will be highest.[87] Some still see aid as a global welfare state; others as an investment for the future. All want to allocate aid more selectively according to the performance of the recipient, which may be a good thing if it is applied consistently and in ways which build capacity for the future.[88] Although couched in different language, old definitions of national interests remain – achieving prosperity and security by promoting democratic capitalism and a stable balance of military power – but offset by greater interest in eradicating absolute poverty and managing global problems such as environmental degradation and financial instability.[89] There is a 'new Washington Consensus' that illustrates this shift well – fiscal discipline remains, balanced by more attention to social expenditure and education, institution-building, global regulation and debt relief.[90] Everyone now speaks the language of participation, gender equity, sustainability and poverty focus, even if they don't practise it. The proportion of total aid spent on human development has started to rise for the first time since the 1960s, up from 19.2 per cent in 1991 to 25.1 per cent two years later.[91] Ninety per cent now goes to countries with per capita incomes below US$3000 per annum, though the proportion going to the poorest parts of the world continues to fall.[92] Less is being spent on aid for infrastructure and technical assistance (after a series of damning reports), and fewer aid contracts are 'tied' to business at home (notwithstanding the occasional spectacular lapse like the British-funded Pergau Dam in Malaysia or the helicopters provided to India that were only fit for scrap).[93] More and more aid is being delivered through private channels, especially NGOs and consultancy companies.[94] Soviet aid has all but disappeared, but there are new donors on the horizon such as South Korea and Taiwan who (like China before them) have learned one thing at least from the West – the value of money in persuading other countries to support your political objectives. After the recession of the 1980s, private capital has started to flow in much greater quantities, except to Africa. By 1995 private flows accounted for over two-thirds of total resource flows to developing countries (see Figure 2.1).[95]

Western governments are confused about how aid relates to private capital flows, and what to do now that the ideological certainties of previous years have disappeared. *'Post Cold-War, there no longer seems any clear compass to guide the international community'* is Joan Burton's judgement.[96] However, the OECD's new 'vision' for the 21st century promises to provide at least some direction for the lost souls of the development world and is rapidly becoming a benchmark for all aid ministries and international organisations.[97] It sets measurable goals like reducing absolute poverty by half and achieving universal primary education by the year 2015. More importantly, it *'sets out an agenda for a model of co-operation that puts developing countries in the driver's seat in planning for co-ordinated support from external partners that enhances local capacity and self-reliance'* – or more crudely, 'more ownership and less donor-ship'.[98] The OECD is honest enough to subtitle the next section 'Vision or Mirage?' It continues like this: *'the principal task now is to define the vision more concretely and translate it into reality...in a way which respects the ideas and opinions of developing countries'.* Unfortunately, the vision suffers from the same schizophrenia that has always afflicted foreign aid – a simultaneous desire for countries to control their development and a reluctance to allow them to do so. Policies '*must be locally-owned*', the OECD says, followed one page later by '*they must adhere to appropriate macro-economic policies, accountable government, gender equity*' and a long list of other things, all defined by the OECD. They can have their own development, but only if it is the kind we approve of seems to be the message. Even where the conditions appear progressive, such a formulaic approach doesn't fit the reality of countries that have eradicated absolute poverty in the past. Despite its good intentions, the new vision is permeated by lingering attitudes of control, inequality and standardisation. 'In the past we were wrong, but *now* we are right.' Until, that is, we are proved wrong again.

CONCLUSION – UNWELCOME GUESTS

Old attitudes are like unwelcome guests – they keep coming back however much you try to get rid of them. One hundred and eighty years separate the quotations at the head of this chapter, but all three embody the same stereotype of the dependent 'other' that requires our help. Nowadays the guests tread more softly and disguise themselves in other people's clothes: the racism of British reactions to India has softened into the paternalism of present-day foreign aid ministries and child sponsorship. '*What can people do except wait for a helping hand to assist them?*' asks Joan Burton. A great deal, as they always have done. As we shall see throughout this book, these attitudes have corrupted the post-war vision at every level, making genuine co-operation impossible by reinforcing unequal notions of power and responsibility. The good news is that, like the unwelcome guests they are, they can be told to go away.

The legacy of the Enlightenment was not entirely negative, but as a historically unprecedented will to control and dominate, a '*world ruled by calculation and wilfulness that is destructively purposeless*', it has done enormous damage.[99] The subjugation of nature for human gain, and the hubris brought on by the West's temporary supremacy in a wider historical perspective, has silenced other voices and alternatives. Standardisation, and an obsession with quick measurable results and size as measures of success, crowds out action on deeper problems. Technocratic approaches to development are still widespread, reducing politics, culture and social realities to bite-sized chunks that 'the experts' can solve. Schooled and trained in zero-sum thinking, we are ill-prepared to deal with complexity and uncertainty.[100] Especially in times of rapid change, we constantly look for things that offer easy answers, and if one easy answer loses its grip, another will be waiting around the corner.

From colonialism, we have inherited a basic inequality in power relations that drives the imposition of standard models across the world. Where power is unequal, double standards abound: Ugandans coerced into AIDS research when they cannot afford to buy the drugs that will be developed; or new measles vaccines tested on Haitian children by the United States Centre for Disease Control which may have *increased* local child mortality levels.[101] Although rarely taken as literally as this, rich-country interests have often used other societies as a testing ground for economic and political experiments they are unable or unwilling to conduct at home. Developing countries have been the instruments of a power play on a much bigger stage. The stereotyping and victimising of the 'other' continues, though this is not a preserve of the West. Malaysian Prime Minister Mahatir Mohammed's blanket description of Western societies as '*riddled with incest and unrestrained avarice*' is a neat mirror image of the gross generalisations practised by the colonisers.[102] This is the age-old mentality of displacing problems elsewhere, making good our damaged selves by externalising doubts and worries. If only we can make 'them' more like 'us', everything will be normal, and all will be well. But treating people as incapable reduces their ability to learn from mistakes, eroding the prospects of change that is sustainable by being rooted in local struggles and realities. Where outsiders perceive crisis and anarchy – an undifferentiated mass of suffering – the reality may simply be a continued struggle to cope and, where possible, advance. This realisation came to me on an early morning walk in a village in Northern Zambia in the autumn of 1984, past mothers engrossed in the daily routine of washing their children, chewing over the news of the day before, and getting ready for the rest of their 14-hour day. A hard life, tough and unfair, but full of its own love and light, and the determination to change it for the better. The moment we realise that others are not waiting for our help, still less relying on it, is the moment we can begin to help them properly.

From the cold war we have inherited a tradition of selective intervention to suit political objectives, mixing humanitarian and other goals in a cocktail that invariably produces poor results. It may be failure through muddle rather than self interest, but the result is the same. Foreign aid has replaced co-operation in the much more important areas of trade and investment, just as humanitarian assistance has replaced international action on the political dimensions of conflict.

In the words of the General Confession, '*We have done what we ought not to have done, and left undone those things which we ought to have done*'. The battle for universal ideologies which must be won or lost; the shifts in fashion from one decade to the next; and the focus on 'the right' policies and models regardless of context – all these things take away from the continuity and learning required for long-term change.

In short, we face a huge inheritance which must be confronted if international co-operation is to work. The future of the world depends on wise collective choices, but such choices can never be made on the back of imposed ideas. That implies a willingness to undertake the search together with those who may disagree with us. Nothing else will secure the collective legitimacy for solutions to hold. Despite our efforts, we have not really tried to help in this deeper sense. Now, with the colonial era at an end, the cold war out of our system, and mounting scepticism about any attempt to engineer universal solutions, the stage is set for a more concerted effort to make the vision of 1945 a reality, informed by the lessons of the last 50 years. That requires new attitudes, approaches and incentives; a switch from converting others to engaging with them; and a deeply-rooted reversal from 'them' to 'us'. '*The future depends on ourselves, and we do not depend on any historical necessity*' was Karl Popper's judgement about the 'Open Society and its Enemies'.[103] That means all of us, and it means together.

Chapter 3

How Do Countries Grow?
It's the Polity, Stupid!

The grafted mango is tastier than the original'
Bernard Ouedraogo, 6-S Movement, Burkina Faso[1]

'It's the polity, stupid'
The Economist, 29 June 1996

When Singapore's elder statesman Lee Kuan Yew visited newly elected Filipino President Fidel Ramos in 1992, he gave him some fatherly advice: restore law and order, build more infrastructure, and concentrate on economics, not democracy. Curious that, it sounds just like...Singapore. No doubt the advice was sincere, for this was a mixture that had turned his own country into one of the world's most dynamic economies in the space of 40 years, making a laughing stock of the World Bank's prediction of imminent collapse if Singapore dared to separate from Malaysia.[2] However, the assumption that what is right for one country is always right for others has never been true. No doubt a Nobel Prize awaits the first economist to come up with the perfect explanation of why some countries grow quicker than others. Sadly for me, I won't be making the trip to Stockholm, but still I find this question fascinating. What lies behind the rise of the West, the success of the 'tiger' economies, and the marginality of Africa? Is there a model that explains it all? Those who have searched for one agree that sustained economic growth requires a systematic reallocation of the factors of production from low-productivity activities like agriculture to high-productivity ones like manufacturing industries (not just an increase in factor inputs, as happened in the old Soviet Union).[3] The key is the ability to invest so that future output is higher than current output, and that means postponing consumption (to generate savings) or borrowing. Eventually the surplus created becomes large enough to provide for everyone's basic needs and finance the health, education and other services that are essential to further growth and welfare. There is no other proven way of doing this other than through a market economy. The conditions necessary for capital accumulation (such as competitive individualism and land reform to boost agricultural productivity) do fracture traditional social and cultural bonds, and they uproot people both physically and emotionally. That is just tough. Governments must push the process through if they are to secure a sustained path to growth. This may involve a period of authoritarian rule, but eventually democracy will consolidate itself as the only political system capable of supporting a pluralistic market economy with freedom of information and association, under the rule of law. *'Slow, cruel, even fearsome'* it may be, but the *'Great Ascent'* to capitalism is *'also irresistible, stirring and grandiose'*.[4] The 'uprooted' may not see it like this, of course, but they don't write the theories.

EXPLAINING ECONOMIC GROWTH

That, however, is where the consensus ends. When it gets to explaining the transition, it's a heavyweight fight between neo-classical (or neo-liberal) economists, and political (or development) economists.[5] According to the neo-liberals, governments need only remove barriers to markets and trade, and comparative advantage will do the rest. If the 'prices are right', resources will be allocated efficiently, enough investment will be generated, and wealth will trickle down through the population. Growth – if there is enough of it to share – will lead to a decline in poverty over time even if inequality increases in the short term.[6] More government involvement is bad by definition because bureaucrats will always look after themselves first. Even if they are imperfect, imperfect markets are better than imperfect states.[7] The only use for international co-operation is to help get the macro-economic policy framework right and ease the integration of developing countries into world markets.

This model is supposed to derive from the experience of the West, though even a cursory glance through history is enough to set some alarm bells ringing. Countries in Europe and North America followed different paths through capitalism in the 18th and 19th centuries. By all accounts the British experience was unique – it was export led with minimal tariffs, a well-developed foundation of market institutions, and a highly-productive agricultural system that had been developing for at least 100 years before 1780.[8] Even here, comparative advantage in textiles rested on the availability of export markets in the colonies and slave labour on the cotton plantations of North America. Germany, the USA and Japan all industrialised strategically behind protective barriers while their institutions were developing – the *'selective de-linking'* favoured by the 19th century German economist Friedrich List, and by early secretaries of commerce in the USA.[9] Sweden and the Netherlands could afford a more open economy with less state intervention because they had the best initial conditions, but still defied comparative advantage by creating a dairy industry using imported food grains.[10] In each case there was a dynamic balance between markets and states, and between protectionism and openness to trade; major investments in economic and political institution building over the long term; a polity that prevented the rising economic surplus from being siphoned off into unproductive use; the accidents of geography; and the exploitation of colonies. As we shall see, these lessons are instructive for lower-income countries, but it is hard to see much neo-classical purity in them. Paul Ormerod goes so far as to say that *'every country which has moved...to strong, sustained growth (except Britain)...has done so in outright violation of free-market principles'*.[11] Japan is probably the best known case of this at work – a country that *'modernised but did not westernise'* by selecting what it wanted from others and co-ordinating an industrial strategy under strong government leadership.[12] There is no basis in Western experience for the neo-liberal revolution which hit Africa and Latin America so hard during the 1980s. Nor is there any evidence from the industrialised world that inequality declines as growth matures, as the theory predicts. Capitalism only survived because social security mitigated its cruelties and women continued to bear the double burden of paid labour and unpaid domestic work.[13]

This is not exactly rocket science, so it is no surprise that development economists spotted the weaknesses of neo-classical theory early on. They recognised that there are many more barriers that get in the way of the transition from low to high-productivity activities – like technology, culture and gender relations, politics and institutions, shortfalls in human skills, and pre-existing inequalities in the distribution of assets – which mean that markets and trade rarely work in the way they are supposed to. Government action is therefore required to propel the economy forward and address the costs of markets (like pollution), their blind spots (a failure to see beyond the short term), and their failings in relation to the needs of people with less purchasing power. The 'free market' itself is a 'public good' that has to be guaranteed by the state in the form of property rights, the enforcement of contracts, and essential infrastructure.[14] The early development economists focused on gaps in savings, investment and technology that needed to be filled by foreign aid in order to kick-start the growth process. Soon it was realised that things were much more complicated. It was the productivity of capital that was the vital factor (not the amount of physical capital on its own), so investment in people and other things which upgraded the economy (like effective institutions) was critical. In order to achieve the economic surplus required for a sustained growth in incomes, countries must make technological or organisational innovations, and/or erect temporary barriers behind which they can become competitive in open markets. Geography and the initial conditions of the country, the shape of government policy, new forms of industrial organisation and management, and the degree of learning and flexibility in the economy, all influence growth. Poor people must participate directly in the growth process if growth is to reduce poverty – building up their skills and assets and ensuring equal access to markets and essential services. Most recently, economists have added a third form of capital (after physical and human capital) as an essential ingredient in the growth process. This is 'social capital', the trust and co-operation that makes markets work.[15]

Despite these innovations, there is no agreement on which theory is best. *'Ugly facts don't fit fancy models'* is Keith Griffin's conclusion after a lifetime studying the subject – there is no best path to development and certainly no single factor that explains variations in economic growth rates.[16] Economies are always evolving, always 'embedded' in culture and social structure,[17] and always 'contingent' – dependent on social and economic forces that change as they interact with each other over time. Every solution produces new problems of its own. Growth is 'non-linear' – think of China's rise, fall and rise again. Felipe Fernandez-Armesto makes the point that, with the advance of East Asia, we are heading back to the world balance that was prevalent 1000 years ago, though whether Western visitors will once again be derided as *'exotic freaks'* is another matter.[18] Nowadays the Russian economy is regarded as a 'basket case', but in the 1920s and 1930s Soviet growth rates outpaced anything in the West.[19] Who is to say that today's success stories will not be tomorrow's failures? Nonetheless, in 1960 South Korea was poorer than Pakistan, Chad

Table 3.1 *Key Development Indicators by Region*

Country	Human Development Index 1993[a]	Life Expectancy at Birth		Infant Mortality Rate		Adult Literacy Rate		Real GDP per Capita[b]	
		1960	1993	1960	1993	1970	1993	1960	1993
East Asia									
South Korea	0.886	53.9	71.3	85	11	88	98	690	9710
Malaysia	0.826	53.9	70.9	73	13	60	82	1783	8360
Indonesia	0.641	41.2	63.0	139	56	54	83	490	3270
China	0.609	47.1	68.6	150	44	na	na	723	2330
Sub-Saharan Africa									
Botswana	0.741	45.5	65.2	116	42	41	68	474	5220
Mauritius	0.825	59.2	70.4	70	18	na	na	2113	12,510
Kenya	0.473	44.7	55.5	124	69	32	76	635	1400
Uganda	0.326	43.0	44.7	133	115	41	60	371	910
Mozambique	0.261	37.3	46.4	190	147	22	38	1368	640
Latin America									
Chile	0.882	57.1	73.9	114	15	89	95	3130	8900
Mexico	0.845	57.1	71.0	92	35	74	89	2870	7010
Brazil	0.796	54.7	66.5	116	57	66	82	1404	5500
South Asia									
India	0.436	44.0	60.7	165	81	34	51	617	1240
Sri Lanka	0.698	62.0	72.0	71	17	77	90	1389	3030
Bangladesh	0.365	39.6	55.9	156	106	24	37	621	1290

Source: All data from UNDP Human Development Report 1996
a The Human Development Index is a composite of economic and social indicators
b Real GDP per capita is in US dollars, adjusted for Purchasing Power Parity

and Haiti; within 30 years it had all but eradicated absolute poverty and joined the ranks of industrialised country donors, while the other three still languish among the least developed countries in the world. What happened?

WAS THERE AN EAST ASIAN 'MIRACLE'?

East Asia covers countries of radically different experience but, as Table 3.1 shows, the most successful countries in the developing world are well represented in the region. Botswana, Mauritius and Chile have been equally successful and Mexico and Brazil have also grown, but with less of an impact on poverty. Sri Lanka and the Indian states of Kerala and West Bengal have spread the benefits of low growth rates widely through the population; but the rest of South Asia and sub-Saharan Africa has achieved neither growth nor equity. Between 1960 and 1990, South Korea grew by seven per cent a year or more, doubling real incomes per head and cutting poverty by two-thirds.[20] Taiwan has achieved the largest reduction in inequality in any non-socialist nation since 1900.[21] With a much larger population, Indonesia cut the number of people below the poverty line from 69 per cent in 1970 to 15 per cent in 1990, before heading into spectacular reverse as a financial crisis exploded across the region. Even East Asian growth rates look small beside those of Botswana (14 per cent a year in the 1970s and ten per cent in the 1980s), which are even more impressive since they were attained under a stable and democratic government.[22] These countries have done in 30 years what took the West 300.

In recent years it has become fashionable to decry these achievements, especially as a result of events that engulfed much of East Asia at the end of 1997. The dramatic slump that originated in a loss of confidence in Thailand spread rapidly through South Korea and Indonesia to reveal the fragility of these countries' banking and financial systems, the dangers of over exposure to foreign loans, and the corrupting effect of close ties (or 'cronyism') between governments and local industry. Critics like the American economist Paul Krugman saw this as proof that the region's growth was unsustainable because it wasn't based on improvements in efficiency, productivity and institutions.[23] The slump came on the back of other weaknesses which were already apparent: political repression in China and Indonesia; high-level corruption,[24] an over concentration of power in the hands of industrial conglomerates, and a failure to deal fairly with strikes in

South Korea;[25] and a rise in organised crime in Taiwan. East Asia is 'a poisoned paradise',[26] especially China, Indonesia and Malaysia, where forest fires blanketed huge areas with smog during 1997.[27] Gender inequalities and wage gaps between men and women persist alongside the predominance of low-skill jobs for women in export manufactures;[28] threats to social cohesion are beginning to grow as younger people become less willing to fulfil their obligations to their parents;[29] high rates of inequality in per capita incomes remain between regions, especially in China; and progress in attacking the hard-core poverty that remains seems to have stalled.

There is no doubt that what happened at the end of 1997 shook the East Asian 'miracle' to its foundations, but the problems don't invalidate the achievements that must be set alongside them. At the time, the *Guardian* newspaper in London claimed that 'an entire philosophy has crumbled'.[30] Was this the same philosophy that had eradicated absolute poverty in record time, produced an economic and industrial transformation unparalleled in history, generated a quantum leap in technology and output, and secured living conditions that surpass all other developing countries?[31] Some countries in the region (like Taiwan and, to a lesser extent, China) escaped the effects of the crisis,[32] and corruption and financial instability are inevitable whenever systems and institutions cannot keep up with very rapid growth.[33] The great depression that swept across the industrialised world in the 1930s was hugely damaging in the short term, but the lessons it taught provided the basis for lasting recovery. Why should East Asia be different? There are already signs that this is happening. President Kim Dae Jung in South Korea came to power on a platform of attacking corruption, deepening democracy, and making markets more efficient.[34] Taiwan has an ambitious programme for environmental clean-up which involves creating a domestic environmental services industry and subsidising less polluting production methods. There is little sign that democracy and 'Asian values' are irreconcilable (as some politicians in the region claim). Ex-President Suharto of Indonesia is the latest leader to find this out.[35] The growth of the middle class, labour unions, and grassroots democracy via village committees and other institutions (even in China), is likely to lead to greater openings. People everywhere demand a greater share of the wealth they help to create, and more of a say in how their lives are run, as incomes rise.[36] The transition to a fully innovation-driven phase of industrialisation depends on the success of the democratisers in creating an institutional environment which encourages more creativity. East Asia is much more likely to return to growth after a few years of austerity than embark on an irreversible slide in its economic fundamentals. Its miracle may have lost much of its shine, but it still has a great deal to teach the rest of the world. The question is, what?

EAST ASIA: THE MECHANICS OF MIX AND MATCH

Reconstructing the past is always dangerous. In retrospect, the mess of life is reinterpreted as a coherent story. Anthropologist Tadao Umesao observes that even Meiji Japan (supposedly the definitive example of planned transformation in the late 19th century) drifted pragmatically with few clear goals and '*no one knowing what would happen next*'.[37] Nevertheless, the strategies that drove poverty-reducing growth in East Asia are well documented. Governments sought to create a 'virtuous circle', with states helping to guide markets in line with long-term national interests and market signals helping to keep governments informed and effective.[38] First came land reform and investment in rural infrastructure to redistribute assets, raise agricultural productivity and encourage rural industry. Large-scale industrialisation followed, with each phase building on the one before. Agro-processing led to labour-intensive manufactured exports, then heavy steel and chemicals, and now high-technology industries, taking goods developed by the West and making them at lower cost and higher standards of quality.[39] This was *manufactured* comparative advantage at its best. The transition was nurtured using tax incentives to industry, subsidised credit, measures to expand domestic demand, and strict performance targets. Rising productivity enabled governments to borrow heavily on international markets without incurring unsustainable debts. States were 'developmental' – disciplined, meritocratic, reasonably accountable and relatively autonomous from the interest groups that could have stifled progress. Citizens worked hard and saved harder, accepting limits on real wages and repressive labour laws in exchange for the promise of future benefits. Levels of investment were exceptionally high – an average of 35 per cent of gross domestic product (GDP) across the region, or almost twice as much as in Latin America in the same period.[40] Growth was widely shared even though formal participation in politics was restricted.

One of the most interesting aspects of the East Asian story is that success – in contrast to economic dogma from Right or Left – came from a dynamic balance between self-reliance and openness to the

world, and the deliberate mixing of government direction, markets
and private enterprise, and social activism. Although government was
quite small (measured by the proportion of GDP devoted to public
spending), it was able to provide a 'central co-ordinating intelligence'
that governed markets wisely and mobilised the resources of all
groups in society to work towards a common purpose.[41] There were
few master plans, but there was planning, in the sense of a conscious
attempt to find the best way to achieve results. Goals and strategies
were constantly adjusted, and learning and flexibility in the economy
were deliberately encouraged, aided by cultures and social structures
which valued self-improvement and education.[42] There were three
areas of state activism that were particularly significant. The first was
prudent macro-economic policy, which secured low inflation, low
budget deficits (aided by private health and education provision and
people's willingness to absorb welfare costs within the family), and
the overall stability essential to savings and investment. Governments
created the confidence required to mobilise domestic resources and
pull in foreign investors.

The second was industrial policy, which aimed to identify firms
and sectors with high growth potential and reward them with preferential treatment such as a protected domestic market or subsidised
credit for productive investment. This becomes inefficient when
taken to extremes, but in the early days performance contracts were
able to promote good results despite these interventions in market
mechanisms.[43] Because there were close links between government,
industry and intermediary groups near to the 'sharp end', the state
had the information it needed to make (mostly) the right decisions.
So although markets were encouraged, market mechanisms were not
trusted as the only mechanism to allocate resources where strategic
goals were at risk. In the 1950s and 1960s, the Taiwanese government monopolised the distribution of fertiliser and exchanged it for
rice from farmers at prices above their world market value. Although
heretical in economic terms, this stimulated rapid increases in
production and savings during the critical early phases of productivity growth. The third focus of state activity was to redistribute
productive assets among the population, and invest heavily in public
services. Secondary school enrolment in East Asian countries during
the 1980s varied between 72 per cent and 94 per cent, compared to
30–50 per cent in Latin America.[44] What stands out from this story
is a refusal to get caught in a false polarity between states and
markets. Both are needed, each overlaps with the other, and the best

results come when markets operate inside a framework set and monitored by a government which keeps in close touch both with industry and with ordinary people.

The second example of this 'mix and match' approach was East Asia's openness to outside technology, ideas, and trading opportunities, combined with a strong sense of national self-determination and a bedrock of self-reliance. The same sense of balance is evident in the use of foreign aid and investment. Aid was certainly important in the early phases of East Asian growth; American aid financed 70 per cent of total South Korean imports between 1953 and 1961 and 95 per cent of Taiwan's trade deficit in the 1950s.[45] It was no accident that Taiwan's Economic Stabilisation Board held its meetings in English to facilitate US participation.[46] Aid helped to finance land reform, allowed the maintenance of military forces without draining the economy, brought in American advisers and technology, and paid for young Koreans to be trained in the USA (who later played a key role in the reforms of President Park). There were furious arguments about economic policy at the height of American aid-giving to South Korea which President Rhee ignored, because he knew that aid would keep on flowing (the cold war would see to that). Rather than a case of good aid well used, East Asia was a case of aid, good and bad, used efficiently by governments that knew where they were heading. The same patterns reappear in other high-performing countries like Botswana, which could and did say 'no' to foreign aid when it judged it inappropriate, and where *local* funds were used to buy in foreign technical assistance within clear priorities set by the state.[47] In any case, the real take-off took place when aid was negligible.[48] Trade and private investment were more important than aid (especially in Hong Kong, which received little aid, and in Singapore, which borrowed most of what it needed, though at preferential rates). Japanese assistance, which increased rapidly in the 1960s and 1970s, was especially important here, in the form of licences to use Japanese technology, consultants from Japanese firms, and trade and investment agreements. If there was a formula to success, it was ten per cent foreign inspiration and 90 per cent domestic perspiration, and even then outside assistance was managed by the state to make sure it did not disrupt progress towards long-term goals.

Although their export orientation has left them vulnerable to sudden shifts in demand from Japan, Europe and North America, the East Asian countries and other high performers like Botswana and Chile have used their success to build up their internal markets, education systems, skills and levels of innovation. Taiwan now registers more patents in America each year per head of its population than Britain does.[49] Because they were late industrialisers, the East Asian countries were able to borrow technology, ideas and management practices from others, though they had to 'get the prices wrong' to do so.[50] All the tiger economies removed domestic trade barriers slowly and selectively so that they could develop higher-productivity industries that would eventually be competitive on world markets. Otherwise they would not have been able to increase savings and investment sufficiently to finance imports and develop exports in the face of open market competition against better-equipped rich-country firms. In the 1960s and 1970s, savings were more important than foreign investment, but when (following the appreciation of the Yen) Japan made large volumes of investment available it too was channelled into the industrial transition and was not allowed to destabilise the economy, unlike in the years preceding the financial crash of 1998. Botswana's rich mineral resources were used strategically by the state to diversify the economy into higher-value exports and develop essential infrastructure.[51] Unlike many other members of the Lome Convention (the treaty which binds the European Union together with the former colonies of its member states), Botswana and Mauritius have put their trade preferences to good effect, responding to rising labour costs (which come with a more educated workforce) by expanding into higher-skilled industries.[52]

The lesson to be learned is that economic integration must be a careful, gradual and strategic process if the gains are to outweigh the costs. That requires understanding and support from the rest of the world, rather than a 'boneheaded' insistence on a 'level playing field' for free trade among economies of radically different levels of competitiveness. Present-day attitudes in the World Trade Organisation would have killed East Asian growth at birth. Recent steps by Chile and Brazil[53] to discourage sudden capital inflows with taxes are much closer to the kind of policy mix developed in East Asia – that is, be open to external opportunities, but not at the cost of long-term domestic goals; engage with the global economy, but do so with all the weapons at your disposal; abandon de-linking as a goal, but don't throw yourself at the mercy of globalisation. Use temporary protection, regional alliances and anything else you can find to get up to speed in the race for international competitiveness, but don't enter the race without your safety gear in working order.

EAST ASIA – HOW DID THEY DO IT?

So much for the mechanics of the East Asian experience. Of more interest to our story is what made these choices possible – 'how did they do it?' rather than 'what they did'. How is it that East Asian states were 'developmental' when so many others were corrupt? Why did ordinary people agree to make the sacrifices growth demanded? Even when you know what the right policies are, how do you persuade business and workers to support them? This is a much more complicated story. The first part of the answer is the most difficult to replicate since it involves culture, geography, leadership and luck.[54] Some East Asian leaders believe the emphasis on 'Asian values' has been overdone, especially since values are changing all the time and many (like family loyalty) are universal anyway.[55] However, the Confucian emphasis on conformity and the needs of the 'social whole', hard work, respect for education, and authority exercised with compassion, were undoubtedly important in underpinning success. In South Korea, an ethnically homogeneous population, linguistic unity, and the weakness of social classes promoted a sense of nationhood, and this was both exploited and rewarded by strong leadership in the guise of 'South Korea's Bismarck', Park Chung Hee.[56] A master at *'conjuring communities out of words'*,[57] Park shared the single-minded determination to achieve production goals that marked East Asian elites out from their counterparts in Africa and Latin America. Like the Japanese before them, people worked ferociously for 60 hours or more each week to fulfil slogans of national improvement. If Theodore Zeldin is right that *'mentalities decide what really happens'*, East Asia is a good illustration.[58] Seretse Khama (in Botswana) and Suharto (in Indonesia) encouraged similar attitudes among their own elites.[59] People wanted success, and believed in themselves. Perhaps colonialism was a factor in strengthening this desire; it was certainly less damaging in East Asia than in Africa.[60]

The second set of factors lie in the international context, which was especially favourable to growth and development in East Asia in the years following the end of World War II. The USA and then Japan provided generous finance to cover temporary import shortfalls and early investments in infrastructure, and when East Asia started to grow more quickly, an expanding world economy offered high rewards for success.[61] Back in the 1950s and 1960s, rich countries were arguably more generous in their aid giving, but they were definitely more frightened by the 'red menace' of communist insurgency into South-East Asia. It was in the interests of the USA to see East Asia succeed, and war in Korea and Vietnam also gave a boost to the regional economy. America's willingness to turn a blind eye to trade barriers and other controls (in stark contrast to today) supported the crucial early phases of industrialisation. Alice Amsden, one of the world's leading authorities on East Asia, describes how, flawed though American assistance was, replete with delays, bungling and inappropriate advice, South Korean firms did gain important experience about quality control and competitive bidding.[62]

The third set of factors centres on politics and governance. Economic growth and the social transformations it demands are tremendously dislocating processes, especially when accomplished in the space of a few decades. Why wasn't change frustrated by vested interests which stood to gain from old power structures and privileged access to a rising economic surplus? The easy answer is that East Asia had 'hard states' that stood firm when faced by opposition to reform.[63] However, other East Asian authoritarian states (like the Philippines under Marcos, or Burma today) did not achieve the same results, and South Korea performed better under the more democratic regime of President Park than his less democratic predecessor, Rhee. Other successful cases (like Botswana and Mauritius) have been democracies since independence, so authoritarianism is clearly not an explanation. Equally important were strong societies which acted as a countervailing force to vested interests. They were not well-developed 'civil societies' in the Western sense (independent associations in opposition to the state), but they did have many intermediary groups which were closely linked to industry and government. They included manufacturers' associations, export promotion councils, and local participatory forums on key policy issues. South Korea's student movement mobilised popular support to help keep government on track, and in Taiwan there were over 11,000 industrial and civic groups with 8.3 million members by 1987.[64] It was these networks that provided the information governments needed to make effective policy and know when to change it, like the early correction of macroeconomic imbalances and the cancellation of heavy industry initiatives in Malaysia, Singapore and South Korea.[65] The same is true of Botswana and Mauritius, where local authorities and village councils participate actively in government planning and budgeting.[66] In Kerala a strong trade union movement and a democratic government forged a series of formal pacts which exchanged voluntary wage restraint and agreement on strikes for high levels of security and welfare benefits.[67]

Industrial relations committees mediate in conflicts that arise between workers and employers, and a huge range of other civic associations act as intermediaries between people and state. Trust, problem-solving abilities and other forms of social capital form a slowly spreading web, though not always defined by Western norms of free association and democratic accountability through elections. These structures exerted at least a modest range of checks and balances on government decisions. They worked differently in different countries, but they worked. In all cases, it was the synergy between a strong and efficient state and a strong and effective society that made the difference.[68]

Most important of all, broadly-based growth gave everyone a stake in success.[69] The benefits of growth-enhancing policies were widely (if unequally) shared. This fostered a sense of solidarity which was vital to the discipline and sacrifice that change demanded. Governments also made it expensive to reverse these policies, thereby giving everyone confidence that they would, in the end, share in the dividends of economic growth. Although labour unions were taken over by the state in all East Asian countries, they did deliver economic benefits to their members, as did co-operatives, which played a significant role in Singapore and Indonesia. And the ethos of shared benefits fed back into a sense of obligation to contribute to the costs of social welfare.[70]

What, in summary, was the secret of success? Clearly, there was no one factor. It was the combination of favourable initial conditions (geography, history, culture, and – in Botswana's case – rich mineral resources), a supportive international context, and the emergence of a strong polity that laid the foundation for effective policies.[71] These policies found a changing mix between state activism, markets, and social obligations on the one hand; openness to the world, and national self-determination on the other. Because the benefits of growth were widely shared, progress was not derailed by opposition from any set of interests. In each case the relative contribution of these factors varied and the end product was unique. But since little could have been achieved without the capacity to make decisions and the broad-based support to push them through, it is those two things that were most important. That conclusion has profound implications for the future of international co-operation.

AFRICA – WHAT WENT WRONG?

Statistics tell us that sub-Saharan Africa is on the way up. In 1995 two-thirds of the region's economies grew by more than three per cent, and some – like Uganda and Ghana – grew even faster, more than keeping pace with continued population growth. Who would have guessed that food production is racing ahead of population in many communities across Africa?[72] However, economic stagnation, war and very poor governance still scar much of the continent, as they have for 20 years or more. A glance through official reports makes depressing reading: poverty in the region up from 29 per cent of the population in 1987 to 33 per cent in 1993;[73] manufacturing output in 1991 less than that of Puerto Rico;[74] and the proportion of children in primary school actually in retreat.[75] Superficially, it is not difficult to see what went wrong. The story of Africa's recent 'development' looks like a mirror image of East Asia: low savings and investment (down three per cent in the last five years),[76] continued dependence on primary exports, spiralling debts, ethnic conflict, corrupt states, and an overall absence of the stability that growth requires. There is no shortage of advice from the experts on what needs to be done: cut tariffs and export taxes on agriculture, slash government spending, and join the world economy, says Harvard economist Jeffrey Sachs. It's all the fault of suicidal domestic policies.[77] Invest in labour-intensive public works and re-emphasise agrarian self-reliance, say many NGOs; its all the fault of a vicious international context. Can they both be right?

It is true that the record of state intervention in Africa since independence has been dismal. Controls on industry and agriculture have discouraged savings, innovation and entrepreneurship. An overblown public sector has shielded inefficient parastatal companies, and incentives have gone to capital-intensive industry instead of labour-intensive growth. This part of the African story is well known, and has been under persistent attack from agencies like the World Bank for at least 15 years. In some areas, however, states have not been active enough. Africa urgently needs more of the public goods that underpin growth, like infrastructure and scientific capacity. Since about two-thirds of growth comes from human and social capital, much more investment needs to go into health, education and training.[78] In the unequal agrarian economies that characterise sub-Saharan Africa, governments must intervene to attack biases in the production and marketing of food and export crops so that small farmers have the land, inputs and credit they need to respond to market incentives. That was what enabled Zimbabwean smallholders to double maize production between 1980 and 1986.[79] Whether this is best done through low-input sustainable agriculture or full-throttle green-revolution techniques is a controversial subject which has divided expert opinion, but since African farming systems are very diverse, a combination of science-based innovations with adaptive research would seem a good way forward.[80] That strategy still needs public investment. More use could also be made of the guaranteed employment and food security schemes which have been so successful in India.[81] It is not a question of more state intervention or less, but of raising the quality of government action in the right areas.

The second set of mistakes attributed to African governments are those that discouraged integration into world markets. The World Bank is clear where the problem lies: Africa's share of global trade has declined consistently because it has not been competitive, and that has been due to domestic policies (including overvalued exchange rates), not protectionism in the rest of the world.[82] All other groups of low-income countries have improved their competitiveness over the same period despite facing higher tariffs than Africa. There has been little diversification into higher productivity exports, and that is the fault of governments. When the walls came tumbling down as a consequence of the debt crisis of the 1980s, Africa's industries followed. Countries that choose to shelter behind high domestic barriers will stagnate: de-linking is fatal to your health.

However, if import substitution didn't work in Africa, how did East Asia grow so quickly by developing selected industries behind protective tariffs? The answer is that these measures were part of a longer term strategy directed at becoming successful as an exporter of high value-added products. They were a means to an end, not an end in themselves, and that is a key lesson for other countries who still face the challenge of integrating into world markets without sacrificing their own goals and visions. Full integration needs careful preparation so that the human resources, research and development capacity, infrastructure and industrial profile are primed for the shock of global competition when it arrives. Countries that are unprepared – as Africa is now – will inevitably suffer. They will need to export more of what they already produce (primary commodities) in order to pay their debts to the rest of the world, but as they export more, the price of these commodities will fall and the cost of what they import will rise. So for Africa some form of temporary protection makes a lot of sense, especially as it will take a long time to develop the conditions required to be competitive in manufactured exports. In giving priority to exports, it is easy to forget that two-thirds of Africans still live on the land, most of them on subsistence farms.[83] For the foreseeable future, investing in smallholder agriculture, labour-intensive rural industrialisation, and higher-value agro-exports (like horticultural products) is the best option since it builds on Africa's abundant natural resources and scarce human skills, so long as this does not become an excuse to abandon gradual, structural change in the economy.[84] Integration into world markets is essential to long-term development, but it is not necessary to do it all at once, or all in one way. International co-operation has a vital role to play in helping countries to do it in ways which suit them best.

AFRICA: WHY DID IT HAPPEN?

Like the bare facts of the East Asian story, this tells us little about what was really going on. As we have seen, no policy recommendation is worth much unless it is rooted in local realities and backed by the capacity and support base to make it work. Why didn't these exist in Africa? Let's look first at the factors African decision-makers inherited from the past: geography and ecology, the colonial legacy, and culture. There is no doubt that the physical isolation of the African interior and the large distances exports must travel to ports place African producers at a relative disadvantage in terms of transport costs. Tropical diseases hit crops, livestock and people especially hard (malaria kills someone every 12 seconds) and the productive potential of large parts of the continent is limited by semi-arid conditions and leached soils.[85] The colonial powers did little to address these natural disadvantages and prepare the way for growth, but more damaging was the assumption that Africans were unfit for self-government. History also left Africa with a legacy of arbitrary borders criss-crossing long-standing ethnic divisions, and that made the task of nation build-ing more difficult. Combined with the cold-war manoeuvres of the Soviet Union and the USA, and the economic and military aggression of the South African apartheid regime, this helped to stack the odds against political stability from independence onward.[86]

Basil Davidson, an especially acute and sensitive observer of Africa over four decades, describes how colonialism *'destroyed the moral order on which people depended for stability'*, but did not replace it with anything capable of bringing them together again apart from rival kinship networks.[87] The post-colonial state in Africa did not operate in any social sense, so it is no surprise that states were ineffective in promoting a sense of national purpose, public good, and collective welfare. Kinship communities (tribes and clans) are still the only workable unit of politics in most countries, and economic lives are organised around fluid social networks, not just markets.[88] That means that state control and the money economy have only a fragile hold. Since these are the two conditions that are essential to capital accumulation, it is not surprising that capitalism in Africa has not been a great success. There are no *'shortcuts to progress'*, as the political scientist Goran Hyden famously declared.[89] Peasants must leave the 'culture of affection' if they want to enter the modern economy, but neither a forced march to capitalism nor Julius Nyerere's disastrously romantic vision of Tanzanian peasants as 'natural socialists' is a viable way forward. Africa must find its own way, though it has been poorly served in searching for it by its leaders. As Nobel Prize winner Wole Soyinka says, *'there is an absolute failure of vision'*.[90] However, under a new generation of leaders like Presidents Museveni of Uganda and Issayas Aferworki of Eritrea this is changing. Such visions will always be more difficult to achieve in those parts of Africa still embroiled in civil war, ethnic violence, and predatory military and economic activities.[91] War is not conducive to development, unless it is someone else's war that boosts your economy and makes you strategic enough to warrant outside attention. In contrast to East Asia during the 1950s and 1960s, Africa has seen no dividend from the cold war or the peace that followed. In terms of its underlying conditions, East Asia had it easy.

The second set of factors lie in the international context. Statistics show a long-term decline in the terms of trade for the primary goods Africa exports (with occasional cyclical upturns) in relation to the manufactures it imports.[92] If this trend had been reversed, Africa could have paid for all of its imports from its own export earnings, and the debts it owes to rich-country banks and governments would have dropped by almost 50 per cent.[93] Current levels of debt in African countries are completely unsustainable: 20 out of 33 owe more to foreigners than their economies are worth.[94] Macro-economic instability has deterred foreign investment, and Africa's failure to make the transition to higher-productivity industries has made sustainable borrowing impossible. Even though Africa's debts will never be repaid, the drain that current levels of repayment place on the exchequer is enormous. Falling export prices plus rising debt repayments means that there is no money to spend on crucial development priorities like infrastructure, health and education. A

combination of oil price shocks, declining terms of trade, rising interest rates for debt repayments, drought and war made the 1980s a
'lost decade' for Africa.[95] In any case, protectionism in the industrialised world and recession on world markets during the same period
would have made it difficult for Africa to sell its goods even if it had
diversified its industrial base.

Set against trends like these, foreign aid would have had to have
been spectacularly successful to reverse the structural weaknesses of
African economies. It was not, and by the end of the 1980s countries
like Mozambique and Uganda were so dependent on aid that whole
sectors of the economy and social policy were financed by outsiders –
70 per cent of Mozambique's GDP in 1988 and 90 per cent of the
health budget in Uganda.[96] The African Development Bank estimates
that Africa will need US$61 billion in external resources each year
for the next five years, just to generate sufficient growth, but the
world total of official development assistance in 1996 was only
US$55 billion, and falling.[97] Even if it were to be provided in such
quantities, the quality of aid would have to improve dramatically to
make any difference. This is partly because donors are always changing their minds, and never allowing enough time for the gradual
development of institutions that is so crucial to development. Roland
Oliver makes the point that it was Africa's misfortune to become
independent just when centralised planning was in vogue and
outsiders were happy to support it.[98] During the cold war, Soviet and
US aid was provided regardless of development performance, even to
'kleptocrats' like President Mobutu who was welcomed to the White
House as a *'voice of good sense and goodwill'*.[99] In the 1980s everything changed, and resources went to privatise and liberalise what aid
had previously built up. Now the merry-go-round has turned again
and investment in health and education is top priority. All this time,
aid was strengthening the social and political structures that stood in
the way of change, buttressing incompetent states, and hampering
the emergence of the capacities and coalitions that are needed for
equitable growth.[100] Despite 40 years of foreign aid, little attention
has been paid by donors to the fundamental weaknesses in African
markets and institutions that reduce their ability to benefit from
international trade and global financial flows.[101] Of course, one can
turn all this around by asking why African countries relied so much
on aid in the first place, failed to diversify out of primary exports,
and took on loans that were out of all proportion to their ability to
repay them, and that gets us to the heart of the problem – the crisis
of governance described below. The unfavourable international

context does not explain what happened to Africa, nor is it an excuse for domestic mistakes, but the cumulative effect of so many external pressures did reduce the room to manoeuvre that all countries need to get things right. Not all aid to Africa was bad, but overall, bad aid was badly used.

Both initial conditions in Africa and the surrounding context were unfavourable to growth and development for much of the post-independence period, but countries like Botswana succeeded in the same context, and policy decisions were rarely dictated by culture and ecology. The real issues lie elsewhere. Although it has devastating economic consequences, Africa's crisis is really one of governance – the absence of the political stability required for economic development to occur. And underlying that problem are social structures based on allegiance to kinship which make the task of nation-building and state autonomy exceptionally difficult, and authoritarian, incompetent states which rarely respond to public pressure. '*Without democracy many African nations are little more than a gambling space for the opportunism and adventurism of power,*' is Wole Soyinka's judgement.[102] Ali Mazrui puts the failure of African states to control their revenue at the heart of the problem.[103] Others emphasise the consequences of personal rule and the constant failure to rise above sectional interests.[104] Mobutu, Bokassa and the rest exemplify a particularly grotesque abuse of power for personal satisfaction. During my own time in Malawi in the 1980s a woman was arrested for 'weeping subversively over the body of her husband' who had been tortured to death in a nearby police cell. It is hard to imagine a more perverted interpretation of state responsibility than this.

Elsewhere in Africa the decline in governance was less extreme, but still it sapped the trust in public action that was crucial to success. Season after season when the fertiliser arrives late, the maize is not collected, the buses don't run, and the schools are empty, confidence erodes. In that situation, 'exit' ('why bother?') seems a better option than 'voice' ('we demand change').[105] '*The wise man bows low to the great lord and silently farts*', as an Amhara proverb puts it in Ethiopia.[106] Sudanese entrepreneurs have given up investing domestically and deposited over US$15 billion in Egyptian banks instead.[107] Lacking any convincing identity beyond their social group, people stick with the politicians who belong to them, and they, in turn, use these social networks to advance. Corruption – the use of formal political institutions for personal gain – is endemic in the way politics is practised. Without autonomy from sectional interests and authority to confront them, states cannot take the decisions economic growth demands.[108] And with the exception of South Africa and a few others, African societies are also weak, with few intermediary organisations to link the grassroots with government.[109] Communication, dialogue, transparency and accountability are impeded. That deprives states of the information they need to make decisions, and erodes the capacity of civil societies to act as a counterweight to a wayward government – or as a support to policy makers facing tough choices. The absence of a competitive political environment also weakens the 'early-warning' systems that have prevented famine elsewhere.[110] NGOs have mushroomed over the past 15 years, but most are too dependent on foreign aid and too involved in delivering services to be of much use in strengthening society or keeping states accountable.[111]

None of this means that Africa needs Western-style democracy, nor even an African version of East Asian authoritarianism. But it does need an effective polity moulded in its own image – an organised society and process of governance that enables decisions to be made in the long-term interests of the whole. Uganda, for example, is making headway using its own system of non-party democratic politics based on 'resistance committees' from the village level upwards. According to President Museveni, this gives people a voice in decision making while avoiding the problems of tribal competition. As in East Asia, what matters is how the system works, not what it looks like to outsiders. In all cases development needs stability, stability requires a legitimate state, and legitimacy rests on transparency, accountability and a level of political participation that is meaningful in local terms.

During the critical period of the 1970s and 1980s, African countries lacked a 'growth coalition' to counterbalance the interests of urban consumers and politicians. Rural producers were exploited by governments in setting crop prices below the market rate, but were rarely organised into an effective movement to exert pressure for change from below. When economic reform did arrive in the 1980s, powerful interest groups hurt most, and that spelt disaster for the changes that still had to be made.[112] Little momentum could be developed in the push for growth. It is the absence of broad-based coalitions of winners (or at least potential winners) that makes progress so difficult, not just in Africa, but in Latin America and South Asia too.[113] Unlike in high-performing countries, the benefits of growth were concentrated among elites, so there was no incentive for ordinary people to make sacrifices in return for long-term gains. Even today, land in Mozambique and Kenya is being given to party leaders and well-connected businessmen in preference to rural communities.[115] In Zimbabwe, funds meant for war veterans have been siphoned off by senior politicians. *'There are so many cabinet members, army and police officers who are claiming funds for serious disabilities, it's a wonder the government can function at all,'* says Margaret Dongo, an independent Member of the Zimbabwe Parliament.[115] Sadly, the likelihood of a developmental state is low in countries that need one most.[116] Bad governance breeds disengagement from the political process, and disengagement allows corrupt politicians to thrive.

Just as there was no one factor at work in East Asia, there is no magic wand that can be waved (especially by outsiders) to put Africa to rights. Luck plays a big role in bringing forth a leader like Museveni in place of a tyrant like Amin, just as it did in replacing Rhee with Park in South Korea. The legacies of geography and history cannot be wished away; nor can foreign aid change African people's deeply-held beliefs about where they belong. Yes, policies were often wrong-headed, but those who believe it was all the fault of policies will have to think again. The real issue is how to get the right policies and steer them through the minefield of African politics and social realities. And the right policies will vary greatly from place to place and time to time. *'Africa is not backward trying to progress, it is different being forced to conform'*: Patrick Marnham's conclusion may be overly romantic, but he has an important point.[117] In reflecting on the prospects for his continent, the Ugandan scholar Mahmood Mamdani sees a future for Africa somewhere between 'liberal modernism' and 'Africanist communitarianism', fusing the best of local traditions with the benefits of the market and liberal democracy.[118] That is an intriguing prospect, and it brings us back to where we started at the head of this chapter – the 'grafted mango'.

CONCLUSION

How do countries grow? In each case one finds a heady cocktail of ingredients shaken and stirred to suit local tastes. Economic growth and social equity both depend on shifting relationships between state, market and people, sometimes with the focus turned inwards and at other times turned outwards to the wider world. Underlying these relationships are some unique factors (geography, history, culture, leadership and luck), and some more general ones (like high savings rates, investment in people, and political stability). It is not a particular model of economy and society that produces good results, but people's capacity to develop their own models by blending outside ideas and opportunities with local realities – *'the grafted mango is tastier than the original'*. There is no absolute truth or ultimate cause in development, only interlocking patterns which lead upwards in a virtuous cycle or downwards to violence and stagnation. But what separates the two?

In each case, a wide range of factors come together to make the whole more than the sum of its parts, enhancing the ability of local institutions to manage internal dilemmas and respond to shifts in the external environment, both of which are changing continuously. But the same parts reassembled elsewhere may produce a very different whole, and the appropriate response to a changing context at one point in time may produce different results at another. That makes it impossible to manufacture success, but what can be done is to support the conditions that make success more likely by giving local forces more of a chance to get things right. That requires international action in two areas. First, encouraging the development of the institutions and institutional linkages that are vital for equitable growth: well-functioning markets; a developmental state; a strong society; a broad consensus in favour of long-term, distributive goals; and active channels of communication and accountability. In that sense the *Economist* was right – *'it's the polity, stupid'* – the collective intelligence and sense of purpose that marks the East Asian experience from most of Africa.

The second priority is to make the international context more favourable by reducing debt repayments, opening domestic markets in the North, facilitating private investment, and improving the terms of trade. That would give African leaders more breathing space so that there is less pressure to make the wrong decisions and more leeway to make the right ones. External support was an important factor in the success of all high-performing countries, especially during the early phase of growth when additional resources were needed to supplement domestic markets and skills, and mitigate the accidents of geography. Temporary help of the right kind gave progressive forces more room to manoeuvre at critical moments, smoothing the transition to a high-productivity economy and a successful society. Because there is no one path to these goals, both these areas for action require outsiders to abandon universal theories and economistic prescriptions. In the past, we have been too concerned with policies, and not enough with the polities that create and sustain them. It's time to reverse the balance.

Calling any society 'successful' is dangerous given the continued existence of exclusion and pollution in all 'high performers', let alone East Asia's recent fall from grace. But high growth rates, broadly shared, do generate the material conditions required to address these problems, and over time they also build the coalitions necessary to see things through. If countries like South Korea and Botswana have not been wholly successful, they are *'good societies'* in the sense that policy has not been subordinated to ideology.[119] They recognised that every member of society must have access to at least a life of economic opportunity with social caring. Securing that goal requires a society that talks, listens, learns and responds. Can a global society be a good society too?

Chapter 4

It's Not Size That Matters: Development Projects Re-examined

'No country in the world has ever developed itself through projects'

Sithembiso Nyoni, Zimbabwe[1]

'Why help trees to grow if the forest is consumed by fire?'

Project worker in Rajasthan, India[2]

When members of the public think about international development, their favourite charity, working away at the coal-face of poverty to 'help people help themselves', normally springs to mind. It is either that, or a showpiece project selected by international agencies to prove how well our aid is being spent. There were few such projects in the early years of foreign aid (like the Marshall Plan), but now they are the bedrock of the development industry. There are projects for everything: cutting down the civil service, for example, and building it up again; or privatising health and education, and then repairing the damage when poor people no longer have the services they need. That's the great thing about projects – even if they fail, new ones can always be started to clear up the mess. In the 1980s, Oxfam-UK had a project that de-stocked and then re-stocked the goat population of northern Kenya like a perpetual motion machine. It worked quite well, though not for the goats that were born in a phase when numbers had to be reduced. Do development projects really change anything?

Disaster stories about aid projects are common in the popular imagination – roads that lead nowhere; agricultural schemes that degrade the environment; tractors left rusting in the African sun; money wasted on high salaries, and sprawling bureaucracy.[3] The general public used to think that NGOs were immune from such criticisms, but recent exposés suggest otherwise.[4] Save the Children-USA spends so much of its donations from child sponsors on internal costs that less than 50 per cent gets to projects in the field.[5] In 1996, CARE-Australia was found guilty by the National Audit Office of inflating the price of relief goods in the field and using the proceeds to finance expansion at home. Canadian NGO specialist Ian Smillie thinks that these top-heavy organisations will be left behind as *'the last cars on the lot with tail-fins'* when the rest of the NGO world moves on.[6] Like the American automobile creations of the 1950s and 1960s, they will eventually go to the scrapyard when no one wants to pay their huge running costs any more, and fashions change. There are other cases of this sort, if one goes looking for them, but in my experience they are not representative of NGO projects as a whole. The more important issue is a less high-profile but much more generalised failure of projects to address the root causes of poverty and violence

To an outsider, the aid industry's focus on projects seems odd. Even a cursory reflection on the past confirms Sithembiso Nyoni's judgement that *'no country in the world has ever developed itself through projects'*. As we saw in Chapter 3, foreign advisers, capital and technology were important in the rise of industrial societies, as they were in East Asia.[7] But they shared little of the bureaucratic project planning and evaluation procedures that are such a feature of the development world today, and none of the external control. The best performers in terms of both growth and poverty reduction have been the least dependent on aid projects, and the most dependent (like Bangladesh or Tanzania) have performed the worst.[8] That's because progress comes, not from the aggregation of small-scale initiatives, but from the interaction between local efforts and broader structural changes, especially in markets and governance. It is the strength of those connections that makes or breaks success at the project level.

Despite these lessons, a world without projects is inconceivable for many aid workers because they offer a controllable delivery system for foreign funds. Even when ineffective, projects can generate some short-term accountability to keep the paymasters content. They provide the perfect framework for a mechanistic vision of development based on inputs and outputs – a security blanket for a system that lacks the trust to give money without strings attached and the confidence to hand over control. Mohammed Yunus, the founder of the world-famous Grameen Bank in Bangladesh, once remarked that donors *'don't want to leave any responsibility to the borrower, except the responsibility for the failure of the project*.[9] That captures the problem in a nutshell. Although much can be done to manage their limitations, the realpolitik of foreign aid means that projects will be with us for some time to come, and they are not irrelevant to success at the national level. The quality of what goes on inside and around them, in families and communities, schools and other institutions, matters greatly. So what if an NGO only educates 40 girls in Pakistan, if one of them grows up to be a great, reforming prime minister? Even when a single person learns to read and write it is a deeply political act, because of what it does to the potential balance of power, near and far. Development work is never insignificant just because it is small in scale. If it is *quality* work that makes the right connections, its impact will diffuse through systems and structures in many unpredictable ways. And if it fails to make those connections it will have little impact, however large it is.

Success in development projects is always difficult to measure, and even more difficult to attribute to foreign aid. There are too many forces at work for that – a sudden fall in crop prices, for example, can wipe out years of careful work in agricultural development. Social and economic change is very dynamic, so what appears successful at one point in time may prove to be unsustainable later on; conversely, failure may produce unanticipated benefits. Some poor performers in a sample of Brazilian agricultural extension institutions studied by political scientist Judith Tendler suddenly did well when threatened by a crisis, whereas previously successful ones stopped performing just as suddenly.[10] Like a stone dropped in water, the impact of good projects ripples through communities, markets and politics to produce lots of other changes which interact with each other. It is these less tangible 'externalities', or 'second and third-order effects' in academic jargon, that are so important in knitting together the underlying fabric of change.[11] But they cannot easily be predicted, and certainly not measured in narrow cost-benefit calculations.

Most projects do some good somewhere along the line, a few do active and significant harm, and most stumble along achieving a mixture of both. Likewise, agencies vary greatly in the quality of their work – some are superb, others dreadful, and most fall somewhere in the middle. If donors still attended school then many would be made to stay after class to catch up on their homework. The Dutch and Scandinavians would be the high achievers, closely followed by the British. The Americans would be stuck somewhere in the middle of the class, and the Japanese would be the new arrivals on the playground, with plenty of enthusiasm but not much street credibility.

These variations make it difficult to generalise, but it is clear that some projects work better than others, and the ones that do have many features in common. I have chosen a few examples that illustrate the general lessons to be learned. It's not that we don't know what breeds success at project level, but that we find it difficult to practise what we do know. It's all the fault of those unwelcome guests again.

WHAT CAUSES POVERTY AT THE GRASSROOTS?

As we saw in Chapter 3, there are no universal relationships between macro-economic performance and poverty reduction. At the grass-roots the situation is just as complex, with people moving in and out of poverty as their circumstances change. Easy generalisations about who is poor, why, and where they live, are regularly challenged by research and experience. Even standard definitions of poverty are difficult to defend in the face of widely-varying priorities about what the 'good life' consists of, at least if cash incomes are the only measure used.[12]

In subsistence economies, risks are high and the margins between success and failure are very narrow. So the first priority is security through sharing and co-operation, not just a better individual return.[13] Ecosystems characterised by diversity demand flexible responses to cope with a constantly shifting set of opportunities and threats – that was the rationale that drove the destocking and restocking of livestock among pastoralists in northern Kenya in the programme supported by Oxfam. In urban areas too, poor people need a basic level of economic and social security before they will invest. That is more difficult in cities of strangers because traditional social bonds are weaker.[14] The factors that underlie poverty are inter-related, so attacking one without the others is unlikely to be effective. Material poverty and the ownership of productive assets, lack of confidence and skills, discrimination according to gender and ethnicity, and exclusion from markets and decision-making struc-tures, all reinforce each other. Poverty is always a political issue, a matter of who holds what power to make decisions, secure advan-tages, and allocate resources. In Indian villages, someone who receives a subsidy from government of Rs1500 may have to hand 50 or 60 per cent straight back to the officials who filled out the appli-cation form, provided the necessary certificates about land ownership, and issued fake receipts for livestock. In Rajiv Gandhi's time as Prime Minister it was estimated that only one rupee out of every six provided through government development programmes actually reached the poor.[15] The same story reappears in Bangladesh, where bureaucrats consumed 75 per cent of the resources intended for employment and income-generating schemes for the poor.[16]

In this situation, two things are needed: first, the systematic strengthening of the assets of poor people, not just material assets like livestock and rights to land and water, but the personal and organisational skills, education, self-respect and confidence that enable these things to be used effectively; second, broader changes in economic, social and political structures so that poor people can participate in markets and governance, and create an atmosphere of peace and stability. As traditional networks of co-operation break down (as they always do under capitalism), these two areas for action become evermore important. The key is to secure, strengthen and diversify livelihoods – or people's 'entitlements' as the economist Amartya Sen calls them – right across the social spectrum and down to the poorest of the poor.[17] However, action should not be focused only on individuals, since structural injustice is something that history shows must be fought collectively – and that means strong organisations of disenfranchised people working together to break the chains of power and exploitation.[18] Just as at country level, it is not a particular set of policies that brings results at the grassroots, but the development of people's capacities to advance themselves and work with others on common tasks against a constantly shifting background of opportunities and constraints.

That requires an institutional framework conducive to a sustained attack on poverty, with property rights that guarantee the security for poor people that investment demands; services that give them the support they need to increase their skills; regulations that favour small producers over larger ones; markets which provide equal access to opportunities and contacts; governments which are transparent and accountable; and NGOs that have the capacity and independence to act as effective intermediaries. With these in place, local-level action can thrive. As more aid agencies have recognised this, projects have begun to focus on institutional development and policy reform. The problem is that a project approach is much less suited to achieving results in these areas. Changing the institutional framework for development is a long and difficult task which requires great sensitivity on the part of those who want to help, flexibility and continuity. In the real world of foreign aid these are rare, and that is why so many projects disappoint.

OFFICIAL AID PROJECTS – FROM 'BLUEPRINT' TO 'PROCESS'

Official aid is aid that is provided by governments. Traditionally, it was given to other governments in recipient countries, though recently the trend is to channel more through NGOs and commercial firms. Let's look at three examples that show how official aid projects have changed over time. Few would question the wisdom of investing in health, education and other areas of human development. Research shows that the returns are extremely high, especially when targeted at girls and women.[19] So the goal of the 'child survival revolution' launched by donors in the early 1980s cannot be faulted – invest in children now for a healthy and prosperous future for all. To achieve this goal the United Nations Children's Fund (UNICEF), the United States Agency for International Development (USAID) and others poured huge sums of money into the rapid expansion of health services, with the emphasis on mass campaigns to immunise all children under five and promote the use of low-cost technologies like oral rehydration salts and nutritional supplements.[20] Later, this effort was joined to the 'Bamako Initiative' (named after the capital of Mali) where the idea of promoting community responsibility and cost recovery in health services was launched, reputedly after having been dreamt up in the shower by the head of UNICEF, James Grant, the night before he was due to speak at a conference of African Ministers of Health. This 'revolution' claimed spectacular success in raising immunisation rates to over 90 per cent in most countries and disseminating the new technologies across millions of villages, contributing substantially to lower rates of infant and child mortality. However, by the beginning of the 1990s criticisms of the approach had begun to surface, especially from NGOs.[21] The critics doubted the statistics that were being cited, with field studies finding discrepancies of up to 40 per cent and coverage dropping significantly after the initial push had come to an end.[22] This raised questions about the sustainability of the improvements because of their dependence on external funding and a failure to build local capacity to keep services going in line with local realities. These questions have taken on starker importance as malaria, tuberculosis and other killer diseases have returned to Africa with a vengeance to confront health systems which cannot cope with the basic tasks of delivery and supervision. UNICEF and other donors have accepted these criticisms, while defending the political gains for children which came from high-profile campaigns.

Even so, this is a useful test case for believers in opposing approaches to project assistance: those who put the emphasis on large-scale, standardised, technology-based solutions to act as a 'locomotive' which pulls the development train forward; and those who believe that without much broader economic and institutional changes such efforts have little chance of making a long-term difference, with the poorest people being left waiting at the station as aid-dependent gains are dissipated.[23]

The second case comes from Uganda, where a World Bank-funded nutrition and early-childhood development project began to take shape in 1996 in discussion with NGOs and government.[24] The problems began right at the start, with the project appraisal being carried out by a visiting World Bank team with little local knowledge and no Ugandan involvement. The benefits from the project (estimated financially at US$54 million) only outweighed the projected costs by US$14 million, a decidedly risky margin given the notorious unreliability of these sorts of calculations in a fragile economy. If the equations were wrong then Ugandans would be paying the consequences for years. Although a task force of local representatives was appointed, it was quickly sidelined, with no resources of its own and little influence over project design. Consultation with the communities who were supposed to benefit was cosmetic, even though they were supposed to appoint two 'volunteers' to spearhead new activities like training. No work was done to test out the feasibility of the proposal or to check whether people had the time and interest to take on the additional work involved. If something so unprofessional happened in your community you would probably have laughed and ignored it. But this is Africa, remember? Local NGOs were given more money than they could handle (an extra US$1 million each), and when they came up with suggestions that were different to those in the project proposal they were ignored and told to get on with doing what they were told. As a result, *'we are all watching the birth of an unloved orphan project from a disgruntled distance'*.[25]

This story could be repeated many times, and in response to such criticisms a new and less bureaucratic approach to government-funded aid projects has been developed, especially by Scandinavian and British agencies. In contrast to the project 'blueprint' imposed from the top, this approach concentrates on a more flexible 'process' approach in which more attention is paid to learning and incremental development.[26] Some of the best examples of this approach come from India and Sri Lanka, where the experience of the Moneragala rural development project (MONDEP) has been especially well documented.[27] This programme began in 1984 with a 20-year time frame, decentralised management, and a rolling schedule of planning, budgeting, and evaluation. Individual projects are discussed and designed at village level, but then reviewed at a higher level to test their feasibility, ensure coherence district-wide, and obtain the necessary funding. Each level does what it can do best but takes care to consult with the others. Unlike other projects, the quality, continuity and commitment of staff in MONDEP are high; performance standards are enforced clearly and transparently; and flexibility is preserved in systems and procedures to allow new problems to be tackled as they arise. Independent evaluations of MONDEP show that it has achieved a far higher level of material and organisational development than comparable projects, and in one of the poorest parts of Sri Lanka. Taking time to get things right brings more sustainable results: in the Indian slum improvement projects supported by British government aid (which follow a similar approach), neighbourhood development committees now meet independently of the project to review progress and plan changes.[28] That is a real sign that something important is happening.

NGO PROJECTS – RURAL REVOLUTIONARIES AND VILLAGE DEVELOPMENT BANKERS

In 1980, two ex-Catholic priests, Jacob Thundyil and Chacko Paruvanany, founded the People's Rural Education Movement (PREM) to work with tribal communities in the Indian state of Orissa.[29] In the space of 15 years their work bore fruit in the shape of a federation of grassroots organisations representing over 800,000 people. PREM's role is to act as a supportive presence for these organisations, helping them to connect with government departments, banks, universities, other NGOs and outside donors who provide money, advice and contacts. But it is the federation that decides on priorities and takes them forward. Already over 400 of their representatives have been elected to different levels of local government. They in turn have directed more public resources to tribal communities, quadrupling the lending capacity of the state-wide 'Women's Savings Society', starting almost 2000 village seed and grain banks to promote food security, financing land redistribution, and investing millions of rupees in schools, clinics and agricultural extension facilities. When government withdrew support from 77 local primary schools, the federation mobilised demonstrations which forced the authorities to reinstate official backing for salaries and other costs. By linking local organisations to national decision makers, PREM and other NGOs have helped people excluded from economic and political structures to challenge discrimination and inequality where it matters most. As a result, the Indian government agreed in 1997 to extend 'self-rule' to 'scheduled areas' with a high tribal and low-caste population. And the amount of external assistance involved in this programme is tiny – about 25 US cents per person per year.

How did a small organisation like PREM do it? It certainly had a favourable context, with socially homogeneous communities and a political climate which allowed mass mobilisation. PREM's donors – international charities like Oxfam and Save the Children – were flexible, loyal, and supportive. But much more important were the choices it made about strategy, and the personal qualities of staff and volunteers. They shared a commitment to the independent development of tribal people, and a sense of solidarity nurtured by long hours of talking and working together. They had a clear long-term goal – a strong people's movement – and had the determination to stick with it over time, even if that meant sacrificing the interests of PREM as an institution. So offers of outside help judged inappropriate were refused, including large amounts of money from other agencies. Requests from government to take over health and education services were rejected in favour of working together to co-manage a comprehensive system. Advances in living standards and social organisation marched along together, so that upgrading the skills and equipment of small-scale fishermen went hand in hand with lobbying government to restrict the activities of commercial trawlers in traditional fishing grounds. More assets and better services maintained people's interest while the process of institutional development continued, and provided the security poor people need to take an active role in organisations. At the same time, rising confidence, sharper organisational skills, and stronger institutions enabled economic initiatives to be managed more effectively at community level, and helped people to discuss with government the sharing of costs and responsibilities of operating services in the future. This balance between social and material development, internal strength and outside contacts, was the key to large-scale, sustainable change. PREM's impact came through the multiplier effect of supporting local organisations to link with, and work through, established structures and institutions.

The second example is a deliberate contrast. This is the current fashion to promote cheap loans as the answer to world poverty. Based on a model pioneered by the Grameen Bank in Bangladesh, hundreds of millions of dollars are being poured into NGOs to lend to small groups of women who agree to abide by certain rules and regulations. These NGOs are expanding at rates unknown in history to work with millions of people in thousands of communities – three million in the case of the Bangladesh Rural Advancement Committee (BRAC), one million for the Self-Employed Women's Association (SEWA) in India, and 7000 villages for Sarvodaya in Sri Lanka. In the process they are being advised to standardise their procedures, borrow management tools from business, and above all 'get real' – charge market interest rates and do the job properly.[30] The advocates of 'micro-credit' are positively evangelical about its potential, as I found to my cost when pinned against the wall at a development conference in Spain by the director of RESULTS, the organisation that arranged a summit meeting in Washington DC during 1997 to mobilise more funds. Despite the midnight hour I was not allowed to go to my bed until I had retracted all doubts that this was indeed a 'magic bullet'. Of course I did retract, but only because I needed my sleep. For the truth is that affordable credit is not the solution to world poverty at all.

No one would quarrel with the need to improve the accessibility of financial systems to poor people, nor with the role of credit and savings in expanding economic assets and opportunities. But there is a downside. Very few NGOs actually reach the very poor despite their rhetoric (since the poorest people lack the basic wherewithal to make use of credit in the first place),[31] and despite the global hype micro-credit reaches less than one per cent of the world's poor.[32] There is also a danger that an obsession with numbers of borrowers and speed of delivery will detract from the slow and difficult changes that are essential for equitable development. After all, industrialised countries have reasonably effective banking systems but they still have deep-seated social and economic problems. Despite its straightforward appeal, the micro-credit revolution has become a subject of controversy, with claims and counter-claims about what is actually happening on the ground.[33]

Arguments about credit projects – just like the 'Child Survival Revolution' – touch on much broader dilemmas about the focus of development assistance, especially the importance of developing capacities to manage change as opposed to delivering standard technical solutions at an ever-larger scale. In an important sense it is unfair to point this finger at NGOs like BRAC or the Grameen Bank, since they have never claimed to be solving world poverty, just doing what they can on particular aspects of the problem in a political context that makes mass-based social organisation dangerous.[34] In that respect their achievements, with high repayment rates across millions of low-income borrowers previously excluded from the formal financial system, are phenomenal. The real problem lies with other agencies who still cling to the idea that there is a solution to poverty that just needs more money. The solution happens to be cheap credit now, because donors have lost confidence in older answers and private provision is popular ideologically.[35] But sooner or later disenchantment will set in with micro-credit too, a new solution will take its place, and the whole cycle will start afresh. As an approach to deep-rooted social and economic problems, this is simply not credible.

The heart of the matter is how to increase the impact of NGO projects without losing the advantages of being non-governmental – being committed to values rather than market share, close to the people they serve, flexible and innovative. Keeping the best from the traditions of the past while moving forward to deal systematically with the underlying causes of poverty is a challenge for every NGO. Doing it when providing a service to millions of people against short-term targets imposed by donors is probably impossible. Engaging with the forces that really effect change requires NGOs to be thinkers and mobilisers, innovators and advocates, and not simply channels for aid or deliverers of services.[36] The example of PREM is important here because it represents an approach that generates material results every bit as impressive as commercial micro-credit programmes, and at the same time promotes the capacity of poor people to fight for their rights.

WHAT BREEDS SUCCESS? THE MECHANICS OF PROJECTS

The first lesson is that things go wrong when common sense is ignored. In some cases projects do not meet local needs, or if they understand these needs they assume that people do not have the competence to deal with them. Yet we know that this is often untrue. There is no shortage of research to prove it: for example, performance indicators are much higher in Kenyan agricultural projects, irrigation programmes in the Philippines, and water supply projects funded by the World Bank when the beneficiaries participate at every stage.[37] Equally basic is the need to make projects respond to local realities. 'The same is never the same' is a catch phrase of the women's movement, even when it seems so on the surface. Organisational issues, human relationships, and basic concepts about planning and progress all vary from one culture to another. Detailed studies of development projects in Lesotho and Kenya show how external agencies disguise deep-rooted cultural and political issues as technical problems, turning projects, in James Ferguson's words, into a veritable 'anti-politics machine'.[38] In the Lesotho case, the World Bank wanted to commercialise livestock management even though tribal rules made cattle a special category of property and a leading source of prestige. In Kenya, Australian agencies misunderstood the most basic economic and environmental realities of the Giriama people, and, like the 'anti-politics machine' in Lesotho, actually left them more vulnerable than when the project began.[39] Even worse were the Norwegian 'experts' who persuaded 20,000 nomadic Turkana tribespeople in Kenya to give up their cows and take up fishing instead. The cost of chilling the fish far exceeded the price it fetched in local markets. Fishing equipment worth millions of dollars was abandoned, and so were the Turkana, left dependent on food aid.[40]

In each of these cases, the analysis of outsiders wasn't just wrong – it was systematically wrong, though it may have been correct in terms of their own blinkered understanding. Successful innovations reduce risks, ensure that benefits outweigh costs, and are affordable both financially and in terms of the demands they place on people's time. It is incredible that such simple advice is ignored. A story related by Robert Klitgaard captures the laconic comedy of generations of projects which have failed for want of basic common sense: *'government officials would show up and demand chickens. Finally there were no chickens left to lay eggs. The project shut down'.*[41] It is easy to laugh at such stories, but they make a deadly serious point – if you can't be bothered to understand the local situation properly and ensure that change is rooted in the social fabric, stay away. Otherwise the consequences may be fatal, like the Bangladeshi villagers now at risk from arsenic poisoning because Western engineers couldn't be bothered to test the water from tube wells funded by foreign aid.[42]

Examples of gross incompetence don't mean that outside help is never required, nor that local answers are always sufficient. Like the high-performing countries analysed in Chapter 3, the most successful projects are the ones that find the right mix between local and non-local knowledge, *inside* a framework of priorities that is locally controlled. Good results are always based on a judicious blend of tradition and challenge – neither a romantic return to a past that was unequal, limiting and discriminatory; nor the energy-sapping dependency that is visible in communities subject to long periods of outside assistance.[43] The best help recognises this and inserts itself carefully and strategically in favour of poor people's long-term interests, reducing dependence and increasing autonomy so that choices can be made from a wider range of options. Peasant federations in Bolivia and Ecuador, for example, play a crucial role in helping people to adapt indigenous technologies to fit market opportunities, and translate modern ones (like improved seeds) so that poor people can use them.[44] If they are prepared to develop long-term, flexible relationships, international agencies can be a very positive influence – teams from Harvard University did this with rural banking in Indonesia from the 1970s onwards, and the Rockefeller Foundation played a catalytic role in supporting the 'Green Revolution' in India.[45] Because they can take more risks, external facilitators can expand the space inside government bureaucracies for internal reformers to develop a constituency for change.[46] The need for outside help increases as the bureaucratic treacle thickens.

In the same way, success is more likely to emerge from a mixture of market mechanisms, public intervention and social pressures. Too much emphasis on the market risks leaving those with fewer assets behind, but too little spells long-term economic stagnation. Too much emphasis on bureaucratic regulation stifles initiative, but social capital alone is rarely enough to attack hard-core poverty and discrimination. As we saw with PREM, there has to be a balance between material, social and institutional development so that each supports the others.[47] Organising in groups helps poor people to solve problems and bridge the gap between individual assets and what is needed to move to the next rung of the economic ladder, like buying an irrigation pump or operating a rotating loan system. When groups link with each other through federations and networks they can influence the wider context to be more favourable to the interests of their members.[48]

WHAT BREEDS SUCCESS? THE REAL ISSUES AT STAKE

Like the bare bones of national experience, these conclusions tell us what can go wrong, but not why. If the secrets of success are this simple, why are they regularly ignored? There are three deeper lessons that show why project aid is often ineffective. The first is the project equivalent of the 'policy problem' described in Chapter 3, with too much of a focus on narrow goals and standard solutions. Successful projects are the ones that strengthen local capacities to identify problems, suggest some answers, and develop the support base to push them through in the face of opposition from vested interests, as PREM and the tribal federation did in Orissa. The successful transformation of health services in North-East Brazil, for example, developed from a strong sense of commitment among government workers and an informed citizenry that monitored their performance.[49] It is the process of innovation itself that needs sustaining, not a particular set of innovations.

Winning short-term gains on the basis of heavy external inputs is not difficult; what is difficult is sustaining them against the background of weak polities, fragile economies, and limited capacities for implementation. This is especially true when projects are financed using loans (as in the World Bank's case), because the need to generate foreign exchange to repay them places more strain on resources that are already stretched. Lasting change rests on institutions that generate outputs valued by many and actively opposed by few, and a framework of laws and incentives that encourages them to flourish.[50] When they feel both secure and valued, local institutions can achieve remarkable results.[51] So as a general rule, successful projects build broad-based demand among the population for improvements in governance, higher-quality services, and the produce and skills of poor people. Projects that focus overmuch on the supply side, by providing large amounts of external resources too quickly, risk losing this momentum and the results that come with it. That means waiting longer for success because demand can't be built up overnight. Donors are often loath to do this, establishing their own project management units to short circuit what they see as inefficient local bureaucracies, and supplementing salaries with aid funds as an incentive to poorly-paid staff. But because these incentives cannot be sustained without aid, they do little to promote performance in the longer-term, and may even erode it. Without strong and active links into civil society, business and politics, small may not be beautiful at all, just insignificant.[52] It is these connections that determine whether projects are a cost-effective catalyst for broader processes of change, or a diversion of resources away from less bureaucratic action. The federation supported by PREM worked because it linked village groups both with each other and with these broader structures, providing channels for innovation, communication and accountability to flow in all directions – the foundation of the 'good society' explored in Chapter 3. Over time, a movement emerged to exert pressure for change from below, improving the wider context in the process as government became more sympathetic to the goals of the movement and banks began to engage with the growing savings and credit society. In Asia between 1952 and 1977, the countries that performed best agriculturally and socially were consistently those that had the strongest links between local communities and central government through a dense network of intermediary organisations.[53]

The third essential condition is the right sort of help. It must be flexible, sensitive, strategic, experimental and achievement based. Small successes are better than large failures. Investment in learning seems expensive until repeated mistakes have to be paid for. There is never any substitute for local ownership, and if this causes conflicts of interest between donors and recipients, long-term imperatives should be chosen over short-term expedients. These are the lessons that 'process projects' and the best NGOs have already taken to heart, and what the rest of the aid system still has to learn. But will it learn them? Unfortunately, lack of co-ordination among donors, too much haste, and standardised solutions impede precisely those things that are required to make projects work, such as time and space to allow lessons to be learned, linkages to develop and capacities to evolve. Even processes like participation become formulaic, with favoured recipes about how they should be organised. The tunnel vision of the project system focuses too narrowly on the short term and the easily measurable, squeezing out the broad-based social and institutional changes that are vital for sustainable results.[54] The demands of a system raised on simple solutions make it difficult to undertake work which is by nature messy and uncertain.

The truth is that heavily administered projects have a very poor record in tackling the real issues. Donors are always changing their minds on the basis of fashion or short-term disappointments. According to Tony Klouda, one of the world's leading authorities in this field, HIV/Aids projects provide a classic case of this general malaise: messianic fervour being followed by intensive action planning, a gradual recognition that the issue is much more complex than first thought, a proliferation of special programmes to deal with the complexity, growing disillusion when they don't work, more new programmes and more disappointments, and finally a return to business as usual, leaving the least powerful constituency (in this case those most at risk) in the same state they were in before stage one.[55] NGOs are not immune from these criticisms, especially those that have abandoned their original *raison d'être*, of building the capacity of others for independent action, in favour of strengthening their own position in the market place. The reason many NGOs are disappointed with their results at project level is that they do not practise what they preach – the need for innovation, accountability, and partnership, not to mention lowering their transaction costs to focus more resources where it really matters. Why are there still five different Save the Children Funds with separate offices in Zimbabwe?

This tendency is exacerbated by donor agencies who see NGOs as instruments of government policy, threatening not only NGO independence and the flexibility to choose different roles for different circumstances, but – because the ruling orthodoxy favours privatisation in economic and social life – posing much wider questions about the social contracts that evolve over time in all societies between states and citizens. If, as in Bangladesh, you are increasingly dependent on NGOs for access to health, education, even finance and telephone connections, you may gain more *entitlements* to these things (if you live in an area that is well served), but lose them as *rights*, especially if the NGOs are only weakly accountable to a weak state.[56] The danger is that countries like Bangladesh end up with aid-dependent social sectors, a patchwork quilt of welfare-provision, eroding government authority, and quiescent NGOs – almost the opposite of the conditions that underpinned success in East Asia. You don't solve problems by throwing more money at them through an ever-spreading web of incoherent projects; problems are solved by polities that have the wherewithal to decide on solutions and finance them from a growing local surplus. The role of outsiders is to support that process, not usurp it – however long and whatever form it takes. At the project level this is certainly possible, but it requires a quality of relationships that is rare in practice. People and their organisations must have room to manoeuvre so that they can learn and change, try things out, and take some risks. And outside help can help greatly in providing a more secure foundation, more *'latitude'* as Albert Hirschman calls it, for this to happen.[57] But that means trusting people to find their own answers. *'We are in no hurry to launch out on an accelerated route to empowerment,'* says Sri Lankan activist Menike Karunawathie, *'do not do anything, even with the best of intentions, that will destroy the power and strength we already possess.'*[58]

Conclusion

On the assumption that quick is good, big is better, and quick and big together are best, it might be true that projects, if there were ever enough of them, could make a real difference to world poverty. But these assumptions have never been true in the 'swamplands' of development. What matters is people's ability to find a path through the swamp, and the existence of institutions that can do the things people can't do for themselves. If projects make the right connections between individual empowerment and institutional development, they can help to lever changes in the systems and structures that reinforce poverty and exclusion. Returning to the second of the quotations at the head of this chapter, the trees – the small-scale successes – will not be *'consumed by fire'* – the wider context that surrounds them. In this task it's not size that matters, it's what you do with the resources you have and the new ones you find along the way.

This is a very complex process, and much less controllable than project planning suggests. Just as at country level, success comes, not from the application of standard models, but from the interaction of different forces over time in each project, such as ecology and environment, culture and social realities, economic constraints and market opportunities, luck and leadership. Making these interactions work for poverty reduction and social progress requires strong local institutions – organisations that represent poor people effectively, governments that respond to their demands, and markets that are accessible; coalitions that can break the stranglehold of local elites; and connections beyond the project to promote sustainability. By contrast, the record of heavily administered project aid weighed down by increasing numbers of preconditions and guidelines is almost uniformly depressing. Under current trends in the aid world, a dangerous cocktail is emerging: a mix of stronger private interests, but weaker governments, marginalised social movements, and co-opted NGOs. Left unchecked, this will lead to a net loss in the bargaining power of the poor and the interventionist power of the state, and that has never been a recipe for successful development anywhere.

The challenge for the future is not an intellectual one. More research is always needed, but we already know the principles of project success: engage with local realities, take your time, experiment and learn, reduce vulnerability and risk, and always work on social and material development together. The real issue is why so many agencies cut corners on these principles, and the answer to that question lies in the attitudes and interests we looked at in Chapter 2 – the short termism, control orientation and standardisation that have infected development work for a generation or more. In this world view, projects are a mechanism to deliver foreign aid, not short-term building blocks of long-term change. Instead of accompanying projects as they evolve, donors use them to generate the results they want to see. There are some difficult issues here about financial accountability and the need to demonstrate rapid gains to keep the aid funds flowing, which cannot be wished away. Chapter 7 suggests some avenues for improvement which do recognise these things. However, if we want projects to deliver better results, we have *to let them go* against a small core of negotiated objectives and performance standards. That is the paradox of achieving more by intervening less. Good projects, like good societies, are the ones that constantly listen, learn and act on what they find, generating social energy to solve problems as well as economic growth to sustain the solutions. That includes the energy to say 'no' to outside help as well as the discrimination to know when to say 'yes'. If we can all learn to accept that 'no *means* no' without abandoning the commitment to work together, we have some hope of making project aid a more powerful tool for development.

Chapter 5

Matters of Life and Death: The Record of Humanitarian Intervention

'Peace is a process, not an event'
Victor Reider[1]

'I am convinced that the Serbs could have been stopped in October 1991 with three ships, three dozen planes, and 3000 men'
Jean Cot, Commander of UNPROFOR[2]

In Cambodia, a Buddhist prophecy tells of a white elephant in blue armour that will rescue the country from a terrible conflagration.[3] After the killing fields of the Khmer Rouge and the instability that followed, UN forces arrived in Cambodia during 1993 to help the country prepare for democratic elections. Their white Toyota land-cruisers and blue UN livery convinced some Cambodians that the prophecy was about to be realised, but this elephant had a very short memory, pulling out as soon as the elections were over. After two decades of war, genocide, invasion and isolation, Cambodia deserved better than this. Four years later, the inevitable coup happened (led by Hun Sen and his party of former communists), followed in 1998 by another round of rigged elections only lightly supervised by foreign observers. Here as elsewhere, the 'international community' has been a fickle friend to those who need its help. Heroic deeds, battles against the odds and the occasional quiet success do form part of the story of humanitarian intervention in recent times, but overall the international response to conflict and famine has been tardy, piecemeal and ineffective. Despite the commitments made in 1945 to nullify the 'scourge of war', 'we the people' stood and watched as genocide unfolded in Indonesia, Cambodia and Rwanda. We did little to prevent 'ethnic cleansing' in former Yugoslavia until it was too late, even though there were UN troops on the ground when 8000 civilians were slaughtered in Srebenica. And 100,000 people have been butchered in the most brutal fashion imaginable in Algeria since 1992, with scarcely a hint of foreign intervention. The life and death of distant strangers never did have much political purchase.

When the cold war ended it seemed that this might change. The withdrawal of Soviet forces from Afghanistan and Cubans from Angola was followed by UN-brokered peace settlements in Central America, Namibia and elsewhere, supervised by a Security Council that, for the first time in 50 years, was veto-free.[4] A new consensus had emerged on the need for intervention in zones of crisis.[5] It was this optimism that underpinned the UN's historic decision to override national sovereignty in order to protect besieged Kurds in northern Iraq in 1991, and which greeted former UN Secretary-General Boutros-Boutros Ghali's 'Agenda for Peace' so warmly one year later. Just as well, for the fall of the Berlin Wall also released a new wave of ethno-nationalist conflicts and forced migrations from the former eastern Bloc and other regions no longer of strategic interest to those who had formerly policed them. These 'complex political emergencies' fuelled a rapid rise in the global number of refugees and internally displaced people, from 22 million in 1985 to 37 million ten years later.[6] In 1995, the equivalent of one in every 115 people on the earth was forced into flight from war, starvation or genocide.[7] However, the spirit of optimism did not last: the debacle in Somalia deterred international action in Rwanda, the Balkans and beyond, and the likelihood of concerted intervention is now highly circumscribed. Emergencies have always been complex and political. What is different about the post cold-war era are the politics of humanitarian intervention itself. They have certainly become more complicated, caught between those who insist on the primacy of universal human rights (enforced if necessary by overriding national sovereignty), and those who worry about the dangers of aggressive military-humanitarian intervention, especially when applied selectively by an international community that is ill-prepared and committed only in fits and starts. The result of this uncertainty is a dangerous muddle, and hundreds of thousands of lives wasted. How did this muddle come about, and what can be done to correct it?

WHAT MAKES EMERGENCIES COMPLEX AND POLITICAL?

People in all societies move in and out of situations where, for a short period of time, they are more vulnerable to a sudden crisis. Subsistence societies are more prone to these crises because there is less of a margin for error when the rains fail or communities are threatened by conflict. So are societies that undergo rapid change or sudden destabilisation, when both traditional obligations to support each other and government capacity to protect people tend to be eroded. Sometimes, as for example when there is a large-scale drought or a full-scale war, the crisis extends for much longer and affects a much larger proportion of the population. Such generalised periods of famine and dislocation have been a regular occurrence in history, though even when widespread their human impact tends to be selective. They have always had complex roots and political causes, and are part of the process of economic and social change, not isolated, abnormal or random events. As the experience of former Yugoslavia demonstrates, crises can reoccur even in industrial societies; they are not simply *'accidents on the highway of development and modernity'*.[8] Peace and stability are more precarious than they appear, but there are reasons why societies break down, and solutions to these problems.

Avoiding large-scale famine and conflict is a matter of effective governance and institutionalised respect for civil and political rights. It is a cliché that democracies do not to go to war with each other, but they also starve or kill fewer of their own citizens: only two million out of the 169 million people killed by their own governments since 1900 have been victims of democratic regimes.[9] Democratic politics provide the best early warning of impending crises, the most effective channels for prevention and response, and the greatest likelihood that differences will be resolved peacefully. This need not mean the Western multi-party system, but any system that combines commitment from government with lines of accountability that enable public pressure to enforce it – what Alex de Waal calls an *'anti-famine political contract'*.[10] The classic example of such a contract is India, which has successfully prevented famine since independence through an effective system of early warning (channelled through a dense network of civic organisations and a free media), and public intervention to protect people's livelihoods when threatened with collapse.[11] When this contract is eroded, crisis ensues.

Famine and war create winners as well as losers. The seizure of assets (like livestock) from vulnerable groups by political and military elites is a well-worn tactic which both government and rebel forces have used in Sudan and other countries to strengthen their position in the struggle for power.[12] Conflict may be exacerbated by the sudden injection of large amounts of cash and food aid, when it can be used as an instrument of war and a factor in fuelling the struggle between rival factions.[13] In Bosnia, between 35 and 75 per cent of total relief assistance was captured by combatants.[14] The Sudanese and Ethiopian governments invented another way of turning famine to their advantage by maintaining parallel exchange rates during the 1980s and thus wildly undervaluing all aid transactions. One estimate suggests that the Sudanese government could have financed half its military expenditure from such gains, while a defecting banker from Iraq claimed that UN relief had contributed at least US\$250 million to Iraq's President Saddam Hussein's treasury.[15] In the absence of political solutions, continued humanitarian assistance can sustain conflict significantly.

Emergencies cannot be solved by technocratic means, standardised packages of food aid, or UN troops, because the processes involved are too local and deep-rooted for that. Food and other material assistance can be useful in plugging temporary gaps in people's entitlements, especially if they form a considered part of a broader strategy. But action on the causes of the crisis is much more important: saving livelihoods not just lives, supporting vulnerable institutions not just people, rebuilding social as well as physical capital, and improving governance not just government. All interventions need to understand and work with local solutions: research in Sudan and Ethiopia shows that people's first priority in a famine is not more food to eat, but preserving the assets they already have (like seeds for the next planting season) so that they can stave off destitution.[16] The importance of outside assistance is usually less significant than it appears. Faced by food shortages in the Indian state of Maharashtra during 1973, government programmes were easily surpassed by the efforts of private individuals who imported more than one million tons of food from neighbouring states.[17] People solve conflicts all the time without recourse to external intervention, but of course they do not make the headlines. The self-organised return of over 600,000 Rwandan refugees from Eastern Zaire – now the Congo – in 1997 is a recent exception.[18]

However, outside help is not irrelevant, and if provided in the right ways it can be crucial in helping to tide people over the worst of times without increasing dependency by rebuilding assets, incomes and skills; supporting local mechanisms for resolving disputes; and strengthening effective institutions. Help must preserve as much autonomy, self-respect and self-determination as possible among those affected so that they can do what *they* think is right.[19] The goal is not a society that never suffers a crisis and is always free from conflict (that is impossible), but one which can resolve conflicts peacefully and work together to protect the most vulnerable during periods of acute stress.[20] This is more difficult where conflict centres on ethnicity, ideology and control of government, and most difficult of all where a fundamental clash of values is involved.[21] According to psychologist Anthony Storr,[22] human violence is always bound up with relationships of power between rich and poor, old and young, men and women, and groups of different ethnic or religious identity, but these relationships are as much the result of socialisation as biology. Johan Galtung, the grand old man of peace research, once said half-jokingly that *'the major carriers of inconsiderateness are males, Protestants and economists, particularly when combined'*.[23] It may be impossible to eradicate the influence of testosterone, but at least we can have a go at the other two, and all the other factors that are amenable to change.

HUMANITARIAN INTERVENTION IN AFRICA: FROM BIAFRA TO RWANDA

Famine and conflict have been regular features of African life for centuries, so it is no surprise that the subcontinent occupies a central place in the practice and mythology of modern humanitarianism. Many relief workers cut their teeth in Sudan and Ethiopia during the 1980s, though the real veterans go back to the seminal experiences they shared together in Biafra in 1968–69. Those experiences marked the beginnings of what Alex de Waal calls the *'humanitarian international, a trans-national elite of relief workers, civil servants, academics and others'* which has since grown to be a powerful and controversial force in defining approaches to emergency intervention.[24] Sudan provides a classic example of how politics, war and famine interact with each other in a downward spiral that outside intervention leaves largely untouched. Since 1983, over 1.5 million people have died there as a result of famine, disease and military activity provoked by civil war between northern government forces and southern rebels.[25]

These famines emerged from a long history of political struggle, and the provision of relief became increasingly entangled in these processes. In the 1980s, donors acceded to government requests to target relief at camps in northern Sudan and Ethiopia, instead of supporting the livelihoods of those who stayed in the south by providing clean water, fodder and guaranteed prices for livestock, temporary employment, and health services. As a result, people moved en masse to poorly-serviced relief camps where they died in large numbers, not from starvation, but from disease. The continuation of the war led government and rebels (under heavy external pressure) to negotiate a 'corridor of tranquillity' called 'Operation Lifeline Sudan', which allowed relief to be delivered to civilians on both sides of the conflict.[26] This worked well for a time, but as it became institutionalised the operating costs spiralled upwards. More importantly, the need for government support to keep the lifeline open made it impossible to return people from the camps (since this would be seen as aiding the rebels), and unlikely that international action would be taken to tackle the causes of the conflict – the consistent failings of domestic governance and a war economy based on foreign aid and the seizure of assets.[27] A qualified and increasingly unsustainable humanitarian success began to obstruct a political solution between the warring parties, leading Larry Minear, an international authority on humanitarian issues, to conclude that it was *'high time to pull the plug'*.[28] Fortunately, the plug wasn't pulled, otherwise the Sudanese famine which hit the headlines in the spring of 1998 would have claimed even more lives. Nevertheless, a power-sharing settlement between North and South remains the key to peace. Although foreign intervention has been instrumental in brokering a temporary cease-fire, international interest in pushing for this settlement is very fragile.

In Ethiopia the story has been similar, with relief aid being systematically manipulated by government forces fighting rebels in Tigray and Eritrea.[29] The Ethiopian famines of the 1980s were caused as much by the war and government attempts to starve the rebels into surrender as by poorly-functioning agricultural markets and lack of rainfall. International NGOs were very active, but the UN failed to support any cross-border operations into Tigray and Eritrea, despite the fact that the humanitarian wings of both rebel movements had a far-superior record in distributing relief and using it to promote long-term development.[30] They had what the Ethiopian government lacked – the 'anti-famine political contract' that comes from popular legitimacy. In contrast, feeding centres established inside Ethiopia helped to support government offensives by providing access to food for the troops, keeping roads open for relief supplies, and making rebel forces more cautious about counter-attacks in case expatriates were killed or injured in the process. The ethical dilemmas involved in *not* providing relief in these circumstances are considered a little later, but without continued access to large-scale foreign aid it is unlikely that the regime in Addis Ababa would have survived for so long.

As the civil war in Ethiopia resolved itself and interest in Sudan declined, the focus of international attention in Africa moved elsewhere, first to the west, and then to Somalia. The crises that unfolded in Liberia and Sierra Leone in the late 1980s illustrate the difficulty of securing peace against a background of internal instability and partisan intervention from neighbouring countries, and the consequent fragility of agreements secured through external mediation – 14 in seven years in Liberia alone. The fighting in Liberia, sparked off by the overthrow of President Samuel Doe by Charles Taylor's forces late in 1989, shows what can happen when even a corrupt central authority is replaced by vicious competition between fragmenting ethnic and political factions: 200,000 people killed, a third of the population displaced, and the widespread deployment of children as soldiers.[31] To stop the war (and prevent Taylor from winning it), 12,000 troops from other West African countries led by Nigeria and Ghana (and known as ECOMOG) intervened in Liberia in 1991. But instead of re-establishing law and order, ECOMOG allied itself with Taylor's enemies and joined in the wholesale plunder of Liberia's natural resources. The economy and administration collapsed as each part of the country was taken over by rival factions. Both regional 'peacekeeping' forces and the UN attempted to broker one settlement after another until agreement was reached in 1996 to hold foreign-funded elections the next year (subsequently won by Taylor). Liberian civic organisations pushed for these elections and took to the streets when it appeared they might be postponed.[32] The same thing happened in Sierra Leone, where elections during 1996 were defended by an informal coalition of citizens' groups (especially the Women's Forum), professional associations and NGOs, which re-formed after a military coup nullified the results in 1997.[33] They were supported by another Nigerian intervention and covert British help that landed Foreign Secretary Robin Cook in hot water for contravening UN sanctions against arms supplies to any side in the war. However, neither has halted the violence that continues to tear the country apart.

In Somalia, the roots of famine lay, as they did elsewhere, in years of misrule, corruption and low-intensity warfare against opponents, this time by President Siad Barre. The toppling of his regime in January 1991 intensified fighting between rival clans which eventually turned into civil war, but at the same time relief was being organised by indigenous organisations at village level and in the capital, Mogadishu. Contrary to the perceptions of many outsiders (like Malcolm Fraser of CARE-International who described the situation as one of '*naked anarchy and the total collapse of social, economic and political structures*'),[34] there were many courageous individuals who kept going a semblance of a health service, primary schools, and other local institutions across clan lines through the height of the fighting.[35] Throughout 1991 and 1992, it was the Somali Red Crescent, in partnership with the ICRC and supplemented by a small number of international NGOs like Save the Children-UK, that fed two million people across the country. Even without a recognised state it might have been possible to develop a network of sub-national authorities – an elemental 'anti-famine political contract' – had these structures been built on. The same thing happened further north in the nascent republic of Somaliland, which had declared its own independence in 1991. Clan-based institutions of elders worked with a fledgling government and new NGOs to take responsibility for governance, reconciliation and reconstruction, but the UN refused to recognise the government or support its efforts at a critical time.[36]

In stark contrast to the NGOs who stayed on, the UN was shamefully absent from Somalia, even after a ceasefire had been agreed between the two key players in the spring of 1992 (General Aideed and Ali Mahdi Mohamed). An earlier resolution had been debated in the Security Council, but this was blocked by the USA, thus missing a crucial opportunity for intervention at a time when local conditions were propitious. It was only later in the year, when the first famine pictures were broadcast in the West by CNN and the BBC, that international interest began to mount and Mohamed Sahnoun was dispatched to Mogadishu as the UN special representative. He immediately set out to bring clan leaders together and encourage civic institutions to take more of a role in the relief programme. Almost alone among UN officials, he saw that peace-building was still possible in the absence of a recognised government, but this insight did him no good. Sahnoun was forced to resign in murky circumstances and replaced by the far more malleable Ismat Kittani. Kittani, in collaboration with Robert Oakley (the US special envoy) and Philip Johnston (seconded from CARE-USA to head the UN emergency programme), reversed Sahnoun's policy and adopted a much harder line on both military and humanitarian issues, aided by the arrival of more UN troops and US marines at the beginning of 1993. They circumvented local structures, became embroiled in partisan support for clan leaders (first in favour of Aideed and then against him), and were unable to control the escalating violence that eventually claimed the lives of 83 UN soldiers, 18 American airmen, and at least 6000 Somalis.[37] It was during this period that Canadian, Italian and Belgian troops were themselves suspected of violating the Geneva Conventions by torturing civilians. US marines turned from the protection of Mogadishu to its virtual occupation, giving up in despair and frustration soon afterwards.[38]

So much for Operation Restore Hope, which spent $4 billion to deliver less than $100 million worth of relief supplies;[39] ironically, the famine was all but over by the time the marines arrived.[40] Four years on, there has been no political settlement, no significant disarmament, and little help for reconstruction.[41] The Somalia experience shows how, after missing the real opportunity for positive intervention in 1991, too authoritarian a mandate effectively disempowered local processes and exacerbated the conflict, a conclusion confirmed by the UN's own commission of enquiry in late 1993 which was suppressed by the Secretary General. '*The UN,*' it said, '*should abandon notions of peace enforcement*', a reasonable conclusion in the circumstances but one which when applied across the board was to have tragic consequences elsewhere.[42]

Stung by criticism of Operation Restore Hope in the USA, the Clinton administration passed a 'Presidential Directive' in May 1994 which laid out new conditions for US military intervention, including a 'sunset clause' which insisted on a specific end date for any new peacekeeping mandate. The difficulty of satisfying these conditions lay behind US reluctance to commit troops in both Rwanda and Bosnia, but all members of the Security Council ignored the warning signals that genocide against Tutsis in Rwanda was being meticulously planned by Hutu extremists throughout 1994, the latest chapter in a long and complex struggle between the two groups which stretched back through the colonial period.[43] Detailed intelligence reports about the preparations were passed to Western capitals and to UN headquarters in New York, but senior officials in the secretariat questioned their validity and made no worst-case contingency plans. Karel Kovanda, the Czech Government representative to the UN, said later that he learned more about Rwanda from NGOs like Human Rights Watch in New York than he did from the entire UN information system.[44] A small UN force had been dispatched to Rwanda at the end of 1993 to oversee peace negotiations between the two parties, but France (a traditional supporter of the Hutu National Republican Movement) lobbied against sending reinforcements at a time when strong intervention would have sent a clear message to those who were planning the killings. In less than 100 days from the beginning of April, 800,000 people were massacred.[45] Many ordinary Rwandans tried to stop the slaughter, and many Hutus helped Tutsis under the most dangerous of circumstances, but their efforts were powerless in the face of the sheer scale and level of organisation of the murders.[46] While the UN dithered (actually reducing its forces on the ground at one point), France launched its own partial intervention ('Operation Turquoise'), which saved about 15,000 Tutsi lives, but did nothing to deter the rest of the killings. By the time a further detachment of 5500 UN troops was dispatched in late June, the genocide was almost complete. What stopped it was the advance of Tutsi troops from the Rwandan Patriotic Front, leading the UN to call without a hint of irony for '*a ceasefire to protect civilians*'.[47] Many of those who were protected turned out to be Hutu killers who fled with two million real civilians across the border into the Democratic Republic of Congo (formerly Zaire) – the notorious 'Interahamwe' militias who continued to regroup, rebuild and spread propaganda about the fate that awaited anyone who returned home to Rwanda from their base in giant refugee camps like Goma. '*We have become the quartermaster for the Hutu militia*' was the conclusion of a senior American aid official.[48] Once again, humanitarian assistance had substituted for political action.

According to official evaluations, the relief programme itself was generally impressive.[49] Although about 80,000 refugees died in the camps during 1994, mainly from cholera and dysentery, this is not considered to be unusual in such a huge influx of people into areas with no clean water.[50] John Seaman, a relief veteran working for Save the Children Fund-UK, was more critical, at least of the many NGOs who '*threw all technical standards to the wall*'.[51] This did not apply to every agency – Oxfam, for example, provided an efficient water supply and others laid on an innovative family tracing and reunification programme. It is easy to be wise from a distance and ignore the stresses and strains that faced decision makers on the ground. Nevertheless, there is clear evidence of waste and duplication among the NGOs that poured into the refugee camps, with far too much energy expended on profile and publicity. This continued during 1996 when both the NGOs and the UN consistently exaggerated the number of refugees at risk of starvation in the Congo as the rebel leader Laurent Kabila and his forces moved closer to Kinshasa. Just as negotiations to send an international military force to the Congo reached fever pitch in November, Kabila's army (supported by Rwandan Government forces) scored a decisive victory against the Interahamwe and 600,000 refugees organised their own return across the border.[52] In a revealing reaction, some relief agencies concluded that the refugees had just been lucky, and continued to claim that millions more still remained at risk.[53] This was untrue, though both Kabila's forces and elements of the Rwandan government were certainly involved in the murder of Hutu refugees and displaced persons.[54]

It is difficult to see anything positive in this saga, but both the official evaluation of the relief programme and Alex de Waal's highly-unofficial critique see Rwanda as a seminal event, *'the beginning of a solution for the people of central Africa but an increasing crisis for the humanitarian international'*.[55] The 'crisis' applies to the institutions that were found publicly wanting, both in the quality of the emergency work they undertook (honourable exceptions notwith-standing) and in their broader failure to intervene in Rwanda to prevent genocide and root out the killers. The 'solution' lies in the hands of a political alliance between civic groups and progressive leaders in the region willing to oversee a solution based on power sharing within the ethnic tensions and political manoeuvrings that still afflict Rwanda, Burundi and their neighbours – notably the Congo, which dissolved into further crisis during 1998. There is plenty for the international community to do in supporting this solution, but if the failings that produced the crisis go unheeded then further humanitarian tragedies are inevitable.

CLOSER TO HOME: HUMANITARIAN INTERVEN-TION IN FORMER YUGOSLAVIA

For politicians in Western Europe it was one thing for Africans to be killing each other in large numbers, and another for the same thing to happen on their doorstep. Yet far from energising the European Union (EU) to prove its worth on the wider stage, the 'death of Yugoslavia' confirmed the fragility of European resolve to work together on a common international agenda, even one of such magnitude so close to home. If this was a 'test for Europe', as researchers Hodge and Grbin put it, the EU failed, raising questions not only about Yugoslavia but about the prospects for future multilateral action in general.[56]

When Josef Broz Tito died in 1980, the bonds that had held the Yugoslav Federation together since the end of World War II began to dissolve, enthusiastically encouraged by nationalist politicians in the different republics. One of those politicians – the Serb leader Slobodan Milosevic – was elected President of Yugoslavia at the end of 1990, and promptly plunged the Federation into a period of economic and political turmoil from which it never recovered. Milosevic was opposed not just by separatists from other republics but by large sections of civil society (including trade unions, students and the media), who were determined to preserve the country as a coherent whole. Although what followed was portrayed as a civil war, it was really a war prosecuted by Serb politicians who used the conflict to fuel the fires of nationalist support for their own agenda. Atrocities were committed by all sides, but Serbian culpability was by far the greatest. The failure of external mediators to grasp this (and their consequent insistence on being even-handed) led eventually to the ethnic division of Bosnia and the over-rewarding of Bosnian Serbs in the Dayton Peace Accords. Serb actions, from ethnic cleansing and rape, through the concentration camps of Omarska and elsewhere, to the massacres of civilians in 'safe havens' like Srebenica, went unpunished by the international community until American patience snapped and NATO forces took the upper hand. At the same time, local attempts to preserve some sort of co-existence were consistently ignored. In Serbia and Croatia, 90 per cent of people displaced by the fighting were accommodated in private homes, most without regard to ethnicity at all.[57] Even after the war was over, thousands of Bosnians defied the nationalist parties by voting to reverse the results of ethnic cleansing in the local elections of September 1997.[58] Yet the conflict was consistently reported as one in which different ethnic groups found it 'impossible' to live together.

By the middle of 1991 the Federation had collapsed. Croatia and Slovenia had declared their independence, and in response Serb forces had entered both, ostensibly to protect the Serbs who lived there. As fighting intensified, the EU attempted to broker one cease-fire after another (14 had failed by the end of September).[59] The UN appointed Cyrus Vance as its first special representative, and international sanctions were agreed – and extended across all parties to the conflict despite extreme inequalities in military capability. By the time UN troops were dispatched to Croatia in November, Serb forces were already redeploying to Bosnia, where they proceeded to take control of two-thirds of the Republic in a matter of weeks. Requests for international help from Alija Izetbegovic (the Bosnian President)

were rebuffed, and continued to be so until September of the following year when a small UN contingent arrived in Sarajevo, despite the
widespread atrocities that had been committed by Serb forces against
Bosnian Muslims during 1992. However, this force was too small to
do much more than accompany relief convoys involving large numbers
of NGOs under the ad hoc but fairly effective umbrella of the UN
High Commission for Refugees (UNHCR).[60] It was also too small to
prevent the widespread theft of relief supplies, especially by the
Serbs, but it was large enough to deter more forceful intervention in
case the troops themselves became targets. This gave Western leaders
(particularly Douglas Hurd, the staunchly non-interventionist British
Foreign Secretary) and the Russian Federation an additional reason
for blocking attempts to agree a more forceful response in the UN
Security Council and the EU.

As the conflict escalated, more UN troops arrived, but their
mandate was neither clarified nor extended as the *'hesitation waltz'*
continued.[61] It was only in September 1994 (when 69 people were
killed by a mortar fired at Sarajevo market) that the Serbs were given
an ultimatum to remove their heavy weapons from a 20-kilometre
exclusion zone around the besieged city. This was ignored, and the
UN then called for a further 10,000 troops to position themselves
along the 600-kilometre border between Bosnia and Serbia. What
they got were 135 unarmed civilians.[62] Serb forces took full advantage, capturing Bihac and Zepa, tying UN troops to flagpoles as
human shields, shooting down British and American aircraft, and
massacring at least 8000 men in Srebenica, the penultimate of the
cruelly-misnamed 'havens'.[63] Only Goradze remained, guarded by
British troops and protected under the terms of the London Peace
Conference, the latest effort at mediation launched in July 1995.
When that too failed to end the fighting, the Clinton administration
forced NATO to initiate a series of air strikes against Serb positions,
finally showing the kind of resolve which might have stopped the
conflict four years earlier, and preparing the way for the Dayton Peace
Accords in November of the same year.

That, of course, was not the end of the story. By the end of the
conflict over two million civilians had been displaced from their
homes or taken refuge in other countries, and under the terms of the
Dayton Accords they were supposed to return to participate in the
forthcoming Bosnian elections (only about 100,000 actually did).[64]
There has been plenty of money from the international community
for reconstruction projects, the establishment of a War Crimes
Tribunal which belatedly began to show its muscle in 1997, and large-

scale military commitments to keep the peace. But the elections were pushed through too quickly, without the conditions necessary for real democratic process such as commitment among all the parties, an environment allowing people to participate without fear, and freedom of expression, information, and movement.[65] Too many resources have been wasted on poorly-designed technocratic quick fixes, and not enough on slower, longer-term initiatives designed to cross the ethnic divide and bring people together. Even the better of these projects (like support for independent media) have been fragmented among competing donors.[66] The Dayton Accords have been praised by some as the only workable response to the conflict,[67] and criticised by others as *'an expedient by which the international community sought to divest itself from the problem, rather than assist in its solution'*[68] – another example of a long-standing tendency to *'divide and quit'*, as previously practised in India, Palestine, Cyprus and elsewhere.[69] This is a harsh judgement, but the half-hearted Western response to Serbian incursions into Kosovo during 1998 suggests that it is not too wide of the mark. When NATO did intervene as this book went to press, their strategy was poorly planned and poorly designed, leaving the Kosovars facing a dangerous and unstable peace with little prospect of longer-term security in the region.

WHAT DO WE NEED TO LEARN?

If the betrayals and the bungling are to be avoided in the future, we need to understand what recent history has to teach. The first lesson is this: responding more effectively to complex political emergencies requires a better balance between conflict prevention and long-term peace-building, 'developmental relief', and international political action. At present, all three are unacceptably weak, and support for relief far outweighs commitment to both of the others.

Preventing crises requires slow, careful, deliberate work on the underlying causes of insecurity: *'peace is an exercise in perseverance'*.[70] Equitable economic development (a secure livelihood for everyone), a polity that respects human rights, and effective governance reduce exclusion and provide more opportunities for differences to be resolved peacefully.[71] However, these are very long-term goals in most societies. In the meantime it is important to focus on more specific initiatives like improving local security (such as by de-mining and arms control); strengthening systems of early warning and timely intervention (like fact-finding missions and proactive negotiations); providing special assistance to communities affected by conflict; training in conflict-resolution, and supporting local dispute-settlement mechanisms (both functioning justice systems and the ways in which ordinary people solve disputes for themselves).[72] The latter are often highly influential, albeit pursued quietly and away from the public eye. Groups like the Quakers, the Moral Re-Armament Movement and the Catholic Church have a long tradition of this sort of 'peace building from below', and have had some success in the Philippines (encouraging a non-violent transition from the Marcos regime to that of Corazon Aquino), Cambodia (the 'peace marches' of the Buddhist monk Ghosananda) and Nigeria (post-Biafra).[73] NGOs like International Alert, the International Crisis Group, and the International Negotiation Network have played a useful role in mediating between rival groups in Ethiopia, Liberia and Sierra Leone, though their impact is sometimes exaggerated for the purposes of public relations.[74] *'Those who own the conflict will know the best approaches to ending it'*,[75] so it is vital to encourage a spreading web of civic organisations and channels for dialogue between committed individuals.[76] When Cyril Ramaphosa of the African National Congress (ANC) and Roelf Meyer of the South African government embarked on a joint fishing trip in 1991, neither had much trust in the other, yet when Ramaphosa pulled a fish-hook out of Meyer's hand a relationship was set in motion that later played a central role in the negotiations that made free elections possible.[77]

At a more fundamental level, peace building means a culture that values diversity and practises dialogue, thus reducing the opportunities for politicians and soldiers to manipulate small-scale conflicts into large-scale wars.[78] The absence of such a culture was a contributing factor in the spiralling violence of Cambodia, Rwanda and Yugoslavia. However, there is no universal model: every society must find its own balance between justice – using war crimes tribunals to punish the guilty – and reconciliation, working through 'truth commissions' like those established in South Africa and El Salvador to air abuses under amnesty, or the village ceremonies held in Mozambique to 'cleanse' returning combatants from both sides of the war.[79] Too much emphasis on judicial proceedings can provoke revenge, especially where a large proportion of the population has been involved in the conflict. Outside help can be important in all these areas, but few donors seem prepared to fund this sort of work on the necessary scale and length of time it needs to be effective. It is sensitive and difficult, provides few short-term returns or visible results, and offers only limited opportunities for profile and publicity. So it is not well suited to the conditions and characteristics of foreign aid.

International political action

Long-term prevention is the best defence against conflict and famine, but to succeed in vulnerable societies it needs as much help as possible from an international climate supportive of equitable development and an international community willing to provide strong and coherent backing in times of need. Neither exists at present. Although diplomatic pressure is often exerted to bring warring factions together on an ad hoc basis (usually when the fighting hits the TV screens), there is no consensus on the criteria for intervention in order to address the causes of the problem, nor for upholding international law as part of the solution. The common perception of low stakes and high risks explains why no major power is prepared to commit large-scale forces to a crisis like Bosnia until it is too late.[80] In that sense it is not the UN's fault if peacekeeping is ineffective, but the responsibility of its member states. The current ambivalence about international responsibilities can only be corrected by the key players – is it peacekeeping, peacemaking, peace enforcement, or something else? It is certainly more than the traditional positioning of military forces between warring parties (as in Cyprus), but quite how much more remains dangerously uncertain.[81] Regional peacekeeping forces (like ECOMOG in Liberia) do not seem to provide a sufficient answer, nor does the imposition of sanctions intended to lever a solution without committing troops. Sanctions against Iraq may have caused the deaths of 500,000 children aged under five since 1991, far more than were killed during the Gulf War.[82] Yet Saddam Hussein is still very much in control. Sanctions against the apartheid regime in South Africa may have added to the pressure for change, but internal dynamics were decisive. External threats seem to work best in a 'middle range' between situations where local factions are strong enough to ignore them and where they are too weak to make threats necessary.[83] Putting enough troops on the ground early in a conflict can prevent an escalation, as when UN forces were dispatched to Macedonia at the end of 1992, but the same lesson wasn't learned in Kosovo six years later.[84]

International help is also vital in the immediate post-conflict phase of an emergency, in order to support economic reconstruction, democratic elections or referenda, and war crimes tribunals. The tribunals for Rwanda and former Yugoslavia have not functioned very effectively. In the Rwandan case this is more a matter of UN ineptitude, and in former Yugoslavia of broader political factors which (until US pressure forced the capture of key Serb military figures in mid-1997) kept the worst criminals safely out of reach.[85] But more resources and pressure would have helped both, just as the Rwandan government needed donors to honour their commitment to speed up a fair trial for the 90,000 genocide suspects languishing in its jails.[86]

Developmental relief

Long-term peace building and solid international action will not do away with crises. When they do break out, it is important that humanitarian relief is provided in ways which also contribute to longer-term solutions – relief, in other words, that is 'developmental'. All relief agencies pay lip service to the need to work with local institutions, to ensure their work is sensitive to gender issues and the environment, to involve people in decision making, and build on local solutions. But the evidence is less impressive. Research has shown that many NGOs in areas of conflict have few local roots, no inclination to act as peace builders, and little capacity to do anything except jump when their donors tell them what to do.[87] Although Western governments say they want to invest in a strong and pluralistic society, '*in Bosnia they have sought and found cheap service-delivery*'.[88] It would be far better to endow a fund for long-term development initiatives through a multi-ethnic NGO federation. Relief consultant Ian Smillie found '*NGOs in Sierra Leone stunted after five years of self-absorbed international NGO activity which has done virtually nothing to build the capacity of local organisations*'.[89] Much more support should go to rebuilding the structures that integrate people across factional lines, like markets and trade, schools and the media.[90] Despite the internal obstacles to reintegration in a case like Bosnia, we may find that large-scale, long-term support now is a better and cheaper solution than an unstable, divided peace settlement. Yusuf Jumale, a trader in Mogadishu, points out that '*the militia don't go after business, they go for the aid – the things that are free...we are trying to make it too expensive for anyone to go to war again*'.[91] Donors must pay attention to these economic basics and be flexible: '*rebuilding health posts is pointless if the nurses have given up and are peddling tomatoes in the market*'.[92] The international relief system is still quite rigid in what it will and will not provide (lucky if you want surplus American grain, too bad if you need something else). *'Misread, standardise the diagnosis, and standardise the response,'* is how researcher Johan Pottier puts it.[93]

It has always been thus. Writing in 1921, the Italian Senator Giovanni Ciraolo complained that *'assistance to those stricken by calamities is...slow, poorly-organised and inefficient'*.[94] But why does this continue to be the case 75 years later when there have been so many advances in the technology of emergency nutrition, health care and sanitation? First, because it is incredibly difficult to stick to best practice when 'all hell breaks loose around you'; second, because technology is only a small part of the solution anyway; and third, because few NGOs or intergovernmental organisations are interested in co-operation when this may lose them precious opportunities for profile and publicity, the lifeblood of agencies that are competing for donations. These institutional imperatives lead NGOs to exaggerate successes and disguise failures, pretend that they are central to emergencies when they are not, cut too many corners on quality, and push for quick results.[95] The role played by the international media in triggering humanitarian action makes NGOs feel *they* must be in the spotlight. Such criticisms touch a raw nerve among relief agencies, not because they know the critics are wrong, but because they suspect that they are right and do not know what to do about it. The hurt and confusion will continue so long as NGOs see themselves as *'ladles in the global soup kitchen'*, cleaning up the mess left by state and market failures on contract to the UN, or dependent on shock tactics to lever money from a guilty public.[96] In response to their critics, NGOs like Oxfam and the Red Cross are trying to improve standards and strengthen accountability using self-regulation. But their codes of conduct lack proper enforcement mechanisms, and that has led some to call for more radical changes such as an international relief commissioner and a world relief corps.[97] This is probably essential to preserve advances in humanitarian assistance (and the agencies that made them) from being undermined by the reputation and performance of the mediocre and self-serving.

Timing

The second general lesson is this: there must be long-term commitment combined with the flexibility to act on 'windows of opportunity' – the secret of success lies in the timing. Because emergencies move quickly, there are always points at which intervention is likely to be more effective, but it is difficult to identify them, still less respond, without continuous involvement. That is something the international community finds very difficult, regularly arriving too late and leaving too soon as crises pop up and disappear from the radar screen of political awareness. The causes of the problem are left unsolved, festering away until they ignite another crisis which prompts the reappearance of the international relief circus. Martin Woolacott of the *Guardian* captures the absurdity of this approach well:

> '*the international formula for dealing with failed states...consists of troops, elections and money. The troops are to restore order, the elections to express the will of the people...and the money to revive the economy. What usually happens is that the troops do not stay long enough, the elections are held too early, and the money is stolen.*'[98]

Insufficient effort is invested in rebuilding the civil administration, the justice system and the economy so that a polity might emerge over time to institutionalise democratic practices.

This fundamental lack of loyalty – the inability to stay the course – makes it more difficult to take advantage of windows of opportunity for outside intervention when they appear. The lack of a long-term presence on the ground dilutes early warning, and the disorganisation of the international community makes a timely response to warning signals unlikely. Recent history is full of examples of these missed opportunities, especially during the early phases of a nascent conflict or at the end when there is a 'peace dividend' to be exploited – as for example in the former Yugoslavia during 1990–92, when both Croatia and Bosnia were recognised without equal recognition of the rights of Serbs living there;[99] Rwanda in the early 1990s, when genocide was being planned; and Somalia in 1991 ('*the year of missed opportunities*').[100]

Consistency

It is not just the timing of intervention that is important, but impartiality – the application of the same criteria to all situations and every party to a conflict, except where one group is guilty of demonstrably greater human rights abuses.[101] To be effective, any system of rules must be applied consistently – otherwise, why should one party make sacrifices if others do not reciprocate? This is exactly what happens in international intervention, where accusations of bias abound: Hutus over Tutsis, Serbs over Muslims, and UNITA over the MPLA government in Angola, where the Western powers seem to bend over backwards to accommodate rebel leader Jonas Savimbi despite his having broken every peace agreement since 1991.[102] US aid to Israel far outweighs support to Palestine despite Israel's violation of the Oslo Accords in its settlements policy, so it is hardly surprising that Washington finds it difficult to play the role of 'honest broker' in the peace process. Croatia achieved international recognition (in circumstances which promoted insecurity), but Somaliland did not (when improved security depended on it). ECOMOG favoured Charles Taylor's enemies in Liberia, the USA took sides between warring clans in Somalia, and the UN's feeble response to pressure from the Khmer Rouge in Cambodia strengthened their position in the run-up to elections. Even the prosecution of war criminals has been partial, allowing the worst offenders off the hook and excluding crimes committed by the interveners themselves.[103]

The problem here is that partiality undermines the willingness of rival factions to support future international action. *'We don't trust them, I can tell you that,'* said Mwenze Kongolo (the Congolese Interior Minister) of the UN in 1997, although in this case he was covering up human rights abuses committed by Tutsis on Hutus which the UN was trying to investigate.[104] So if the international community is part of the solution to this puzzle, it is also part of the puzzle itself, damned when it does intervene (as in Somalia) and when it does not (as in Rwanda). The only way through this maze is to be more sensitive to the conditions under which intervention is likely to be effective, and then implement these criteria consistently. Unfortunately, that requires outsiders to be clear and unambiguous about what they are trying to achieve, and then stick to principles once they have been agreed collectively. In the real world of foreign policy-making this is unlikely.

Do it properly, or stay away?

That brings me to the final lesson to be learned, and the most uncomfortable: if you cannot intervene systematically, it may be better not to do so at all, since half-hearted action can exacerbate conflict and prolong the crisis. There *are* examples of long-running stand-offs between factions where a continued international presence is probably essential (like Cyprus), but few cases where external intervention has been instrumental in gaining a lasting settlement. The exceptions to this rule, like the Mozambican peace accords of 1992[105] or the end of civil war in Guatemala and El Salvador, are situations where deep-rooted ethnic conflicts are absent or the parties involved have themselves been ready to reach a settlement.[106] Even then it took US$ 2.5 million to bribe rebel leader Alfonso Dhlakama into participating in the 1994 Mozambican elections – money well spent given the largely successful reconstruction of the country since then. In El Salvador and Guatemala, the UN and its 'Group of Friends' (including Mexico, Colombia and Spain) played an important role in bringing the different factions together, fostering trust, disbanding the rebel forces, demobilising two-thirds of the national army, smoothing the way for peaceful elections, and getting the 'truth commissions' up and running.[107] Significantly, UN forces arrived there in sufficient numbers to be credible before the peace settlement, and did not leave until 1995.[108]

Unfortunately these conditions are rare; most conflicts are much more difficult to resolve until the internal dynamics have worked themselves out. The dilemma they present is stark: do we intervene in the messy way that international realities dictate, sure in the knowledge that this will complicate matters even further; or stay away while people suffer on the ground because we know we cannot do the job properly? The veteran American diplomat George Kennan answered this question in the context of Somalia by admitting that since '*our action holds no promise of correcting the situation*', US marines should not have been sent.[109] They could neither resolve the problem by achieving victory for one side over the other, nor secure a lasting peace through mediation. Instead, they left behind a permanently unstable middle ground – a grey area stained with red. To various degrees this has been the situation in Liberia and Sierra Leone, Sudan, Rwanda and Iraq and now the Balkans. Should we therefore leave people to fight it out among themselves, as Kennan's advice suggests? While attractive to some, this sits uneasily with humanitarian ethics and the dilemmas of real-time decision-making, hedged around by politics, media pressure and other influences. If we were to decide what to do solely on grounds of the problems that might result from doing it, we would end up doing nothing at all, and that would not be a viable basis for a co-operative future. However messy they are, we have got to get to grips with the practical issues of making intervention more effective.

CONCLUSION

It may seem obvious that prevention is better (and cheaper) than cure, but this message has not yet convinced those who need to hear it most. In Angola, the largest peacekeeping force in history cost US$5 million a day,[110] and Operation Restore Hope in Somalia cost the USA more than its entire foreign aid budget for Africa.[111] Had this money been invested in a standing international intervention force of sufficient size, and in long-term peace building to limit the need for its deployment, millions of lives might have been saved. They might not, of course, especially where the internal dynamics of conflict are so fierce, and certainly not in the absence of clear and consistent criteria for intervention. However, not to try is equivalent to moral surrender, and leaves all of us with blood on our hands. A more forceful and intelligent response is essential, but the two must go together – the ethical defence against criticism is not to abandon intervention but to undertake it having analysed all the ifs and buts, made the most informed judgement possible, and struggled long and hard to get things right – *'to be faced with the hardest of choices and still protect human life in ways which constantly challenge evil'.*[113]

   'Citizens must ultimately rebuild their own societies, but they need breathing space to do so', and that, at the very least, is something international co-operation can help to provide, by securing the foundations people need to build their own solutions before they start killing each other in large numbers.[113] In the short term the key is to secure a window for peace – like a ceasefire – guaranteed by international forces for long enough to be effective in finding common ground. In the longer term, peaceful societies are those that celebrate differences when they are healthy and attack them when they are not, and if international co-operation is not encouraging these things, then what is it doing? Each component of the humanitarian trilogy is vital, but thus far relief has been a substitute for peace building and international political action. *'We have chosen to respond to major unlawful violence not by stopping that violence but by trying to provide relief to the suffering...but our choice of policy allows the suffering to continue.'*[114] Reversing that policy requires robust diplomatic and military action as well as humanitarian relief in a coherent overall framework. What is needed is not just a better military response, but global co-operation to address the increasing divisions that lie at the root of insecurity and obstruct the peaceful resolution of differences. That requires a depth, continuity and courage of engagement that has

defeated the international community for 50 years. And that represents a poverty of the imagination that disgraces all of us at a time when so many resources and opportunities are available.

Chapter 6

Summary: Sticks, Carrots and Room to Manoeuvre

'We want them to own the programme, of course, but they must do what we want. If not, they should get their money elsewhere.'

Senior World Bank official,
talking about the Tanzanian Government[1]

'If appropriate aid is put to good use in a satisfactory policy context, and if all the other components of growth are present, the statistical relationship between aid and growth will be positive.'

Robert Cassen et al[2]

In the early 1990s, Western governments financed an exhaustive study of foreign aid. Its conclusions, summarised in the second of the above quotations, don't exactly set the pulse racing, but they do capture the reality of outside help, and not just foreign aid. There may be little similarity on the surface between the experience of a country like South Korea, the work of NGOs such as PREM in India, and the complex political emergencies examined in Chapter 5, but the lessons they teach are remarkably alike. External assistance is never the key factor in promoting internal change, and always a blunt weapon in the fight against poverty and violence. Nevertheless, the right sort of help at the right time can be very influential in creating more space for local forces to get things right. US aid and trade preferences with South Korea and Taiwan in the 1950s, or the support given to PREM by international NGOs in the 1980s, were important in giving early development efforts the extra push they needed. When local efforts break down, outside help can be even more important in fostering the basic conditions required to get them going again. The support provided by the UN and its 'Group of Friends' to the nascent peace process in Central America is a good example. So we *can* help in important ways, even though our help is never the deciding factor. Finding better ways to resolve this paradox is the central challenge facing international co-operation in the 21st century.

DOES MY MONEY MAKE A DIFFERENCE?

Everyone wants a simple answer to this question, but because of the complexities involved it is impossible to provide one. Let's take foreign aid first. There are lots of methodological problems which make it difficult to generalise between different countries, donor agencies and types of assistance.[3] Aid with ill-defined objectives (like most programme aid) is almost impossible to evaluate anyway.[4] Scandinavian aid comes out best among government donors in terms of its quality and focus on the poorest countries, the USA the worst,[5] and Japan somewhere in the middle.[6] NGO aid tends to be more poverty-focused than official aid, but faces increasing questionmarks about its own impact that replicate doubts about aid on the wider stage. Emergency assistance and food aid have a more obvious function in times of acute need, but they rarely play a decisive role in the longer term.[7] *'Negative elements loom rather large'* in the record of food aid according to Robert Cassen and his colleagues;[8] *'a marginal positive effect with huge transactions costs'* is the judgement of the EU.[9] Technical assistance has fallen out of favour since a series of critical evaluations in the early 1990s showed that most expatriate advisers had little positive impact on local institutions despite the huge costs involved, for example US$4 billion a year in Africa alone.[10]

An enormous amount of research has been carried out to test the aggregate impact of these different types of aid, and the conclusion is always the same: where the objectives are clearly and unambiguously developmental, good aid works when it is well used in the right climate over a sufficient length of time.[11] Under these conditions its effects will be *'positive, not insubstantial, but not dramatic'*;[12] *'all things being equal, good aid helps'*, as the Dutch government puts it.[13] However, in the real world all things are rarely equal, so the correlation between aid, economic growth, and poverty-reduction tends to be weak, especially in the most aid-dependent economies. Here, there is more evidence that aid goes to finance consumption rather than investment, displaces domestic savings, and acts as a disincentive to local producers or decision makers facing tough choices.[14] In Bangladesh, for example, *'policy-makers continue to wait upon decisions in Washington before they formulate their budgets...or even decide how many children should be born'*.[15] In such aid-dependent countries the capacity to absorb more aid and use it effectively is very limited, so much so that at the end of the 1980s the Swedish government was holding undisbursed funds for Bangladesh equivalent to five times the value of the country's annual allocation.[16]

The influence of political and commercial considerations, lack of co-ordination between donors, and the tendency to keep on adding new conditions make failure almost a self-fulfilling prophecy where recipients are weak. World Bank research shows that non-developmental objectives among donors reduce economic growth among recipients by as much as 1.5 per cent.[17] Aid is more effective when dealing with temporary gaps in financing than with deep-rooted social and political problems, but it could do more to eradicate poverty if this was made the overriding objective.[18] At present only about 20 per cent of total aid is used to finance activities which benefit poor people directly.[19] Overall, the record is bad enough to lead US Senator Patrick Leahy to conclude that foreign aid is *'exhausted intellectually, conceptually and politically'*.[20] *'The truth is that debt, not economic development, has been the legacy of 40 years of foreign aid.'*[21] This judgement may be too sweeping, but donors have themselves to blame for foreign aid's shortcomings.

If evaluating the impact of foreign aid is difficult, calculating the net effect of international co-operation as a whole is even more so. Yet those who have tried to measure the impact of trade concessions, debt relief and so on find the same pattern. *'Development co-operation generally does not seem to have had a decisive influence on the evolution of developing countries'* is the European Commission's conclusion.[22] Despite European rhetoric that the Lome Convention is the *'finest and most complete instrument of development co-operation ever'*, the African, Caribbean and Pacific (ACP) countries who are members actually lost market share in their trade with the EU between 1976 and 1994.[23] At the same time, the administrative burden of implementing the Convention on the ground has become *'a nightmare'*.[24] There is also evidence that the ACP countries' dependence on the EU has stifled the growth of trade among themselves, marginalising their economies from world markets and tying them too closely to a single consumer.[25]

Elsewhere, the influence of trade pacts varies. As we saw in Chapter 3, concessions were vital in the early growth of East Asia; NAFTA is too young to judge; and arrangements between equals (like MERCOSUR in Latin America) may do better to strengthen less competitive economies in the early stages. In all cases it is not trade concessions by themselves that make the difference, but how they interact with other factors at home and abroad. Chapters 2 and 3 showed how these interactions determine the net cash flow to and from developing countries, and how this has fluctuated markedly over the last 50 years. It was negative throughout much of the 1980s even for the stronger economies of Latin America, because the losses from falling export prices and rising debt repayments outweighed the gains from foreign aid, loans and private investment.[26] UNCTAD estimates that the developing world lost US$42 billion from the terms of trade alone between 1982 and 1986.[27] Since then, trade and investment have improved for some but debt relief has yet to bite, and the net benefits of international co-operation for the poorest countries (especially in Africa) remain precarious.

A charitable conclusion would be as follows: international co-operation in the form we have known it has been more important to successful performers than its critics have claimed, but more damaging to bad performers than its defenders have admitted. What explains this paradox is the ability of local institutions to incorporate external opportunities into their own long-term development framework – the very thing that co-operation is supposed to strengthen but often erodes.

WHY DOESN'T CO-OPERATION WORK BETTER?

Why hasn't international co-operation produced the desired results? The easy answer is because we haven't tried it, preferring to intervene, impose and interfere instead. Nearly all 'co-operation' is based on the use of 'sticks' – threatening countries with aid cuts, sanctions of various kinds, military intervention, and commercial or diplomatic retaliation; and 'carrots' – the promise of more aid, trade concessions, a seat at the international negotiating table or protection by foreign troops. Sticks and carrots are applied according to the recipients' performance in doing what has, theoretically at least, been agreed with the donor – like cutting public expenditure or holding elections. All help is conditional on one thing or another. The conditions may be milder among some agencies than others, but they will be there somewhere, if only in the form of specified reporting requirements, demands for information, or project targets. In all cases the conditions are set by the more powerful of the parties, and the sticks and carrots are there to encourage these conditions to be observed. Most recipients know this and are quite willing to play the game, so long as the benefits outweigh the costs. But do they? Conditions work best when they approach the *spirit* of co-operation – agreed jointly, implemented collectively, and involving sacrifices on all sides. Then they have the legitimacy required to make them work. Otherwise, conditionality becomes a *'ritual dance around the Tower of Babel'*,[28] incapable of generating any ownership over change and corrupting the relationships on which authentic partnership is based.[29] That spells disaster for lasting results.

STICKS AND CARROTS AT WORK: STRUCTURAL ADJUSTMENT

The classic example of conditionality is 'structural adjustment', along with its close companion, 'economic stabilisation'. The debate that has grown up around these policies has consumed acres of paper and gigabytes of numbers for crunching by computer. Because they illustrate so much that has gone wrong with international co-operation in recent years, it is worth taking a closer look at the theory and practice of how they were applied. First of all, let's be clear on what this debate is not about. As Chapter 3 demonstrated, successful economies adjust all the time to the changing international and domestic contexts. At times they may run a rising budget deficit or protect an overvalued currency, but in the long term they practise prudent macro-economics to ensure the stability that growth and investment require. Both 'economic stabilisation' (correcting short-term domestic imbalances by curbing demand and cutting public spending) and 'structural adjustment' (aligning the domestic economy with the demands of international competitiveness over the medium term) are normal aspects of managing any economy that wants to keep on growing. As David Knox (ex-Vice President of the World Bank) once told me, *'If you've been on the bottle you'll have a hangover, and if you don't learn from the hangover you might become an alcoholic.'*[30] Economic reform was supposed to cure the headaches caused by years of overspending, and wean countries away from the drink – the bad economic habits that lay at the root of the problem.

A cold shower (stabilisation), followed by a period in rehabilitation (adjustment), would do the trick. Like conditionality, the real question was never 'do we stabilise or adjust?', but how such changes were implemented – who decided what was done when, how the programmes were designed, who paid the costs and enjoyed the benefits, and how fast things were pushed through. And that's where the problems arose.

The IMF and the World Bank began to lend money to countries experiencing severe economic difficulties in the early 1980s, with the Fund concentrating on stabilisation and the Bank on adjustment.[31] In both cases, loans were made on condition that recipients undertook a wide-ranging programme of reforms designed to stabilise the economy and promote future growth. That meant deep cuts in public expenditure, devaluation and other measures to promote exports, higher crop prices and the freeing of agricultural markets from government control, and privatisation. The results of these reforms varied from one social group, country and time period to another, and these comparisons are still the subject of considerable debate. It will take many years before the long-term impact on growth and poverty can be assessed, but overall things have not worked out as the Bank and Fund expected, especially in sub-Saharan Africa.[32] As of 1993, only six (out of 29) adjusting countries in Africa had achieved '*decisive improvements in macro-economic policies*'.[33] Internal studies stuck to the line that short-term pain would produce long-term gain, but almost all the independent research that has been carried out disagrees: there is little evidence of significant structural change in the economies of adjusting countries, the competitiveness of non-traditional exports, the efficiency of production, or levels of savings and investment – all the things that would have to change to make the economy stronger in the long run.[34] In some of the more success-ful cases (like Ghana), imbalances are starting to re-emerge after a period of growth.[35] The only cases where adjustment has stimulated a return to sustained growth are those where it was self-imposed (as in parts of East Asia), or in a few middle-income countries where initial conditions were favourable (like Colombia).[36]

If the economy returns to long-term health, then the short-term social costs that result from reform might be an acceptable price to pay.[37] But since the key economic indicators have shown no lasting improvement it is hard to make this argument for most countries, especially when there were less painful alternatives available. These social costs were immense. Inequality increased in nearly all cases and poverty in most, especially among very poor people in rural areas who lacked the assets and skills to take advantage of market incentives, and in the cities, where the axe fell heavily on people in government jobs and on others whose wages fell in real terms against a background of rising food prices. Those who did not have relatives to fall back on were affected especially badly, and women bore the brunt of coping for their families.[38] When the scale of these social costs became apparent, the World Bank launched a series of welfare projects to create a temporary safety net for the poor. Their impact varies, but generally they came too late to stop the worst damage or provide protection on a scale that was sustainable.[39]

What was going on here? Why did the reforms not have the effects that were intended, and why did international institutions insist on persevering with them in the face of so much contrary evidence? At the most basic level, the adjustment paradigm was not based on empirical evidence but on economic theory, regardless of whether the conditions existed for the theory to work.[40] It was weakest in the areas where all neo-liberal thinking is weak – regarding long-term change simply as a series of unconnected short-terms; obsessed with securing stability by deflating demand; retrenching states while ignoring market imperfections; bypassing local institutions, culture and social realities; and getting the politics of change completely wrong.[41] More compensation should have been provided to those who suffered in the short term, since they were able to organise political opposition to continued reform.[42] Adjustment relied on theoretical stabilisation effects that never arrived; links between growth, employment and poverty that didn't work; local commitment that rarely materialised; and regulatory and supervisory mechanisms that didn't exist.[43] The sequence of the reforms was poorly-designed, and complementary measures to protect poor people and the environment were not incorporated at the right time.[44] In the words of one leading authority on the issue (Professor Lance Taylor) the *'prescriptions were simply ridiculous'*.[45] Does this sound familiar? It's one thing to have unwelcome guests, but quite another for them to take over the housekeeping and insist that they know best.

So what was the alternative for economies that were faced by bankruptcy? The consensus is that macro-economic policy should have been less deflationary (to preserve more growth), social policy more active (to protect the poorest and maintain political support), reform carefully graduated, control kept in the hands of local institutions, and poverty reduction central to everything.[46] In the longer term, adjustment needs to be integrated into the strategies explored for Africa in Chapter 3, with temporary de-linking based around agriculture and rural industrialisation while the preconditions for international competitiveness in non-traditional exports are developed.[47] Then it might be adjustment to poverty-reducing growth rather than growth-reducing poverty – structural transformation, as some have called it.[48]

CONDITIONALITY GONE MAD

The IMF and World Bank did not invent conditionality (the Marshall Plan had some conditions attached to it and President Kennedy's Alliance for Progress in the 1960s had many more),[49] but since 1980 the number and severity of the conditions have increased enormously, and with them, the level of responsibility assumed by outsiders over other people's affairs.[50] The old conditions have been joined by new ones based around gender equity, environmental sustainability, poverty focus, democracy and 'good governance'.[51] Less emphasis is now placed on the sticks, and more on the carrots – giving more aid if the conditions are met.[52] Some countries (like France) ignore the politics so long as the economic conditions are respected; others (like Germany) only apply them when recipients are weak. As the conditions multiply, the time frame for meeting them tends to shrink, imposing an impossible burden on local institutions.[53] The overall picture is one of increasing complexity and disorientation on the ground. The World Bank, an organisation with *'plenty of ideas but no priorities'*, set 111 conditions in its policy framework paper for Kenya alone.[54]

On the surface, these new conditions might sound positive, but the real test lies in their impact. If there is no single route to eradicate poverty it is difficult to see how more focused pressure from aid agencies will help countries to succeed, unless there are much deeper changes in the kind and level of support provided. Do societies become determined to eradicate poverty because loans or grants contain a clause to that effect? Unlikely, isn't it? There is increasing evidence that 'progressive' conditions only increase the influence of international institutions over recipient countries – a charge recently levelled at international NGO coalitions in their attempts to persuade the World Bank to adopt tougher social and environmental criteria.[55] This is fundamentally incompatible with local ownership over the changes which do promote equitable growth in different contexts. The evidence on conditionality shows this to be true. In a recent study of aid and democracy, political scientist Gordon Crawford concluded that 18 of the 29 cases of conditionality he studied were *'wholly ineffective'*; there were only two (in Malawi and Guatemala) where threats to withdraw aid had any impact at all.[56] *Plus ça change* – 20 years earlier, research on economic conditionality imposed by USAID found no impact in 22 out of 25 examples.[57] Other studies have found slightly more evidence that conditions can influence economic policy more than social and political change, and that 'positive' conditions (the carrots) work better than 'negative' ones (the sticks). But these conclusions only hold true where local groups are already committed to the changes required – in which case the conditions are redundant.[58] Overall, the links between outside influence, internal compliance, and results on the ground are generally weak.[59] Where outside assistance is of little importance to the recipient (or can be replaced easily by other sources of funds), or where it is so important that withdrawal would do significant damage to the loan portfolio of the donor (like the World Bank and the IMF in Mexico), sticks don't work anyway.[60] Examples of the former include China, Indonesia (where Dutch pressure on human rights was ignored, partly because other Western donors continued with their support),[61] Burma, where Western withdrawal was nullified by the 'constructive engagement' policies of the Association of South East Asian Nations (ASEAN),[62] and Kenya, whose government kept agreeing to conditions about democracy and corruption, banked the resulting aid, and then found plenty of reasons for non-compliance.[63]

As a result of these disappointments, some donors (like Canada) have abandoned conditionality completely.[64] It is not difficult to see why. Most conditions require a local support base, which isn't there, to see them through, and as conditions multiply, a technical capacity, which is usually weak, to ensure compliance. There is no necessary link between the different conditions that donors think are related – economic reform and Western democracy for example, or market liberalisation and poverty reduction. In any case, everyday resistance – James Scott's famous *'weapons of the weak'*[65] – is used all the time by recipients to play the conditionality game to their advantage, frustrating the impact of conditions long after they have been officially 'accepted'. To have any chance of success, donors must agree to work together: this they rarely do in practice.[66] Conditions have to be applied consistently to be legitimate, but political and other interests make their application selective. There are four conditionality clauses in the Lome Convention, but the EU has only applied them to the poorest ACP countries in Africa, not to more strategic 'partners' like Algeria, China and Indonesia.[67] In any case, the incentive of more aid, or less, is rarely strong enough to convince a recalcitrant government to implement painful reforms.[68]

To summarise, one can have unanimity among outsiders without sufficient local leverage to be effective (like Kenya), leverage without the unanimity to apply it (like Burma), neither of the two (like Iraq), but very rarely both. Where conditionality is necessary it probably won't work, and where it might work it is usually unnecessary. Why should governments need to be bribed to persuade them to do things that are supposedly in their interest?[69] Sometimes external pressure can tip the balance in favour of progressive local forces (like Malawi during the fall of President Banda in 1992–93),[70] but home-grown recipes are still the best. The only conditions that are truly effective are those that are recognised as legitimate by all the parties involved, and that requires a level of dialogue that hardly exists anywhere.[71] The key – taken up in Chapter 7 – is a system of mutually-agreed performance standards for all the parties, not ideological conditions set by one for the other; 'light but firm' criteria, not 'heavy but loose' arrangements in which conditions multiply but are never implemented consistently.[72] Good riddance to the sticks – they never work in the long term. But positive conditionality in its present form is no solution either: no more carrots, please!

HOW CAN WE HELP?

If the stick-and-carrot approach doesn't work, what does? As we've seen in previous chapters, the transmission mechanisms between outside help and results on the ground are immensely complex. Peace and prosperity come from three interrelated levels of causes. The first is the appropriate mix of policies in a flexible economy – constantly adjusted between self-reliance and openness to the outside world: competition, co-operation, and an active state. The second is an intelligent polity – the capacity and willingness to identify what mix is appropriate in different circumstances and secure the political support to see it through. The third consists of all the things that vary so much from one society to another, like culture, leadership, geography, and the prevailing international context. Each one determines success at the next level up – the 'right policies' require a polity to sustain them, and a strong polity requires the right underlying conditions to support its development. Yet, as the stick-and-carrot approach demonstrates, the dominant approach to this complexity has been incredibly simplistic, focused overmuch on the first of the three levels, wedded to standardised solutions imposed from the outside, and (when war or famine hits the headlines) pushed into partial and ineffective intervention. Standardisation implies that we can predict how internal and external forces will combine over time to produce the best net outcome, but we cannot know such a thing in advance and it does not fit the evidence we do have. If that is true, the standard approach won't be effective, and if it is ineffective it cannot be ethical to enforce it through conditionality. Personal experience tells us that nothing changes in any lasting or meaningful way unless the internal conviction exists to carry change forward. We don't need vast amounts of research to confirm this, but we have it anyway, and the results are the same.

What is it, then, that determines whether external help is genuinely supportive of these deciding factors? Experience across the board reveals three principles: consistency (with local realities), continuity (over the long term), and coherence (between different types of help). Consistency implies a full and sensitive understanding of culture, social structure and political realities, and a willingness to fit into and around them even where they differ from outside expectations. Dudley Seers, a pioneer in development studies, pointed this out 35 years ago in his article *'Why Visiting Economists Fail'*, and his strictures are just as necessary today.[73] The architect Stewart Brand observes that:

> *'evolution is always and necessarily surprising. You cannot control adaptability. All you can do is make room for it. Let the mistakes happen small and disposable. If you let things flourish, you get a wild ride, but you also get sustainability'.*[74]

Not for nothing is the word 'development' translated as 'chaos', and 'planning' as 'dream of the white man' in Cameroon.[75]

Continuity means a commitment to work together over the long term, de-linked from the volatile selectivity imposed by shifting foreign policy concerns, ideological fashions, and disagreements along the way. This doesn't imply slavish adherence to partnership, but it does require the flexibility to respond in different ways at different times. Getting things right on the ground sometimes requires U-turns or unforeseen compromises that do not fit into predetermined contracts and agreements. In real life, politics rarely converges on an unchanging set of policy options, and success comes from lots of small changes interacting with each other over time.[76] The transformations development requires (especially in culture, social norms and institutions) take generations to evolve. In that respect the East Asian story is unique. Expecting results in Africa in a matter of years is absurd, *'as if the Renaissance, the Reformation, the Scientific Revolution, the French Revolution and the Industrial Revolution were all telescoped into a single lifetime'* as Arthur Toynbee puts it.[77] Except in this case even a lifetime seems too long to wait. Most donor agencies have little sense of loyalty, abandoning adult literacy and community development in favour of micro-credit in the 1990s, for example; pulling out of Latin and Central America as soon as the cold war ended; and switching aid funds from sub-Saharan Africa to the Mediterranean region to stem the expected 'flood' of immigrants into the EU from North Africa and the Middle East.[78] By contrast, the most successful helpers are those who stay in for the long haul, accompanying people and organisations as their efforts evolve. That was what underlay the success of the Rockefeller Foundation in helping to strengthen national agricultural research capacity in India between 1953 and 1990. It helped that, as a private foundation, it didn't have to show quick results.[79] The World Health Organisation says leprosy will be eradicated by the year 2000, so aid agencies can then withdraw. Let's hope someone discussed it with the bacillus, unlike the uncooperative germs and mosquitoes that have brought tuberculosis and malaria back to Africa when officialdom said they were finished too.

The third principle is coherence. Coherence means a unified framework for all development-related decision-making in donor countries, including aid, trade, debt, investment, diplomacy and domestic policies that have a knock-on effect internationally – this is the *'full span of government instruments'*, as the Canadians put it.[80] At present, losses from some outweigh gains from the others – the lopsided 'humanitarian trilogy' described in Chapter 5 is a classic example; aid, trade and debt another. In the 1980s, over 50 per cent of the US$210 million provided in aid to the government of Corazon Aquino in the Philippines each year came straight back to the USA in the form of quotas on imported sugar and textiles; in the Dominican Republic such trade losses were even higher.[81] Political and strategic interests have long dominated development goals in the US aid budget, with aid to Egypt and Israel taking four times the total amount allotted to sub-Saharan Africa in 1994.[82] Coherence is written into the EU Maastricht Treaty and forms a key plank of the Green Paper on the future of EU development co-operation, but this message hasn't yet made it through the minefield of European domestic politics.[83] Reforming the Common Agricultural Policy (CAP), described by UK Development Minister Clare Short as *'crazy economics'*,[84] would do more for developing-country growth than increasing the aid budget, but not according to French farmers. At present the EU is providing aid to encourage beef production in Namibia while simultaneously restricting imports of Namibian beef into Europe and exporting subsidised European beef to the whole of southern Africa.[85] Coherence at the policy level is one thing. On the ground, increasing co-ordination between different donors is also essential to reduce the administrative burden on recipients. There is no reason why Burkina Faso should have to endure 350 separate aid missions a year,[86] nor why Africa needs 22 different aid instruments from the same government in the Netherlands, nor why EU emergency aid should be put in the same basket as fish and mad cows instead of being integrated with the European Development Fund.[87]

CONCLUSION

Consistency, continuity and coherence: put these three principles together and you have the foundations for good help. Good help assists people to solve problems with fewer costs to themselves and more benefits to the rest of the world by expanding the range of choices available, illuminating alternatives, and providing more opportunities to develop and apply win-win solutions. *'Every nation must solve its own problems,'* said Senator Robert Taft in 1945, *'but we can help them over the worst',*[88] by expanding the room to manoeuvre decision makers need when faced by difficult choices. How can this principle be made the centrepiece of the international system?

Part 2

Looking Forward

Chapter 7

Creativity Plus Opportunity: A New Formula for Foreign Aid

'We must find room-to-manoeuvre and space to develop, faced by a choice between death by de-linking and a world economy in which we may not survive. With this space, and human creativity, solutions will be found, little by little'

Jean-Bertrand Aristide[1]

Like ex-President Aristide of Haiti, we all know how it feels to be caught 'between a rock and a hard place' with no obvious escape route. In his case the 'rock' was the stagnation caused by Haiti's marginalisation from the world economy, the result of poor resources and a long history of meddling and exploitation. The 'hard place' was the added risk of dislocation and instability if Haiti were to integrate into world markets when ill-prepared to compete with others and manage the changes integration requires. Such choices are characteristic of economic and social transitions, but they are much harder to resolve against the background of domestic weaknesses and a hostile international context. Admonished by the World Bank for his failure to implement government reforms in Sri Lanka, ex-President Julius Jayawardena made a similar point: *'with a civil war in the north, an uprising in the south, my neighbour rattling her sabre, and plummeting commodity prices, do you honestly think I can afford to set the civil service on fire?'*[2]

In cases like these, what is needed is not another set of standard solutions, but more breathing space and the capacity to use it creatively. Long-term progress is not achieved by *'piling short-term results on short-term results'* – that leads to a spreading web of contradictions from which there is no escape.[3] Real success requires a vision of the future and the ability to realise it through all the challenges and reinterpretations that lie ahead. The problem for poor countries is that weak institutions and external pressures deny those with vision the room to manoeuvre they need to pursue it.[4] Suitably reformed, foreign aid can address those institutional weaknesses, while other forms of international co-operation can make the global context more supportive. Together, creativity and opportunity will breed solutions *'little by little'*, as Aristide puts it. In this way, we can encourage efforts to attack poverty and violence without imposing foreign agendas.

This may be true in theory, but given the deficiencies outlined in the first part of the book, isn't there a case for getting rid of outside help completely? The answer is no, for two reasons. First, poor countries need US$40 billion every year just to meet their basic needs in health and education – never mind the other investments that development requires. These resources have to come from foreign aid, because private capital continues to pass these countries by. Second, the international context has a critical influence over each country's development, but it can't be reshaped by anyone acting alone. International co-operation is essential. Therefore, the correct response to the failings of the past is not to abolish outside help, but change the way we provide it. As we shall see in this chapter, that requires a revolution in the way foreign aid is given and used.

FOREIGN AID PRIORITIES

Fostering creativity and enhancing opportunity will take different forms according to the context. Strengthening the hand of smallholders in sub-Saharan Africa obviously requires a different mix of support to the challenge of a nascent computer industry in India. If roads are what is needed, build them; if building a culture of peace is the priority, then do that; and if both are vital, don't sacrifice one for the other. Room to manoeuvre means getting the help you need, when you need it, and always in a form that gives local institutions the chance to use their talents and be accountable for the results.

In the poorest countries, the priority is still to build up public goods (like technology and communications) and basic endowments of skills and abilities.[5] Investment in people from cradle to grave is a prerequisite for the success of any economy, though better health care, education and access to safe family planning are not automatic routes to poverty reduction. As we saw in Chapter 4, problems of sustainability arose when the expansion of services ran ahead of local capacity to manage and pay for them. The Norwegian government steered clear of standard remedies when it reviewed its own aid programme in the mid-1990s, arguing that there are many ways to reduce poverty and that each society must decide which ones it wants to pursue. Where public goods and private skills are reasonably well-developed, the priorities for aid will be more specific, focused on building up particular export sectors or institutions (like financial systems), or environmentally-friendly production processes, or areas of social policy that have been neglected in the dash for growth.

External help is especially important during periods of rapid change, when constraints close in and progressive decisions are endangered. These are the moments when room to manoeuvre is most important, but most difficult to preserve without additional support. They might be critical points in the transition from war to peace, or from dictatorship to democracy, when extra help can make a difference to the quality of political participation. US support helped to stave off repression by the South Korean government against the mass demonstrations of 1987, and bolstered Taiwan's determination to hold its first free elections in 1990.[6] Ten billion dollars loaned to Russia by the IMF prior to elections in mid-1996 certainly helped President Boris Yeltsin's cause, though similar support four years earlier might have strengthened the hand of moderate reformers even more.[7] More broadly, outside help can soften the costs of integration into world markets (like sectoral unemployment and rising inequality between workers with different levels of skills), and smooth out the other structural changes which characterise unbalanced growth in its early phases.[8] In a sense, structural adjustment was easy; the next 25 years of deeper reform will be much more difficult, as countries struggle to diversify their exports and move away from primary commodities.

This is even more important where gradual change will hurt less and be more sustainable politically. Policies that upset elites (like land reform), or lose elected governments votes (like macro-economic austerity) can be strengthened using outside support to compensate the losers at the right time.[9] Extra aid to Egypt in the form of a social safety net, early retirement packages and share ownership schemes has helped to spread the benefits of privatisation over the last seven years and maintain public support.[10] In 1997, President Mugabe proposed that Britain should cover the £150 million cost of compensating white farmers in Zimbabwe so that their land could be redistributed to smallholders. This was rejected by the UK government on the grounds that land allocations were unlikely to be either

fair or efficient, but the principle involved is important.[11] The economist Paul Streeten[12] advocates *'radical adjustment loans'* in situations
where giving into populist demands might increase macro-economic
problems but resisting them would erode political support for continued reform – a classic case of building room to manoeuvre. At the
grassroots level the same principle applies: the Oslo Action Plan on
Child Labour signed in 1997 recommends temporary support to the
families of working children to replace the income lost when they
attend school.[13] These are all ways of providing more breathing space
at critical times so that local groups have more opportunity to pursue
difficult decisions while retaining responsibility for the consequences.
However, they require international help to be highly strategic, with
resources made available quickly and without lots of strings attached.

Foreign aid is best used in a supporting role to a broader, and
more coherent, framework of international co-operation. That means
excluding anything that is unhelpful to poor countries (like aid that is
tied to commercial contracts in the North), and linking policies on
aid to policies on debt reduction, trade and diplomacy.[14]
Unsustainable levels of debt are an albatross around anyone's neck,
and it is difficult to think of anything that could compete with debt
relief in enhancing room to manoeuvre in the poorest countries. There
are always 'moral hazards' in debt forgiveness when no one is sure
how resources will be used, but they can be managed by negotiating
achievement targets between debtors and creditors, and investing the
proceeds in things (like credit for small borrowers) that do not incur
more debts for the future.[15] With countries like Uganda spending 35
times as much on debt repayments as on education, the arguments
for withholding relief are hardly convincing.[16] There are plenty of
precedents, like Germany in 1953, Indonesia in 1969, and countries
in the Eastern Bloc (like Poland) more recently.[17] Unfortunately the
sceptics have yet to be convinced. The agreements reached between
the IMF, the World Bank and the major creditor nations over the last
three years revolve around the sale of gold reserves to finance soft
loans to 'highly-indebted poor countries', on condition that they
undergo a further six years of rigorous adjustment *before they might
qualify* for debt relief, up to a maximum of 80 per cent of what they
owe. How generous! At the last count only seven of the world's 41
poorest countries have been approved for this scheme, starting with
Uganda and Bolivia in 1998. While the rich world poured billions of
dollars into East Asia's financial crisis, the same countries – led by
Germany, Italy and Japan – squabbled over a mere US$350 million to
write off Mozambique's massive debts.[18]

Even in the most optimistic of scenarios, debt forgiveness would only reduce Africa's current external resource gap by about 25 per cent – improved terms of trade and more inward investment are much more important.[19] So if we are concerned about room to manoeuvre, that is where more international action should be directed, for example in abolishing the trade tariffs that remain in the industrialised world (like the CAP), and facilitating access to private capital in the high-risk or low-return markets that characterise the poorest countries. That can be done by using the financial reserves and high credit rating of international institutions to provide guarantees to private investors, subsidising the infrastructure that makes a country more attractive to foreign capital, and enhancing local capacities to absorb, manage and regulate capital inflows without crushing incentives. Reducing private risks raises questions about the distribution of public benefits in the longer term, but these measures can be combined with commitments from investors on social and environmental criteria to ensure that foreign companies behave responsibly.

Just as influential would be easier access to powerful trading blocs like NAFTA and the EU, and security alliances such as NATO. Extending membership of these bodies might be much more important to development and security than any increase in foreign aid, and is often what countries actually want from the West instead of continued handouts. Promoting coherence between aid and other forms of help requires donors to develop a unified strategy for all development-related decision-making in place of the ad hoc arrangements of the present. This will take the heat off recipients who currently face a plethora of competing, conflicting and partial interventions, allowing them to concentrate on what they should be doing in the first place, long-term planning and management. Recent attempts in the UK to break down departmental barriers in government and construct a single response to social exclusion provide an interesting model here – pointing the way for an 'international co-operation unit' under the cabinet rather than (or in addition to) a Ministry of International Development constantly at loggerheads with the Treasury, the Foreign Office, and the Department of Trade and Industry.

CAPACITIES FOR CHANGE

Making the most of room to manoeuvre requires strong institutions that foster the economic flexibility, social solidarity, and strong polities development demands. Institutional creativity underpins the notion of a win-win future in which new possibilities appear over every horizon. Mention 'institutional development' to aid agencies, however, and before long there will be hundreds of uncoordinated projects, missions and consultants, all claiming to build the capacity of one thing or another, like the seven separate projects currently 'strengthening' the Ministry of Finance in Malawi.[20] Too much outside assistance treats institutions as instruments to deliver predefined objectives instead of agents of decision-making in their own right. Institutional development needs long time-scales, great flexibility and high levels of co-ordination among those who want to help. All aid resources should be integrated into local planning and budgeting procedures so that governments can bring public expenditure into a coherent framework, not a patchwork quilt of projects financed by different donors. Aid agencies need to agree among themselves on what they mean by institutional development and ensure consistency in doing it; in a single district of Uganda (Rakai) there are currently four conflicting approaches to 'building the capacity' of the same departments of local government.[21] Trust and continuity are more likely to motivate strong institutions than micro-management or searching for scapegoats to blame. In Rakai, local government accountability, financial discipline and tax collection all improved when donors learned to confront failure with encouragement rather than short-term sanctions and penalties.[22]

Foreign aid can be useful here, but it must cover all the factors that promote strong institutions, not just salaries or the technical skills required to implement aid-funded projects. Internally there has to be a culture of performance – and concrete incentives – to encourage results; accountability and responsiveness to citizens, members or users; and the ability to learn and form partnerships with others.[23] Externally there has to be a strong constituency to monitor performance and take an active role in governance. Without strong local demand no institution will survive. It's no good increasing the capacity of the Treasury to manage the national debt if the value of fiscal responsibility is not accepted by government as a whole. Brazilian cities like Curitiba and Porto Alegre are often cited to show how public administration can be made to work efficiently at relatively low levels of resources, *if* the necessary political leadership, public support, and channels for dialogue are present. In Curitiba rigorous performance standards are enforced for all public functions and every planning application has to be dealt with within two weeks of submission.[24] Likewise, it is vital to root all NGOs in their own society so that they can develop a constituency to finance their work and generate popular legitimacy.[25] The record of donors in this respect is appalling, with little support to promote sustainability (through local fund-raising, corporate links or endowments); strengthen internal accountability, learning and research; or deal more effectively with the external environment – all the things that are crucial to long-term success.[26]

There are no universal truths about how big states should be or what civil societies should look like, but all societies need strong public, private and social institutions working together for long-term goals. Only governments can guarantee the legal and regulatory framework other institutions need to flourish, the infrastructure and macro-economic stability growth requires, and the fundamental rights of citizens.[27] Decentralisation and partnerships between public and private sectors usually pay dividends, but states must retain the authority to maintain standards.[28] The structural adjustment programmes analysed in Chapter 6 backfired by imposing public-sector cuts at a time when civil servants were paid at a fraction of the private-sector rate.[29] This eroded the very capacity that was required to manage the intended changes – a neat if disturbing illustration of the stupidity of an approach which allows itself to be driven by standard prescriptions. Too many capacity-building efforts in the public sector have suffered from these internal contradictions, pre-packaged to fit Western models and focused too narrowly on pay and conditions in selected government ministries.[30]

Civil societies play a key role in keeping states accountable and effective, cultivating social energy, and mobilising citizens, but they work differently in different places.[31] Civil society is an arena, not a thing, so it is vital that those who wish to encourage civic institutions are specific and strategic about who they want to help and why. Support to organisations that represent poor people helps to secure outcomes that are favourable to their interests, but building the capacity of fundamentalist organisations would be a strange thing to do even if they do form part of civil society in some countries.[32] To judge by the amount of money going into health, education and micro-credit NGOs, it seems that donor agencies are interested in civic groups primarily as service-providers, but other roles such as protecting human rights, defending the independent voice of lobby groups, supporting a dynamic media, promoting citizen education, organising workers, and nurturing a culture of dialogue and peace are just as important. Foreign aid can support these roles, but must be careful not to distort the authenticity of pluralism by favouring one group over another with large financial and technical inputs. By and large, successful civil societies take care of their own strengthening over hundreds of years, as political scientist Robert Putnam has argued for Italy.[33] It is better to support a range of groups working synergistically to defend and advance their visions of civic life, providing extra resources and opportunities for them to find their own ways of marrying flexible, humane service with independent critique. This is what the most sensitive of donor agencies are already doing. In Bangladesh, for example, the Asia Foundation is supporting both service-providing NGOs and rights-based activists to work together in networks and alliances. One of these, the Environmental Lawyers Association, won a landmark decision from the Supreme Court in 1996 to enable it to bring public cases on behalf of aggrieved citizens.[34]

If it is difficult to strengthen civil society responsibly, it is even more so in the private sector, yet nurturing the capacity of market institutions like entrepreneurs, banks and insurance systems is obviously vital – the recent financial crisis in East Asia shows how important these institutions are to sustained growth.[35] Some critics of foreign aid (like Sir William Ryrie, ex-head of the International Finance Corporation) believe that private-sector capacity building is the most important task of all, given the dangers of promoting unsustainable social and political change on the back of outside resources and ideas.[36] If people have jobs and incomes of their own, the argument goes, they can use the resources prosperity gives them to invest in their own solutions in the non-economic arena. There is merit in this argument, especially the recognition that someone, somewhere, has to pay for institutions and the services they provide. As many township councils in South Africa have discovered to their cost, creating more accountable political structures is no guarantee that urban basic needs will be satisfied when the local economy is weak.[37] But Ryrie's approach has obvious defects: the choices that come with market-led growth are unequally distributed, so the political decisions that result will be skewed in favour of the better off; and growth produces social and environmental problems that require intervention by strong non-market institutions that often don't exist. To participate effectively in a global economy, poor countries need a much stronger legal, regulatory and policy-research capacity. US trade negotiator Charlene Barshefsky takes an army of experts with her to the World Trade Organisation (WTO) but Bangladesh can afford only one. Many donor agencies assume that the capacity required to oversee the market is already present in low-income countries, or can be developed quickly as whole swathes of industry and services are privatised. This is never true, and the result is always second best: monopoly rather than competition, more corruption not less, dividends skewed to foreign shareholders, and exclusion by income in place of access by right.[38] In Pakistan, aid-funded subsidies to private investment in the energy sector have been taken up entirely by foreign corporations.[39] Using foreign aid to develop these capacities is a risky business, but it can be an exceptionally useful form of support because of the multiplier effect improved regulation has across a whole range of institutions.

COALITIONS FOR DEVELOPMENT

It is one thing to foster creative institutions, and another to persuade them to work together for the common good. Even if you do have more 'room', how do you ensure it is 'manoeuvred' toward development goals instead of the agendas of elites? Development requires a coalition of institutional interests that will fight for poverty reduction, peace and human rights, like the alliances we looked at in Part I between state government and trade unions in Kerala; tribal federations, banks and politicians in Orissa; and the cross-society coalitions that lay at the heart of East Asian success. Remember – 'it's the polity, stupid'. Poor people need to be actively involved in these coalitions if their concerns are to be advanced. This doesn't necessarily mean representative democracy at every stage of economic transition, but it does mean that grassroots interests have to percolate upwards through the machinery of decision making. Not surprisingly, it is usually those who are themselves exploited, excluded and discriminated against that are most committed to doing something to reverse their condition, but they cannot do this on their own. Historically, rich people and states have only prioritised meaningful action on poverty when their interests have been directly threatened, as for example by popular protests on their doorstep, rising crime and epidemics of infectious disease.[40] In more recent times the threats have become less direct but the basic principle applies: development needs a political constituency that cuts across different sections of society, and that can only come from coalitions which perceive a common interest in attacking the threats posed by poverty and exclusion. Thus far, foreign aid has done little to foster these coalitions and much to destroy them.

As we saw in Part I, institutional linkages advance development by bridging the divide between public, private and social action. Outside help can be important here, at least in subsidising the extra costs of meeting and working together for a while. Support to networks of institutions can help to avoid the potentially destabilising effect of strengthening single-issue groups or special interests.[41] At the local level it is increasingly common for civic groups, governments, businesses and donor agencies to come together and develop action plans for economic development and natural resource management, but sooner or later these partnerships must develop or link into a national coalition to push change through. The importance of these coalitions to economic and political reform has been intensively studied by scholars.[42] They have found that successful reformers diffuse the costs of change and spread the benefits, adopting a pragmatic approach to policy, avoiding sudden and significant damage (like the removal of subsidies overnight), and building legitimacy by honouring the tacit social compromises that develop among governments, businesses and different groups in civil society – *'you scratch my back'* by supporting change, *'I'll scratch yours'* by delivering results.[43] Someone always loses out in this process, but as long as no one loses so much that the reforms are overturned then the coalition can hold. Democracy may make reform more difficult in the short term, but it is better at securing the compromises that long-term success demands, by persuading the middle classes to finance the expansion of social services through progressive taxation, for example, or encouraging employers and workers to adopt voluntary restraints on wages and other costs.[44]

Building a consensus on these issues is difficult in any society, particularly in those with entrenched interests and fractured institutions, but the initiative for coalition building must come from within:

> *'if democracy flourishes in Africa it will not be because outsiders would like to see Africa become democratic, but because Africans themselves wish to tread that path, and because civil society is willing to struggle for it, accepting the inevitable sacrifices along the way.'*[45]

Nevertheless, outside help is not irrelevant. At the very least it can 'do no harm', as the Hippocratic Oath puts it, taking care not to expose reform-minded leaders to the political instability that enforced austerity measures can breed, making sure that foreign aid does not dilute the relationship between states and citizens by substituting for domestic taxation, and avoiding the imposition of sanctions which distract attention from the need for domestic reforms by providing a common external enemy to fight.[46] Political scientist Janine Wedel has shown how Western support allowed the St Petersburg Group headed by

Anatoly Chubais to circumvent parliamentary processes in Russia.[47] This made economic liberalisation easier, but in the longer term it may erode the domestic constituency for lasting change by identifying reform with foreign interests. The key is to strengthen the process of coalition building across society, not just the favoured candidates of outsiders. In that way, foreign aid can support a platform on which new coalitions can be built, especially by opening aid negotiations to broader participation. Unfortunately this rarely happens, because such negotiations are confidential to foreign agencies. Even southern governments are excluded from most debt negotiations, consultative groups, donor round-tables and the like.[48] Civil society representation is almost non-existent, unless you are prepared to abseil down from the rooftops, as environmental NGOs did at the annual meetings of the World Bank and IMF in the mid-1990s. Since large sections of society are excluded, why should they buy into the proposals that result? Bad politics leads to unsustainable economics. The World Bank's 'Country Assistance Strategy', the key document in designing overall lending policy for each recipient, isn't even publicly available, apart from a few that have been approved for release by governments. It is remarkable how closed these things are despite the acknowledged importance of coalition-building to success.[49] All negotiations should be open and transparent, with extra support provided to groups whose voices might otherwise be excluded. Where it is really necessary, confidentiality can be preserved (for example, in protecting market-sensitive information), but this should be the exception, not the rule.

A COMPACT FOR THE FUTURE

As we have seen, there is much that can be done to make foreign aid a more useful resource for development, but all of it requires a different system for aid giving that trusts in people's ability to find their own solutions – a system based on demand, not supply, in which aid is valued as an investment for all our futures, not a gift from the rich man's table. Is this possible? There are plenty of ideas already under discussion, built around a single, negotiated development framework for each country, consolidated funding (all assistance in one pot), and a long-term 'compact' to integrate domestic and international action on all the things that influence success, from debt relief, through graduated trade protection, to co-ordinated programming in the field. Every participant would be required to sign the compact in order to play a role in global decision making and receive an 'investment entitlement' from an international development fund, channelled through independent local foundations with cross-society representation. The wording here is important – investment, not aid; compacts, not conditionalities. This may sound far-fetched – about as distant from current realities as one could get – but in different disguises it has already been suggested by a wide spectrum of thinkers and activists in both North and South.[50] A combination of consolidated funding (to promote continuity), mutually-binding international agreements (to strengthen coherence), and cross-society decision making (to maintain consistency with realities on the ground) could build the local ownership development demands without sacrificing the accountability donors require to keep the aid funds flowing.

If this system is to work, the first requirement is a more reliable way of raising money so that a basic minimum can be guaranteed to every participant for a period of about 25 years, independent of the fashions and fluctuations that characterise the world of foreign aid. The obvious candidate is global taxation, an idea that stretches back over 100 years and a favourite topic of discussion at the end of World War II, when it was seen as a prerequisite for the new United Nations.[51] The basis of the system could be a mandatory income tax (or tax credits on contributions to an international development fund), the so-called 'Tobin Tax' on all foreign exchange transactions, or taxes levied on polluters (especially for car use) and the use of the 'global commons' (like a levy on air travel).[52] Alternatively, money could be raised from 'development bonds' issued to governments or private investors by an international agency; debt conversions; payments for services rendered by one country to another (like preservation of the biosphere or control of the drug trade); and compensation for 'economic injury' (like the 'brain drain' from Africa and South Asia, or the use of local genetic material by corporations).[53] Since contributions would come from a wider range of countries than the current OECD membership, this would help to erode the pernicious inequality between donors and recipients that corrupts the current system. Whatever the mechanisms used, the funds should sustain themselves over a targeted period of time by recycling repayments on favourable terms.[54] Since there would be massive savings on transactions costs (only one delivery mechanism instead of hundreds), they could also be ploughed back into the fund. UNDP has recently proposed consolidating all development finance under two headings: one for resources designated for the national development programme of each country, and the other as a central fund for 'global housekeeping' to finance the costs of common problems like environmental protection or bailing out bankrupt countries.[55] The World Bank has made a similar proposal to divide resources between balance-of-payments support, debt relief and specific development priorities, country by country. That would fit nicely into the model proposed here, so long as significant funds were held in reserve at both national and global levels to deal with unforeseen emergencies and other periods of exceptional stress, without the strings attached to current World Bank standby loans and the IMF's various 'structural adjustment facilities'.

Each country's initial investment entitlement would be based on their per capita income, human development index and attractiveness to private capital (with more refined calculations where there are large geographical inequalities within countries). At the country level, each development fund would be governed by a board of directors appointed from government, business and civil society, and decentralised to districts or municipalities where participation would be more meaningful. National indicative funding frameworks with lower-level decision-making but strong accountability mechanisms already work well in many areas of administration, being small enough to build local ownership but large enough to blow the whistle if necessary.[56] Cross-society representation is especially important where formal democracy is weak. International agencies could be represented too, but without majority voting rights, since the whole point is to encourage countries to produce and defend their own development strategies in public, as they did in the days of the Marshall Plan.[57] Each fund would be open to applications across the board to make sure that priorities responded to genuine demand. There would be no guarantee that resources would be used for the priorities described in this and other chapters, but neither (in contrast to the current system) would there be prior restrictions, it being better to let people make their own decisions since this is a capacity and coalition-building process in itself. Applicants (whether government departments, NGOs or others) could also use the fund to purchase technical assistance from Oxfam, UNDP or a local consultancy company. One cannot approve of market economics and allow suppliers to determine the allocation of resources.[58] In emergencies (or cases where basic agreements were violated) there might be a phase when the normal procedures of the fund would have to be suspended, but generally a system like this would provide a much better framework to encourage long-term investments and the peace and stability they help to create.

What about accountability? The most important task is to find a better balance between pressure for short-term results, and the long-term learning, flexibility and innovation required to support risky and difficult work like institutional development. That can be done by using iterative planning procedures where objectives evolve over time and resources can be switched from one heading to another on the basis of what works best.[59] Since funding is likely to involve the use of contracts, there will inevitably be conditions to be fulfilled, but they and all other performance targets must be negotiated, not imposed.[60] If there is disagreement about targets and results (as there nearly always is), don't hide it under a false consensus. Face up to it with honesty, argue it through, and if necessary refer the matter to an independent arbitration or mediation mechanism embedded in a reconstituted global authority, like a network of 'development ombudsmen' or an improved version of the World Bank's inspection panel.[61] Funding decisions cannot be based solely on results achieved, since the horizon of future possibilities is never fixed: we don't know whether what will be needed in ten years' time is the same as what seemed to work in the past. Targets that reflect long-term outcomes are more important than short-term outputs, but clearly the latter have to be included to preserve prudence and transparency. No one objects to financial accountability in principle, only when in practice it begins to drive programme decisions. That is accountancy, not accountability.[62] Progress should be monitored using 'social auditing' techniques or other ways of involving all stakeholders in making reasoned judgements about achievements.[63] Factors beyond the control of the implementing organisations can be controlled for using statistical techniques, by averaging performance across groups of similar countries, and by gathering and systematically comparing a wider range of opinions about what has happened, and why.[64] Major retrospective evaluations could be carried out every ten years prior to replenishment of the fund, shadowed by independent studies to provide a 'reality check' from outside the system.

Clearly, a network of national development funds like this implies a high degree of trust in people's ability to find their own ways forward despite the mistakes they will make, and there are some circumstances where the risks involved might be too high to proceed. They involve countries (like Afghanistan or Burma) where domestic realities block the minimum level of participation and accountability required to make the system work. A higher authority would be required to arbitrate in such cases, but trust works both ways, and to preserve the legitimacy of the system the same authority would have to arbitrate in cases where contributing countries fall short. At the global level, all participants would, therefore, be accountable for meeting the goals of the compact, so there must be negotiated targets for both net contributors and net consumers. Progress on poverty reduction and access to health and education would be obvious candidates for the latter; trade liberalisation, resource flows and debt forgiveness for the former. To be meaningful, the compact must be comprehensive, so all international institutions would have to sign up, including regional mechanisms like the European Development Fund, and others like the IMF and the WTO which currently consider themselves above democratic jurisdiction through the UN. To reduce accusations of partiality, representatives from different countries could be selected at random to monitor progress in implementing the compacts. A failure to achieve targets (where failure could reasonably have been avoided) would result in penalties for whichever of the parties were responsible – reduced contributions to the fund, for example, if local interests had blocked their own poverty-reduction initiatives consistently; temporary suspension from international agreements, or tougher targets for the next round of globally-agreed pollution controls, if contributing countries had reneged on their commitments; and a mixture if (as is likely) both were implicated. That would generate a new set of incentives and alter the dynamics of political debate about international co-operation in the industrialised world.

Wouldn't exceptions need to be made in this system for NGOs and other special cases, where there is an 'added value' through direct people-to-people links and a plurality of funding sources? Much of this added value is assumed rather than demonstrated, but even so there would be no reason to prevent local organisations from using the channels they prefer, so long as this did not degenerate into the duplication and ineffectiveness of current practice. Separate funding could be preserved for non tax-derived funds and areas of work (like advocacy) which are particularly sensitive politically, and would be better funded independently. In a demand-based system unwanted providers will go to the wall, NGOs or not. Plurality would not be endangered, but quite the reverse, because people would be able to buy what they wanted from a wider range of suppliers. Even so, these proposals are more radical than any that have been proposed before. Judging by the howls of protest from UNICEF and others that greeted Secretary-General Kofi Annan's attempts to merge the specialised agencies of the UN into a single economic and social organisation in 1997, few institutions are ready to pool their resources, let alone take part in a global compact for development.[65] The arguments made at the time, that separate agencies are needed to protect special interests, are spurious, since these can be defended as effectively in a unitary or matrix structure, but institutional inertia backed by powerful political contacts will always stifle reform.

Dig a little deeper into current experience, however, and one finds more encouragement for the future. There is already a gradual move to harmonise the procedures of different donors by enforcing codes of conduct, common implementation arrangements and co-ordinated strategies for aid to different parts of the world.[66] A landmark paper presented to the World Bank's board of directors in 1998 argued strongly in favour of 'partnerships for development' in which all foreign donors would co-ordinate their activities in a framework directed by recipient governments, and rooted in a dialogue with business and civil society.[67] This radical move – what World Bank President James Wolfensohn calls a 'comprehensive development framework' – is already being implemented in Bolivia, so the mood is clearly changing. Almost any improvement is worthwhile given the low point from which we are starting, and incremental change will avoid the danger of creating something which turns out to be just as bureaucratic as the systems we have already. Go slowly, experiment and learn, find out what works best, and build on it. Is this really too much to ask for? What is stopping us from being more imaginative – those unwelcome friends we encountered in Chapter 2? After all, these reforms only take us back to the spirit of the Marshall Plan, but this time applied to everyone, not just our close friends in the West. And perhaps that, at root, is the real issue at stake. A world development fund and a global compact are closer than we think, if we have the desire to make them work.

CONCLUSION

Whether we end up with a system like this or a different set of solutions matters less than finding something that works better than what we have. It is time we stopped focusing so much on the quantity of foreign aid flowing through the existing system. The target of 0.7 per cent of GNP set for industrialised countries by the UN was only a back-of-the-envelope calculation when it was first mooted in the 1940s,[68] and the argument that a 'critical mass' of aid is crucial to its effectiveness becomes less convincing as aid declines even as a proportion of financial flows. It's the quality of aid and its place in a more effective system of international co-operation that are important. Since money is the only thing that makes donor agencies sit up and take notice, tying agreements on their resources to demonstrated improvements in the way they work together is a good way of motivating change – let them sample some conditionality for a change! No international institution or government aid ministry should have their funds increased without demonstrating what they have done to resolve the inadequacies of the foreign aid machine.

Suitably reformed, there is no shortage of ways we can use outside resources without incurring the problems of the past; nor are there any unanswerable questions about the concrete changes required. The concept of room to manoeuvre provides a useful framework for thinking about these issues, uniting lots of disparate threads around a bottom line that is meaningful across different contexts. Would a new framework for foreign aid be enough to attack deep-rooted problems of global poverty and injustice? It would certainly bring local needs and outside help into closer alignment, and in that sense it gets us to the starting line in the race for improvements. But it is clearly insufficient to win any of the major prizes, like managing the costs and benefits of globalising capitalism or responding more effectively to humanitarian emergencies. Those challenges require deeper and broader action, so let's move on to deal with them.

Chapter 8

Humanising Capitalism:
Which Way Forward?

'Take the long view, and fight like crazy'

Inner City Foundation[1]

'The test of any economic system must be the type of individual it tends to reproduce'

J R Bellerby[2]

People everywhere dream of better days to come, when poverty is no more, discrimination and violence have been banished for good, the air is clean and all are free to enjoy life to the full. Of course, we all wake up to a very different reality, but that has never stopped us from trying to change it for the better. Utopians apart, we know that we can never have a perfect world, but why can't we find a better balance between economic growth, political freedom, social cohesion and the preservation of what we care for in ourselves and the world around us? In theory this is an easy question to answer, but in practice we have not been able to demonstrate a viable non-capitalist route to sustained economic growth. There is nothing in history to suggest that capitalism is anything but disruptive, dirty and unequal, however many material and technological advances it brings. Yet the alternatives we have tried have turned out even worse (like centrally-planned economies), and the others we still talk about (like co-operative self-reliance) lack a constituency to put them into practice. So we are left with the task of humanising capitalism, that is, preserving the dynamism of markets, trade and entrepreneurial energy while finding better ways to distribute the surplus they create and reshape the processes that produce it.

Economic growth is not sufficient for development, but development needs growth, growth needs markets, and markets always impose costs and inequalities. Does that mean, however, that basketball player Michael Jordan has to earn 31,000 times more for advertising Nike sports shoes than the workers who produce them, despite the fact that should the wages be doubled the cost of production would still fall below US$1 a pair?[3] – or that all the hydroelectricity in Laos has to be produced from large dams and exported to Thailand instead of from a range of large and small ones that do less damage to the environment and bring more benefits to local industry?[4] Of course not! There is plenty of room to manoeuvre in the market economy, and if in exploring it we find more radical alternatives that people will vote for, so much the better. Inequalities result from political decisions about the distribution of gains from economic activity. What is allocated to private consumption, public spending, and social responsibilities is never fixed, and it is democracy's job – not the role of markets – to determine our collective goals and common interests.[5] The journalist Matthew Parris once observed that *'our morality does not mesh with our economic system, but because we need both they cohabit in an awkward marriage based on silence'*.[6] Why settle for silence when an active conversation could make the marriage happier and more fulfilling?

There are three reasons why international co-operation is central to a 'conversation' of this kind. The first is that integrated markets dictate a co-ordinated response to social and environmental questions. Few governments will impose eco-taxation or insist on improved labour standards unless other countries agree to do the same. Second, there is no consensus on how to humanise capitalism, now that the traditional ways of doing so through trade unions, welfare states, a large public sector with extensive market regulation, and expanding, progressive taxation have been eroded.[7] The measures recommended to replace these things, like better education and training or partnerships between the public and private sectors, seem inadequate when set against the inequality-producing power of real markets and the systematic discrimination that is built into current economic models on grounds of gender and age, especially in the global context.[8] There is unlikely to be any universal answer to these questions across so many different national contexts, but we can support each other to find some answers by fostering the creativity and opportunity described in Chapter 7. Third, it is hard to have a dialogue when you are starving, and difficult to innovate without a basic level of security, voice and equality of rights. The preconditions for successful 'conversation' have not yet been established in most poor countries. Humanising capitalism is not just a matter of market reform; it means tackling the interlocking structures of social, economic and political power that exclude particular groups of people. As security and voice increase, the possibility of meaningful dialogue grows, and with it the likelihood that people will find solutions that distribute the costs and benefits of change more equally across society. In such a situation, 'short cuts to progress' may still be possible.

'Empowering the poor' is well-worn territory in development debates. As the first of the quotations at the head of this chapter puts it, *'take the long view, and fight like crazy'* to improve the situation of those who are excluded from services, jobs and political influence. However, any serious attempt to humanise capitalism depends on changing the ways people use the power they gain, not just for themselves, but also in the service of the common good. As J R Bellerby[9] put it long ago in his book on the *'Contributive Society'*, it is not just a case of regulating systems of power, but transforming them to reproduce a different set of power relations and a new kind of individual: competitive where that makes sense but co-operative where it does not, protective of the environment, committed to an equal sharing of paid and household work, and willing to defend the rights of strangers as fiercely as their own. And that is a much deeper challenge, especially in societies which have yet to reach a minimum level of economic security.

THE IMPORTANCE OF REDISTRIBUTION

As we saw in Chapter 3, countries that reduce poverty and inequality while maintaining a high economic growth rate and a reasonable level of peace and social cohesion always make redistribution a priority – by spreading the ownership of assets and opportunities widely through the population. This is especially important in the high-risk economies that are emerging under globalisation, since individuals who do not possess an increasing portfolio of marketable skills will be excluded from higher-wage jobs and the rewards that go with them. The minimum required to make the market economy more inclusive is to guarantee equal access to the opportunities it provides, and that cannot be done where the majority of the population lack the basic wherewithal to participate. Third World countries (especially the agrarian economies of Africa and South Asia) are still characterised by extreme inequalities in the distribution of land, work and other assets, and these inequalities reinforce other forms of oppression based around gender and ethnicity.[10] Without land reform and more equal access to other productive assets there is no possibility of eradicating absolute poverty, broadening the base of market-led growth, or promoting sustainable resource management, since ownership is a precondition for conservation. High levels of inequality make intergroup conflict inevitable and deny people the basic security they need to participate in governance and civic life, so redistribution is much more than an economic measure.

Just under one billion absolutely poor people live in the rural areas of the developing world, and poverty of assets is the prime reason for their condition. Landlessness is actually increasing in countries like Bangladesh, up from 35 per cent of rural households in 1960 to 45 per cent 25 years later, and is especially acute among women.[11] '*We want land, all the rest is humbug*' was one woman's response to Indian researcher Bina Agarwal,[12] though she might have added the other things that allow farmers to make more productive use of this most precious of assets, like irrigation, electricity, and credit.[13] In countries that have a large labour surplus, land reform is insufficient; they need activities that expand productivity and the demand for labour simultaneously.[14] Although 'green revolution' techniques can do this, they are often outperformed by low-input farming practices which have the added benefit of conserving soil, water and forests.[15] In cities, access to jobs is the most important requirement, along with a secure claim on property, such as titles registered in a woman's name, not just her husband's.[16]

Equally important are less tangible assets that enable people to bargain, negotiate, and advance their interests. In Arabic, poverty has two meanings: the first is destitution, and the second, literally translated, means 'piercing a camel's nose with a metal ring tied to a rope in order to suppress it'.[17] Collective action is vital in attacking exclusion, since '*power and privilege do not willingly submit to popular control or market discipline*'.[18] If poor people's voices are excluded from decision making, their interests will be ignored. That is why community organisations and other civic groups are so important. Trade unions are currently out of favour with aid agencies, but they were vital to success in Kerala and East Asia. The Landless Movement in Brazil and the Union of Rubber Tappers led by the murdered activist Chico Mendes achieved huge gains for their members, and there is no reason why unions cannot reinvent themselves to suit a changing world, perhaps as members of wider civil-society alliances which mediate between business and workers.[19] Underlying the ability to organise in any group are the most basic assets of all, such as self-belief, human ingenuity, and independence of thought. *'If people feel good about themselves they can start to create change'* and participate in the fundamental task of defining alternatives – perhaps the *'supreme instrument of power'* as some have called it.[20] Building these less tangible possessions is vital because inequalities based on gender or race can withstand the effects of education, training and even the redistribution of material assets like land and jobs.[21]

At the national level, governments need to prioritise agrarian reform, public intervention to guarantee basic food security and employment on public works, and investment in essential services like health care, education and agricultural extension.[22] These are tried and tested strategies, but they are difficult to sustain in weak economies without international support, and that implies redistribution at the global level through foreign aid. A full-scale attack on inequality is a necessary condition for poverty eradication, but it is far from sufficient. Rising economic participation stimulates competitive behaviour as well as co-operation; increased political participation brings more disagreement as well as consensus; and empowerment strategies may reinforce anti-developmental notions of power over others if they neglect the need for inner transformation. The fact that poor people share in decision making does not mean that the outcome will always be better, even for them. As a representative of the Native American community in the USA once joked, *'what we want is the same right as everyone else to screw things up'*.[23] In the same way women *'will be as difficult and diverse and as daft as men, in power or out of it'*.[24] We cannot assume that more participation will generate the best results, since people's access to information may be imperfect and the views of one group might have to be overridden in favour of others, as for example when natural resources of value to the broader common interest must be given up by those who own the land on which they sit. As a right, participation is incontestable; as a practice, it is essential in generating more sustainable solutions; but as an alternative paradigm it is unconvincing.

TRANSFORMING SYSTEMS OF POWER

If redistribution is not a sufficient condition for humanising capitalism, how do we make material advancement the handmaiden of much broader social, environmental and personal goals? The answer lies through measures that increase security while encouraging people to surrender at least some of their ambitions to the concerns of others, whether they be present or future generations.[25] Many commentators have observed that co-operation declines as people grow in wealth and status. This produces a *'culture of contentment'* as J K Galbraith describes it, and the ebbing away of the *'habits of the heart'*.[26] In these circumstances, rising incomes do not lead to sustainable development; they reinforce competition, exclusion and pollution instead. Addressing this problem requires all systems of power to be regulated and reconstructed in ways which encourage three things: a better distribution of what they deliver, less costly ways of producing it, and more co-operative attitudes which encourage people to set some limits to their self-interest.

Put like this it sounds an impossible task, but lots of experiments are already underway: new forms of business which compete effectively but distribute work and profits more equally; social policies that provide what children need but place less of a burden on women; and formulae for decision making that achieve a less damaging set of trade-offs between growth and the environment. In an era of integrated markets and increasing cross-border influences, mainstreaming these experiments implies co-ordinated action from the local to the global level, but it is the grassroots that provides the foundation for sustainable change. It is here that we can see the impact of decisions in our own lives, and that acts as a powerful incentive to personal responsibility. The UN cannot prevent global warming unless people judge that their own environment has to be protected from their own actions.[27] So the transformations we are searching for should be easier to find in neighbourhoods, local authorities and firms.[28] Humanising capitalism is partly a matter of localising more activity so that we enjoy a new level of intimacy in our jobs, decision making and relations with each other: a connectedness that shows us the destructive consequences of our uncooperative actions. There can be no escape into blaming anonymous corporations or governments if firms, schools and communities have the wherewithal to govern themselves.[29] That does not mean limiting our horizons to the local, which would be a recipe for stagnation, but self-reliance need not reject outside resources or contacts unless they actively erode autonomy and choice.[30] However, since these are threatened by unaccountable power in a globalising economy, grassroots action must be strongly connected to a supportive framework at the national and international levels if it is to thrive. What does this mean for the way we practice economics, politics, and social policy?

DO WE MEAN BUSINESS?

In economic terms, the most important structures of power are markets and firms, and if we are serious about humanising capitalism that is where we should begin. Complex societies are best governed by feedback from individuals to decision makers through prices – which means markets – and votes.[31] But prices must reflect social and environmental costs if the common interest is to be protected, and markets must be tied down to their signalling role and not extended into governance or social life.[32] At present, some resources (like air) are not priced at all, and others (like oil) are priced without regard to their scarcity, so markets will not necessarily correct destructive practices over time. Labour rights (like all human rights) are too important to be left to the price mechanism, especially when – as is universal – markets are permeated by power relations of various kinds.[33]

Fortunately, markets can be influenced to work in different ways. At one extreme that means attacking monopolies and oligopolies so that the price mechanism can operate more efficiently. At the other it means a completely different set of market principles, like Islamic economics in which interest is outlawed.[34] The most likely situation lies between these two extremes, when social and environmental goals are inserted into the mechanisms of the market as we know them. That can happen in a number of ways.

First, access to information among consumers and producers on how things are made and what they really cost can be increased – the foundation for ethical consumption, investment and trading. Good citizens do not switch off their citizenship when they go shopping or arrive at work, and few people are *'interested in wearing clothes made by exploited workers'* as the US Labour Committee put it in 1997.[35] Consumers cannot make these judgements unless they know how goods are produced, so that means more labelling systems like the 'Fairtrade mark' and footballs that are certified free of exploitative child labour. The information revolution makes fair trade much easier, since purchasers can deal direct with producers over the Internet. Artisans in Guatemala, for example, are already using it to get feedback from consumers in North America on their designs.[36]

This process raises much wider questions about business accountability, though criticisms of corporations are nothing new. As far back as 1909, reformers in the USA demanded that all firms be regulated toward 'constructive goals', with everyone affected by their operations having a say in company decisions (including consumers and employees).[37] Ninety years later this remains a challenge to a system of corporate governance dominated by shareholders, especially large institutions like investment funds which may care little for non-economic goals. An increasing number of businesses are recognising that they must establish decent working conditions for their employees, contribute to the life of the communities in which they operate, and hold themselves accountable on social and environmental criteria as well as profitability. In the USA the Social Accountability 8000 standard developed by the Council on Economic Priorities provides one way of doing this, though its compliance procedures are weaker than the independent verification measures that are being piloted in coffee production, clothing, footballs, and timber supplies.[38] Accountability implies specific commitments that few large companies are prepared to make. As pioneers like the Body Shop have discovered, this is risky because claims to fairness must be publicly tested, and that requires a degree of transparency that goes against the grain in competitive institutions that guard information jealously. The commercial benefit is that consumers will repay adherence to standards with their loyalty in the marketplace, but that requires a huge expansion of 'ethical demand'. In the meantime even small victories are valuable, like the gains made in Sri Lankan clothing factories under pressure from local NGOs: the reinstatement of a worker sacked for writing poems that lamented her life; increased compensation for another who put a needle through her eye; and the formation of a support group for a colleague raped on her way to work on Christmas Day.[39]

Second, markets can be made to work to the benefit of smaller consumers and producers by reducing the benefits that are siphoned off by intermediaries. In South India, over 90 per cent of crop storage capacity and 80 per cent of credit disbursements are controlled by the richest ten per cent of merchants – the *'masters of the country-side'* as economist Barbara Harriss-White calls them.[40] International NGOs have helped peasant foresters in Mexico to negotiate higher prices directly with the timber companies, just as rubber tappers in Brazil have been able to retain a higher proportion of the surplus they create by clubbing together to sell their produce at a main depot.[41] The Inter-American Foundation finances a joint marketing organisation for small producers in MERCOSUR which increases their bargaining power in negotiations over prices and conditions of sale.[42] Collective action like this stimulates both equity and efficiency, and builds a sense of solidarity among people who are sharing risks as well as benefits.[43] That reverses the normal position in markets whereby the rich protect themselves against exposure by purchasing insurance or taking expensive legal action, while the poor bear the costs of market failure.

Third, it is possible to change the structure of business so that goods and services are produced in ways which build co-operation, and profits are distributed with a social purpose. Community-based economic activities are nearly always excluded from national accounts, but according to futurist Hazel Henderson they already make up 25 per cent of global transactions.[44] Thousands of businesses in North America recovered from the great depression of the 1930s by issuing their own local currencies and tax-anticipation notes so they could retain more of the surplus they produced, just like the growing numbers of 'Local Exchange and Trading Schemes' that are springing up around the world today.[45] Mohammed Yunus, the founder of the Grameen Bank in Bangladesh, was once asked whether *'the capitalist system has to be the handmaiden of the rich'*.[46] His reply was 'no', so long as a 'social conscience' could be mainstreamed into banks and businesses – as his own organisation is trying to do by making loans affordable, adding in a fixed amount for health insurance and savings, and using credit groups as a vehicle for education and raising of awareness. John Bird, who founded the 'Big Issue' movement in the UK (a movement which supports homeless people to earn money through the sale of its magazines), has called for a huge expansion in 'ethical social businesses' which are *'capitalist in creating profits but socially-supportive in their distribution'*.[47] Some economists think that low-income countries can bypass the sweat-shop stage of production altogether by concentrating on micro-economic reforms that boost productivity and raise living standards, while adhering to Northern standards of social protection and environmental sensitivity.[48] However, many 'social enterprises' find that they must be less social and more commercial over time as markets become increasingly competitive, just as a highly-responsible company like Levi Strauss still has to close plants when cost pressures increase in the global marketplace.[49] Co-operative production requires an unusual set of circumstances to be successful in open markets, especially as the scale of the enterprise increases.[50] But it can work if it builds on pre-existing collective work arrangements that still meet market standards of cost and quality, like the firms in Papua New Guinea that work on both commercial and community tasks together,[51] or the Native American businesses in Canada which are owned collectively but work in partnership with large corporations who offer them access to global markets.[52]

Experiments like these need support from macro-economic policies that integrate social and environmental criteria into decisions over prices, interest rates, industrial policy and labour markets; rewarding behaviour that is beneficial, like labour-intensive production; and penalising what is undesirable, like pollution. In Latin American cities, infrastructure is now routinely provided through labour-intensive works co-managed by communities, NGOs and private companies, which makes design more relevant and keeps more of the economic surplus local.[53] Decision makers must assess the impact of fiscal measures on vulnerable people, protect public expenditure for the poor, stabilise the prices of key consumption goods, and integrate gender considerations into decision making so that the hidden costs of public-expenditure reform on women and children can be addressed.[54]

Since resources are obviously limited in low-income countries, most of these measures will need temporary support in the form of foreign aid, along with graduated agreements to level up working conditions and environmental standards around the world. This must be done carefully. For example, in Bangladesh an estimated 55,000 children lost their jobs in the garment industry as a result of a US trade boycott during 1996. None of the children went back to school, and at least half ended up in much lower-paid jobs or prostitution.[55] It is better to work with local producers on codes of conduct, and provide additional support for factory inspections and compensation if children lose their jobs.[56] Although it is multinational companies that are usually criticised for exploitation, conditions are often worse among small local firms. This poses problems for global regulation, but research in Asia shows that even small firms can improve their standards if they get enough support to improve production processes and submit themselves to local regulation more sensitive to the need for flexibility.[57] Encouraging corporations to adopt some minimum standards and enforce them along their supply chains is a sensible strategy so long as it is applied fairly, as sportswear giant Nike did when it severed ties with four Indonesian contractors in 1997 for gross abuses of labour rights.[58] Most governments already support the principle of core standards, though they argue about how big the core should be. An irreducible minimum (already protected in the International Bill of Human Rights) should include the right of workers to organise and bargain (since that provides the basis for locally-appropriate standards in other areas) and a ban on forced labour, slave labour, and exploitative child labour, defined – as in the Bangladesh example – following a dialogue with parents and their children.

Finally, changing the way economic decisions are made requires a new framework for national accounting which reflects the real costs of production and exchange (not just the level of economic activity). The current system is based on GNP, which as Senator Robert Kennedy once noted, *'measures everything except that which makes life worthwhile'*. There can't be much sense in a system that confuses goods with bads and addictions with cures; counts weapons production on a par with investment in schools; treats child care as valueless, and discounts the costs of pollution. When these costs are revealed and quantified there will be stronger incentives to steer clear of decisions which damage the things we want to protect, like our human and natural resources. And that will stimulate the transition to an economy which grows without increasing the throughput of non-renewable resources or placing an unfair social burden on women. There are many possibilities on offer, like 'green GDP' and the index of sustainable economic welfare. All have problems of methodology, but most can be handled by developing a system of 'satellite accounts' to run alongside the normal ones.[59] The more we can change the language of economics and the measurement of prices in this way, the easier it will be to use the market to advance social and environmental objectives. And that will take us closer to a win-win future where economic efficiency does not have to be traded off against long-term common interests.

WHO CARES?

Success in caring for one another is a precondition for the health of any economy, but it is also an end in itself because of the intrinsic value it adds to all our lives. So how should caring be organised and financed in societies that want to be just? As the feminist scholar Nancy Folbre asks, *'who pays for the kids?'*[60] Market-based solutions to this question are inadequate, especially in low-income countries, because access to services is based on purchasing power and incomes are unequally distributed. The majority of citizens don't get the nurturing, health care and education they need to make society as a whole safer and more productive, and that harms everyone in the longer term. Market mechanisms are also systematically biased against women and children because they assume the supply of domestic labour is inexhaustible, and discount the value of unpaid work and learning, even though high-quality child care and the time children spend in school are crucial to future economic success. We say that childhood is important, but in the world of decision making it is adult life that counts.[61] The structures of social power – gender, age, ethnicity, and disability – both strengthen these biases and are reinforced by them, distributing the costs of growth and change unequally across the population. That denies some groups – especially women – the opportunities enjoyed by others – especially men, and there is nothing very human about that. If we are serious about humanising capitalism we must find better ways of attacking discrimination and sharing out social responsibilities, without imposing unsustainable costs on the economy. Capitalism individualises these responsibilities but denies most people the means to meet them on their own, so preserving or reconstituting a collective approach to care is a vital part of the agenda. However, co-operation of this sort is not sufficient to remove discrimination. That requires much deeper action to transform the systems of social power from the bottom up (by changing values and attitudes) and the top down (by enforcing equal rights and removing any obstacles that prevent their realisation). We don't want a society where everything is turned into a commodity, even the parts of our lives, like love, that have never been for sale. But how do we make the *'economy of care and the commodity economy mutually supportive'*?[62]

In societies in the developing world there are some traditions that help us to answer these questions, and others that pose more questions in themselves. Gender discrimination, stereotypes about people with disabilities, and the exclusion of children from decision making were all present in indigenous cultures before the transition to the cash economy. On closer inspection, there is usually less that is 'moral' about the 'moral economy' than first appears. In any case, long-established bonds of family and community inevitably break down under capitalism, as do traditional values of stewardship over natural resources. *'Today only the parents are responsible for their children's upbringing; before, the whole community was involved'*, reports an oral history project in Senegal and Niger, *'land used to be sacred; now fields are bought and sold like any other piece of merchandise'*.[63] As the nature of community changes under the influence of global economic forces, traditional ties have to take their place in a wider setting of 'networks of opportunity', as the sociologist Ray Pahl calls them.[64] Strong traditions provide a secure foundation to meet this challenge, but people must grow beyond them to forge relationships with others if they are to retain security and belonging in a flexible labour market and a rapidly changing social milieu.

When adapted to these changing conditions, values of collective responsibility and co-operative problem-solving have considerable potential to resolve the social and environmental questions that face all societies. Land rights regulated at community level, for example, provide more security to poor people; older people have a higher status and play more of a role in caring, especially in areas ravaged by the AIDS virus where younger generations of parents and relatives have passed away; and ethnic and religious obligations have always provided a safety net in times of need.[65] There are many aspects of village life that need not disappear in the rush to commercialise caring – like consensual methods of resolving disputes, a vision of time not wholly eaten away by the short term, and a deep-rooted resilience.[66] The ability of grassroots groups to manage their affairs has been *'blocked by bureaucrats since the days of the pharaohs'*,[67] but people soon learn the value of co-operation when they see that selfishness is an irrational strategy. The famous 'prisoner's dilemma' in game theory shows how two people in isolation can make rational short-term decisions that turn out to be against the long-term interests of both. Experiments have shown, however, that co-operation becomes the rational thing to do when the game is played more than once.[68] This is exactly what happens in real communities, like the Sri Lankan farmers who have developed a successful collective management scheme for canal irrigation. Each farmer gets water without depriving others further downstream, something that would be impossible in a market system where the richest landowners would take as much water as possible, both for themselves and to sell to others.[69] Under these conditions there is no conflict between rational behaviour by individuals and social ethics favouring solidarity.

Poor people have always supported each other, in all societies, using social networks, kin, neighbours, employers and voluntary associations to tide them over the worst of times before turning to charity. French traders were 'building social capital' 400 years ago by allowing lavender sellers to accumulate 12 months of arrears before calling in the bailiffs.[70] The same tradition of mutual support was tested to the limit when communities had to provide their own social services as government was retrenched under the structural adjustment programmes described in Chapter 6.[71] Rotating credit-and-savings associations, welfare societies and other groups provide invaluable material help, and enhance social energy for use in other settings. Trust and co-operation have to be cemented and extended by building upwards and outwards into markets and politics from groups that already practise them.[72] So different ways of organising social provision have major economic implications, just as the way in which economic systems are transformed will influence the quality of care.

The fact that the Grameen Bank includes social insurance in its loans promotes access to health and education among borrowers, just as codes of conduct adopted by businesses can help to enforce more effective child-care provision. Even better are approaches that attack discrimination as well as welfare needs. In Lesotho, village-based rehabilitation programmes run by community groups and NGOs have successfully integrated children with disabilities into mainstream primary education.[73] The links that develop through initiatives like these do not simply replicate community traditions, but challenge and extend them into new areas.

This process of adaptation is the key to building networks of care that are rooted in community but not stifled by tradition, for trust and co-operation are not unalloyed 'goods'. The radical thinker Geoff Mulgan points out that individuals achieve most when they are *'cautious reciprocators'*, predisposed to co-operate but retaliating when others take advantage of them.[74] This is why strong NGOs and other civic groups are so important when marrying individual action with collective responsibilities, like SEWA (the Self-Employed Women's Association in India), which strengthens the position of its members in the marketplace but also promotes the joint provision of child-care facilities. It was this sort of part-social, part-commercial provision in health, education and welfare that allowed East Asian governments to keep public spending low while their economies grew rapidly.[75] It isn't necessarily better than a full state system, but it is certainly easier to finance.

Much has been written about the privatisation of welfare in countries like Chile, which have developed a system that is financially sustainable but excludes those who lack a secure income. Other countries (including Argentina) have opted for a mixed system of the private and public sectors which is more difficult to finance, but more effective in meeting the needs of the whole population.[76] That will be more efficient in the long term too, because it enhances more of the human skills and resources on which future prosperity and caring will be based. Any serious effort to reduce poverty and vulnerability requires a large safety net, and in the end that means tax-based systems with cost recovery limited to the better off.[77] In China, the switch from a highly organised health system to a weakly regulated market has been disastrous for the poor, and gaps in access have not been closed through the use of insurance, which is the route recommended by most economists when faced by the sustainability problem identified in Part I – that is, the large gap that exists between the costs of service provision and the ability of the population to pay.[78] It remains a government responsibility to institute a framework of laws and social policy that does what communities, NGOs, and commercial providers cannot do: to ensure comprehensive access and standards of care, and intervene where necessary to protect the rights of individuals.

The underlying priority is to find ways of helping men and women to combine their market and non-market roles to better effect, using schemes like SEWA, after-school facilities and subsidies to employer provision. Unfortunately, societies dedicated to profit rather than human potential are bound to be reluctant to afford a comprehensive child-care system which uses the strengths of commercial and social provision but backs them up, as it must, with a full-scale commitment of public resources though progressive and corporate taxation.[79] Where domestic tax revenue is scarce, international assistance is obviously vital, but aid agencies must avoid pressurising countries in the developing world to privatise welfare if this means losing the opportunities that traditional obligations provide. Then there would be more chance for everyone to get the care they need without reinforcing unequal systems of social power.

DIALOGIC POLITICS

Transforming systems of political power is a prerequisite for social and economic change. Decentralised, democratic governance provides the best framework for people to exercise their citizenship rights over the power of prejudice and the market, nested within larger systems that do the same at national and global levels. How to connect new forms of local governance with global institutions is considered in Chapter 9. Decentralisation is important because, as we have seen, transforming other systems of power is most effectively rooted at the local level. Democratization is important because new trade-offs must reflect the views of everyone to be sustainable, and that can't happen without political mechanisms that allow everyone a voice in debate and decision making. As participation in politics increases, the legitimacy and effectiveness of state authority also grows, providing a strong hand to protect the rights of those discriminated against by systems of social power, or exploited in the economic arena.

The first task is to increase the voice of poor people, women, children and other groups that are under-represented in decision making so that all have the same opportunity to participate. Political skills can be nurtured in civic organisations, but as we saw in Chapter 7, they must be translated into the formal political arena to make a real difference. A failure to do this has been a consistent problem for grassroots action throughout the developing world. Young people are especially excluded despite the fact that they are the citizenry of the future who should be learning the skills of democracy now.[80] Decentralisation does not imply de-linking. The Zapatista rebellion in Mexico's Chiapas region has received much global publicity, but there are other experiments nearby which, by contrast, are winning large-scale electoral support at the centre of the economy. In Guanajuato, for example, Governor Vicente Fox is opening municipal government to much broader participation, and reinvesting tax revenue locally instead of seeing it siphoned off to Mexico City.[81] Similar experiments are taking place in many other Latin American municipalities, like Recife, where neighbourhood councils bring communities, government and business representatives together. Other alliances have developed around 'Agenda 21', the action-planning process that emerged from the Rio de Janeiro Earth Summit, and experiments like the 'Panchayati Raj' system of local government in India.[82] The best of these experiments engage with mainstream politics in order to redirect the costs and benefits of change, rather than withdrawing into the trenches to preserve a vanishing way of life. Dialogic politics must also make room for those, like the Zapatistas, who do want to withdraw, but in the long term de-linking is unlikely to provide a viable route into the future.

Democratic politics teach people the skills of dialogue and co-operation that are essential for new partnerships in social and economic life. It is no coincidence that new forms of municipal governance make heavy use of pre-existing traditions to bring people together – like the *'minga'* (collective workdays) used in the Ecuadorian city of Curicama, and the community round-tables that drive decision making in Peruvian cities like Cajamarca.[83] The coalitions that develop through these experiments illustrate how political power can be regulated in ways which promote co-operation and deliver benefits for everyone: more voice, and consequently a better deal, for citizens (for example, water connections and other services have improved dramatically in municipalities that practise dialogic politics); a stronger local economy with more opportunities for business and joint partnerships of the private and public sectors; and the political support and growing tax revenues that reforming governments require. This is win-win politics at its best.

THE IMPORTANCE OF CIVIC LEADERSHIP

Governments and businesses are unlikely to be enthusiastic about increased public spending or lower consumption levels, so the pressure for change in these areas is likely to come from civil society. Civil society is the common denominator in all the innovations described thus far, whether organising collective responses to welfare, pressuring businesses to be more responsible, or creating a counterweight to vested interests in decentralised politics. This is not surprising, since civil society is traditionally the repository of the social virtues, the prime source of social energy, and the strongest advocate of the benefits of co-operation. But it does mean that any weakening of civil society, any co-option, erosion or distortion, is likely to make the task of humanising capitalism much more difficult. Among writers and politicians doubly disenchanted with the ideologies of Left and Right, civil society has assumed the status of a 'solution' writ large. American writer Jeremy Rifkin calls it our *'last, best hope'*, despite the fact that the USA's deep-rooted social problems coexist with the most active associational fabric on the planet.[84] Echoing the communitarians, psychologist M Scott Peck saw civic life, especially in the form of community, as *'the salvation of the world'*.[85] And many British political commentators now view civic organisations as the key to reinvigorating democracy and the birth of a new 'project' to reunite fragmented societies against the onrush of globalising markets.[86]

The more extreme of these claims are wildly unrealistic, especially in countries in the developing world. Real civil societies are fragmented, most citizens are energised only during periods of crisis, and civic institutions are often undemocratic and uncooperative themselves. The ideal of a self-initiated civic organisation with strong accountability to its members is rarely matched by the practice. The *'iron law of oligarchy'* identified early in this century by Swiss political scientist Robert Michels catches up with most organisations somewhere along the line.[87] In the foreign-aid business, many NGOs are tied to donor agendas rather than a constituency or to each other, and that makes them a poor conduit for social connectedness and the nurturing of co-operative values.[88] Dependence on foreign resources has allowed them to grow without earning the trust of their supporters, reducing their potential to transform social and economic relations from a mass base.[89] In the world of international development, too much is being asked of civil society: pausing only to do the washing up on their way to their fourth meeting of the week, poor people (which usually means women) are now expected to organise social services, govern their communities, evaluate projects, solve the unemployment problem, and save the environment. But most poor people are too busy making a living to do these things and most of the others are too lazy. *'Don't ask us to carry more than our capacity,'* says Peruvian NGO leader Mario Padron, *'and then blame the failure of the next development decade on us. We can't carry the load.'*[90]

Is there a civil society at all in most developing countries? Some doubt it, seeing Western enthusiasm as a plot to spread liberal democratic values to other cultures. It is true that civil society has been popularised by Western writers, most recently by Robert Putnam's famous study which linked the economic success of northern Italy to its strong civic culture and dense web of interconnecting organisations.[91] By contrast, *'the fate of the Mezzogiorno is an object lesson for the Third World today: social capital may be more important than economic capital for social, economic and political progress'*.[92] It is clear, however, that co-operation is not the property of Western culture, and that civic groups are developing rapidly in Africa, Asia and Latin America, in many cases independent of outside support.[93] The largest-ever survey of the 'non-profit sector' during 1996 found over one million such groups in India, 210,000 in Brazil, 17,500 in Egypt and 15,000 in Thailand, not counting all the informal or non-registered groups that are just as important.[94] Despite the defects and the differences, enough remains in these organisations – if they work together – to become a powerful motor for change, helping to *'re-vision the world as an ever-growing web of less exploitative relationships'*.[95] As researcher Jenny Pearce says:

> *'For those of us who retain a commitment to social change and still want to do things despite the collapse of the big idea in socialism, civil society does legitimate the collective activities which are still the only means to bring about such change.'*[96]

At their best, civic groups are a unifying influence, a bulwark against the abuse of power, and a practical vehicle for the transformation of values and behaviour. But if this is to be the case, they must put their own house in order to become genuine exemplars of the society they want to create, and work much harder with business and government to make the social virtues less the property of one section of society, and more the defining characteristics of society as a whole. The goal is not just a strong civil society, but a society that is just and civil in all that it does.

CONCLUSION

Capitalism offers poor people both gains and losses, and it is up to them to decide how far they want to resist these forces, how far to reform them, and how far to accept them as they are. Every society must make its own trade-offs between equity, efficiency, and the sacrifices sustainable development demands.[97] Meaningful participation in decisions like these requires a basic level of economic security and political voice for everyone, and in that sense the Inner City Foundation was right. As a first principle, outside help must '*fight like crazy*' to strengthen the position of those excluded from the benefits of growth or discriminated against by prejudice, and never give up. However, this is not an end in itself. If all we do is fight, there will be precious little energy left over to form partnerships with others. A focus on empowerment must be balanced by innovations in economics, politics and social policy which encourage people to use some of the power they gain for the common good. And international co-operation can play a vital role in supporting these innovations through foreign aid, global networks, and multilateral standard-setting.

The most interesting innovations in politics, economics and the social world occupy the middle ground where the logic of competition meets, and mixes with, the logic of co-operation. The solutions that emerge from this process show that progress is possible in all three of the areas we want to change: the distribution of the surplus economies create – using fair trade to increase producer prices, for example; the processes that produce it, by finding better ways to combine people's market and non-market roles; and the values and attitudes that underpin these changes, by using dialogic politics and co-operative management. These innovations use market mechanisms, but they are not captured by them; what is left to markets is socially regulated; and information gathered through the market is only one source of knowledge in decision making.[98] Gradually, as the language of economics shifts and markets provide their own incentives (like increased demand for renewable energy technologies), change becomes self-reinforcing. Extending these virtuous cycles further into the mainstream is the key to humanising capitalism.

The assumption underlying 'win-win' strategies is that everyone benefits when the social virtues are injected into markets, and the principles of market efficiency are injected into the way societies meet their social responsibilities. All modern societies depend on the co-existence of these market and non-market rationalities, since otherwise markets could not work and complex societies would fall apart.[99] Competition and co-operation are both inescapable parts of our lives, and there is nothing to stop us from changing the balance between the two in favour of long-term goals. However, market economies still need incentives, and preserving those incentives places limits on their reformability. The job of business is to be a business. It is the job of politics to redistribute the surplus business creates, but if too much is redistributed there won't be enough incentive to produce it in the first place. It would be wonderful if businesses only produced products that we actually needed, but who needs 52 kinds of vodka or yet another generation of high-technology warplanes?[100] Industry produces the goods it wants society to need, and we shouldn't be surprised that there are limits to corporate reform. Priorities in the 'triple bottom line' are clear (financial, social and environmental goals), and when hard choices have to be made between different interests, market forces and hierarchical management are pretty good at making them.[101] But that doesn't mean the same forces will be good at making choices elsewhere, so why not declare some parts of life a market-free zone, defending those things we judge to have an infinite value that cannot be traded-off against the costs of production?[102] That was the core of Richard Titmuss's famous defence of voluntary blood donations in the UK, in which he argued that commercialisation would inevitably undermine the '*gift relationship*' on which the system depended.[103] Defending this position comes at a price (often in terms of increased public expenditure), but that too is a political choice. It would be better to be honest and find ways of raising more tax revenue than disguise the debate with spurious rhetoric about the superiority of market solutions, and easier to do this in many countries in the developing world where the option of redistribution with international help is still a political possibility.

Co-operation requires us to set some voluntary limits to our self-interest, and to accept collective responsibility to care for each other and the environment – an attitude of stewardship over the human and natural resources on which all our futures depend. In that sense, humanising capitalism means recreating rationality on the basis of caring; and that requires, not a romanticising of care, but building the conditions under which caring becomes rational.[104] At the minimum, they include a more equal sharing of endowments and the regulation of all exclusionary systems of power, since '*it is only from security that we feel able to reach out and make connections with others*'.[105] As Matt Ridley concludes, exchange between equals is the raw material of trust, and trust is the foundation of virtue.[106] The challenge of a virtuous society takes everyone into uncharted territory, but we don't need to stumble blindly in the dark. There are lots of signposts which show how economics, politics and social policy can be suffused with incentives for co-operation without losing the competitive rationality that economic growth requires.[107] As the benefits of co-operation feed through via dialogic politics, new forms of enterprise, and shared social responsibilities, the incentives for change become self-reinforcing, eventually reproducing that *'different kind of individual'* that J R Bellerby and others have dreamed of.[108] *'We live in crowds,'* he said, *'and if some people use their elbows, others will suffer.'*[109] In an increasingly crowded but competitive world, it is natural for people to use their elbows all the time, even if they erode their own security in the process. The only solution to that dilemma lies through international co-operation, but co-operation at the global level, just like in firms, neighbourhoods and local politics, won't take root without concrete incentives that reward contributive behaviour and penalise selfishness. That raises huge question marks about the future of global governance, especially in a world of such unequal powers.

Chapter 9

Light But Firm: The Future of Global Governance

'Good governance requires that legislation be the last step
in regulating human affairs'

Davinder Lamba[1]

'The problem with current global institutions is that they
are dead but not yet buried'

Denis Goulet[2]

During the 1990s, workers in South Wales celebrated the benefits of
large-scale inward investment in manufacturing industry, especially
from East Asia. Late in 1997, a wave of stock market and banking
collapses swept through Thailand, Indonesia, Malaysia and South
Korea, and threatened the health of the Japanese economy too. As the
panic spread to Europe and North America, billions of dollars were
wiped off the value of leading corporations, and East Asian manufacturers shelved plans to expand their factories abroad.[3] The celebrations
in South Wales were cut short, providing a useful reminder that globalisation carries risks as well as opportunities.[4] In this increasingly
interconnected world of cause and effect, where problems spread
across national frontiers and security threats leak from one location to
another, there are three ways for decision makers to react. The first is
a continued free for all, but that produces self-destructive behaviour
in the form of the 'prisoner's dilemma' we mentioned in Chapter 8.
Alternatively, some will take a 'free ride' on the back of sacrifices made
by others, undermining the impact of collective agreements to
preserve the biosphere and protect human rights. Self-evidently, this is
a stupid strategy because it endangers the common social and environmental heritage on which all our futures depend.

The second response is to go the opposite extreme and regulate everything globally, but that erodes incentives too much and imposes intolerable limits on human freedom. In any case, the world government it requires exists only in the realms of fiction. The third and best approach is the one explored in this chapter: a set of core agreements that rein in the most destructive of behaviours but preserve room to manoeuvre elsewhere, backed up by voluntary regulation and other non-coercive alternatives. This is global governance – a generally accepted set of rules, norms and institutions that shape behaviour across national boundaries.[5] Discussions about global governance quickly turn to the global institutions we already have (such as the UN Security Council) and how unprepared they are to deal with the challenges of the 21st Century. There are many reasons for this, but underlying them all is the gulf that has opened up between international regimes and the people whose co-operation is required to enforce them. In real life, human activity is regulated as much by consensus from below as by laws from above, especially those that are seen as unfair. Paraphrasing the introductory quotation from Kenyan activist Davinder Lamba, legislation is the last resort of good governance. Laws and formal institutions are required to arbitrate in disputes, enforce unpopular decisions, and protect the rights of those whose voices are ignored, but the citizens of a democracy will not accept regulations they cannot control.[6] And therein lies the problem, since few of us feel we control the UN or the IMF – institutions that seem dominated by elites, detached from their constituents, and run by self-serving bureaucracies. If global institutions are 'dead but not yet buried', should we administer the last rites and begin afresh, work to revive global institutions with a new infusion of energy, or simply let them waste away?

Rules work best when they are fair and enforceable, but that is difficult to achieve in a world of unequal powers and declining state authority. So the future of global governance is likely to rest not on a single system like the UN, but on a new mixture of bottom-up and top-down authority; public, private and civic institutions; and informal norms as well as formal laws and standards. The result will be 'light but firm': less bureaucratic, but with more chance of being implemented. What would such a system look like in practice?

GOVERNANCE FOR WHAT?

Pollution

International co-operation has been a reality in some areas of life for a century or more, since there have always been issues that self-evidently require a collective response which benefits everyone. Examples include the regulation of air traffic and telecommunications, the treatment of civilians in wartime, and the work of the Atomic Energy Authority.[7] These initiatives proceed largely unchallenged in the background of international affairs – no one froths at the mouth at the mention of the International Postal Union, for example, but tempers soon start to rise when regulation is suggested in environmental affairs, trade, and human rights. In fact, pollution is already subject to over 180 multilateral agreements, and some have been very successful.[8] The Montreal Protocol has reduced damage to the earth's ozone layer substantially, but it benefited from a special set of circumstances that is difficult to replicate: everyone fears skin cancer but few are prepared to give up their cars in order to combat global warming. Only a small number of manufacturers produced ozone-depleting substances, alternatives were readily available, and there was no real North-South fault-line to frustrate negotiations.[9] By contrast, the agreements reached at the Earth Summit in Rio de Janeiro are either non-binding or subject to too many loopholes to make them work.[10] Part of the problem is that countries at different stages of industrialisation have different environmental priorities. China has little incentive to make sacrifices now for the benefit of future generations in the rich world; its priority must be to reduce poverty by all means possible. Although rich nations are currently the world's biggest polluters, why should they clean up their act if poorer countries like China will be even bigger offenders in ten years' time? The same problem arises over biodiversity, and in particular the genetic material in plants and animals that provides the basis for new medicines. Countries in the tropics (with the greatest biodiversity) argue that corporations should pay handsomely for genetic material, which has taken centuries to evolve, to be extracted for human use.[11] Corporations (and Northern governments) reject these claims, arguing that knowledge, like any other commodity, can be patented and traded on international markets. So it is no surprise that Southern delegates who negotiated the Biodiversity Convention accepted only limited commitments on conservation in return.[12] This is a travesty of governance, in which no one really wins.

Addressing these conflicts of interest requires a co-operative response which benefits each participant in different ways, such as pollution permits that can be traded on international markets, or 'joint implementation' arrangements like the Arctic Council, where countries as diverse as Canada, Russia and Malaysia co-operate to limit deforestation and its impact on pollution thousands of miles away.[13] The idea of tradeable permits is a controversial one which dominated the Kyoto Conference on Climate Change in 1997.[14] The principle itself is simple: since what matters is stabilising the overall production of greenhouse gases at a level compatible with manageable global warming, holding individual countries accountable for meeting fixed quotas is less important than reducing emissions wherever that can be done most cost-effectively.[15] So if Russia is polluting less than its permitted quota, it can sell some of its unused emissions to another country which can meet its own targets without cutting pollution – the net result would still be a reduction in world carbon dioxide production, especially if the payments received by Russia were used to clean up local industry. Like many market remedies, this sounds too good to be true. Sure enough (its critics argue), not only are there too many loopholes to make permits work, but there are fairer and more effective alternatives, such as international eco-taxation, and environmental regulation through the WTO.

The WorldWatch Institute estimates that a tax on carbon emissions could raise between US$700 billion and 1.8 trillion at its peak, stabilising global warming over the same length of time as tradeable permits and reducing annual economic growth by a mere 0.04 per cent.[16] Unlike permits, taxation would be more comprehensive and predictable, and place responsibility on the shoulders of those in the North who consume and pollute most of all.[17] In the example given above, Russia might only have permits to sell because it was in recession, not because it had increased the efficiency of energy use in its economy; and since the other country involved could meet its targets by doing nothing at all to reduce pollution, this approach is akin to rearranging the deckchairs on the *Titanic* as it sinks beneath the waves. A real market-based solution would make polluters pay directly for the damage they inflict; if global warming raises sea levels sufficiently to flood a large part of Bangladesh, then the industrialised world should meet the costs of erecting dykes along the Bay of Bengal, since most of the problem is the result of pollution it has caused in the past. Only part of the Kyoto targets can be met using permits, but the suspicion remains that they are a device for the rich world to buy its way out of its international responsibilities. And if that is the case, why should poorer countries make their own sacrifices?[18]

The second alternative to a permit system involves amending the rules of the WTO to mandate protection of the global commons, and allow exemptions to free trade in favour of environmentally-friendly production methods, as the Montreal Protocol did.[19] This would be most effective if rich countries agreed to three complementary measures. First, there is a clear need for long-term support and technology transfer so that poorer countries can clean up their agriculture, industry, energy and transport. One estimate suggests that Indonesia alone needs US$20 billion to conserve its forests, compared to the US$2 billion agreed at the Earth Summit for the *world-wide* Global Environmental Facility.[20] Second, a long grace period would be necessary before they have to comply with targets (ten years in the case of the Montreal Protocol, longer for the Convention on Climate Change). Third, global regimes should incorporate measures which are inversely proportional to a country's per capita income or skills base.[21] Graduating rules and supporting compliance emerge as key principles in making international regimes fairer and more effective.[22] Underlying these principles is the need for public pressure for results from below. The Brazilian city of Cubatao, for example, was transformed from one of the most polluted urban areas in Latin America to one of the cleanest by an alliance between government officials and civic groups which pressed local industry to implement environmental legislation.[23] It is this combination of 'hard law' with 'soft law' that makes the difference; in other words, community action, NGO lobbying, and media pressure as well as written rules.[24] If environmental regulation is to work, the North must pay more, the South must demand less, and all of us who care about the future have to make our views known in the political process.[25]

Trade and finance

Conflicts of interest are just as entrenched in international economics. There are few advocates nowadays of completely unregulated markets or uncoordinated macro-economic policy making, but there is much less agreement on how to govern world trade, commodity prices and multi-national corporations. The least contentious area is financial regulation, since recent experience demonstrates the havoc that uncoordinated capital movements can cause. *'While you have monetary chaos it is very difficult to have order of any other kind'*, as Keynes once remarked.[26] Gullermo Ortiz, Mexico's Finance Secretary, must have been thinking the same thing when he telephoned Washington DC in January 1995, with the news that his country was about to default on its debts. His call triggered rapid disinvestment and devaluation of the Peso, and sparked what became known as the *'first crisis of the 21st century'* because of its international causes and consequences, with vast capital flows sweeping into and out of economies ill-prepared to deal with them.[27] The crisis stemmed from weak banking systems, overreactions among foreign investors, and built-in incentives to destabilise exchange rates in order to make quick profits for speculators. Even though Mexico's economic fundamentals had changed only slightly, investors panicked.[28] The same pattern reappeared in East Asia two years later, when speculators sold large quantities of Thailand's currency on the expectation that they would be able to buy it back cheaply after devaluation. Like a contagious virus, the erosion of confidence this produced spread within weeks to neighbouring markets. At least this time the IMF was better prepared, having adopted new procedures to provide help quickly from a larger bail-out fund.[29] Other elements of a more effective monetary regime remain to be put in place: temporary controls on capital movements, more effective banking supervision, closer co-ordination between central banks in different countries, and tougher measures to discourage irresponsible lending (like limiting the value of insured loans or instigating a bankruptcy procedure for countries *in extremis*).[30] These would help to guarantee the stability that long-term investment and employment growth require – expansionary policies free of the threat of destabilisation by capital flight or speculative attacks on a country's currency.[31] The point of global governance is not to organise world affairs for the benefit of speculators, but to promote reforms that are in the common interest, and despite the claims of some economists there is no guarantee that markets will do this better than governments.

Foreign investment flows to markets where profits are secure, and multilateral agreements can increase the attractiveness of economies in the developing world by 'locking in' government policies on taxation and investor rights. But investors have responsibilities too, especially in terms of the proportion of production they export, the repatriation of their profits, and social and environmental standards in their factories. The problem with current economic thinking is that these responsibilities are forgotten in the race to 'level the playing field' for corporate interests. For example countries that do not ratify the

Multilateral Agreement on Investment (MAI), which was temporarily shelved in 1998, will be disadvantaged in attracting foreign investment, but once they do, it will be impossible to treat foreign investors differently from domestic ones: to give low-interest loans to local businesses, tax breaks to labour-intensive industry, or preferential treatment to community construction contracts – all highlighted in Chapter 8 as part of the economic agenda for the future. The MAI will give investors freedom to move their funds at any time, preventing countries from imposing exchange controls to halt capital flight. Renato Ruggiero (head of the WTO) calls this a *'constitution for globalisation'*; the *San Francisco Bay Guardian* describes it as *'NAFTA on crack'*.[32] In any case, poor countries are excluded from negotiating the Agreement, which is a strange way to draw up a constitution if the goal is to elicit their co-operation further down the line. As the OECD puts it in characteristically haughty tones, *'whether and to what extent the high standards of the MAI could be relaxed in non-member country accession negotiations has yet to be determined'*.[33]

What the MAI intends to do for investment, the WTO is already doing for trade as a whole, though trade agreements have a much longer history. Over the past 50 years, there has been a gradual reduction in barriers to free trade under the General Agreement on Tariffs and Trade (GATT), culminating in the 'Final Act' of the Uruguay Round of trade negotiations signed by 145 countries in 1994. That agreement established the WTO and extended the principles of trade liberalisation to services (which make up an increasing proportion of production costs), intellectual property (like copyrights and patents), and other areas.[34] The short-term objective is to abolish all barriers in the industrialised world to imports from the poorest countries; the longer-term goal is to make it impossible for any country to impose restrictions on international trade. Proponents of free trade argue from economic theory that liberalisation will benefit everyone in the long term, since resources will be allocated more efficiently at the global level. Computer modelling shows a small gain for developing countries as a whole in the next century, but substantial losses for Africa.[35] The world is not, however, a model in which all things can be made equal on the computer screen. In reality, the benefits of free trade depend on how different countries integrate into the world economy and what steps are taken to manage the social and environmental costs of production and exchange. Free trade is not an end in itself, but a means to prosperity, security and well-being, so trade agreements are as much about how trade affects people as about who sells what to whom.[36]

Article 20 of the GATT/WTO already provides for protection of the environment and human rights, but not as a form of disguised protectionism, which is what Southern countries fear about Northern intentions.[37] A 'social clause' in trade agreements imposed without regard for local conditions would make poor countries fall further behind in the race for competitiveness. Northern countries can afford to implement tighter regulation, but it would be extremely difficult for Bangladesh to improve standards in the clothing industry, for example, without being priced out of the market by less scrupulous competitors. However, as we saw in Chapter 8, regulation is still possible at the local and regional levels using codes of conduct and other measures negotiated between government, workers and industry. The key issue is preferential treatment, which poor countries need so that they have enough time to diversify their exports and prepare themselves for full integration into the world economy. The seeds that drove the green revolution in Asia were developed by international research institutions and made available to anyone who wanted them, but under a binding agreement on intellectual property-rights farmers would not be able to reuse varieties that 'belonged' to Unilever or Shell, for example.[38] Nor would India be able to force corporations to transfer patents to local producers in order to stimulate a nascent pharmaceutical industry.[39] This is particularly dangerous to late industrialisers because it makes it much more difficult to borrow technology from abroad, which was one of the cornerstones of East Asian success. The West developed by borrowing, so why should a different set of rules be imposed on poorer countries now?[40] Knowledge that benefits humanity is a public good, not a private privilege, and any attempt to restrict its availability is simply *'institutionalised theft'*.[41]

Membership of the GATT/WTO obliges each country to extend 'Most-Favoured-Nation' status to all the others, enshrining non-discrimination as a fundamental principle. However, there are legitimate exceptions to this rule that make it possible to treat poor countries differently, so it is perfectly legal to abolish trade barriers in the North while keeping them in the South for a time, especially in the key areas of agriculture and textiles.[42] Part of the problem in making sure this happens is the way trade rules are made. The WTO is democratic in that decisions are made by consensus in its ministerial conference (one country, one vote), but the enforcement of judgements is left to the complainant, so weaker countries (acting alone at least) are automatically disadvantaged.[43] When the EU complained about America's 'Helms-Burton Act' (which threatened sanctions against countries trading with Cuba), the US government refused to co-operate with the WTO's arbitration panel.[44] But when banana producers in Central America complained about preferential treatment for European corporations involved in the Caribbean banana trade, the EU accepted the WTO's ruling despite the dire consequences for growers.[45] Accusations of double standards were strengthened by the fact that the complaint was backed by the US government and multinationals like Chiquita who stood to benefit. Parties with no material interest in the EU banana trade had full participation rights on the appeal panel, which was headed by a former US Congressman and had one delegate supposedly to 'represent' the developing world; but Caribbean producers had no right to ask questions even on factual or legal matters, or submit rebuttals.[46] Groups campaigning in support of the growers were sidelined while Chiquita received an invitation to the White House after donating US$500,000 to Democratic Party funds the day after the complaint was filed.[47] At this point you might be wondering whether it's the product that is bananas or the procedures, even if their outcome (as in this case) was legally correct. Poor countries need special help to develop to the point at which world trade can be fair as well as free. Legitimising that help is the role of global governance. Without it, liberalisation simply accelerates the international transmission of inequality.[48]

HUMAN RIGHTS AND HUMANITARIAN INTERVENTION

Good governance in economic and environmental affairs will reduce the likelihood of conflict over resources, but other forms of conflict and human rights violations require rules of their own: codes of conduct for arms exports and weapons regulation, a coherent framework to deal with complex political emergencies, and consistency in applying sanctions to non-civilian targets. There have been some successes in this field: biological and chemical weapons have been formally outlawed;[49] nuclear weapons have been subjected to tighter regulation, though the Comprehensive Test Ban Treaty faces opposition from India, Pakistan and others on the grounds that the major nuclear powers are not disarming quickly enough;[50] and trade restrictions on some conventional weapons are being actively discussed. Although a small number of countries refused to sign the Ottawa

Treaty on anti-personnel mines in 1997, the award of the Nobel Peace Prize to the International Campaign to Ban Landmines signified a stunning victory for worldwide efforts to halt the trade in these most indiscriminate of weapons.[51] Compared to the failure of the UN's Inhumane Weapons Convention, the campaign shows what can be achieved when a cross-society coalition comes together to lobby from below and connect with politicians at the top. The five permanent members of the UN Security Council want world peace, but are responsible for 85 per cent of global arms exports, so it is obvious where the prime responsibility for regulation lies.[52]

We saw in Chapter 5 what is needed to deal with emergencies: a better early-warning system channelling intelligence into a unified command structure at UN headquarters; stronger levers to make sure this information is acted on at the right time; a standing military intervention force equipped with aircraft and helicopters and backed by quick-release funding to support Security Council resolutions;[53] an international police force specially trained for ethno-nationalist conflicts and minority-rights protection; an international relief corps to reduce dysfunctional competition between agencies, with expertise in peace building, economic reconstruction and the use of the media as well as the delivery of humanitarian assistance; stronger accountability, perhaps through a relief commissioner; and an international criminal court (launched in the face of US opposition in 1998). What of these other priorities? Money is one obvious problem: the UN's global peace-keeping budget has fallen from US$3 billion to one billion since 1995 – about the same as the budget of the New York Police Department or the amount of money spent each year by Americans on cut flowers.[54] The UN's own structures are another, since *'it can no more conduct military operations on a large scale on its own than a trade association of hospitals can conduct heart surgery'*.[55] A division of labour between the UN and regional blocs (like NATO) may be the most pragmatic way forward, because none of the major powers *'will put troops into the firing line by committee'*.[56] This assumes that NATO would commit the necessary forces at the right time and agree to be held accountable to the terms of UN resolutions in order to preserve the legitimacy of international action – NATO at the service of the wider community of states, not the other way around.[57]

Even in this scenario, what would trigger intervention? Political realities dictate that large-scale military force is only likely in exceptional circumstances. That puts the onus on building a constituency to ensure that, at the very least, human suffering on the scale of

Rwanda or Bosnia is included in this definition, and acted on. Sanctions are a tempting alternative to intervention for the major powers (involving fewer body bags, for your own countrymen at least), but they are rarely a satisfactory solution unless restricted to non-civilian targets.[58] In most circumstances, constructive engagement and 'multi-track' diplomacy will be more effective – a combination of peace building from the bottom up and pressure from the outside in, backed up by long-term investments in equitable development and conflict-resolution capacity.[59] The best way to influence 'rogue states' is by surrounding them with international pressure that is seen to be legitimate (not a cloak for great-power interests), coupled with support to organisations lobbying for change inside the country; working collectively on a steady and patient basis; and communicating terms that are clear and predictable in their consequences.[60] Respect for rules will come over time if they are agreed democratically, applied consistently, and supported with financial and other help to encourage compliance. There is no point in bombing Iraq if Saddam Hussein remains in power while other sources of instability in the Middle East are ignored. Double standards destroy the legitimacy on which international alliances are built. To say, as Secretary of State Madeleine Albright did in February 1998, that the USA *'would pursue its national interests if Kofi Annan comes up with a deal we don't like'* is hardly a recipe for encouraging other states to co-operate.[61] In the same way, there is no reason to withhold food aid from starving North Koreans because their government is non-democratic. After all, *'when they get their strength back, they may decide to do to their rulers what the East Germans did to theirs'*.[62]

Whenever states are struggling for survival or supremacy, the opportunities for morality in international affairs will be limited.[63] This is especially true for 'lower-level' human rights violations – the daily round of discrimination and mistreatment that scars so many societies. The Western powers rushed to defend democratic values in Kuwait when threatened by Iraqi invasion, but are largely disinterested in pressing for democracy in the Arab states now that the Gulf War is over; after all, political reform might transfer power to democrats who would use oil reserves to their own advantage.[64] After the killing of Chinese students in Tiananmen Square in 1989, Western executive directors on the World Bank's Board decided to veto new loans to China, but they were blocked by the same countries that have protected China from censure in the UN.[65] A change of name from the State Law and Order Committee (SLORC) to the even more Orwellian 'State Peace and Development Council' has not stopped the Burmese junta from imposing slave labour on its population. But never mind, ASEAN still welcomed it into the fold.[66] The same depressing story is retold in Nigeria, East Timor, Algeria and other countries where human rights abuses have been relegated to economic interests.

Does this mean that human rights cannot be used as the fulcrum for global governance? At the Vienna Conference on Human Rights in 1993, 171 states recommitted themselves to the *'universal nature of the rights and freedoms'* contained in the International Bill of Human Rights.[67] This may be so in theory, but in practice the sheer diversity of cultures and capacities requires some room to manoeuvre, *without* losing the power of international law to hold abusers to account. States are obliged to do as much as they can to adhere to standards to which they have publicly signed up, even if what they can do is constrained by resources and conditioned by culture. Once that is accepted, North-South conflicts over human rights begin to fall away. The UN Charter recognises both economic and social rights, and civil and political rights, and treats them as indivisible. Civil rights are realisable for individuals through the courts, whereas guarantees of a decent standard of living require more complex solutions, but both signify that there are minimum standards that must be respected. Many non-Western cultures view rights through the duties and obligations individuals owe to groups (like the family or society at large), not just individual freedom, but there are few cases where the rights and duties of groups and individuals are irreconcilable in practice.[68] International law is a body of norms (not just rules), made up from many overlapping sources. Some are 'hard' (like international conventions), and others 'soft' (like customs and customary usage).[69] So the role of global governance is not always to apply the 'big stick' of international law but to facilitate the emergence of 'an authoritative consensus' on what is correct in different circumstances – what the lawyer Philip Alston calls *'localised conventions'*.[70] The fact that rules about morality change from place to place does not equal moral relativism; a core of universal principles is still possible, but not a universal interpretation of what they mean in practice.

This does not apply to all rights. Without an irreducible core, the concept of human rights becomes meaningless. 'Life integrity' is part of that core – the fact that I am starving or hacked to death is not a grey area, nor is it negotiable according to culture. So are the two conditions listed in the Introduction: the right to have rights, and an equal voice in deciding how they are expressed. If that is accepted, global conventions can be negotiated between communities of rule users, as is happening now over the environment, humanitarian law and different visions of democracy.[71] The results of this dialogue show that people in non-Western societies usually want more of the rights traditionally labelled as 'Western'. There are few volunteers for imprisonment without trial,[72] and as the writer Fatima Mernissi points out, it is not Islam that rejects democracy, but leaders who fear its consequences.[73] Over time, new loyalties emerge from discussion and struggle, and that is where outside help, pressure and encouragement are important. Re-legitimising a global core of moral standards in this way is vital, but even if we 'dis-invented' the International Bill of Human Rights we would probably end up with something very similar. So it is better to work together on interpreting the ones we already have. *'The UN Charter is full of possibilities, but they can only be realised if states want to do so'*, with the agreement of their citizens.[74] A combination of core standards – negotiated and graduated according to circumstances – support for compliance, and room to manoeuvre will never be a wholly satisfactory solution for anyone, but that doesn't really matter: the absence of such solutions is characteristic of any real-world expression of global governance, since compromise is inherent to co-operation and some element of inconsistency is inherent to compromise.[75]

INSTITUTIONS FOR GLOBAL GOVERNANCE

Linking the local with the global

In each of these areas – the environment, international economics, and human rights – it is possible to identify a small core of universal standards that preserves enough flexibility to gain support across different countries. That still leaves the problem of implementation. The implausibility of world government has led many writers to speculate about new forms of global governance based around more fluid arrangements, which recognise that different tasks are best dealt with in different ways at different levels: pollution, for example, can be challenged locally, regulated nationally, supervised regionally against cross-country standards, and globally evaluated for its impact on others.[76] This is impossible through governments alone, but nation states do not disappear in this vision. They play a more specialised role in a larger system, ceasing to monopolise representation but, as custodians of the rule of law, continuing to hold both local and global institutions to account.[77] *'International governance does not mean the end of nations, any more than an orchestra means the end of violins,'* said the late Prime Minister of Israel Golda Meir,[78] but if centralised authority is the only instrument we have it will inevitably play to the tune of the already powerful. The future lies in a better distribution of power through the international system, expressed in a wider variety of channels, with many more checks and balances.[79] That requires the exercise of *'multiple citizenship'*, as sociologists call it,[80] realising our rights and exercising our responsibilities as members of communities and local pressure groups, citizens of our national polity, consumers in the global marketplace, and – for the future – constituents of international regimes.

Strong local roots are vital to this form of governance, since global problems have local origins and no solution will last unless it has grass-roots support. Local charters on employment rights, human-rights conventions and environmental planning have to be rooted in new partnerships between civil society, governments, businesses, and international agencies. There are two ways this could be done. The first lies through formal politics, like the municipal structures we looked at in Chapter 8 or the decentralised development funds outlined in Chapter 7. The problem is that few of these innovations are connected to similar structures at the national level, never mind globally. That increases the importance of the second source of local roots: pressure groups, membership associations and specialised authorities. Some of these organisations are formally representative of a constituency, but most are not; some work only at the local level while others are already part of global networks. All help to build the preconditions for democracy by injecting a wider range of views and voices into the political arena. Powerful interest groups can also distort the democratic process, but those dangers can be managed by ensuring that no interests are excluded and that all are transparent and accountable for what they do and who they claim to represent.

All systems of democratic governance are a mixture of these two routes – the formal and the informal. There is no reason why global governance should be different, especially given the difficulties of representative democracy at the international level. However, since the leap from local to global is too large to bridge directly, there is increasing interest in the potential of intermediary structures to artic-ulate relations between the two.[81] By limiting the number of voices and agendas around the negotiating table, these structures increase the possibility of consensus and raise the resolution of differences above the lowest common denominator. Getting small groups of countries together to negotiate face-to-face over regular intervals has always been crucial to successful co-operation. The first way to do this centres on regional associations of states, building upwards from new experiments in local politics and constitutional reform at the national level.[82] Regional solutions have been suggested for military and humanitarian intervention,[83] environmental governance,[84] human rights monitoring,[85] and economic regimes (like an 'Asian monetary fund').[86] *'What countries do for themselves (individually and together) is much more important than dreaming about new global institutions.'*[87] Regional trading blocs are seen by many as an ideal way to balance self-reliance with integration into the world economy, though not everyone agrees.[88] The economist Jagdish Bhagwati[89] calls them *'a pox on the world trading system'* because they distort the economic advantages of free trade, but this ignores the political difficulties of gaining agreement over trade liberalisation at the global level and the confidence-building impact of organisations like ASEAN or MERCO-SUR. Over time, associations like these may evolve into more formal structures like the EU, linking downwards to grassroots democracy and upwards to global institutions. From Scotland to Eritrea, relations between states and citizens are already changing against the background of devolution. Regionalism of this kind offers a pragmatic middle way between the *'enlightened Cro-Magnons standing in the UN Plaza, and the slope-headed Neanderthals with clubs raised, ready to isolate America from the world'*.[90] As such, it is less threatening to isolationists, 'new protectionists', and others who fear both globalisation and world government, but still see advantages in grouping together to face the future.

However, because it is so difficult to democratise formal politics at higher levels of the world system, transnational networks of interest groups and specialised authorities may offer an easier way to link the local with the global. Civic organisations are already interacting with each other across national borders to create a nascent international civil society,[91] held together by common values and concerns – not just NGOs like Greenpeace, Oxfam or Amnesty International, but 'virtual communities' of all shapes and shades, business and trade union networks, and parts of states that co-operate with their counterparts in other countries (like banking regulators, law-enforcement agencies, judiciaries,[92] and local authorities).[93] If these organisations are to play a greater role in global governance, there need to be many more members in the South and new South-North alliances so that transnational networks are less dominated by rich-country interests. Many civic groups are tied to self-generated agendas rather than a global democratic process. Research on NGO alliances has shown how initiative can be taken away from local groups by more articulate and well-resourced agencies in the North who have more access to information technology and the media.[94] Networks don't have to be formally representative of a constituency to play a legitimate role in debates – Oxfam's voice is valuable, as Oxfam – but global governance must differentiate between the views of special interest groups (however well-intentioned) and formal representation from below. For NGOs, that means more attention to transparency and accountability both within themselves and in their relations with others, and no more unsubstantiated claims to 'represent the people'. There *are* examples of responsible North-South linking – like the 'Common Frontiers Project' which brought NGOs together from Mexico, Canada and the USA to consider strategies for NAFTA – but they don't involve financial transfers.[95] Working as equals is much easier outside the world of foreign aid.

Reforming global institutions

Every financial system needs a lender of last resort, just as every legal system needs a supreme court. Otherwise there will be no way of ensuring that decisions arrived at democratically by one set of groups do not impinge on the equal rights of others. So we still need global institutions to do the things that can't be done at other levels. However, our current institutions, like the UN and the IMF, are confused and unresponsive. The first problem is one of overlapping functions, and the second is a mismatch between what these institutions do and the way they are governed. The UN was set up to govern world affairs, not to operate relief and development programmes, and in fact it has been quietly successful in this international standard-setting role: conferring legitimacy on international intervention, codifying a substantial body of human rights law, and setting global goals. But there are other institutions that can *implement* these things more effectively, without the combination of high costs and low levels of innovation that characterises organisations lacking both market discipline and social pressures to perform.[96] Universities and think-tanks can outperform the UN in research; non-profit and commercial providers can take on most of the service-delivery activities; and we can do without 90 per cent of the turgid meetings and conferences that occupy so much of the UN's time. This is less a matter of size than of style and comparative advantage. Far from being a gigantic bureaucracy, the UN has fewer permanent employees than

Disneyland,[97] but they devote their energies to the wrong things, and fall into the *'mere frothing of words'* that the UN's founders expressly warned against.[98] The Independent Working Group on UN Reform estimates that 75 per cent of the budget could be cut from these areas without any loss of quality and be redirected to more effective human-rights monitoring where it could really make a difference.[99] The UN is not central to any of the innovations on the ground described in earlier chapters, but it is crucial to the future of global governance. In any case, decision-making by disagreeable member states is not conducive to the effective delivery of programmes and services.

Rebuilding the UN's global governance function still requires a strong central capacity, and that can be retained by building around parts of the organisation that already perform well – like the Human Development Report Office at UNDP or the newly-revitalised UNCTAD. Other specialised agencies which combine protection with implementation – like the United Nations High Commissioner for Refugees (UNHCR) and the United Nations Children's Fund (UNICEF) – should concentrate on the former and do it properly. All overlapping mandates (like the eight separate bodies which oversee food security and humanitarian assistance) should be merged, as recommended in Secretary General Kofi Annan's reforms of July 1997.[100] Dubbed a 'quiet revolution', they aimed to consolidate all the specialised agencies into a 'UN Development Group' with a single office in each country, a no-growth budget, a 25 per cent cut in staffing, a 33 per cent reduction in administrative costs and paper, and a 'development dividend' to make use of the resources these measures release.[101] This is probably the best that can be hoped for in the face of continued opposition from agencies inside the system, and a lack of support for more fundamental reform from the outside. As a UN press release put it with typical diplomatic understatement, *'the natural complement to these proposals would be certain changes of a more fundamental nature, which can be undertaken only by member states'*.[102] The end result of these changes would be a UN of two major parts: one to govern social and economic affairs (and oversee a world development fund), and the other for peace and security (with responsibility for humanitarian action). Both would report to an expanded Security Council and a more democratic General Assembly. Proposals in the diplomatic pipeline already make provision for five new permanent members (including one each from Africa, Asia, and Latin America) and four non-permanent members elected from the same regions together with Eastern Europe.[103] Ideally, voting in the General Assembly should also be reformed to reflect the shifting balance of world population, though the Western powers object to this and would probably build up alternative institutions (like the IMF) over which they could exert continued control. The most pragmatic solution is to weight voting power according to an average of a country's share of world population and GDP, or to the material interest each country has in a particular subject.[104] There is no need for the same authority to regulate everything since different issues are subject to different time scales, regional priorities, and implementation requirements.[105] Since direct participation by civil society and business is unlikely, many commentators have suggested a second non-elected chamber to stand alongside the General Assembly. Arrangements would need to be put in place to prevent domination by any one region or interest group, and for delegates to have a clear role and a degree of real influence over decisions – for example, the freedom to demand more information on General Assembly proposals and the authority to monitor Security Council resolutions.

Articles 57 and 63 of the UN Charter already require all international bodies to be brought into a formal relationship with the Economic and Social Council of the General Assembly, but this has never been supported by member states. The WTO doesn't even mention the UN in its Articles of Association, but the World Bank and the IMF are listed as sister institutions. Constitutionally, both are part of the UN system, but they are very different animals – confident, secure in their funding, and more competent technically, but still confused about their mandates. As the IMF has entered the traditional territory of the World Bank, the Bank has moved closer to the core concerns of the UN, and that has left the UN even more unsure of what it is supposed to be doing. The latest spate of World Bank reforms – christened the *'strategic compact'* by its President (James Wolfensohn) – see the organisation as an anti-poverty machine for the 21st century, capturing an increasing slice of the UN's work in social development and governance as international banks and fund managers finance more of the lending the Bank used to provide. Does this make sense? The poorest countries don't benefit from private capital flows, so the Bank's traditional role is still valid there, by providing or guaranteeing affordable finance to fill temporary resource gaps, facilitating private-sector development to close these gaps over the medium term, and advising on general economic policy. This was recommended by governments' own commission on the future of the development banks,[106] and is why the World Bank was designed as a Bank, not as a surrogate social service agency. Its funding mechanisms are based on compulsory repayments of the loans it makes, which give it a reliable surplus each year and a high credit rating to borrow on international capital markets. But social and institutional development, and sustainable natural resource management, may not generate the foreign exchange required to repay them in the relevant timescale.[107]

The Bank counters this argument by emphasising the declining importance of traditional lending in its portfolio, and the increasing importance of grants from the IDA. But is the Bank the right home for IDA? Because it is self-financing, any tendency to insularity and inflexibility (qualities its critics say it has in abundance) is much more dangerous in the World Bank than in the UN.[108] It has changed its mind so often about development that no one can rely on its future direction.[109] Despite the rhetoric about listening to its stakeholders, the Bank lacks any democratic mechanisms for decision making or accountability since voting in its Board is dominated by rich-country representatives. And it is only just beginning to gain the expertise required to be effective outside the field of economics. Although Bank research is strong on theory, it took outsiders to make it see sense on all the most important issues, from structural adjustment to participation.[110] Wolfensohn's efforts to reform the Bank have not been matched by a coherent vision of what the institution is for, and if its purpose is to be the world's premier development agency then it should stop being a bank. The choice is clear: either move IDA to a world development fund in an energised UN and leave the World Bank to do what it does best, until it is no longer needed; or change the way the Bank is governed and financed so that it can do its new job properly.[111]

A similar process is at work inside the IMF, which is encroaching on World Bank territory as its own role is increasingly challenged by international capital markets.[112] Like the Bank, the IMF lacks proper accountability mechanisms, being governed by a secretive 24-member inner council. It wants to be the world's macro-economic policeman, but lacks the expertise to do so and the discrimination to tailor its advice to different circumstances. The Fund has only one remedy – tight fiscal and monetary policy in an open trading regime – even though excessive austerity is often counter-productive because it prolongs recession.[113] In the recent East Asian financial crisis, the IMF insisted on rapid liberalisation and the abolition of all local restrictions on foreign takeovers – an opportunity likened by journalist Mark Atkinson to the *'January sales where bargains can be picked up on the cheap'*.[114] East Asia's problems were more to do with an inefficient financial system than high inflation or poor interest-rate management. The IMF needs to focus on what it was designed to do – act as a lender of last resort and smooth out destabilising capital flows – but gear up to do it more effectively against the background of globalisation.

No institution can reform itself through death by a thousand cuts, so the continued withholding of UN funds by the US Congress is a pointless exercise in machismo (as well as a violation of the Charter). However, because the World Bank, IMF and WTO have the support of the industrialised world to do their jobs and the UN does not, there is a danger that that we will end up with an increasingly powerful set of undemocratic and unaccountable institutions which all think alike, and a UN constantly leaking authority and resources. That is unlikely to produce a satisfactory framework for global governance. Instead we should opt for a simultaneous recommitment to UN principles and a deep reappraisal of their practice as a platform for global governance in the 21st century. It is hard to resist the symbolic significance of the millennium as an opportunity for a new beginning of this kind. *'Why waste political capital on retooling an old jalopy when a new cart can be designed to fit new needs?'* asked UN insider Mahbub ul Haq before his death.[115] If global institutions do not respond to the changing world context, new structures of authority will take shape outside and around them.

CONCLUSION

The future of global governance rests on moulding an international system in which all countries can be stakeholders and whose essential fairness is recognised by all. The best way to do this is by negotiating a set of core agreements which enjoy enough support to prevent the most destructive of behaviours. Elsewhere, countries should be free to pursue their own ways of realising rights and protecting standards. The combination of the two – 'light but firm' – leads over time to the levelling up of conditions as countries become wealthier and more democratic, and to a stronger consensus on what is non-negotiable in international affairs. This is not a matter for states alone, since they do not control the forces that damage and exploit people, so governance is best exercised through a combination of public, private and social action – the *'gentle morality'* of civil society, the disciplines of the market, and the authority of governments.[116]

Countries in the developing world are more likely to buy into this system if global rules are graduated and backed up by support to encourage compliance. Industrialised countries must move in step (otherwise no one will take the risk of imposing eco-taxation or higher labour-market standards), but countries in the developing world must be allowed to opt out for a while, just as the North did in the 19th century and high performers did after 1945. That requires sacrifice and moral leadership in the North, for eventual security gains for all.[117] Despite the constant shadow of hubris, the USA remains the 'one indispensable nation' in global governance, so if it remains a reluctant multilateralist there is little prospect that a more co-operative world order will be created in the wake of the cold war, let alone that the superpowers that replace it in the next century (like China) will learn to use their position wisely.[118] Global governance does require the sacrifice of short-term national interests, especially by rich countries. However, it is unlikely that this will be voluntary – governments need permission to do things differently, and that requires constituencies for change in politics, public opinion and professional life. How are we going to build them?

Chapter 10

Building Constituencies for Change: The Rise and Fall of Third-World Charity

*'At the Cannes Film Festival, Demi Moore emerged from
a screening of "Welcome to Sarajevo" to ask "wow, did
that stuff really happen?"'*

The Observer, London[1]

'We are strangers only by the fact that we have never met'
Modern Times, BBC2[2]

Imagine three whales stranded on a beach, in desperate need of help.
As soon as the word gets around, the whales are surrounded by
crowds of people straining every sinew to keep them alive. Yet when
the crisis has passed, the same people refuse to involve themselves in
the international environmental movement. Sounds familiar? The
biologist Daniel Suzuki tells this story to explain how our brains are
insufficiently developed to trigger action in response to distant events,
or threats that are diffuse. Like the whales, *'we learn to love humanity not in general, but through its particular expressions,'* says the
communitarian writer Michael Sandel.[3] Life is lived through the
smaller solidarities of friends and family, neighbours and colleagues –
not according to the suffering of strangers. If children in our own
community were being butchered we would intervene, but when it
happens in Algeria or Rwanda we wring our hands, and then forget.
It's tragic of course, but what can we do? Sometimes the distance is
so great that brutality simply goes unnoticed, like Demi Moore's
incredulous reaction to events in Bosnia. Unless there is a menace we
can see and feel, we don't react, but most of us will never live next

door to Chernobyl or Three Mile Island. Even when people do feel insecure, they are just as likely to retreat into isolationism as co-operate with others in finding solutions. The unholy alliance between right-wing 'economic nationalists' like Pat Buchanan in the USA and 'new protectionists' on the left of politics does touch a raw nerve among voters frightened by globalisation, despite the bogus nature of most of their arguments. Physical and psychological distance, ignorance and media manipulation, and the pressing priority of our own short-term problems, make international co-operation an unlikely option in all but the most pressing of circumstances.

This obviously creates a problem for the agenda laid out in previous chapters, since even if the case for change is convincing, we lack the constituencies required to push it through – to stiffen the hand of limp-wristed foreign secretaries, organise a quantum leap in ethical consumption, underpin the activities of an international polity, mobilise taxpayers to contribute to a world development fund, or even push for reforms in foreign aid. Like all social causes, slavery was eradicated because it became ethically and politically impossible to sustain, but how do we achieve the same priority for an end to poverty and violence in the world?[4] We may dream of global community but we don't live in one, so by themselves the moral claims of Africans or Asians have little purchase over our decisions.[5] The long-term costs of not co-operating to tackle global problems may be clear in theory, but the short-term benefits of selfish behaviour are much more tangible. Is there a route out of this impasse? One way forward is to nurture new solidarities between people who are physically separate but increasingly interconnected in other aspects of their lives, both moral and prudential. A sense of the underlying unity of things is characteristic of spiritual experience, but in the material world it is also true that we are *strangers only by the fact that we have never met*. Our welfare is affected by events from Mexico to Thailand, decisions taken in distant capitals, and threats from enemies we may never see. An exodus of refugees from global trouble spots, the knock-on effect of an environmental disaster, and the need to help others if we want their help when our turn comes – all these things make international co-operation the increasingly rational choice. Conflicts and differences do not disappear in this scenario, but underneath them we share a common interest in managing the costs and benefits of global change. My development is part of yours, and yours is part of mine, but neither is safe unless we recognise and build on this reality. It's just that we don't see it this way.

Persuading people to see things differently cannot be done with the tired clichés of the foreign-aid lobby. As we have seen, aid is as much a problem as a solution, and will continue to decline in importance as other forms of co-operation grow up around global regimes. We need a more engaging story with new messages, positive images, and concrete avenues for action now. And we need a much greater effort to communicate it across business, government and civil society. Who will lead it? The organisations with the most experience and public trust are international NGOs like Oxfam and CARE, but are they up to the job? A focus on constituency building would bring few of the financial rewards that come with foreign aid, but would still require major changes in the way these organisations work. That's why building support for international co-operation is so bound up with the rise and fall of Third-World charity and its replacement by new ways of working designed to meet the challenges of the 21st century.

THE IMPORTANCE OF ETHICS

The first requirement for a successful campaign is a cause that is seen to be right. However, the ethics of international development are never straightforward, since there are different views about what development is and ought to be, and how best to foster it in practice. Philosophers of development accept that all definitions have an ethical foundation, but disagree on what it is.[6] Some favour human rights, and others prefer income, wealth, and basic needs (distributed in such a way as to maximise the situation of the least well-off).[7] Some talk of 'capabilities and entitlements' (everyone should have the minimum they need to function effectively), while others use autonomy, or 'negative liberty' (equal freedom from government interference or the denial of choice by other means). And there are still utilitarians who believe in the greatest good for the greatest number. 'Universalists' (like utilitarians) argue that development goals are valid for all societies; 'relativists' (especially the post-modern variety) see this as a cover for cultural imperialism, there being no such thing as a universal value system. For our purposes, these arguments are less important than the underlying question of how ends and means are decided, which itself is an ethical issue. The gap between different systems of ethics can be bridged if we agree that each society should have the freedom to make choices about its own development, on two conditions: first, that every individual can share equally in that process; and second, that the choices that result should not come at the expense of the same conditions for people in other countries.[8] Although this approach still leaves questions unanswered, it resolves the apparent incompatibility between a universal framework of minimum standards and a system rooted in respect for diversity.

We don't need a philosophy textbook to see that this approach is more likely to be acceptable across different cultures. After all, it is only a reworking of the 'Golden Rule' that is common to all traditions – '*do as you would be done by*', from Christianity to Confucius.[9] The Golden Rule emphasises two things that are especially important to the ethical case for international co-operation. The first is reciprocity, the key to agreements that are seen to be fair. The second is a conviction that human development is an end in itself, not just a means to growth, so no one should be used as an instrument by others.[10] Both these qualities echo a sense of basic justice, which is the lifeblood of trust and the wellspring of co-operation. It is hard to imagine a better *leitmotif* than this: the right to one's own journey, and the obligation to support others on theirs. It's as simple, and as difficult, as that.

THE PERSONAL AND THE POLITICAL

Ethical arguments are ineffective unless they are connected to a political constituency for change. Constituency building is not a matter of briefing a few politicians or distributing an education pack to schools on how children live in Africa, since making co-operation work in the ways I have described implies deep-rooted changes right across society in order to persuade governments, businesses and individuals to make short-term sacrifices for long-term gains, and engage actively in global regimes. International co-operation is not just a matter of relations between countries; it also concerns the costs and benefits that arise within societies when countries deal with each other in different ways.[11] It makes no sense to expect people to be global citizens when they feel disenfranchised in their own polity, nor rein in their living standards when they have pressing economic problems of their own. It is difficult to be co-operative on a 60-hour week, surrounded by fears of unemployment and an increasingly fragile family life.[12] These problems must also be addressed, and in a global economy the best way to do so is through international co-operation. Broadcasting this fact (and compensating people who lose out as a result of adjustments to global change) is essential if we expect ordinary citizens to act as 'new internationalists'.[13]

Ultimately, constituency building requires deep-rooted changes in personal behaviour. As the experience of Scandinavian countries shows, attitudes toward helping abroad are intimately related to attitudes toward helping at home. Progressive social policies and a culture of concern are closely associated with support for international co-operation; conversely, high levels of domestic inequality correlate with low levels of foreign aid.[14] In 1991, citizens of the USA spent more on cleaning-products for their homes than on federal contributions to education, training and employment, so it is no surprise that they also spent three times more on cigarettes than foreign aid.[15] There won't be a constituency for international co-operation unless there is a commitment to co-operative living generally, for why should people co-operate with distant strangers if they do not do so with their neighbours? After all, global regimes impose clear limits to autonomy and consumption. This presents us with a dilemma, since capitalism tends to encourage the opposite of these attitudes – competition, insularity, and selfish individualism;[16] the triumph of the sensate (short-term material gratification) over the ideational (long-term moral values).[17] The negative effects of capitalism are balanced to some degree by the possibilities affluence creates, and there is no guarantee that different attitudes would emerge under other systems since the problem lies in human consciousness rather than economic organisation.[18] However, as I showed in Chapter 8, it is possible to alter economic structures in ways which both feed from and support the changes we are looking for in values and behaviour, while at the same time achieving a universal level of material security that makes a radical change of human heart more likely.[19] Instead of wishing it were otherwise, we should focus on the opportunities globalisation presents to advance a more co-operative agenda.

For that to happen, we need vision and leadership in politics. The tragedy is that this has been so lacking in the major powers since the the end of the cold war. Opposition to international taxation comes less from the public (who might not mind paying a few pounds extra for their air tickets or dedicating a similar amount to something useful like a world development fund) than from politicians who refuse to cede sovereignty over revenue. Nevertheless, in democracies the bottom line is always a public constituency willing to make new issues matter in the political process. Domestic politics are always vulnerable to chronic short-termism, restricting government strategy to four- or five-year electoral cycles and making long-term vision a risky commodity, unless there is consistent backing from voters. The problem is that, although successive opinion polls reveal a steady level of public support for foreign aid and humanitarian relief, this has never been translated into meaningful political pressure nor extended to embrace a broader international agenda.[20] As a result, the citizens of the rich world are woefully unprepared for a co-operative future.

MESSAGES AND METHODS: BREAKING THE MOULD

In addressing this situation, the first priority is to break the mould of stereotypes that do so much to erode support for genuine co-operation. Doing that requires a 'new story' that engages its listeners on grounds of self-interest as well as ethics. These two things always go together: it is not possible to build a coalition on ethics alone, but without a moral centre it is unlikely that self-sacrifice will be part of the political agenda. The moral case for helping others is based on a simple set of assumptions laid out by the philosopher Peter Singer: *'if it is in our power to prevent something bad from happening without sacrificing anything of comparable moral significance, we ought to do it'*.[21] Since starvation and genocide are undoubtedly bad, and there is much we can do to address them without any sacrifice at all, then the moral imperative for doing so is clear. In less extreme situations, this argument is muddied by the fact that international co-operation (especially foreign aid) does not always produce the desired results. Nevertheless, it is clear that gross inequality and oppression are morally unacceptable even if we fall short in our attempts to remove them. Nor can it be ethical for one group of people to be denied the same chances in life as others because they happen to be born in a place with fewer natural resources, a longer history of exploitation, or more of the accidents of geography.[22] If others do not have the minimum required to sustain themselves, then we in the rich world have a moral obligation to set aside some of our resources to help them reach that level. That applies to future generations too.[23] No one would willingly allow children to be denied the same opportunities as their parents, but this is what is happening by default as the earth's resources are depleted. There is a basic unfairness about this which is easily grasped, and that – especially if it is focused on our own children – is a powerful message for constituency building. In communications, a connection with the heart is just as important as with the head. *'The Marshall Plan was never focus-grouped'* – it worked by touching a hidden chord in the public imagination.[24] The world does what it feels, not just what it thinks.

It would, as the veteran economist Sir Hans Singer once remarked, be a *'happy coincidence'* if by following our self-interest we could also achieve what is best for the communities we live in, both near and far.[25] This was Adam Smith's argument in *The Wealth of Nations* (1776) but at the international level the 'invisible hand' is less influential than the conscious manipulations of the powerful. It is certainly possible to bring self-interest and community interest together, if enough people recognise that co-operation is to everyone's long-term benefit; in other words, that we are part of a unity that stands or falls according to the welfare of the whole. For some it is obvious that we are already one in the spiritual sense: *'the delusion that we are separate,'* said Albert Einstein, *'is a kind of prison for us, restricting our affection for a few persons who are nearest.'*[26] Escaping from this prison requires a redefinition of human solidarity on the basis of a new affinity of interests.[27] *'We are not simply people set in isolation from each other, but members of the same community, the same human race,'* said British Prime Minister Tony Blair in 1997.[28] However, building a community means more than just belonging; it requires an active process of sacrifice and working together – a new vision of citizenship in which rights and responsibilities at different levels of the global system are integrated into a single framework, made real through the practice of ethical consumption, international political action, and joint planning for sustainable development. Without these practical expressions, 'global citizenship' is a meaningless concept since it involves no concrete obligations.[29] In any case, our duties to communities in other countries are only additional to the obligations we owe to our own.[30]

For some in the West these are sufficient arguments in themselves, but most people need more immediate evidence that co-operation is 'good for business', or at least is compatible with a good material life. That means convincing voters that what they want can only partially be met within existing structures of international relations.[31] The more real these connections – in global communications, international flows of capital and jobs, and threats from pollution abroad – the easier it is to argue the case for change. When 'your problem' and 'my problem' are recognised as 'our problems', new solutions are possible.[32] That is why it is vital to improve the quality of public debate about globalisation, environmental change and the benefits of a co-operative response. At the Kyoto Conference on Climate Change, the Australian government produced evidence that 90,000 jobs would be lost at home as a result of emission controls, but all their evidence came from research funded by the industries who would lose out if controls were introduced.[33] Contrary to the fears of many in the North, there is no evidence that jobs are being lost overall as a result of global regulation or competition from exports from the developing world. Nor is domestic protection a cost-effective way of dealing with unemployment. It costs over US$40,000 each year to protect one job in the US textile industry, far more than average annual earnings in the same sector.[34] Why not use these resources to compensate, support and retrain those affected by global industrial restructuring? That would simultaneously increase their chances of finding work in higher-wage jobs and help to maintain their belief in the value of global co-operation. European farmers (the main sticking point to reform of the CAP), and workers in low value-added manufacturing industry, would be obvious candidates for this sort of help. As ex-US Labour Secretary Robert Reich has said, the best way to build a constituency for internationalism is to *'enhance the capacities of one's own citizens while at the same time working with other nations to ensure that these improvements do not come at their expense'*.[35] At a deeper level it can be argued that caring for each other is part of our own welfare, it being more fulfilling to live such a life than continue in servitude to selfishness and shopping.[36] An increasing number of people in the industrialised world are recognising the benefits of working less and playing more, so that they are less rich in financial terms but less poor in terms of time spent with family and friends. Most of us know that our true self is compassionate and loving, but feel we must disguise it in the street-fighting of everyday life. On rare occasions we allow the mask to fall, but why not make this experience the norm, once our basic needs are met? After all, we might actually enjoy it.

The rewards for competitive behaviour are short-term in nature, whereas the benefits of being a good global citizen are visible over generations, so we need more imaginative ways of bringing the two together. This is more difficult with international development than with themes people can relate to in their daily lives (like the environment or discrimination at home). Part of the problem is that 'development' is too abstract and aid is too dull. It is also quite complicated, given the fact that the record of aid is so patchy in practice. 'Global housekeeping', a war on global poverty, and a fair deal for everyone – all these might be marketable to a sceptical audience. The most important thing is to move away from an attitude that 'the problems are over there' and embrace an inclusive message that co-operation matters both at home and abroad, as the environmental movement has done. It is no coincidence that the German parliament has responded consistently to pressure from the green movement, but until the election of a new government in 1998 ignored the development lobby on developing-world debt; nor that membership of environmental and human-rights groups continues to rise as support for development charities stagnates, especially among the young. In the UK, Greenpeace increased its membership from 80,000 in 1987 to 420,000 in 1995, and Amnesty International from 39,000 in 1987 to 109,000 seven years later.[37] The story is the same in the USA, but the only part of the development sector that is growing is child sponsorship, and that, as we shall see, has little to do with constituency-building at all.[38]

However this new vision is expressed, it must be connected to practical actions that people can take to put it into practice. They must feel, not just that the cause is important, but that there is something they can do about it in the short term. *'Once society accepted the broad environmental critique,'* says Chris Rose (communications director at Greenpeace-UK), *'people asked "So what, what can we do?", and we said, "Give us more money and we'll think about it."'* – just like charities such as Oxfam or Save the Children Fund.[39] Progress on environmental issues depended on practical innovations like 'green refrigerators' to protect the ozone layer, bottle banks for recycling, dolphin-free tuna in the supermarket and industrial clean-up to reduce acid rain.[40] These did not solve the problem in themselves, but they provided symbols that encouraged people to move to the next step in the campaign. It is much more difficult to find equivalents for global poverty, but as the focus is broadened to co-operation at least it is easier. That's where ethical consumption and action on human rights can be useful, building support for the international dimensions of these issues from a solid foundation in local practice. If I perceive an advantage in making my own neighbourhood safer, my workplace fairer, and my shopping more responsive to moral concerns, I am more likely to extend this logic to other people in other countries. Opportunities for action move the discussion beyond a succession of negatives (the starving-baby syndrome), to the positive affirmation of co-operative lifestyles.[41]

Traditional arguments about foreign aid have produced a constituency that may be supportive in principle, but is largely ill-informed and inactive in practice. In Australia only five per cent of respondents polled in 1997 thought that international factors were important in causing poverty in the developing world; two-thirds felt that government aid did not help the poor, and almost 50 per cent said the same about NGOs.[42] In Britain, less than 40 per cent of those polled in 1997 had even a vague idea of how much aid the government actually provided.[43] Contrast that with the environment, which voters in 1996 put as one of their top three electoral issues.[44] What is needed is a systematic process of *'coming to public judgement'*, as Daniel Yankelovic, the guru of public-opinion formation in the USA, puts it.[45] That means a continuous effort to deepen understanding and commitment through a deliberate series of stages. At present, public opinion in most industrialised countries is stuck in the middle stage of 'resistance', somewhere between 'awareness' and 'resolution'. The missing link is 'judgement', the process of working through complex issues instead of responding to simplistic messages or the hard sell of charity fund-raising. Shock tactics are less useful than guidance on how everything fits together in what to most people is a mystifying debate: jobs at home and jobs abroad, industry in one country and pollution in another, distant killing fields and one's own government's responsibility.

This is true for both adults and children, who are the key target group if we want to build a constituency to confront the challenges of the 21st century. Internationalism, global citizenship, and the ethics and practice of co-operation should be central components of every national curriculum; education means more than acquiring the skills required to compete in the global marketplace.[46] We need a huge increase in energy and resources in this area, moving far beyond the traditional development themes used by charities to educate children about the developing world. However, this comes at a time when most NGOs are cutting their education budgets, and government support is only just beginning to resurface after the insularity of the Thatcher–Reagan years.[47] In 1993, only one quarter of one per cent of the total income of the 25 largest development NGOs in the USA was spent on development education.[48] By contrast, countries that spend properly on international education have already secured a stronger base of public support for international co-operation: the Dutch government spent more than US$17 million in 1997 and Sweden US$15 million, compared to US$3.9 million in the USA and US$1.2 million in Japan for much bigger populations.[49] We should double spending over a five-year period in order to kick-start a new phase of education for international co-operation, and require any development charity that receives public aid funds to earmark 25 per cent of its voluntary income for constituency-building activities. That, combined with legal restrictions and penalties on dishonest, offensive or misleading advertising, would make charities sit up and take notice of their responsibilities.[50]

It is much easier to be a cog in a destructive wheel if you are insulated from the consequences by physical or psychological distance. That's why community or local authority linking schemes, student exchanges, volunteering, and international community service are so important. I well remember the impact of visits by Oxfam shop volunteers to their 'partners' in Zambia when I worked there in the 1980s. Many arrived with a mixture of ignorance and subtle prejudice, but that soon dissolved when they made a direct connection with villagers who, despite all the surface differences, were just the same as they were underneath. Most returned to the UK full of enthusiasm for the tasks ahead, *'arriving where they started, but knowing the place for the first time'*, in T S Eliot's words.[51] In Australia, Community Aid Abroad is training hundreds of activists with experience in the developing world to work as constituency builders in their own communities. Oxfam and other NGOs have built a network of local campaigners dedicated to mobilising support for international issues. And new organisations like Community Networks International are supporting activists in the UK and the developing world to exchange ideas on homelessness, community action and local economic development across very different contexts.[52]

Business and trade unions, domestic charities and international campaigners rarely see themselves as part of a global movement that links international development with domestic concerns. In the UK, the first stirrings of such a movement were felt in the general election campaign of 1996, when a broad coalition of development, environment and other groups came together to form 'Real World'. The aim of this coalition was to inject a common agenda of green and social issues into the policy proposals of all the major parties, but it was largely ignored by the media and dismissed by politicians (though behind the scenes many of its proposals chimed with official thinking, especially in the 'new' Labour party).[53] This was partly due to the myopia of mainstream politics, but there were also internal weaknesses, principally the fractious nature of much of the alliance (a bit like 'herding cats', as one member put it), and the refusal of its members to involve their two million supporters. This was an indictment of the failure of development NGOs to mobilise their supporters as a political force, as opposed to a mailing list of donors. Most development NGOs in the UK and the USA are only weakly connected to other civil society groups, many of whom have more genuine international partnerships despite (or perhaps because of) the fact that they are not directly involved in providing aid to groups in the developing world.[54] We saw in Chapter 9 how difficult it is to forge North-South alliances without falling prey to old patterns of domination, but outside the world of foreign aid this is much easier. Friends of the Earth already has more member organisations in poor countries than rich ones, and a new wave of global movements is taking shape around trade and investment issues without the asymmetries of power and voice that have affected NGO networks in the past.[55] These experiments are laying the foundations for an eventual 'red-green alliance' to campaign worldwide for equity and justice.[56] It is important not to be carried away by rhetoric, but this may take less time than we think: campaigns against landmines and 'sex tourism' have succeeded in less than ten years. Where the issues are clear and powerful, connected to practical solutions, and linked into government and business, resolution can come more quickly than for more contentious causes like the women's or environmental movements.[57]

THE ROLE OF CIVIL SOCIETY

Governments and businesses are crucial players in constituency building, but they are unlikely to be the bearers of radical change in the absence of large-scale support from voters and consumers, which isn't yet in place – a severe case of the chicken and the egg. Business has a natural interest in global co-operation since it needs long-term security and expanding markets to protect its profits, but this is only just beginning to emerge in any coherent way. Universities, think-tanks and the media are also potential allies, but thus far have shown little inclination to advance an internationalist agenda. In any case, academia is too detached and most of the media too commercialised to be leaders of public opinion. So other organisations in civil society must take on this role, forging alliances to spearhead change in markets, politics, and public attitudes. The problem is that few of the organisations that have a natural constituency in the international arena are able or willing to do this at present. Even giants like CARE and World Vision show little interest in investing enough of their time and resources to have much chance of success. Spending on development education is down in both the UK and the USA, volunteering and other forms of public involvement are declining, and the focus of engagement is fixated on foreign aid.[58] Why is this?

When charities like these were established (usually in the kitchen of someone's house or, like Oxfam, in the cramped quarters of an old church), they had an understandably straightforward view of the world: projects overseas were the motor of development, financial transfers were the best means of support, and people in the rich world were seen as contributors of funds. As time went by, all three assumptions were challenged by the lessons of experience, and a changing global context. Project successes (and there were fewer than expected) achieved little without wider changes in systems and structures; money was found to be the least important factor in promoting change; and NGOs wanted their supporters to be activists at home, where many of the real problems lay.[59] As a result of this growing mismatch, NGOs began to experience more and more confusion about their roles and identity, and by the mid-1990s this had produced a constant stream of rethinking and reorganising for the future. Some NGOs are moving further into the global service-providing marketplace, while others see themselves as part of international social movements. And that is not counting those that end up managing a muddle in the middle, desperately trying to be innovative in tackling fundamental problems while holding on to traditional ways of raising and spending their money. This is an attractive strategy for those who don't want to rock the boat too much, but is unlikely to remain viable beyond the next 10 or 20 years. We can't fudge our way into the 21st century.

Even the most entrenched of organisations must respond to changes in the external environment (otherwise they go out of business), and the context for international development NGOs is changing dramatically. Globalisation makes traditional North-South, donor-recipient relationships increasingly redundant. The decline of foreign aid and its replacement by a wider agenda of global co-operation opens up new avenues for influence, but raises question marks about existing roles. More aid contracts are being managed by commercial firms and consultancy companies, and official donor agencies are looking to an increasingly confident NGO sector in the developing world to deliver their aid programmes on the ground. If organisations like CARE don't add much value to the aid relationship, why pay their overheads? Better to give the money direct to the Grameen Bank, for example. Even without these external changes, international NGOs would be asking themselves some serious questions. Many are children of the post-1945 period, so by now are well into their inevitable mid-life crisis. Designed to deliver relief from rich to poor (or from poor people in rich countries to rich people in poor countries, to use a well-worn jibe), they are ill-suited to the new roles that have appeared over the horizon – like mobilising ethical consumers or taking part in new forms of global governance.

These pressures are real, but they also provide a route out of the anxieties of the present: a rationale which can help NGOs to move away from unequal relationships based on money, to genuine partnerships based on complementary roles and responsibilities; a chance to engage with the forces that really effect change instead of being marginalised as *'ladles in the global soup kitchen'*;[60] and an energising mission instead of an increasingly fractious foreign aid lobby. If they are to grasp these opportunities, NGOs must transform themselves into vehicles for international co-operation and accept their share of the responsibility to build the constituencies co-operation requires. They must also be good civic actors themselves, since otherwise they won't be able to encourage co-operation in others; nor will they be legitimate players in an emerging international civil society. This poses major organisational questions for development NGOs since constituency building is not primarily about raising money, but the understanding and commitment to be an agent of change in and from one's own society. It means creating an 'agenda for concern' using diffuse channels over the long term, whereas NGOs focus on narrow policy lobbying within the international aid system, usually reacting to issues of current but passing importance. In any case, the rapid and unpredictable nature of change in the modern world (and the fact we have few convincing answers) makes traditional campaigning less relevant than public engagement – working with people to find solutions, not just telling them what they should believe. None of this is possible unless NGOs agree to work together, yet rising competition for money and profile sets them apart in an increasingly aggressive charity marketplace.

NGOs are reacting to these dilemmas in one of two ways. The first is to market the NGO 'brand' across the world in order to capture a larger slice of the foreign-aid cake, both public and private. The brand may be franchised out to local organisations in countries in the developing world (the equivalent of McDonald's in Bombay or Bogota), or the international body can implement programmes in the field directly. Contracts are won or lost on commercial terms, mostly for service provision in humanitarian relief, small-scale credit, health and education projects. Funds are raised wherever it is cost-effective, so if there is money to be made in India or Brazil (even at the cost of support for local NGOs) that becomes the goal. In this model, links with business are used to extract corporate donations, and increasingly the charity becomes a business itself, reshaping decisions around a bottom line of market share. The priority is to build support for one's own organisation, not the cause. There is little room for constituency building since this is a slow and expensive business with little guarantee of a payback in financial terms – it is considered an overhead rather than a core programme activity. The emphasis is on project work in the developing world as the answer to global poverty, and size and numbers as indicators of success. The fact that this makes little difference to the structural problems which cause violence and exclusion is not a very important consideration if the aim is to pump as much money through the system as possible. Domestic responsibilities in the industrialised world are ignored, or dealt with cosmetically with a little lobbying on debt and a stab at development education. And if pictures of starving babies raise more cash, don't worry too much about the consequences of using them or the ethical questions involved. '*Choose a child. Inquire at desk,*' says Save the Children in the USA.[61] '*Your sponsorship can save them,*' trumpets Plan-International.[62] The message is clear: the problems lie 'over there', and the solutions are in your pocket – it is your five pounds that will 'make the difference'.

Most people in these organisations are uncomfortable with the implications of this approach. International co-operation implies relationships between equals, and the acceptance of responsibility to put one's own house in order. By contrast, traditional fund-raising images elicit sympathy, but not solidarity.[63] Under the guise of bringing people closer together, they force them further apart, increasing the psychological distance between giver and receiver, rich and poor, and more and less powerful. It is easier to remain passive in the face of injustice when we treat people as objects for pity, rather than as subjects of a struggle in which we are also implicated. NGOs claim that child sponsorship encourages an understanding of the deeper issues involved, but there is no evidence to support their case.[64] Paternalistic attitudes spell disaster for co-operation because they reinforce the conviction of separateness that underlies our failure to take responsibility. '*Caught in the models of the limited self, we end up by diminishing one another. The more you think of yourself as a philanthropist, the more someone else feels compelled to be a supplicant*',[65] and the less inclination we both have to co-operate together as equals.

The second response to global trends accepts that the future of charities like Oxfam lies largely in their role as change agents in their own countries, and in working from them as members of an international social movement. In this scenario, NGOs become equal members of networks spanning the globe, coalescing around common goals and values but working synergistically to achieve and advance them. This is the lesson to be learned from the environmental and women's movements, which have been much more successful in creating change than any development agency. They have achieved all the things that development NGOs have not: a focus on attitudes, not projects; a spirit of collaboration; powerful connections from their supporters out into business, government and other areas of civic life; and a genuine global reach, not a cancerous division between donors and recipients. As a result, they have made their issues matter in the political process, and changed all our lives for the better. By contrast, international development remains a boring backwater dominated by a narrow professional elite.

In this approach, NGOs emphasise the impact they can make by effecting change in larger structures, such as markets, politics and the media. Constituency building is a natural component of this model, since all movements need strong domestic roots that can activate a concerned citizenry to work for change in a wide range of settings. Charity shops become centres for civic action and training as well as fund raisers; links with business are used to forge an agenda for economic transformation, not just as a cash cow; much more investment goes into learning and research as the foundation for influence; and domestic development work is pursued along the same principles as programmes overseas, as Save the Children has done for 50 years and as Oxfam decided to do on a small scale in 1995. This raised predictable outrage in the tabloid press ('Scotland joins the Third World'), but a recognition that poverty and discrimination exist in Western society is crucial to internationalism. Grassroots projects, and financial support to 'partners' overseas, are not abandoned in this approach. If there is a problem with village food security, it would be odd to start by lobbying Western supermarket chains. The real question is who does what best, and how different parts of the problem are addressed by different parts of the movement in a co-ordinated fashion. In that respect the answers are clear: the role of outsiders is always to support local capacities to innovate and make connections. Sometimes there is a role for special expertise that local organisations do not have, or for an operational response by foreign NGOs where local structures have been destroyed (in some humanitarian emergencies, for example), but these occasions are declining, even in Africa, the last refuge of white men in shorts.

The differences between these two approaches have been deliberately exaggerated in order to make the point that choices do exist for NGOs in the North, each of which carries a different set of implications. The questions they raise, like the ethics of fund raising and the balance of spending between activities at home and overseas, have been the subject of heated debate among charities for decades – old chestnuts that are roasted at Oxfam's Christmas party every year.[66] But the changing global context provides an opportunity to deal with them properly instead of burying the issues in the closet and hoping they will go away. The first approach promises continued organisational growth but with little impact, and only while the supply of foreign aid lasts and NGOs remain competitive against alternative providers. The second promises more impact but little growth, since constituency building is less attractive to donors and the focus turns to building the capacities of others, not the organisation itself. This poses an acute dilemma for NGO staff and trustees, none of whom wants to be first to see their organisation shrink, cede control over governance to more democratic structures, or risk the wrath of charity regulators in becoming more active, socially and politically. Nevertheless, the decisions they make over the next ten years on these questions will determine whether development NGOs play a central role in shaping the 21st century, or linger in the memory only as a footnote to the history of the post-war world. Are they agents of foreign aid or vehicles for international co-operation? As supporters of charities like these, this is a question as much for you and me as for the organisations themselves. We are unlikely to agree on the best way for NGOs to tackle global poverty, but we can all press for more transparency on how these decisions are made. Do you really know where your money goes? Are you satisfied that the organisation is telling the truth about the impact of its work? Do you honestly believe that child sponsorship will make the difference? You wouldn't settle for second best on questions like these from your political representatives or the companies you buy from, so don't do it with the charities you support. By all means give your hard-earned cash to Oxfam or World Vision, but not as a substitute for action in your own life or your obligations as a future global citizen.

CONCLUSION

Anyone who spends time drumming up support for unpopular causes knows how difficult it is to achieve real progress in public attitudes. Since international co-operation is one of the least popular of causes (outside the occasional world of the collecting tin), its proponents must think that they are fighting a losing battle on a full-time basis, especially against the background of globalising capitalism and the material values it inspires. But a major part of this problem, I have argued, lies in the messages we have used to communicate the case and the methods and techniques employed. With courage and imagination, these things can be put right, but that requires important changes in the institutions that dominate the field: moving from donors and recipients to relations between equals; from charity to co-operation, negatives to positives, and the abstract to the concrete. The 'new story' we need to tell is part moral, part spiritual, and mostly prudential – persuading people in all walks of life that their future, and the well-being of their children, is best provided for in a world that co-operates to manage global problems and maximise the opportunities of an integrated economy. The historian Arnold Toynbee once said that *'apathy can only be overcome by enthusiasm, and enthusiasm can only be aroused by two things: an ideal which takes the imagination by storm, and an intelligible plan for carrying that ideal into practice'*.[67] Foreign aid and Third-World charity provide neither of these things, but the vision of a co-operative world can do so, starting with ourselves, and building outwards to embrace the whole of humanity. True freedom is attainable only through relations with others, since in an interconnected world I can never be safe until you are secure; nor can one person be whole unless others are fulfilled. That is only possible in a co-operative world. Is that the kind of world we want to live in and bequeath to those we love? If so, our responsibilities are clear.

Chapter 11

The Getting of Wisdom: Institutional Reform and Personal Revolution

'Open up, loosen up, listen up, speak up, and don't work weekends on anything you don't enjoy'

Herman Daly, ex-World Bank economist[1]

'When you get it right, it's better than sex'

Anonymous fieldworker, Zambia[2]

After toiling away in the nether regions of an international bureaucracy for 20 years, most of us would probably echo Herman Daly's advice in his farewell speech to the World Bank: for goodness sake 'loosen up'. The organisation would be much more effective as a result, and its employees would be happier, though maybe not so happy as the fieldworker in Zambia who thought his work was *'better than sex'* – a reference to the high that comes from helping people escape from any form of oppression. This feeling is the opposite of the paternalism that infects so much in international development. It springs, not from a sense of responsibility for the achievements of others, but from participating in a process which liberates everyone involved. This is real co-operation, but in a world of unequal power and resources it demands continuous self-development on the part of those who want to help. There is no other way of gaining the inner security we need to let go of predetermined outcomes, nor the self-knowledge to identify and deal with the interests and agendas that mark out all human relationships.

Building a political constituency for international co-operation along the lines sketched out in Chapter 10 is an essential task for the longer term. In the meantime, improving the performance of organisations already involved in the field requires a *professional* constituency for reform. All development workers have room to manoeuvre, but using it requires imagination, a willingness to take risks, and the courage to *'speak truth to power'*, in the words of the American academic, Aaron Wildavsky.[3] Effective institutions grow from developed individuals, just as institutional cultures and incentives shape the skills and attitudes of their staff. The intertwining of the personal, the institutional, and the political is as obvious as it is neglected, perhaps because professionals are embarrassed by talk of the inner dimension, or discomforted by the thought that operational problems require change inside themselves. In the international context, where the focus is always on the development of others, it is probably the most important lesson we have to learn. At the deepest level, we help by what we are, not what we know or even what we do.[4]

In this Chapter I look at the qualities required to help others effectively, and at how they can be fostered among NGOs, government aid agencies, and multilateral organisations like the UN. The rhetoric of these organisations already speaks volumes about the need for change, expressed in the current vogue for participation, partnership, and the primacy of local ownership over decisions. In most cases the reality lags far behind, and not just in huge bureaucracies like the World Bank. NGOs face similar questions, albeit on a smaller scale. Are they prepared to put their own house in order, and if so, what might that involve? The answer is to nurture wisdom. This may seem a strange word to use, especially in the institutional context, but the mixture of knowledge and discrimination wisdom embodies makes it the perfect description of what needs to be developed: institutions that combine technical efficiency with attitudes of service; a new generation of 'reflective practitioners' schooled in the skills of thinking as well as doing; and a better all-round balance between expertise, and the humility to use it properly. The author of *Small is Beautiful*, E F Schumacher, once said that *'we are much too clever to survive without wisdom'*.[5] He wasn't talking about the arrogance of international development agencies or the hubris of the jet-setting consultant, but his words ring true in this context too. Institutional reform depends on personal revolution, personal revolution depends on institutional reform, and both depend on 'the getting of wisdom'.[6]

Development work needs people and institutions that listen, learn, innovate and make connections. These characteristics are essential to success because development is complex and dynamic, involving constant dialogue and bargaining against a shifting background of politics, culture and economic interests. Those who want to be useful in this process must be sensitive to real-world conditions of uncertainty, diversity, local control and extended timescales, and comfortable in dealing with them. Development professionals are *part* of the ongoing negotiations of development, so the quality of their interventions is an important influence over success. It is never possible to evaluate the impact of a development project without asking questions about the agencies involved, all the way down the line to their headquarters in Brussels or New York.[7] Unfortunately, the answers often show that they are ill-equipped and ill at ease. At the minimum, those who want to elicit co-operation must be seen to practise what they preach. Otherwise they can influence events only through coercion, which is not a strategy for sustainable change. The problem is that many have been found wanting in this respect, lecturing others on 'good governance' but being secretive and unaccountable themselves. Closing the gap between rhetoric and reality requires action in three areas: learning, accountability, and incentives.

INSTITUTIONAL REFORM

Learning

The underlying problem in most institutions is a view of the world fundamentally at odds with realities on the ground. Development is messy and conflict ridden, but bureaucrats thrive on prediction and control. In a world that seems evermore unstable, development agencies seek security in its mirror image, often going to ridiculous lengths to quantify, codify and plan what is going to happen in the field.[8] It never does, of course, since we don't even know what will happen in the morning, but reports and results can always be massaged to satisfy the donors. It's like walking through a maze whose walls rearrange themselves with each step you take.[9] Problems are caused by a multitude of factors that change as they interact with each other; communities are fractured by different interests and perceptions; and unintended consequences are often the most influential of all. In this context, learning is the key to results.

As successive management gurus tell us, organisational learning is vital to performance.[10] Learning is essential to understand what works best in different circumstances, to anticipate and prepare for threats and opportunities, and to keep the organisation alive to innovation and challenge. Because development is dynamic, connections must be made continuously between learning and decision making throughout the organisation.[11] Even if we know what produced good results in one situation, we can't assume the same course of action would do so elsewhere. Knowledge advances through the observation of unexpected phenomena as well as reflection on what is already familiar.[12] So building the capacity to learn is much more important than accumulating information. The problem is that learning implies honesty and change, and it is difficult to admit to failure in public when fund raising is based on the image of success. Many organisations feel that learning is too expensive, until they have to pay for their mistakes.

The first step is to recognise the difference between information (the raw material), knowledge (information that is systematically analysed), and wisdom (the application of knowledge to practical problem solving). Development agencies usually spend too much time on the first of these things and not enough on the last, and that is partly because they are caught in the separation of thinking from doing that is the legacy of the Western academic tradition. In this tradition, abstract ideas are elevated and muddling through is suspect: 'it's all very well in practice,' as someone once said of the newly-opened bridge across Dublin's River Liffey, 'but how does it work in theory?'[13] Learning *requires* action because many of the mechanisms responsible for poverty are invisible until they are activated by attempts at change. Uniting action and understanding in this way requires concrete incentives to connect the two – like more resources for programmes that demonstrate effective learning, staff appraisal systems that value time spent in this way, and accountability to ensure that space for learning doesn't mean the freedom to repeat mistakes. Oxfam-UK, for example, has an innovative 'learning fund' to which any member of staff can apply.[14] Learning means a search for the truth, not a confirmation of what the organisation wants to hear, so relationships with universities, think-tanks and other knowledge brokers are vital to provide a source of independent challenge.[15] The problem is that researchers and practitioners find it difficult to work together. Their worlds are ruled by mutual suspicion, and even where they are not, they lack the practical tools required.[16] This is where the 'bridging' role of NGOs can be crucial.[17]

We know from experience that bureaucratic, hierarchical institutions find it very difficult to learn, since rapid feedback is blocked by too many layers between decision makers and the field. That's why the UN's early-warning systems are so weak, compared to the decentralised NGO systems that enabled decisions to be made very quickly, for example, in the northern Kenya drought of 1990–91.[18] So long as mechanisms are in place to ensure accountability for common goals and standards, devolving authority will always pay dividends. It is no surprise that decentralisation figures so highly in the reform of international institutions. UNIDO (the industrial development arm of the UN) achieved a 22 per cent increase in productivity on the back of a 38 per cent cut in staffing and resources.[19] The World Bank's 'strategic compact' includes such subversive ideas as siting the Mexico team in Mexico, and getting senior managers to spend a day in a slum – hardly the stuff of revolution, but important nevertheless. In less top-heavy and more democratic structures it becomes rational for staff to co-operate and exchange information, because there is less to be gained from disguising mistakes. The writer Charles Handy likes to think of organisations as communities of individuals planning and working together for long-term goals, rather than the property of a managerial elite.[20] This may be somewhat romantic, but a clear and common vision is certainly more important than elaborate strategic planning models, which are often a refuge for bureaucrats with too much time on their hands and not enough immersion in grassroots realities.[21] The process of planning is important, but the plans themselves are less significant.

Effective institutions combine the autonomy of field units with the gains of overall co-ordination through various forms of federalism.[22] Task groups and multi-skilled teams work across organisational boundaries; internal structures are loose, pragmatic, and often temporary, designed to facilitate co-operation and mutual accountability for results, not make staff feel secure and protected.[23] The International Potato Research Centre in Peru, for example, started to produce much better research (and potatoes) when anthropologists and engineers began to work together.[24] Contrast that with the monochromatic nature of World Bank staff, where the ratio of economists to other social scientists is 28:1,[25] and the impossibly complicated and competitive subdivisions of the UN.[26] The rising power of information technology means that development agencies can act as hubs of networks rather than isolated hierarchies.[27]

No development agency can afford to be 'fundamentalist', in the sense of defending a rigid ideology or a universal set of prescriptions. They all need '*more asking and less telling*', as Aaron Wildavsky puts it.[28] Flexibility and responsiveness are all, and 'accompaniment' (long-term support) is a much better approach than imposing blueprints and deadlines from the top.[29] In this approach, staff are encouraged to follow processes on the ground rather than rush in and out on short consultancy visits, so that they can create stronger feedback loops between field realities, practice and policy. The emphasis moves from control to dialogue, helping groups to solve problems for themselves instead of fixing on one answer that is deemed to be correct. Insiders and outsiders become *'critical friends'*, as Brazilian NGOs call it, retaining a sense of loyalty so that disagreements can be accommodated in a supportive yet challenging relationship.[30] Effective organisations encourage debate and allow differences to coexist, so long as they generate results in accordance with the overall mission. Alfred Sloan, past-chairman of General Motors, always delayed decisions that appeared to have unanimous support in the boardroom, since this indicated that colleagues weren't voicing their true opinions. *'Without dissent, you don't know what the problem is,'* says the management guru Peter Drucker.[31] This may be true in theory, but dissent inside the World Bank (or even a large international NGO) is more likely to lead to early retirement than promotion.

Accountability

Learning requires an active conversation between institutions and their clients. As Theodore Zeldin once observed, this is a quality which is absent from most modern institutions, *'distanced by their professionalism from the concerns of everyday life and lacking any sense of human warmth'*.[32] As a result, there is little to stop them focusing on their own survival as opposed to the needs of those they were set up to serve – a common problem among international agencies. If 'local ownership' is the key to results (as all development agencies say it is), then this is a serious problem. Correcting it requires accountability to those who are supposed to benefit from interventions as well as those who fund or regulate them. In reality, development agencies rarely take their lead from poor people, despite the problems that ensue when institutions do not listen to their customers.[33] This is partly because they are unsure who their customers are: are they the public or governments that fund them, the volunteers who sit on the boards, their staff, or the people in the village whose development is the real issue? The truth is that all these constituencies are legitimate stakeholders, but no organisation can be equally accountable to all of them at one time. Since 'money talks', accountability to donors tends to be the bottom line. As a result, too much attention is paid to external agendas when setting objectives and evaluating progress. Indicators are skewed toward bean counting and narrow measurements of cost-effectiveness. The *'tunnel vision of the project system'* compresses timescales and discourages experimentation, and attempts to inject more room to manoeuvre into the 'project cycle' tend to be cosmetic.[34] Development agencies cannot be completely accountable for the impact of their interventions, since they don't control the other factors that determine what happens at the end of the line (like the wider economic and political environment). But they can and should be held responsible for using their resources in a reasonable way.[35] *'Always ask how we can do what we already do better,'* is Peter Drucker's advice, so long as we also ask whether we should be doing other things as well.[36]

This has to be a consultative process, since what is reasonable to a manager in New York may be extremely unreasonable to a villager in Namibia. That means broadening the base of participation in monitoring and evaluation using techniques such as social audits, reciprocal evaluations, surveys of service users, and two-way monitoring, like the NGOs in Mexico which feed information on World Bank projects to the grassroots and reactions from the grassroots back to the Bank.[37] The social audit is a particularly interesting innovation pioneered by the UK-based New Economics Foundation and its counterparts in other countries. It works on the assumption that all the stakeholders of an organisation have a right to participate in monitoring its performance. A number of NGOs are using social audits (like Traidcraft, a fair-trade organisation based in Newcastle), and they have found them very helpful in improving programme quality.[38] Oxfam-UK has recently launched a less ambitious version of this process – an annual 'assembly' at which stakeholders can ask questions of staff and engage in a public debate on the agency's achievements. However, it is significant that none of the largest international NGOs – and certainly no multilateral agency – has agreed to a social audit. Concessions to democratic accountability made by the World Bank (through its inspection panel) and some UN agencies like UNDP (on the public disclosure of information) are limited. We have already looked at some of the ways this could be improved – like an 'international relief commissioner' to govern humanitarian assistance and an ombudsman for development NGOs – but even a simple complaints procedure with some external scrutiny would be better than what we have now.

Incentives

Many of these problems can be traced back to inadequate or perverse incentives in organisations, and to the pervasive influence of organisational cultures. Perverse incentives are those that reward staff for behaviour that is antithetical to the stated mission of the organisation, or act as a barrier to the qualities that underpin success. In aid agencies, the obvious source of perverse incentives is 'disbursement pressure' – the need to spend the budget by the end of the financial year come what may, in order to avoid cuts next time around.[39] This leads to poor-quality work and the temptation to rush proposals through – the opposite of the demand-led approach recommended in Chapter 7. No one is rewarded for taking the time to get things right. High salaries (over US$120,000 a year for middle managers in both the UN and the World Bank) and feather-bedded conditions of work encourage staff to put job retention before self-criticism, reinforcing a longstanding tendency to worship internal audiences and ignore those outside. Both the Bank and the UN's specialised agencies have issued forests of directives on social development, participation, gender and the environment, but they still lack the incentive systems to make them work.[40] People talk the talk but do not walk it. One way of changing this is to audit a random sample of programmes independently, place the results in the public arena, and hold staff accountable for their performance in a way which influences their future career in concrete ways.

The culture of an organisation is extremely important in sanctioning some types of behaviour and frustrating others.[41] Development agencies often have an activist culture which sees learning as a luxury when compared to the 'real work' of operations, or moving money. Innovation and challenge are unlikely to be valued by managers unless there is a tradition of self-criticism. This may be present in theory but is heavily circumscribed in practice. According to a recent independent study of the UN, its specialised agencies have no cohesive culture at all, apart from a love of bureaucracy and prehistoric management systems – the *'last of the organisational relics of the Cold War'* as its authors conclude.[42] Another independent survey found the UN civil service *'a disgrace, lacking a career structure, inflexible, under-skilled and over-manned, and alien to the concepts of productivity or rewards for merit'*.[43] Its recruitment procedures don't help matters, stifled as they are by the political correctness of the quota system and corrupted by patronage from member states. A broader nomination process would be a good start, inviting names from NGOs and the private sector as well as governments. Mandatory work in the field for ten years outside the UN system or the World Bank would provide another useful filter. One difficulty is that the UN's long-standing recruitment freeze (the result of America's failure to pay its dues) has led to increasing pressure on middle managers, there being no money to pay off dead wood at the top of the system nor recruit new blood on permanent contracts at the bottom.

If things are this bad, what hope is there for improvement? Institutions never reform themselves voluntarily. Six presidential commissions have come and gone without much change in the US Agency for International Development; the 'strategic compact' is only the latest in a long line of upheavals at the World Bank; and the UN has been in continuously unsuccessful reform since 1945.[44] The last two attempts at management reform (led by UN Undersecretaries Dick Thornburgh and Joseph Connor) failed for want of an internal constituency to push them through. The UN's management information system is three years behind schedule and US$60 million over budget; and its Office of Internal Oversight has only ever acknowledged one incident of fraud in public, and that was handed over for investigation by London's Scotland Yard.[45] Institutional reform comes from the combined effects of internal and external pressure exerted strategically and over long periods of time. External pressure often comes from NGO networks that lobby the international financial institutions continuously, since they are the main source of policy and funding.[46] An internal constituency is just as important, chipping away at the status quo until a critical mass emerges to push change through. Strong leadership is vital. The increasing influence of social-development concerns inside the World Bank fits this pattern particularly well, beginning with a few lone voices on the inside (like that of the anthropologist Michael Cernea) and gradually expanding its constituency both internally and in alliance with NGOs, bilateral aid agencies and academics.[47] This model is less likely to work inside the UN because it is a much more diffuse organisation with fewer political openings for the 'big bang' approach employed by James Wolfensohn at the World Bank. The UN is naturally more attuned to incremental change, but that is likely to be dissipated by institutional inertia. The only way to tackle this problem is for Northern governments to make sufficient funding available to push through more radical reforms – as they did with the 'strategic compact' – accepting the costs of large-scale redundancy and restructuring along the way. That might not make the UN wise, but it would certainly encourage less stupidity.

PERSONAL REVOLUTION

It is a truism that institutions change when people do. No amount of theorising or displacement-activity by development workers can change the fact that our personal behaviour will make or break any attempt to facilitate positive change in the world. Develop yourself if you want to be of service to others should be our mantra. There is no other way of dealing with the 'unwelcome guests' described in Chapter 2, for it is us who are the guests and our own attitudes that are unwelcome. This is an unfashionably puritanical view at a time when the private peccadilloes of political leaders are not supposed to influence the quality of public decision-making: you don't need a department full of saints to administer an ethical foreign policy. But one cannot argue generally that personal behaviour is irrelevant to institutional performance, nor that it doesn't influence the trust people place in the professionals who are supposed to help them. The writer Alice Miller makes this point about the hidden agendas of parents and their impact on their children.[48] If our own practice is autocratic, closed and chauvinist, it is unlikely that we will be able to encourage others to be democratic, open and egalitarian.[49] This is especially relevant for those in the helping professions, because their motivations are always ambiguous. Adolf Guggenbuhl-Craig, the psychotherapist who has studied this issue in detail, concludes that ego and power-drives are often strongest when cloaked by moral rectitude.[50] Development workers who preach participation are often autocratic in their own behaviour, despite the fact that consistency between words and actions is the fundamental tenet of social organisation.[51] If we really want to make a difference, it's not just what we do but the way that we do it that is important.

Learning and Wisdom

In this situation, the minimum required is to practise what you preach, and be accountable for it – just like the institutions we looked at earlier. Humility, patience, sensitivity, continual self-development, and an openness to learning are the qualities of successful helpers at any level – the peculiar combination of arrogance and ignorance which infects so many expatriates in other people's societies is a guaranteed recipe for failure. One of the biggest problems in this respect is the cult of the expert. Anthony de Mello, an Indian writer on spirituality and development, tells the story of a man who lived his life as a world-famous authority in his field, proud of his expertise and dismissive of those who did not share it. One day he had a massive heart attack and was left for dead by his friends. The following morning he woke up and was taken to visit the local doctor. But the doctor, just as much an expert as he was, pronounced his recovery from the grave as medically impossible, re-signed the death certificate, and buried the poor chap. Nonsense, of course, but instructive in exposing a widespread tendency to pay too much respect to technical expertise. This is especially common in developing countries where, for example, one can be a bank manager in Britain but an expert on micro-finance on stepping off the plane in Malawi. The problem lies not with expertise itself (which is invaluable in development work) but with the attitudes that surround it. Expert thinking is often adversarial, assuming that facts are unambiguous and that each case is there to be won. This discourages intellectual complacency, but can also lead to the exclusion of dissenting voices and the downgrading of the new and unorthodox.[52] Yet creating alternatives is as much a part of development as testing out the things we already know. '*In the beginner's mind there are many possibilities. In the expert's there are few*'.[53] Humility turns out to be the threshold of insight.

The idea that experts know best makes it more difficult for professionals to identify and accept their weaknesses, but unless we do that it is impossible to unravel our own involvement in the power relations of international development, and put right what might otherwise interfere with our ability to be helpful.[54] No help is completely unconditional, but we can be honest about our interests so that they can be negotiated in a relationship between equals.[55] Until recently, development professionals ignored or downgraded the indigenous knowledge of people in the developing world, branding it as unreliable and unscientific – a barrier to progress, not a resource. This began to change in the 1970s with new methodologies that emphasised the value of participation, listening instead of preaching, and the untapped ability of poor people to identify and analyse problems for themselves using simple techniques and visual expressions such as maps and drawings. These methodologies go by many different names, but the most popular description is 'participatory learning and action' (PLA, or sometimes PRA [participatory research in action]).[56] The influence of the British scholar-activist Robert Chambers and his growing band of colleagues deserves special mention here, though 'action research' of this kind has a much longer history, dating back at least to American pioneers like John Collier (at the Bureau of Indian Affairs in the 1930s), Kurt Lewin, and Ronald

Lippitt.[57] What unites these efforts is a conviction that those directly involved in social change are best placed to analyse what is happening around them, and feed the results back into practice. So action research is a vehicle for both programme effectiveness and personal empowerment. This vision influenced later generations of social activists, including Saul Alinsky and his *'rules for radicals'*, and Paulo Friere and his *'pedagogy of the oppressed'* in Latin America.[58] The PLA movement took the basic principles of these philosophies, combined them with elements from other traditions (like farming-systems research), and codified them into an expanding menu of tools and techniques that could be disseminated quickly through the training of trainers and the production of low-cost 'self-improving' materials. As a result, PLA has spread rapidly across the world, potentially revolutionising the philosophy and practice of development work in the process. If there was a Nobel Prize for international development, then Chambers and his colleagues would be first on the list.

However, a note of caution is required here. Part of the reason for the rapid uptake of these methods is that they offer easy solutions to complex dilemmas. If people focus on techniques rather than the philosophy that underpins them, participatory research is just another way to capture information. Development workers sometimes romanticise tradition and ignore the power relations, inequalities and limitations that exist in all communities, and they can't help but be caught in the 'games people play' when the development circus comes to town. Part of the outsider's job is to help people make connections between what they know and what is new, unfamiliar, or just a better option in the circumstances. It is the combination of local and non-local knowledge that makes the difference. Donald Schon, one of the pioneers of new forms of education and training in the USA, likens the world to a swamp surrounded by the high ground of problems that can be managed using technocratic means – *'The irony is that the problems of the high ground tend to be relatively unimportant...while in the swamp lie the problems of greatest human concern'*.[59] So professionals need to help people navigate a safe passage through the swamp, acting as a bridge between different views and backgrounds, and a channel for information. Schon describes this as 'reflective practice'. I prefer wisdom: *'the ability to think and act utilising knowledge, experience, understanding, common sense and insight'*.[60]

The 'getting of wisdom' is crucial to professional effectiveness, but it cannot be taught in the classroom. Important technical skills can obviously be learned in this way, but the current university system does not produce the reflective practitioners we need: people who

are skilled in both fieldwork and higher-level analysis, able to inter-
pret indigenous as well as 'modern' knowledge, and prepared to be
self-critical as well as to challenge others. This subject demands a
book in itself, questioning as it does the whole basis of professional
education and training in the West, but there are already some interesting innovations to build on. The key is for all development agencies
to support their staff in a continuous, structured process of learning,
both from experience and from more formal exposure to the cutting
edge of academic research. As we have seen, this is weak at present
because time, resources and incentives are absent and there is too
much of a gulf between the worlds of action and understanding. Save
the Children-UK has experimented with sabbaticals and end-of-
contract write-ups for its field staff, joint programmes of research
with universities, and job descriptions and staff development systems
which emphasise thinking as well as doing. The UK Development
Studies Association has a permanent programme to help academics
and practitioners work together on common problems through
'framework partnerships', staff exchanges, a code of practice, and the
redesign of university development management courses (making use
of distance learning through Britain's innovative 'Open University'
for example).[61] Part of the World Bank's 'strategic compact' involves
doubling the amount spent on staff training using prestigious universities like Harvard, though in the Bank's case this money would be
better spent in persuading reluctant technocrats to spend more time
in the field.[62] All these innovations show promise, but they need to
be scaled up dramatically.

Personal Accountability

Ultimately, professional development requires much deeper changes
in attitudes and behaviour. The philosopher Zygmunt Bauman calls
this a shift to *'being and living for the other'* – a move from *'power
over'* others to *'power to'* facilitate their self-development, with no
strings attached.[63] Of course, no one wants to be the *'sort of woman,'*
as C S Lewis put it, *'who lives entirely for others. You can tell the
others by their hunted expression'*.[64] However, all of us need to find a
better balance between self-preservation and selfless service. A solid
sense of humour is surprisingly important in this respect, along with a
'lightness of being' even in the most difficult of circumstances and a
sense of detachment from the fruits of our actions. This may seem a
paradox, since most development workers are attached to particular

visions of the world as they want it to be – a certain set of economic, social and political outcomes. Without a clear vision it is unlikely that most of us would continue in our jobs, but when applied without discrimination it can make us rigid and autocratic. Real effectiveness requires a level of inner security strong enough to support a lifetime of struggle and sacrifice, without being unduly affected by the results. That sort of security comes only from constant self-development.[65] Unless we change ourselves, our efforts to change the world will be infected by the anger, frustration, jealousy and urge to control that lie inside.[66] Just because we work for Oxfam doesn't mean we are delivered from evil, but at least we can learn to deal with it.[67] It is in this sense that self-development and service to others are linked in a common purpose – the liberation of all parties from their limitations. It is certainly possible to help others effectively, but only if we realise that in doing so they help us to grow to a fuller, more independent knowledge of ourselves.

This is all well and good, but it is exceptionally difficult to institutionalise at any level. Whatever else it brings, you don't get humility from an MBA (Master of Business Administration). Can anything be done to nurture these attitudes, or is it all down to the individual? In a neat inversion of Paulo Friere, Robert Chambers has called for a *'pedagogy of the non-oppressed'* to liberate development professionals from the constraints of their background, education and training.[68] Others see the question in feminist terms. Hilary Rose has written convincingly of *'a rationality of responsibility for others'*, driven less by the competition and hierarchies of the masculine world and more by the intimacy and interdependence that characterise relations between women and children.[69] There are other practical things that seem to help, like allotting a small amount of time each day for quiet reflection and meditation, and the conscious contemplation of the day's events – 'could I have done this differently?', 'what did I learn?', and so on. Long hours in a Land Rover are especially good for this technique! Most important of all is the recognition that there are limits to what we can achieve.

> *'On the large scale of society no one person has enough knowledge to change one thing without creating more problems than they solve...but if each person will take on the responsibility of being open to all the information available and allow it to change them, this will bring about gradual changes in society which are vastly more intelligent.'*[70]

Once liberated from the conceit that we know best, we can get on with the job of using the gifts we have in a more constructive way. This takes hard work, and then more of it. '*It is only through repeated confrontations with the shadow of the Self that we can fulfil our task,*' is Adolf Guggenbuhl-Craig's advice, '*the struggle for blessing must last a lifetime.*'[71] In a profession that talks constantly about impact and results, personal accountability is often forgotten. But the real 'bottom line' is in our hearts, and our hearts will tell us when we cross it. Institutions may not have a heart to listen to, but we do. 'Am I part of the problem?' At some stage in their career, all development workers ask themselves this question. To answer it truthfully and with an open mind is the beginning of a journey of liberation, first for ourselves, and then for the world around us.[72]

CONCLUSION

Change in institutions and change in individuals supports and flows from the other. So the important thing is to start somewhere and not worry too much where in the cycle it happens to be. After all, our plans are only 'works in progress'.[73] Are development agencies wise? Not especially, but at least there is more interest in being so now, and a richer repertoire of tools and techniques to help them along the way. The first priority is not to be stupid. This is more of a challenge for some in the development business than it appears, since it means no more standard solutions imposed from the outside, and an end to rushing, disbursement pressure, arrogance about who knows best, and ignorance about local realities. The best way to develop these qualities is to strengthen learning, accountability and incentives to good practice. There are some simple things that could be done in the short term, like a social audit for every development agency and ring-fencing a portion of each loan or grant for learning, analysis and debate. In the longer term, change requires much deeper reforms in institutional structures and cultures, and in the way professionals are educated and trained. Personal change is the biggest challenge of all. International co-operation requires development professionals to recognise that it is not just others that must be developed, but themselves, and to live life from this premise. If we can do that (even in the imperfect way that is inevitable), the skills, experience and resources we do have will be accepted more readily and used more productively to the long-term benefit of everyone involved. In its unconditionality, loyalty and strength to challenge and be challenged, this means that we must love each other in our professional as well as our personal relationships. In this world at least, that is probably impossible, but there is no reason why we can't like each other more than we do, and work together more effectively as a result. And if we can't even do that, then it is better that we stay out of each other's way.

Chapter 12

Conclusion: How Can I Help?

'True steadfastness sparkles with flexibility'
Gurumayi Chidvilasananda[1]

*'A gift truly pure is offered without a sense of obligation,
and with the simple feeling, this should be given'*
The *Bhagavadgita*[2]

How can I help? It's a simple question with no straightforward
answers, even after a lengthy journey through the highways and
byways of international politics and economics, personal psychology,
and a few other detours along the way. The easier question is how *not*
to help – by imposing ideas on others, ignoring your own responsibilities, avoiding accountability, and manufacturing universal solutions.
At its worst, the international 'system' acts like the stereotypical
Englishman abroad: if only we shout loud enough, the foreigners will
understand, and do what we say. Laughable, of course, but not so far
from the reality of bungled development projects and bucketfuls of
inappropriate advice. *'True steadfastness sparkles with flexibility,'* says
the spiritual master Gurumayi Chidvilasananda; the determination to
work together is what matters, despite the differences and disagreements that arise along the way. Contrast that with the response of
governments and aid agencies, consistently intolerant of different
views and voices but inconsistent in their support for those who need
it most. Heedless of the *Bhagavadgita*'s instructions, the gifts of the
rich world always come with strings attached. As a result, they rarely
achieve the desired results. If these basic errors were put right, the
possibilities of being helpful would be transformed. Since that
requires confronting vested interests, this is unlikely to happen in the
short term, but, as we have seen, there is no shortage of incremental

improvements waiting to be made. There *are* successes to build on, and ideas and possibilities aplenty. What we lack are the constituencies to put them into practice. 'How can I help?' The first part of the answer is obvious: if you are not already part of that constituency for change, then start work now.

Over the last 50 years, the record of international co-operation has been disappointing, for at least four reasons. First, it has failed to get to grips with the fundamental challenge of our times: reshaping global capitalism to spread the benefits of economic growth more evenly across societies, reduce its social and environmental costs, and achieve a basic level of security for everyone. Second, it has failed to establish the conditions required to make co-operation work: a sense of equality and mutual respect in international affairs, reciprocity, and the legitimacy that comes from democratic participation in setting the rules of the game. Third, it has neither halted the abuse of basic rights and freedoms, nor encouraged different ways of realising them in practice. Fourth, it has failed to engage with the forces that really change things, becoming over-dependent on action by recalcitrant governments and detached from the dynamism and innovation that marks out the best in business and civil society. Correcting these systemic weaknesses can't be engineered from the top down. All solutions start with you and me, not just by donating money to good causes but by demonstrating co-operative behaviour as the wellspring of our daily life. So don't switch off your internationalism when you go shopping, or face difficult decisions at work, or have the opportunity to be active in politics, or give to charity. If you really want to help, be an advert for the virtues of co-operation in all these arenas, and always look for connections between action at home and solutions abroad.

A conviction that we share obligations as citizens of overlapping worlds provides the key to the future of international co-operation, and chimes with the new spirit of social responsibility that is spreading rapidly through business and politics. One of the problems of constituency building has always been the unimportance of international development to the political mainstream, but the changing global context makes questions of international poverty and conflict increasingly relevant to all our futures. The need to manage the costs and benefits of global change in an increasingly interconnected world economy makes international co-operation matter in the political process. That is already happening, though pronouncements from Western capitals are stronger on rhetoric than reality, and hesitant and confused in their details. This is partly because the links between domestic and international policy agendas have yet to be worked out and communicated in any convincing way. Now that the cold war is no more, there seems no grand narrative to motivate foreign policy, in contrast to the search for a 'third way' between free-market idolatry and state socialism that drives the centre-left in power. Prime Minister Blair and President Clinton speak far more confidently about these issues in Wisconsin or Liverpool than in global forums, though both recognise that solutions at home are inextricably bound up with a framework of international co-operation. One of the aims of this book has been to explore these links and map out a 'third way' in the international context. Crucially, this does not mean a new social and economic model to be exported across the globe, but a shared effort to create the conditions in which everyone can participate in finding their own ways forward, without imposing unsustainable costs on anyone else. It is that vision, messy and difficult to communicate as it is, that provides the philosophical framework we need to guide us into the 21st century. In place of universal prescriptions, we should focus on the things that all societies need to make choices about their future from a wider range of options: strong institutions and institutional linkages, coalitions of interest groups that use them for constructive ends, and an international setting favourable to local efforts.

Building the case for third-way policies is difficult enough in the domestic context. At the international level it is even more challenging, since short-term interests vary so much between one country and another. However, it is easier to identify solutions as the climate of ideas moves on, away from the complacency of 'globalisation as panacea' and the naiveté of 'de-linking as solution'. *'Davos man'*, Samuel Huntington's shorthand for the international elite who gather together in the Swiss Alps each January to discuss world affairs, seems ready to abandon his blind faith in globalisation in favour of managed markets and renewed social concern;[3] just as the thrust of radical critiques and NGO campaigns is turning toward constructive engagement. To be sure, the transition is slow and the details of what needs to be done are hazy, but the centrepiece of the debate is clear: globalisation has costs as well as benefits; both must be managed more effectively than in the past; and we can't do that without new ideas and institutions.

International co-operation is central to these ideas and institutions. It will not be co-operation as we have known it – a cloak for great-power interests, more or less successfully disguised – but a framework of rules and standards established and implemented through more democratic means. Peter Sutherland (one-time director-general of GATT) has called for a 'globalisation summit' to ensure that the poorest countries have a fair say in negotiating this framework.[4] Otherwise there will be few dissenting voices, little real debate, and no answers that enjoy enough support to make them work. But the mood is changing here too. Calls for transparency and accountability in international institutions are mounting, participation by business and civic groups is no longer controversial (though it remains weak in practice), and sooner or later the changing balance of power will be reflected in who sits where at the global negotiating table. History does not start in the year 2000, just as it did not end in 1989 (despite Francis Fukuyama's claims to the contrary).[5] But if international co-operation does become the defining characteristic of the 21st century it will be a new beginning in one sense – the first time that human beings have actively codetermined their future on the world stage. Except, of course, that life is never so simple. 'The devil is in the detail', and the detail is what has frustrated substantive progress towards a more effective global system. So let's briefly review what the last 11 chapters tell us about the practice and potential of international co-operation, past, present and future.

SUMMARY: LOOKING BACK

The first part of the book explored the role of outside assistance in promoting peace and prosperity. At the national level, success comes from a flexible economy, a polity that is strong enough to take decisions in favour of long-term goals, and a minimum level of satisfaction of everyone's basic needs. Countries that achieve these things do so, not because of a standard model, but because they have the capacity to manage change, coalitions of interest groups that push change through, and room to manoeuvre to find the appropriate balance between self-determination and outside opportunities; market competition, social co-operation and an active state. There are no universal mixtures that work across boundaries of context and culture. The best examples of this pattern at work are in East Asia, and a small number of countries or states elsewhere (like Botswana and Kerala). Despite the recent tarnishing of their 'miracle' status by the financial crisis that exploded at the end of 1997, countries like South Korea stand out from the rest in having addressed the basic questions of economic and industrial transformation that determine whether progressive social and political goals are achievable. Simplistic jibes about 'crony capitalism' cannot alter the fact that absolute poverty has been eradicated in these countries, and in record time. The question is, what role did international co-operation play in this process?

The evidence shows that foreign aid, technology, investment and trading opportunities did play an important role, especially in the early stages of economic and social transition. External resources were needed to supplement domestic markets and skills, and mitigate the accidents of geography; temporary help with the balance of payments smoothed the way for difficult decisions; and a favourable international context provided the markets and political support that were essential for success. However, the contrasting experience of most African countries shows that none of this is automatic. Sub-Saharan Africa received as much foreign aid as East Asia (though much less in the form of investment and technology), but inherited a more difficult set of initial conditions and a less supportive global context – declining terms of trade, rising levels of debt, and a depression of world demand just at the time it needed expanding markets. Even so, it would be perverse to blame the 'international system' for Africa's problems, given the shortcomings in domestic governance that underlay decision-making throughout this period. It didn't help that outside assistance was poorly designed and shot through with the wrong incentives (*'bad aid, badly used'*, as Chapter 3 put it), but even if it had been better, African countries would have been hard-pressed to replicate the virtuous interaction of domestic and international factors that was present in the high performers. In both cases, it wasn't *policies* that made the difference on their own, but the *polities* that created and sustained them, and nurturing those is a much more delicate task than pushing money through the pipeline of foreign aid or forcing countries to accept the conditions that go with it.

At the project level, it is tempting to see the same pattern writ small, and in some ways this is true: the best development projects create social energy to solve development problems as well as material advances to sustain the solutions. However, national success is not simply the sum of successful projects. What really counts are the connections that develop between small-scale innovations and structural changes in economic systems and governance, and fostering those takes great sensitivity, flexibility and continuity over long periods of time. The problem is that international agencies need quick results to keep the aid funds flowing, and that leads them to prioritise the supply of external inputs over the demand to use them effectively. Rushing, lack of co-ordination, and an unwillingness to hand over control have been characteristic of project aid for decades. As a result, outside intervention often undermines the foundations of the 'good society': a strong central authority, independent civil society groups, well-functioning markets, active communication to promote learning and accountability, and a framework of local ownership over mistakes as well as success.

When societies break down under the impact of famine, war, and civil strife, the need for external help may seem obvious. Yet the evidence reviewed in Chapter 5 shows that this is far from the case. Well-timed and properly-constructed intervention in humanitarian emergencies has been vital in saving lives, but in most cases both timing and strategy have been lacking. Rwanda and the Balkans are the two most recent examples, and the catastrophic loss of life in both has led some to question the future of humanitarianism as a whole. Improving the international response to 'complex political emergencies' rests on a combination of three things: long-term peace building (a society that accommodates differences when they are healthy and attacks them when they are not); developmental relief (short-term interventions that strengthen the conditions for long-term development), and international political action to address the external causes of insecurity and intervene with sufficient force at the right time. Unfortunately, none of these things are satisfactory at the moment, and support for relief far outweighs action on both of the others. The international response has been tardy, piecemeal and partial, creating more complications than solutions and leaving the causes of the problem to fester away. The reason is obvious – there is no consensus among the great powers on the desirability of intervention, and little stomach for the potential sacrifices involved in a more active, intelligent stance. The dilemma this creates is stark: do we intervene in the messy way international realities dictate, sure in the knowledge that this will complicate matters even further, or stay away while people suffer on the ground because we know we cannot do the job properly? There is only one moral answer: we must do better.

In all these areas, external help is never the key to internal change, and it is always a blunt weapon in the fight against poverty and violence. Yet the evidence shows that the right sort of help at the right time can be very influential in creating more space for local forces to get things right. So the obvious question is what sort of help is the right sort of help, and how do we ensure it is provided at the right time? In theory, the answer to the first part of this conundrum is simple: good help assists people to solve problems with fewer costs to themselves and more benefits for the rest of the world by expanding the options available, illuminating alternatives, and providing more opportunities to develop and apply win-win solutions. It keeps responsibility in local hands, supports decision makers facing difficult decisions, and uses its influence to encourage more room to be 'manoeuvred' in favour of development goals instead of the interests of elites. This is partly a matter of the right support to local institutions, and partly a matter of reshaping the global context so that it is more favourable to local efforts. When these come together, the prospects for success are high.

The second part of the conundrum is more difficult, because it strikes at the heart of the problems that corrupt the effectiveness of international co-operation. Nearly all foreign aid, and most other forms of help, are based on the use of sticks and carrots to persuade the recipient to conform with conditions set by outsiders. Over time the conditions have grown, and, on the surface at least, become more progressive, but they are still applied in a framework of unequal power and responsibility that erodes local ownership over change. The results are predictably disappointing – the dysfunctional children of an unhappy marriage. What does breed success are three qualities conspicuous by their absence from the programmes of most rich-country governments, NGOs and international agencies. The first is consistency with local realities; the second is long-term continuity of support, de-linked from the volatile selectivity imposed by foreign policy concerns, unreliable funding, and donor fashions; and the third is coherence between all the things that influence development performance, from debt relief to diplomacy. Developing these three qualities means putting our own house in order and adopting an attitude of 'critical friendship': a loyal but challenging relationship in which both sides practise what they preach, and each trusts the other to find ways forward which fit their reality best. Successful collective action is difficult outside of relationships like these, but they are rare in the practice of international relations. The influence of the system created in 1945 dwindles along with its reputation, unwilling to break free from the security blanket of the foreign aid system, uncomfortable in the shades of grey that characterise development, and incapable of the reforms required to be of true service to others. Fifty years of foreign intervention have left us ill-prepared to face a co-operative future. So what's to be done?

SUMMARY: LOOKING FORWARD

Imposing universal models never works, but for those of us who are simultaneously committed to universal human rights and to the right of others to decide things for themselves, what sort of international system should we be looking to build? The second part of the book answered that question by reversing the traditional order of things and refocusing international co-operation around a very different formula: competition between different paths to the same destinations (there are different ways of meeting social and economic goals); co-operation to reduce the costs they impose on individual societies and the world as a whole (collective action is required to protect universal rights and standards); and principled dialogue to decide which costs are acceptable and which are not. 'Principled dialogue' means an equal voice for everyone, and that is impossible without a redistribution of the skills and assets people need to participate in economic and political life, and the regulation of all exclusionary systems of power. International action in both areas can put the 'stake' into stakeholding at the global level, and build the incentives required to make co-operation work. Our leitmotif for the 21st century is simple: the right to one's own journey through life, and the obligation to support others on theirs, now and for future generations. But that implies wholesale changes in our approach to global problems and the institutions we've created to deal with them.

The first part of this new formula implies long-term support for each society to find its own ways of dealing with social and economic problems, in line with local realities. Chapter 7 explored how to do this by using foreign aid in a supporting role to a broader agenda of international co-operation, fostering the capacity of hard-pressed institutions and increasing their room to manoeuvre. The best way to achieve these goals would be a global compact for the future, supported by a world development fund independent of great-power domination: a single, negotiated framework of development co-operation for each country; consolidated funding (all assistance in one pot); and binding agreements on domestic and international action. Commitments to economic and social policies to help the poor by institutions in the developing world would be balanced by specific goals on debt relief and trade liberalisation in the industrialised world. Most important of all, the same rules would be applied to everyone: democratic participation in setting objectives and reciprocal accountability for results, whether you are the IMF or the Ugandan government. The agencies that benefit from the current system will scream and shout, of course, about how unrealistic this is, and that requires a strategy to deal with opposition. We will come to that a little later.

A new framework for foreign aid would give countries more chance to get things right without abandoning accountability, but since change is inevitably painful and they are certain to make mistakes along the way, the second part of the formula is just as important: helping others to develop with 'fewer costs to themselves'. Chapter 8 explored this challenge in the context of humanising capitalism – preserving the growth-producing potential of markets and trade while finding better ways to distribute the surplus they create and reshape the processes that produce it. This is not because capitalism as we know it is the best economic system we can hope for, but because eradicating world poverty requires a level of growth which is impossible outside of a market economy and an integrated world trading regime, albeit implemented over time. Conventionally, 'empowerment' has been seen as the answer to poverty and social exclusion, but the real breakthrough comes from solutions that both empower people and encourage them to use some of the power they gain for unselfish ends: firms that are successful in markets but distribute work and profits more equally, for example, or collective approaches to caring which provide children with the support they need without placing an unequal burden on women. Foreign aid has a role to play in supporting innovations like these, but more importantly they need a system of rules-based co-operation at the global level to ensure that one country's sacrifices are not exploited by others. No government is likely to impose substantive 'green taxation' unless its competitors do the same. That raises fundamental questions about the future of global governance.

For sceptics, 'global governance' means 'world government', but as Chapter 9 points out, there is no necessary connection between the two. What is required are norms and standards that govern public and private behaviour across national boundaries. The costs of uncoordinated action can then be managed to reduce their impact on the 'world as a whole'. Gaining assent to rules and standards doesn't come through global regulations, but through a messy mixture of top-down and bottom-up authority; formal and informal pressure for compliance; and market mechanisms, social action, and government intervention. Reconstituting a legitimate sense of global authority (highlighted in the Introduction as one of the key challenges for the 21st century) is much more likely to come from the interaction of these things over time, than from the decisions of the UN General Assembly, however much it is reformed. Global governance will only be effective when it is solidly rooted in ordinary people's lives, and connected upwards into international institutions that are closer to us, and which we trust. Nothing else will generate the incentives required to enforce changes in destructive behaviour. Respect for rules will come over time if they are negotiated democratically, applied consistently, and accompanied by support for compliance – unlike the Multilateral Agreement on Investment, say, or bombing Iraq while ignoring the transgressions of others.

The examples explored in Chapter 9 show how this might work. Global regimes work best when they are 'light but firm', not 'heavy and loose' – a small core of negotiated rules and standards, graduated by each country's ability to meet them, and backed by the necessary support and incentives. To be sure, there are few examples that fulfil these conditions, but on paper agreements already exist to prevent the most destructive of behaviours without interfering overmuch with market mechanisms or personal freedom: global pollution targets, minimum labour standards, rules for international intervention when populations are threatened by war or famine, and the provisions of the International Bill of Human Rights. More concerted action in these areas rests on the combined efforts of governments, business and civil society. It's not the UN that will save the earth or protect refugees – it's you and me. The international ban on landmines agreed at the end of 1997 shows how influential international civil society groups can be in exerting bottom-up pressure on official negotiations. Generally though, the problem is that 'you and me' don't feel involved in the structures and processes of global governance, nor are we likely to with the institutions we have today – a collection of overlapping mandates, top-heavy bureaucracies, and unaccountable decision-making procedures. The symbolic opportunity of a new millennium provides the ideal platform to address these problems through a simultaneous recommitment to UN principles and a deep reappraisal of their practice.

These proposals are persuasive in theory, but are they politically feasible? All change will be met with stiff resistance from vested interests, so the most that can be done is to outline a set of options that have an internal logic, linked to a strategy for generating the necessary public and political support. That was the subject of Chapter 10: how to build a constituency for international co-operation in the industrialised world. In many ways this is a thankless task, since most people's immediate interests have little to do with global citizenship.

But it is not impossible, with the right mix of moral messages and legitimate appeals to self-interest, and new communications strategies to back them up. The first step is to break free from paternalistic images of Third-World charity and the message that global issues can be tackled through foreign aid, and replace them with strategies that convince people to take action in their own lives to build a more co-operative world – as ethical consumers, agents of change in their communities, and active citizens of an increasingly internationally-minded polity.

The moral case for co-operation takes us back to the quotation from the *Bhagavadgita* cited at the beginning of this chapter. Simply put, we know that there are things in life that should be done, and one of them is making sure that everyone has the minimum required to live a life that is fulfilling. No other justification is required. *'The art of being kind is all this sad world needs.'*[6] However, that is not enough in practical terms. Most people need to be convinced that co-operation is in their interest, and that is a matter of making the costs of living in an uncooperative world much clearer to them. The increasing visibility of trans-boundary problems like pollution and financial instability makes this easier, but we need to work much harder to get the connections across, and be more active in compensating those who lose out from the domestic changes international co-operation demands. As the economist Lester Thurow points out, the contemporary world lacks any unifying ideology to provide a common sense of purpose to our collective struggles.[7] Competition offers nothing to bring us together, yet unite we must if we are to prosper in a web of increasingly interconnected relationships. The vision of a co-operative world which manages its differences and disagreements to mutual benefit could be a powerful leitmotif for the future, providing a source of meaning and a sense of purpose which does not require the wholesale surrender of self-interest or self-determination. We may never share a common vision of ends and means across so many cultures and generations, but we can all be committed to a process that allows everyone to share in defining how these different visions are reconciled. Co-operation does require some sacrifices, but once our basic needs are met they are not, in the end, very large ones to exchange for the prospect of a better future. We would enjoy it too – the global equivalent of an end to noisy neighbours and the driver who always ignores the rules on the highway.

None of this will happen without leadership, and where is that to come from in these times of discredited ideology and diminished public figures? Chapter 10 argued that this is the job of NGOs like

Oxfam, who have the contacts and credibility required to spearhead a global movement for change. What they sometimes lack are the courage and imagination to strike out in new directions, especially when these offer less security than the comfort of the foreign-aid system. Tarnished, as all heroes are, by the real world demands of compromise, pressures to conform, and internal failings, it is still civil society that reappears in every chapter of this book as innovator, facilitator, bridge builder and counterweight: providing channels for accountability and communication in the 'good society'; supporting poor people to organise and fight for their rights; experimenting with new social and economic models; and helping to underpin the norms of an emerging global polity. The challenge to civil society groups is to put their own houses in order so that they can do more of these things, more effectively: not as contractors to a shrinking supply of foreign aid, but as active partners in the broader networks and alliances that will spearhead change in the next century. To do that they must forge more equal relationships with each other across the changing boundaries of North and South, and engage strategically with states and markets to effect changes where they matter most.

An active global citizenry that uses its muscle to promote co-operation in all areas of life is a prerequisite for a positive future of this kind, but in the meantime there is much to be done to make the institutions we already have work more effectively. That requires a professional constituency for reform on the inside, as well as greater political pressure to perform from the outside. Institutional change is partly a matter of the right systems, structures and incentives; and at a more fundamental level, an issue of personal change – helping professionals to be exemplars of the qualities they wish to encourage in others. Chapter 11 called this 'the getting of wisdom', meaning a combination of knowledge, technical skills, and the discrimination required to use them effectively. That comes only from long experience and constant self-enquiry, especially in a profession fixated on the problems of others, and others as problems, and defensive about its own part in creating the world that it then tries to change. The result is a yawning gap between rhetoric and reality in all development agencies which requires concerted action in three areas: better learning, with more feedback loops into policy and practice; stronger accountability, especially to users or beneficiaries; and positive incentives to perform in ways conducive to long-term impact, not short-term financial results. Institutions succeed far more by letting go against a clear bottom line than through micro-management. There are plenty of ways this could be done, but none which ignore the most personal of bottom lines, which is honesty. After serving an apprenticeship of self-development, we qualify to be 'critical friends' with others. Once liberated from the conceit that we know best, we can get on with the job of using the gifts we have in a more constructive way.

No FINAL WORDS

Much of the world has developed at breakneck speed over the last 200 years, but we are still incapable of living at peace with ourselves or with each other, and unwilling to eradicate the scandal of global poverty and hunger. We have the resources, the technology, the ideas and the wealth, but we don't yet have the will and imagination to harness these things to a higher purpose. I have tried in this book to explore what this purpose might be – the vision of a co-operative world – and how we might get there in practice. Hundreds of detailed proposals have been made, and hundreds more have been made by others, but none has the slightest guarantee of success. The only certainty is the certainty of struggle, and life, as M Scott Peck is fond of saying, '*is what happens when we plan something else*'.[8] What lies ahead is the still-constant movement of engagement and retreat, two steps forward and one step back, that demands the courage and conviction to carry on regardless.

Underlying all the details and uncertainties are some issues of principle that will make or break the prospects for a more co-operative world. The devil may be in the detail, but the '*power and magic*', as Goethe puts it, lie in '*boldness and simplicity of vision*'.[9] The first principle is this – co-operation requires the exercise of co-operative values: putting your house in order; practising what you preach; being transparent, consistent, and accountable for your side of the bargain; and showing that you have the strength to challenge and be challenged without wrecking the relationship as a whole. The world will never be secure if our goal is to wipe out the differences that exist between us; we have to find ways of uniting with our positive differences intact.[10] So co-operation means talking, listening, learning, and always reaching out to make connections with others. These are the foundations for a positive future. Second, co-operation doesn't work unless all those involved have the basic essentials of a fulfilling life: voice, security and equality of rights. With those things in place, people can make their own choices about the good life, and the sacrifices that are necessary to make more room for others. Eradicating absolute poverty and all forms of gross oppression is therefore a precondition for a co-operative future, as well as the outcome of co-operative practice now. We can't make other people happy, but we can support each other in our attempts to lead more fulfilling lives and help to create an environment in which wholesome choices are more likely.[11] Perhaps that is obvious in our relationships with those we love, but it is no less true of relations between countries.

'*The last word is that there is no last word,*' as Robert Chambers tells us, and thank goodness for that.[12] It relieves me of the obligation to pull any rabbits out of hats, reveal the ultimate answer to global problems, or find the final key that unlocks the mess and uncertainty of life. However, to accept this stance without surrendering the determination to move on is itself a key of sorts, and the basis of the critical friendship on which all our futures depend – the loving but forceful encounters between equals who journey together into the unknown but dreamed-of world of the true and the beautiful. '*Any mindful action undertaken in a spirit of love will help the transformative process along,*' as the writer Elise Boulding once remarked.[13] We are co-creators of the world we live in, and must take responsibility for doing what we can to make it worthy of ourselves and a fitting legacy for future generations.[14] That is real co-operation – '*helping others to escape*' from constraints and limitations as Fredrich von Hugel wrote to his niece, not digging them further into the mud like the hermit and his friends who were cited at the beginning of the Introduction. Any relationship that is truly principled will lead upwards to a more fulfilling conclusion, even though we can never be sure what it will look like at any level of detail. Co-operation will show us a better way forward; never to a future perfect, but always to a future positive. Now, let's get back to work.

References and Notes

PREFACE

1 Zeldin, T (1994) *An Intimate History of Humanity*, Sinclair-Stevenson, London, p334

CHAPTER 1

1 Ridley, M (1996) *The Origins of Virtue*, Viking, London
2 Salman Rushdie, cited by van den Berg,M and van Ojik, B (1997) in *Rarer than Rubies: Reflections on Dutch Development Co-operation*, NOVIB, The Hague
3 Cited in Goulet, D (1995) *Development Ethics*, Zed Books, London, p19
4 Ormerod, P (1994) *The Death of Economics*, Faber, London
5 UNDP (1997) *Human Development Report*, New York
6 The UK Government announced small increases in the aid budget in 1998 and 1999
7 Maren, M (1997) *The Road to Hell: the ravaging effects of foreign aid and international charity*, The Free Press, New York
8 Kaplan, R (1996) *The Ends of the Earth: A Journey at the Dawn of the 21st Century*, Random House, New York
9 OECD/Development Assistance Committee (1997) *Development Co-operation 1996*. For a more dated but similar view see Hancock, G (1989) *Lords of Poverty*, Atlantic Monthly Press, New York
10 Thompson, D (1996) *The End of Time: Faith and Fear in the Shadow of the New Millennium*, Sinclair-Stevenson, London
11 See for example Escobar, A (1995) *Encountering Development*, Princeton University Press, Princeton; and Sachs, W (ed) (1992) *The Development Dictionary*, Zed Books, London
12 Cited by Mulgan, G, in *The Guardian*, 1 February 1997
13 Horsman, M and Marshall, A (1994) *After the Nation State: Citizens, Tribalism and the New World Disorder*, Harper Collins, London
14 Huntington, S (1993) 'The Clash of Civilisations', *Foreign Affairs*, Summer
15 Korten, D (1995) *When Corporations Rule the World*, Earthscan, London

16 Athanasiou, T (1996) *Slow Reckoning: the Ecology of a Divided Planet*, Secker and Warburg, London. WorldWatch Institute (1996) *State of the World*, Earthscan, London. See also Grieder, W (1997) *One World, Ready or Not* (1997), Penguin, Harmondsworth; Martin, H and Schumann, H (1997) *The Global Trap*, Zed Press, London; and Gray, J (1998) *False Dawn: the delusions of global capitalism*, Granta, Cambridge
17 Hirst, P and Thompson, G (1996) *Globalisation in Question*, Polity Press, Cambridge
18 Korten, D, op cit, (note 15), p221
19 Krugman, P (1996) *Pop Internationalism*, MIT Press, Cambridge
20 Kaul, I (1996) *Globalisation and Human Development*, EADI Annual Conference, Vienna, September
21 Barber, B (1996) *Jihad versus McWorld*, Penguin, Harmondsworth
22 Micklethwait, J and Wooldridge, A (1996) *The Witch Doctors*, William Heinemann, London, p247
23 Cockburn, A and Silverstein, K (1995) 'The Demands of Capital', *Harpers Magazine*, May
24 Korten, D, op cit (note 15) p180
25 Giddens, A (1991) *Modernity and Self-Identity*, Polity Press, Cambridge; Beck, U (1992) *Risk Society: Towards a New Modernity*, Sage, London; Castells, M (1997) *End of Millennium*, Blackwell, Oxford; Rodrick, D (1996) *Has Globalisation Gone too Far?* Institute for International Economics, Washington DC
26 Letter from Ralph Nader to Bill Gates, August 1998 (downloaded from the NEXUS Global List)
27 Cited by Stewart Wallace, Overseas Director of OXFAM-UK in an address on 'Beyond Capitalism', Oxford: 20 May1997
28 Kofi Annan, UN Secretary-General, New York: UN Press Release, 12 May 1997
29 Nader, R, op cit (note 26)
30 Thurow, L (1996) *The Future of Capitalism*, William Morrow, New York, p1
31 Drucker, P (1993) *Post-Capitalist Society*, Butterworth/Heinemann, Oxford; Giddens, A (1990) *The Consequences of Modernity*, Polity Press, Cambridge
32 Wood, A (1994) *North–South Trade, Employment and Inequality: Changing Fortunes in a Skill-Driven World*, Clarendon Press, Oxford.
33 McRae, H (1994) *The World in 2020: Power, Culture and Prosperity*, Harper Collins, London
34 UNDP (1997), op cit (note 5); Singer, H and Jolly, R (1995) 'Fifty Years On: the UN and Economic and Social Development', *Institute of Development Studies Bulletin* 26 (4)
35 UNDP (1996) *Human Development Report*, New York
36 Zadek, S et al (1997) *Building Corporate Accountability*, Earthscan, London; Elkington, J (1997) *Cannibals with Forks*, Capstone, London
37 Thurow, L, op cit (note 30); Mulgan, G (1997) *Connexity*, Chatto and Windus, London
38 Archer, R (1996) *Should Private Aid be Reconsidered?* TransNational Institute, Amsterdam, p13
39 Soros, G (1996) in *The Atlantic Monthly*, December

40   Cited by Kennedy, P (1993) *Preparing for the 21st Century*, Fontana, London

41   Korten, op cit (note 15); see also Lang, T and Hines, C (1993) *The New Protectionism: Protecting the Future Against Free Trade*, Earthscan, London; and Mander, J (ed) (1996) *The Case Against the Global Economy*, Sierra Club Press, Washington

42   Micklethwait and Wooldridge, op cit (note 22), p217

43   Burke, T (1997) in *New Statesman*, 20 June

44   The New Club of Rome Report Weizacker,E, Lovins, A and Lovins, E in *Factor Four: Doubling Wealth, Halving Resource Use*, Earthscan, London

45   Fukuyama, F (1995) *Trust: the Social Virtues and the Creation of Prosperity*, Hamish Hamilton, London, p13

46   Hutton, W (1995) *The State We're In*, Jonathan Cape, London and (1997) *The State to Come*, Vintage, London

47   Etzioni, A (1993) *The Spirit of Community*, Fontana, London; and (1997) *The New Golden Rule*, Profile Books, London; Sandel, M (1996) *Democracy's Discontent*, Belknapp Press, Cambridge

48   Reich, R (1992) *The Work of Nations*, Vintage, New York; Thurow, L op cit (note 30); Rifkin, J (1995) *The End of Work*, G P Putnam, New York; Drucker, P (1993) *Post-Capitalist Society*, Butterworth/Heinemann, Oxford; Handy, C (1997) *The Hungry Spirit: Beyond Capitalism*, Hutchinson, London

49   Putnam, R (1993) *Making Democracy Work: Civic Traditions in Modern Italy*, Princeton University Press, Princeton; Kelly, G, Kelly, D and Gamble, A (eds) (1997) *Stakeholder Capitalism*, Macmillan, London

50   Kay, J (1997) in the *New Statesman*, 16 May

51   Etzioni and Sandel do recognise this problem in their works.

52   Giddens, A, op cit (note 25); Giddens, A (1994) *Beyond Left and Right: the Future of Radical Politics*, Cambridge University Press, p17; Gray, J (1995) *Enlightenment's Wake: Politics and Culture at the Close of the Modern Age*, Routledge, London; Bauman, Z (1993) *Post-Modern Ethics*, Basil Blackwell, Oxford; Barry, B (1995) *Justice as Impartiality*, Clarendon Press, Oxford;

53   Bernstein, R (1983) *Beyond Objectivism and Relativism*, Basil Blackwell, Oxford

54   Mernissi, F (1993) *Islam and Democracy*, Virago, London

55   Arendt, H (1958) *The Human Condition*, Chicago University Press; Jelin, E and Hershberg, E (1996) *Constructing Democracy, Human Rights, Citizenship and Society in Latin America*, Westview, Boulder

56   Escobar, A, op cit (note 11); Kothari, R (1988) *The Amnesia of Development*, Zed Books, London; Nandy, A (1983) *The Intimate Enemy*, Oxford University Press, New Delhi

57   Kaul, I, op cit (note 20)

58   Editorial in the *New Statesman*, 28 August 1996

59   Goldblatt, D and Held, D (1997) *New Statesman*, 10 January

60   George, S (1996) *Development in Practice* 6(4)

61   World Bank (1997) *World Development Report 1997*, Oxford University Press, Oxford

62   Horsman and Marshall, op cit (note 13)

63   Ignatieff, M (1994) *Blood and Belonging*, Vintage, London, p2

64   Ibid, p9
65   Edwards, M and Hulme, D (eds)(1992) *Making a Difference: NGOs and Development in a Changing World*, Earthscan, London; Hulme, D and Edwards, M (eds) (1997) *Too Close for Comfort? NGOs, States and Donors*, Macmillan, London and St Martin's Press, New York
66   See for example Mathews, J (1997) 'Power Shift', *Foreign Affairs* Jan/Feb; and Salamon, L *The Global Associational Revolution*, Institute for Policy Studies, Johns Hopkins University. For a sceptical view see Putnam, R (1995) 'Bowling Alone: America's Declining Social Capital', *Journal of Democracy* 6(1)
67   See Edwards, M and Hulme, D (eds) (1996) *Beyond the Magic Bullet: NGO Performance and Accountability in the post-Cold War World*, Earthscan, London and Kumarian Press, West Hartford
68   Hirst, P and Thompson, G, op cit (note 17) p171; see also Commission on Global Governance, (1995) *Our Global Neighbourhood*, Oxford University Press, Oxford; Hirst, P (1994) *Associative Democracy*, Polity Press, Cambridge
69   Sachs, W (ed) (1992) *The Development Dictionary*, Zed Press, London
70   Bauman, Z, op cit (note 52), p245
71   Beck, U (1996) *The Risk Society*, Polity Press, Cambridge
72   Bauman, Z, ibid
73   See Etzioni, A, (1997) op cit (note 47)
74   Giddens, A (1994) op cit (note 52)
75   Huntington, S, op cit (note 14)
76   Cited in Tarock, A (1995) *Civilisational Conflict?* Third World Quarterly 16(1)
77   Daly, H (1992) *Steady-State Economics*, Earthscan, London, piii
78   Sachs, W, op cit (note 69)
79   Cited in *The Guardian*, 16 February 1996
80   *The Economist*, 16 November 1996; see also WorldWatch Institute, op cit (note 16)
81   Garrett, L (1996) 'The Return of Infectious Disease', *Foreign Affairs* 75(1)
82   Radford, T (1997), *The Guardian*, 5 April
83   Allison, G (1996), *New Statesman*, 11 November
84   Speech given at the Institute of Directors, London, July 1997
85   Burke, T (1997), *New Statesman*, 7 March
86   *The Economist*, 16 November 1996; Overseas Development Institute (1997) *Global Hunger and Food Security After the World Food Summit*, London
87   Vidal, J (1997) *The Guardian*, 8 March. For an overview see Newman, L (ed) (1990) *Hunger in History*, Blackwell, Oxford
88   Burke, T (1997) *New Statesman*, 7 March

CHAPTER 2

1   Cited in Dharampal (1983) *The Beautiful Tree: Indigenous Indian Education in the Eighteenth Century*, Biblia Index, New Delhi, p76

2   Presidential Inauguration Address (1949) Washington DC
3   TROCAIRE Conference on 'Poverty Amid Plenty', Dublin, February 1997
4   Cowen, M and Shenton, R (1996) *Doctrines of Development*, Routledge, London, p7
5   Lyon, D (1994) *Postmodernity*, Open University Press, Buckingham
6   Anderson, B (1991) *Imagined Communities*, Verso, London; Giddens, A (1990) *The Consequences of Modernity* and (1991) *Modernity and Self-Identity*, Polity Press, Cambridge; Mann, M (1986 and 1993) *The Sources of Social Power*, vols 1 and 2, Cambridge University Press, Cambridge
7   Hite, S (1989) *Women and Love*, St. Martin's Press, New York; Mumford, L (1970) *The Pentagon of Power*, Secker and Warburg, London; Sbert, J (1992) 'Progress', in Sachs, W (ed) *The Development Dictionary*, Zed Press, London; Seidler, V (1994) *Recovering the Self*, Routledge, London; Tarnas, R (1991) *The Passion of the Western Mind*, Pimlico, London; Zoja, L (1995) *Growth and Guilt*, Routledge, London
8   Zerubavel, E cited in Crosby, A (1997) *The Measure of Reality*, Cambridge University Press, Cambridge, p230
9   Davies, N (1996) *Europe: A History*, Oxford University Press, Oxford; Blackburn, R (1997) *The Making of New World Slavery*, Verso, London; Ferro, M (1997) *Colonisation: a Global History*, Routledge, London; Fernandez-Armesto, P (1995) *Millennium: a History of the Last Thousand Years*, Bantam, London
10   Cunninghame Graham, R (1988) *A Vanished Arcadia*, Century, London
11   Pakenham, T (1991) *The Scramble for Africa*, Weidenfeld and Nicolson, London, p 18; Ponting, C (1991) *A Green History of the World*, Penguin, Harmondsworth, p199
12   Chowdhury, B (1964) *The Growth of Commercial Agriculture in Bengal 1757–1900*, Past and Present Publishers, Calcutta; Cockcroft, L (1990) *Africa's Way: a Journey from the Past*, I B Tauris,London
13   Hobsbawm, E (1987) *The Age of Empire*, Weidenfeld and Nicolson, London; Foreman-Peck, J (1995) *A History of the World Economy*, Wheatsheaf, London; Kennedy, P (1988) *The Rise and Fall of the Great Powers*, Fontana, London
14   Cited in Ponting, C, op cit (note 11) p222
15   Cited in Said, E (1993) *Culture and Imperialism*, Chatto and Windus, London, p268
16   Fernandez-Armesto, F, op cit (note 9) p252
17   Pakenham, T, op cit (note 11) p615
18   Nandy, A, op cit (note 56, Chapter 1)
19   Dharampal, op cit (note 1)
20   Ibid, p75
21   Ibid, p75
22   Judd, D (1996) *Empire: the British Imperial Experience from 1765 to the Present*, Harper Collins, London, p67
23   Davies, N, op cit (note 9) p853
24   Chomsky, N (1993) *Year 501: The Conquest Continues*, Black Rose Books, Montreal, p201
25   Said, E, op cit (note 15) and (1995) *Orientalism*, Penguin,

Harmondsworth. See also Larrain, J (1994) *Ideology and Cultural Identity: Modernity and the Third World Presence*, Polity Press, Cambridge; and Latouche, S (1993) *In the Wake of the Affluent Society: an Exploration of Post-Development*, Zed Press, London

26   Blackburn, R, op cit (note 9)

27   See Ferro, M, op cit (note 9)

28   Zinkin, M (1993) 'Neo-Colonialism, Today and Tomorrow', *International Relations* XI (4), pp347–58

29   Said, E, op cit (note 15); Burman, E (1994) 'Innocents Abroad: Western Fantasies of Childhood and the Iconography of Emergencies', *Disasters* 18 (3), pp238–53

30   Hodgson, G, (1995) *People's Century*, BBC Books, London (2 Volumes)

31   Davies, N, op cit (note 9) p950

32   Arndt, H, (1972) 'Development Economics Before 1945', in H Arnott (ed) *Development and Planning: Essays in Honour of Paul Rosenstein-Rodan*, Allen and Unwin, London, p25

33   Staley, E, Rosenstein-Rodan, P, Mandelbaum, K and Kohler, G (1995) 'The UN and Development Thinking: from Optimism to Agnosticism and Back Again', *IDS Bulletin* 28(4), pp54–63

34   Arndt, H, op cit (note 32)

35   United Nations Charter

36   ul Haq, M et al (1995) *The United Nations and the Bretton Woods Institutions: New challenges for the 21st Century*, Macmillan, Basingstoke; Patel, I G (1995) 'Global Economic Governance: some thoughts on our current discontents', *Discussion Paper* 9, Centre for the Study of Global Governance, London School of Economics

37   Ruttan, V (1996) *United States Development Assistance Policy: The Domestic Politics of Foreign Economic Aid*, Johns Hopkins, Baltimore

38   Toye, J (1987) *Dilemmas of Development*, Basil Blackwell, Oxford

39   Singer, H (1995) 'Rethinking Bretton Woods: an historical perspective', in Griesgraber, J and Gunter, B (eds) *Promoting Development: Effective Global Institutions for the 21st Century*, Pluto Press, London; and Singer, H (1997) 'The Golden Age of the Keynsian Consensus – the Pendulum Swings Back', *World Development* 25(3), pp293–5

40   Meier, G, (1984) *Emerging From Poverty: The Economics that Really Matters*, Oxford University Press, Oxford ; Kennedy, P, op cit (note 13)

41   Hobsbawm, E, op cit (note 13); Foreman-Peck, J, op cit (note 13); Hackett Fisher, D (1996) *The Great Wave: Price Revolutions and the Rhythm of History*, Oxford University Press, Oxford

42   Foreman-Peck, J, op cit (note 13) p245

43   Kunz, D (1997) 'The Marshall Plan Reconsidered', *Foreign Affairs* 76(3), pp162–70

44   Hodgson, G, op cit (note 30) p271

45   Foreman-Peck, J, op cit (note 13) p246; Hodgson, G, op cit (note 29) p282; Galbraith, J K (1994) *The World Economy Since the Wars*, Sinclair-Stevenson, London, p160

46   Allen, G (1981) *A Short Economic History of Modern Japan*, Macmillan, London

47   Bauer, P (1971) *Dissent on Development*, Weidenfeld and Nicolson, London

48   Galbraith, J K, op cit (note 44); Foreman-Peck, J, op cit (note 13)
49   Rostow, W (1997) 'Lessons of the Marshall Plan', *Foreign Affairs*
     76(3), pp205–12
50   Kindleberger, C (1997) 'In the Halls of the Capitol', *Foreign Affairs*
     76(3), pp185–90
51   Schelling, T (1997) 'The Cost of Facing Global Warming', *Foreign
     Affairs* 76(3), pp8–14
52   Bienfeld, M (1991), 'Karl Polanyi and the Contradictions of the
     1980s', in Mendell, M and Salee, D (eds), *The Legacy of Karl Polanyi*,
     Macmillan, London
53   Escobar, A (1992) 'Planning', in Sachs, W (ed), op cit (note 7)
54   Ibid, p135
55   Hettne, B (1990) *Development Theory and the Three Worlds*,
     Longman, Harlow; Kay, C (1993) 'For a Renewal of Development
     Studies: Latin American Theories and Neo-liberalism in an Era of
     Structural Adjustment', *Third World Quarterly*
56   Jones, E (1988) *Growth Recurring: Economic Change in World
     History*, Clarendon Press, Oxford, p191
57   Reich, R, op cit (note 48, Chapter 1) p64
58   Hobsbawm, E, op cit (note 13) p434
59   Chomsky, N (1966) 'The Responsibility of Intellectuals', in Peck J
     (ed) *The Chomsky Reader*, Pantheon, New York, p63
60   Opeskin, B (1996) 'The Moral Foundations of Foreign Aid', *World
     Development* 24(1), pp21–44
61   *The Guardian*, 1 January 1996
62   Including those killed in East Timor: Hobsbawm, E, op cit (note 13)
63   Reich, R, op cit (note 48, Chapter 1) p64; Curtis, M (1995) *The
     Ambiguities of Power: British Foreign Policy Since 1945*, Zed Press,
     London; Jonas, S (1996) 'Dangerous Liaisons: the US in Guatemala',
     Foreign Policy 103, pp144–60
64   *The Guardian* 10 July 1997
65   Jonas, S, op cit (note 62)
66   Horsman, M and Marshall, A, op cit (note 13, Chapter1), p25
67   Mumford, L, op cit (note 7) p269; Burnell, P (1997) *Foreign Aid in a
     Changing World*, Buckingham, Open University Press
68   The Covenant on Civil and Political Rights was added in the same year
69   Hodgson, G, op cit (note 30)
70   Toye, J, op cit (note 38) p179; Benn, D (1996) *South–South Co-
     operation and External Resource Flows*, Netherlands Economic
     Institute Workshop on External Resources for Development
71   Hettne, B, op cit (note 55); Esteva, G (1992) 'Development', in
     Sachs, W (ed), op cit (note 7); Himmelstrand, V, et al, (1994) *African
     Perspectives on Development*, James Currey, London
72   Friere, P (1972) *Pedagogy of the Oppressed*, Penguin, Harmondsworth;
     Wignaraja, P, (1993) *New Social Movements in the South*, Zed Press,
     London; Rahman, A (1993) *People's Self-Development: Perspectives on
     Participatory Action Research*, Zed Press, London
73   Toye, J, op cit (note 37); Gilbert, C (1996) 'International Commodity
     Agreements: an obituary notice', *World Development* 24(1), pp1–19
74   Singer, H, op cit (note 39), p6
75   Burnell, P, op cit (note 67)

76   Figures compiled by Miyoshi, T from annual DAC reports
77   Burnell, op cit (note 67)
78   Singer, H, op cit (note 39); Hobsbawm, E, (1994) *Age of Extremes: The Short Twentieth Century*, Michael Joseph, London
79   John Williamson of the Institute for International Economics in Washington DC
80   Cited in Singer, H, op cit (note 39) p7
81   DAC reports
82   Toye, J, op cit (note 38)
83   Hobsbawm, E, op cit (note 78), p423; Bienfeld, M, op cit (note 52)
84   DAC (1997) *Development Co-operation 1996*, OECD, Paris
85   Kohler, G, op cit (note 33)
86   DAC (1997 and 1998) *Development Co-operation Reports 1996 and 1997*, OECD, Paris
87   Chase, R et al (1996) 'Pivotal States and US Strategy', *Foreign Affairs* 75(1), pp33–51
88   Graham, C and O'Hanlon, M (1997) 'Making Foreign Aid Work', *Foreign Affairs* 76(4), pp96–104
89   Cox, M (1995) *US Foreign Policy after the Cold War: Superpower without a mission?* Royal Institute for International Affairs, London
90   Funaro, R (1997) 'Balancing Out the Development Equation', *Grassroots Development* 21(1), pp48–50
91   DAC Annual Reports
92   DAC (1997), op cit (note 85) p102; and *The Reality of Aid*, ActionAid, London
93   See Berg, E (1993) *Rethinking Technical Co-operation*, UNDP, New York; Fukuda-Parr, S (1995) 'Redefining Technical Co-operation', *IDS Bulletin* 28(4), pp64–7; Moore, M (1994) *Institution-building as development assistance method*, SIDA, Stockhom; Bossuyt, J (1995) *New Avenues for Technical Co-operation in Africa*, European Centre for Development Policy and Management, Maastricht
94   Hulme, D and Edwards, M (eds) (1997) *Too Close for Comfort? NGOs, States and Donors*, Macmillan, London
95   DAC (1997) op cit (note 86)
96   Burton, J, op cit (note 3)
97   DAC (1996) *Shaping the 21st Century: the Contribution of Development Co-operation*, OECD, Paris; DAC (1998) *Development Co-operation in a Global Age*, OECD, Paris; DAC (1997) *The World in 2020*, OECD, Paris
98   DAC (1996 and 1997) op cit (note 97)
99   Hollinger, R (1995) *Postmodernism and the Social Sciences*, Sage, London; Gray, J, op cit (note 52, Chapter 1), p146
100   Uphoff, N (1992) *Learning from Gal Oya: Possibilities for Participatory Development and Post-Newtonian Social Science*, Cornell University Press
101   Adler, M (1996) *The Guardian*, 21 February; Cockburn, A (1996) *New Statesman*, 18 October
102   Cited in *The Guardian*, 5 January 1996
103   Popper, K (1945) *The Open Society and its Enemies: The Spell of Plato*, Routledge and Kegan Paul, London, p3

CHAPTER 3

1   Pradervand, P (1989) *Listening to Africa*, Praeger, New York
2   Root, H (1996) *Small Countries, Big Lessons: Governance and the Rise of East Asia*, Oxford University Press, Oxford
3   Adelman, I and Morris, C (1997) 'Development History and its Implications for Development Theory', *World Development* 25(6), pp831–40; Porter, M, (1990) *The Competitive Advantage of Nations*, Macmillan, London; Streeten, P (1995) *Thinking about Development*, Cambridge University Press, Cambridge; Griffin, K (1989) *Alternative Strategies for Economic Development*, Macmillan, London; Seers, D (1983) *The Political Economy of Nationalism*, Oxford University Press, Oxford; North, D (1990) *Institutions, Institutional Change and Economic Performance*, Cambridge University Press, Cambridge; and North, D and Thomas, R (1973) *The Rise of the Western World: A New Economic History*, Cambridge University Press, Cambridge
4   Heilbroner, R (1963) *The Great Ascent*, Harper and Row, New York; Huntington, S (1991) *The Third Wave: Democratization in the Late Twentieth Century*, University of Oklahoma Press
5   Toye, J, op cit (note 38, Chapter 2)
6   Lal, D (1983) *The Poverty of Development Economics*, Institute of Economic Affairs, London
7   Colclough, C and Manor, J (1991) *States or Markets? Neo-liberalism and the Development Policy Debate*, Clarendon Press, Oxford. See also White, G (ed) (1993) 'The Political Analysis of Markets', *IDS Bulletin* 24(3)
8   Hobsbawm, E (1975) *The Age of Revolution 1789–1848*, Weidenfeld and Nicolson, London; Kennedy, P (1988) *The Rise and Fall of the Great Powers*, Fontana, London
9   Senghaas, D (1985) *The European Experience: a Historical Critique of Development Theory*, Berg, Leamington Spa. De-linking is defined as the erection of trade and other barriers to protect the domestic economy from open market competition.
10 Jones, E, op cit (note 56, Chapter 2); Sinha, R (1995) 'Economic Reform in Developing Countries: some Conceptual Issues', *World Development* 23(4), pp557–75; Adelman, I and Morris, C, op cit (note 3)
11 Ormerod, P (1994) *The Death of Economics*, Faber, London
12 Fernandez-Armesto, F, op cit (note 9, Chapter 2); Hobsbawm, E (1962) *The Age of Capital 1848–1875*, Weidenfeld and Nicolson, London
13 Galbraith, J K, op cit (note 44, Chapter 2); Miles, R (1988) *The Women's History of the World*, Michael Joseph, London
14 Goldsmith, A (1995) 'The State, the Market and Economic Development: a Second Look at Adam Smith in Theory and Practice', *Development and Change* 26(4), pp633–50; Sinha, op cit (note 10); Mosley, P (1995) 'Development Economics and the Underdevelopment of Sub-Saharan Africa', *Journal of International Development* 7(5), pp685–706; Krugman, P (1995) *Development, Geography and Economic Theory*, MIT Press, Cambridge

15 Putnam, R, op cit (note 49, Chapter 1); Fukuyama, F, op cit (note 45, Chapter 1)
16 Chowdhury, A and Islam, I (1993) *The Newly-Industrialising countries of East Asia*, Routledge, London; Griffin, K, op cit (note 3) p242
17 Granovetter, M and Swedberg, R (eds) (1992) *The Sociology of Economic Life*, Westview Press, Boulder
18 Fernandez-Armesto, F, op cit (note 9, Chapter 2)
19 Hobsbawm, E, op cit (note 80, Chapter 2) p251
20 Johansen, F (1993) *Poverty-reduction in East Asia: the Silent Revolution*, The World Bank, Washington DC
21 Chowdhury, A and Islam, I, op cit (note16)
22 Maipose, G and Somolekae, G (1996) *Aid Effectiveness in Botswana*, Overseas Development Council, Washington DC
23 Krugman, P (1994) 'The Myth of Asia's Miracle', *Foreign Affairs* 73(6), pp62–78–summarised and repeated in *USA Today* 31 December 1997
24 Kong, T (1996) 'Corruption and its Institutional Foundations: the Experience of South Korea', *IDS Bulletin* 27(2), pp48–55
25 Ogle, G (1990) *South Korea: Dissent within the Economic Miracle*, Zed Press, London
26 Bello, W (1990) *Dragons in Distress: Asia's Miracle Economies in crisis*, Institute for Food and Development Policy, San Francisco
27 *The Guardian*, 28 September 1997
28 Chant, S and McIlwaine, K (1995) *Women of a Lesser Cost*, Pluto, London
29 Mulgan, G, op cit (note 37, Chapter 1)
30 *The Guardian*, 1 January 1998; *The Observer* 18 January 1998
31 Wade, R and Veneroso, F, letter to *The Economist*, 10 January 1997
32 *The Economist*, 3 January 1998
33 Radelet, S and Sachs, J (1997) 'Asia's Re-emergence', *Foreign Affairs* 76(6), pp44–59
34 *The Economist*, 31 January 1998; *Financial Times*, 17 January 1998
35 Ibrahim, A (1996) *The Asian Renaissance*, Kuala Lumpur
36 Chalmers, I (1995) 'Democratisation and Social Change in Indonesia', *Development Bulletin*, 32, pp28–30; Dahrendorf, R (1996) 'Economic Opportunity, Civil Society and Political Liberty', *Development and Change* 27(2), pp229–49
37 Jacobs, J (1984) *Cities and the Wealth of Nations: Principles of Economic Life*, Vintage, New York; Mann, M (1993) *The Sources of Social Power*, Cambridge University Press, Cambridge, vol II
38 Amsden, A (1989) *Asia's Next Giant: South Korea and Late Industrialisation*, Oxford University Press, Oxford; Haggard, S (1990) *Pathways from the Periphery: the Politics of Growth in Newly-industrialising Countries*, Cornell University Press; Page, J (ed) (1994) 'The East Asian Miracle', *World Development* 22(4); Wade, R (1990) *Governing the Market: Economic Theory and the Role of Government in East Asian Industrialisation*, Princeton University Press; Root, H, op cit (note 2); Chowdhury, A and Islam, I op cit (note 16)
39 McRae, H, op cit (note 33, Chapter 1)
40 *The Economist*, 1 March 1997, p24

41   Weiss, L and Hobson, J (1995) *States and Economic Development: a Comparative Historical Analysis*, Polity Press, Cambridge

42   Killick, T (1995) 'Flexibility and Economic Progress', *World Development* 23(5), pp721–34

43   Amsden, A, op cit (note 38)

44   Baer, W and Maloney, W (1997) 'Neoliberalism and Income Distribution in Latin America', *World Development* 25(3), p323; Wood, A and Ridao-Cano, C (1997) 'Skill, Trade and International Inequality', *IDS Working Paper* 47

45   Grindle, M and Thomas, J (1991) *Public Choices and Policy Change: the Political Economy of Reform in Developing Countries*, Johns Hopkins University Press, Baltimore, p108; Bello, W, op cit (note 26) p4

46   Root, H, op cit (note 2) p34

47   Dahlgren, S (1994) *Support for Independence: an Evaluation of 27 Years of Development Co-operation with Botswana*, SIDA, Stockholm; Maipose, G and Somolekae, G, op cit (note 22)

48   Chowdhury, A and Islam, I, op cit (note 16)

49   *The Economist*, 18 May 1996, p102

50   Amsden, A, op cit (note 38)

51   Riddell, R (1990) *Manufacturing Africa*, James Currey, London; Maipose, G and Somolekae, G, op cit (note 22)

52   ECDPM, (1996) *Beyond Lomé IV*, ECDPM, Maastricht

53   Agostin, M and Ffrench-Davis, R (1996) *Managing Capital Inflows in Latin America*, UNDP, New York

54   Diamond, J (1997) *Guns, Germs and Steel*, WW Norton, New York

55   Kim Dae Jung (1994) 'Is Culture Destiny?' *Foreign Affairs* 73(6), pp189–94; Ibrahim, A, op cit (note 35); Root, H, op cit (note 2); Perkin, H (1997) 'The Third Revolution', in Kelly et al (eds), *Stakeholder Capitalism*, Macmillan, London

56   *New Statesman*, 31 January 1997

57   This phrase comes from Eric Young, an Ottawa-based consultant, to describe the prime task of a leader. See also Weiss, L and Hobson, J, op cit (note 41)

58   Zeldin, T, op cit (note 1, Preface) p136

59   Leftwich, A (1996) *Democracy and Development*, Polity Press, Cambridge

60   Kohli, A (1994) 'Where do High-Growth Political Economies Come From? The Japanese Lineage of Korea's Developmental State', *World Development* 22(9), pp1269–93; Haggard, S et al 'Japanese Colonialism and Korean Development: a Critique', *World Development* 25(6), pp867–81

61   Page, S (1990) *Trade, Finance and Developing Countries*, Harvester-Wheatsheaf, London

62   Amsden, A (1994) 'Why Isn't the Whole World Experimenting with the East Asian Model to Develop?' *World Development* 22(4), pp627–33; Cassen, R et al (1994) *Does Aid Work?*, Clarendon Press, Oxford; Burnett, S (1992) *Investing in Security: Economic Aid for Non-Economic Purposes*, Institute for Strategic and International Studies, Washington DC; Chan, S and Clark, C (1992) *Flexibility, Foresight and 'Fortuna' in Taiwan's Development*, Routledge, London;

Krueger, A (1989) *Aid and Development*, Johns Hopkins University Press, Baltimore

63   Migdal, J (1988) *Strong Societies and Weak States*, Princeton University Press; White, G (1988) *Developmental States in East Asia*, Macmillan, London; Gills, B et al (eds) (1996) 'The Developmental State?' *Third World Quarterly Special Issue* 17(4); Wade, R, op cit (note 38)

64   Root, H, op cit (note 2) p32

65   Ibid

66   Carroll, B and Carroll, T (1997) 'State and Ethnicity in Botswana and Mauritius: a Democratic Route to Development?' *Journal of Development Studies* 33(4), pp464–86

67   Heller, P (1996) 'Social Capital as a Product of Class Mobilisation and Government Intervention: Industrial Workers in Kerala, India', *World Development* 24 (6), pp1055–71

68   Tendler, J (1997) *Good Government in the Tropics*, Johns Hopkins University Press, Baltimore; Evans, P (1996) 'Development Strategies across the Public-Private Divide', *World Development* 24(6), pp1033–7; Taylor, L (1996) 'Sustainable Development: an Introduction', *World Development* 24(2), pp215–226; Weiss, L and Hobson, J, op cit (note 41)

69   Campos, J and Root, H (1996) *The Key to the Asian Miracle: Making Shared Growth Credible*, Brookings Institution, Washington DC

70   Workers across East Asia pay a much higher proportion of their earnings into provident funds or their equivalent – 22 per cent in Singapore and ten per cent in Malaysia: DEMOS (1996) *The Age of Asia*, London

71   See Diamond, J, op cit (note 54)

72   Wiggins, S (1995) 'Change in African Farming Systems between the mid-1970s and the mid-1990s', *Journal of International Development* 7(6), pp807–48; Thirtle, C (ed) (1998) 'The Hesitant Recovery of African Agriculture', *Journal of International Development* 10(1), pp71–128

73   World Bank (1997) *IDA in Action 1994–96*, Washington DC

74   Mosley, P, op cit (note 14)

75   ECA (1996) *Report on the Economic and Social Situation in Africa 1996*, ECA, Addis Ababa

76   Ibid

77   *The Economist*, 29 June 1996

78   UNDP (1996) *Human Development Report*, New York

79   Eicher, C (1995) 'Zimbabwe's Maize-Based Green Revolution', *World Development* 23(5), pp805–18

80   Borlaug, N and Dowdswell, C (1995) 'Mobilising Science and Technology to get Agriculture Moving in Africa', *Development Policy Review* 13, pp115–29; Jiggins, J, et al (1996) 'A Response to Borlaug and Dowdswell', *Development Policy Review* 14, pp89–103

81   Fisher, T and Mahajan, V (1997) *The Rural Non-farm Sector in India*, IT Publications, London

82   Ng, F and Yeats, A (1997), 'Open Economies Work Better: Did Africa's Protectionist Policies Cause its Marginalisation in World Trade?', *World Development* 25(6), pp889–904

83   *The Economist*, 7 September 1996, p11
84   Cornia, A et al (1992) *Africa's Recovery in the 1990s*, Macmillan,
      London; Putterman, L and Rueschemeyer, D (1992) *State and Market
      in Development: Synergy or Rivalry?* Lynne Rienner, Boulder;
      Helleiner, G (1995) 'Africa in the Globalised Economy', *Copenhagen
      Conference on Sub-Saharan Africa*, November; Stewart, F (1995)
      'Biases in Global markets: can the Forces of Inequity and
      Marginalisation be Modified?' in ul Haq, M et al (eds) *The UN and
      the Bretton Woods Institutions: New Challenges for the 21st Century*,
      Macmillan, London; Bryceson, D and Howe, J (1997) 'African Rural
      Labour and the World Bank: an Alternative Perspective', *Development
      in Practice* 7(1), pp26–38
85   *The Guardian*, 10 April 1997; Sachs, J (1996) 'Growth in Africa: it
      can be done', in *The Economist* 29 June and 'The Limits of
      Convergence', in *The Economist* 14 June 1997; OECD (1995)
      Whither African Economies? Paris
86   Judd, D, op cit (note 22, Chapter 2); Oliver, R (1991) *The African
      Experience*, Pimlico, London
87   Davidson, B (1992) *The Black Man's Burden: Africa and the Curse of
      the Nation State*, James Currey, London, p297; Cockcroft, L (1990)
      Africa's Way, I B Tauris, London
88   Bevan, P and Ssewaya, A (1995) *Understanding Poverty in Uganda*,
      Centre for the Study of African Economies, Oxford; Ellis, S (1996)
      *Democracy in Sub-Saharan Africa: Where did it come from and can it
      be Supported?* European Centre for Development Policy and
      Management, Maastricht
89   Hyden, G (1980) *Beyond Ujamaa in Tanzania*, University of
      California Press, Berkeley; and (1983) *No Shortcuts to Progress*,
      Heinemann, London. See also Spalding, N (1996) 'The Tanzanian
      Peasant and Ujamaa: a Study in Contradictions', *Third World
      Quarterly* 17(1), pp89–108
90   Soyinka, W (1996) 'The National Question in Africa', *Development
      and Change* 27 (2), p279
91   Green, R (1992) *Africa 1975–95: the Political Economy of Boom,
      Decline, Conflict, Survival and Beyond*, UN NGO Liaison Service,
      Geneva; Swift, J (1996) 'War and Rural Development in Africa', *IDS
      Bulletin* 27(3), pp1–5
92   Jamal, V and Weeks, J (1993) *Africa Misunderstood or Whatever
      Happened to the Rural-Urban Gap*, Macmillan, London; Sarkar, P and
      Singer, H (1991) 'Manufactured Exports of Developing Countries and
      their Terms-of-Trade since 1965', *World Development* 19(4), pp333–40
93   Pettifor, A and Wood, A (1996) *A Fresh Start for Africa*, Debt Crisis
      Network, London
94   DAC (1996) *Development Co-operation Report*, OECD, Paris, Table
      III-5
95   Murshed, S and Raffer, K (1993) *Trade, Transfers and Development*,
      Edward Elgar, Aldershot
96   Hanlon, J (1991) *Mozambique: Who Calls the Shots?* Zed Press,
      London, p6; LaFond, A (1995) *Sustaining Primary Health Care*,
      Earthscan, London
97   ECA, op cit (note 75)

98   Oliver, R, op cit (note 87) p241
99   *The Economist*, 7 September 1996
100 Van de Walle, N and Johnston, N (1996) *Improving Aid: the Challenge to Donors and African Governments*, Overseas Development Council, Washington DC
101 Ndulu, B (1995) 'Africa's Development Challenges in a Changing World Economy', *Copenhagen Conference on Sub-Saharan Africa*, November
102 Soyinka, W, op cit (note 90)
103 Mazrui, A, 'The African State as a Political Refugee', *OAU Symposium on Refugees and Forced Displacement, Addis Ababa, September*
104 Healey, J and Robinson, M (1992) *Democracy, Governance and Economic policy: Sub-Saharan Africa in Comparative Perspective*, Overseas Development Institute, London
105 Hirschman, A (1970) *Exit, Voice and Loyalty*, Harvard University Press
106 Cited by Hawthorn, G (1993) 'Sub-Saharan Africa', in Held, D (ed) *Prospects for Democracy*, Polity Press, Cambridge
107 Ellis, S, op cit (note 88)
108 Haggard, S and Kaufman, R (1995) *The Political Economy of Democratic Transitions*, Princeton University Press; Nelson, J (1990) *Economic Crisis and Policy Choice*, Princeton University Press
109 Bratton, M (1994) *Civil Society and Political Transition in Africa*, Institute for Development Research, Boston; Ndegwa, P (1996) *The Two Faces of Civil Society: NGOs and Politics in Africa*, Kumarian Press, West Hartford
110 Sen, A (1983) *Poverty and Famines*, Clarendon Press, Oxford
111 Edwards, M and Hulme, D (eds) (1996) *Beyond the Magic Bullet: NGO Performance and Accountability in the post-Cold War World*, Kumarian Press, West Hartford and Earthscan, London; Sachikonye, L (1995) *Democracy, Civil Society and the State: Social Movements in Southern Africa*, SAPES, Harare
112 Morrissey, O (1995) Politics and Economic Policy Reform, *Journal of International Development* 7(4), pp599–618
113 Grindle, M (1996) *Challenging the State: Crisis and Innovation in Latin America and Africa*, Cambridge University Press, Cambridge; Diamond, L and Plattner, M (1995) *Economic Reform and Democracy*, Johns Hopkins Press; Bates, R and Krueger, A (1993) *Political and Economic Interactions in Economic Policy Reform*, Blackwell, Oxford; and the works by Haggard and Kaufman, Williamson, Nelson, and Grindle and Thomas already cited
114 *The Guardian*, 20 September 1996
115 *The Guardian*, 19 April 1997
116 Putterman, L and Rueschemeyer, D, op cit (note 84)
117 Marnham, P (1980) *Dispatches from Africa*, Abacus, London p88
118 Mamdani, M (1996) *Citizen and Subject: Contemporary Africa and the Legacy of Late Colonialism*, Princeton University Press. See also Pradervand, P, op cit (note 1) and Platteau, J (1996) 'The Evolutionary Theory of Land Rights in Sub-Saharan Africa', *Development and Change* 27(1), pp29–86
119 Galbraith, J K (1996) *The Good Society*, Sinclair-Stevenson, London

CHAPTER 4

1   Currently a Minister in the Zimbabwe government
2   A remark made in passing on a visit I made to Rajasthan in 1989
3   Hancock, G (1989) *Lords of Poverty*, Atlantic Monthly Press, New York
4   Edwards, M and Hulme, D (eds) op cit (notes 65 and 67, Chapter 1);Fowler, A, (1997) *Striking a Balance*, Earthscan, London
5   Maren, M, op cit (note 1, Chapter 1)
6   Smillie, I (1995) *The Alms Bazaar – Altruism Under Fire*, IT Publications, London, p59
7   See Chapter 3 references
8   Mosley, P and Hudson, J (1995) *Aid effectiveness: A Study of the Effectiveness of Overseas Aid in the Main Countries Receiving ODA Assistance*, Department for International Development, London
9   Cited in Hodson, R (1997) 'Elephant Loose in the Jungle: the World Bank and NGOs in Sri Lanka', in Hulme, D and Edwards, M (eds) op cit (note 65, Chapter 1)
10   Tendler, J 'Tales of Dissemination in Small-Farm Agriculture: Lessons for Institution-Builders', *World Development* 21(10), pp1567–82
11   Uphoff, N (1995) 'Why NGOs are Not a Third Sector: a Sectoral Analysis with some Sceptical and Affirmative Thoughts on Accountability, Sustainability and Evaluation', in Edwards, M and Hulme, D (eds), op cit (note 67, Chapter 1)
12   Chambers, R (1995) 'Poverty and Livelihoods: Whose Reality Counts?' *Environment and Urbanisation* 7(1), pp173–204
13   Cashdan, E (1990) *Risk and Uncertainty in Tribal and Peasant Economies*, Westview Press, Boulder; Scoones, I and Thompson, J (1994) *Beyond Farmer First: Rural People's Knowledge, Agricultural Research and Extension Practice*, IT Publications, London
14   Amis, P and Rakodi, C (1994) 'Urban Poverty: Issues for Research and Policy', *Journal of International Development* 6(5), pp627–34
15   Awasthi, R (1989) 'Poverty Alleviation or Doling Out Illusions?' *FRCH Newsletter* 3(2), p5
16   Kramsjo, B and Wood,G (1992) *Breaking the Chains: Collective Action for Social Justice among the Rural Poor in Bangladesh*, IT Publications, London, p33
17   Sen, A (1986) *Poverty and Famines*, Oxford University Press, Oxford; Chambers, R (1984) *To the Hands of the Poor: Water, Trees and Land*, Ford Foundation, Delhi
18   Esman, M and Uphoff, N (1984) *Local Organisations: Intermediaries in Rural Development*, Cornell University Press
19   Psacharopoulos, G (1994) 'Returns to Investment in Education: a Global Update', *World Development* 22(9), pp1325–43
20   Black, M (1996) *Children First: The story of UNICEF*, Oxford University Press, Oxford; LaFond, A (1995) *Sustaining Primary Health Care*, Earthscan, London
21   LaFond, A, ibid; Edwards, M (1996) 'New Approaches to Children and Development', *Journal of International Development* 8(6), pp813–28

22   Chen, L and Singh, S (1995) *Sustainability of the Children's Summit Goals*, UNICEF/International Child Development Centre, Florence
23   Rifkin, S and Walt, J (1986) 'Why Health Improves: Defining the Issues Concerning Comprehensive and Selective Primary Health Care', *Social Science and Medicine*, 23(6), pp559–66
24   Mawer, R (1997) *Developing the World Bank Nutrition and ECD Project from an SCF-UK Perspective*, Save the Children Fund-UK, Kampala
25   Ibid
26   Moris, J (1981) *Managing Integrated Rural Development*, International Development Institute, Bloomington
27   Bond, R (1997) *Operationalising Process: the Experience of the First Decade of the Monegagala IDRP in Sri Lanka*, IDPM, Manchester; Moore, M et al (1995) *MONDEP Mid-term Programme Review*, NORAD, Oslo
28   Internal project documents, Vijayawada Slum Improvement Project (1996) Department for International Development, London
29   Edwards,M (1996) *NGO Performance: What Breeds Success?* Save the Children Fund-UK, London, Working Paper 14
30   Dichter, T (1997) 'Appeasing the Gods of Sustainability', in Hulme, D and Edwards, M (eds), op cit (note 65, Chapter 1); Hulme, D and Mosley, P (1996) *Finance Against Poverty*, Routledge, London
31   Kabeer, N and Murthy, R (1996) 'Compensating for Institutional Exclusion?' *IDS Discussion Paper*, 356
32   Dichter, T, op cit (note 30)
33   Hulme, D and Mosley, P, op cit (note 30); Goetz, A and Sen Gupta, R (1996) 'Who Takes the Credit?' IDS Sussex; Hashemi, S, et al (1996) 'Rural Credit Programmes and Women's Empowerment in Bangladesh', *World Development*, 24(4)
34   Rutherford, S (1995) *ASA: the Biography of an NGO*, Association for Social Advancement, Dhaka
35   Edwards, M and Hulme, D, op cit (see note 112, Chapter 3)
36   DAC (1997) *Searching for Impact and Methods: NGO Evaluation Synthesis Study*, OECD, Paris; Uphoff, N et al (eds) (1997) *Reasons for Hope*, Kumarian Press, West Hartford; Riddell, R and Robinson, M (1996) *NGOs and Rural Poverty Alleviation*, Clarendon Press, Oxford; Fowler, A, op cit (note 4); Wiggins, S and Cromwell, E (1995) 'NGOs and Seed Provision to Smallholders in Developing Countries', *World Development* 23(3), pp413–22
37   Chambers, R (1994) 'The Origins and Practice of PRA', *World Development* 22(7), pp953–70; Korten, F and Siy, R (1988) *Transforming a Bureaucracy: the Experience of the Philippine National Irrigation Administration*, Kumarian Press, West Hartford; Narayan, D (1994) *The Contribution of People's Participation: 121 Rural Water Supply Projects*, The World Bank, Washington DC; Ostrom, E et al (1993) *Institutional Incentives and Sustainable Development*, Westview, Boulder
38   Ferguson, J (1990) *The Anti-Politics Machine: Development, Depoliticisation and Bureaucratic Power in Lesotho*, Cambridge University Press, Cambridge

39   Porter, D et al (1991) *Development in Practice: Paved with Good Intentions*, Routledge, London

40   *The Economist*, 7 September 1996

41   Klitgaard, R (1990) *Tropical Gangsters*, I B Tauris, London, p 104

42   *The Guardian* 19 February 1998

43   Mosse, D (1994) 'Authority, Gender and Knowledge: Theoretical Reflections on the Practice of PRA', *Development and Change* 25(3), pp497–526; Peet, R and Watts, M (eds) (1996) *Liberation Ecologies: Environment, Development, Social Movements*, Routledge, London; Garforth, C (1994) 'Rural Peoples' Organisations and Agricultural Extension in Thailand: who benefits?' *Journal of International Development* 6(6), pp707–20; Rahman, M (1993) *People's Self-Development*, Zed Press, London

44   Bebbington, A (1996) 'Organisations and Intensifications: Campesino Federations, Rural Livelihoods and Agricultural Technology in the Andes and Amazonia', *World Development* 24(7), pp1161–77; Dudley, E (1993) *The Critical Villager*, Routledge, London

45   Hulme, D and Mosley, P, op cit (note 30); Lele, U and Goldsmith, A (1989) 'The Development of National Agricultural Research Capacity', *Economic Development and Cultural Change* 37 (2), pp305–44

46   Thompson, J (1995) 'Participatory Approaches in Government Bureaucracies', *World Development* 23(9), pp1521–54

47   Tendler, J and Alves Amorim, M (1996) 'Small Firms and their Helpers: Lessons on Demand', *World Development* 24(3), pp407–26; Ndegwa, P (1996) *The Two Faces of Civil Society: NGOs and Politics in Africa*, Kumarian Press, West Hartford; Smith-Sreen, P (1995) *Accountability in Development Organisations – Women's Organisations in India*, Sage, New Delhi

48   Burkey, S (1993) *People First: a Guide to Self-reliant Participatory Rural Development*, Zed Press, London; Wignaraja, P (1993) *New Social Movements in the South*, Zed Press, London; Brass, T (ed) (1995) *New Farmers' Movements in India*, Frank Cass, London

49   Tendler, J and Freedheim, D (1994) 'Trust in a Rent-Seeking World: Health and Government Transformed in North-East Brazil', *World Development* 22(12), pp1771–92

50   Uphoff, N, op cit (note 11); Brinkerhoff, D and Goldsmith, A (1992) 'Promoting the Sustainability of Development Initiatives', *World Development* 20 (3), pp369–83

51   Wade, R (1988) *Village Republics: Economic Conditions for Collective Action in South India*, Oxford University Press, Oxford

52   Annis, S (1987) 'Small-Scale Solutions and Large-Scale Problems', *World Development*, special supplement on NGOs; Friedmann, J and Rangan, H (eds) (1993) *In Defense of Livelihood: Comparative Studies on Environmental Action*, Kumarian Press, West

53   Uphoff, N (1993) 'Grassroots Organisations and NGOs in Rural Development: Opportunities with Diminishing States and Expanding Markets', *World Development* 21(4), pp607–22

54   Carroll, T (1992) *Intermediary NGOs: the Supporting Link in Grassroots Development*, Kumarian Press, West Hartford

55 Klouda, A (1995) 'Responding to AIDS: Are There Any Appropriate Development and Health Priorities?' *Journal of International Development* 7(3), pp467–87

56 Wood, G (1997) 'States without Citizens: the Problems of the Franchise State', in Hulme, D and Edwards, M (eds), op cit (note 65, Chapter 1); Mackintosh, M (1997) *Public Management for Social Inclusion*, IDPM, Manchester

57 Hirschman, A (1967) *Development Projects Observed*, Brookings Institution, Washington DC, p186

58 Karunawathie, M (1993) 'People's Empowerment from the People's Perspective', *Development in Practice* 3(3), p177

CHAPTER 5

1 Smillie, I (1996) *Sierra Leone: NGOs in Complex Emergencies*, mimeo CARE-Canada, Ottawa, p25

2 Hodge, C and Grbin, M (1996) *A Test for Europe: Confidence-Building in Former Yugoslavia*, Institute of Russian and East European Studies, Glasgow, p51

3 Prior, M (1994) *Shooting at the Moon: Cambodian Peace-workers Tell Their Stories*, MPA Publishers, Canberra

4 Roberts, A and Kingsbury, B (eds) (1993) *United Nations, Divided World: The UN's Role in International Relations*, Clarendon Press, Oxford; Slim, H (1995) 'Military Humanitarianism and the New Peacekeeping: an Agenda for Peace?' *IDS Bulletin* 27(3), pp86–95

5 Halliday, F (1994) *Rethinking International Relations*, Macmillan, London

6 International Federation of Red Cross and Red Crescent Societies (1996) *World Disasters Report 1996*, Oxford University Press, Oxford, p9

7 Weiss, T (1997) 'Rekindling Hope in UN Humanitarian Intervention', in Clark, W and Herbst, J (eds) *Learning from Somalia*, Westview Press, Boulder

8 Donini, A (1995) *Beyond Neutrality: on the Compatibility of Military Intervention and Humanitarian Assistance*, The Fletcher Forum (Summer/Fall), p33

9 Evans, G (1994) 'Co-operative Security and Intra-State Conflict', *Foreign Policy* 96 (Fall), pp3–20; Riggs, F (1994) 'Ethno-Nationalism, Industrialism and the Modern State', *Third World Quarterly* 15(4), pp583–611

10 de Waal, A (1997) *Famine Crimes: Politics and the Disaster Relief Industry in Africa*, James Currey, London; Davies, S and Hossain, N (1997) 'Livelihood Adaptation, Public Action and Civil Society – a Review of the Literature', *Working Paper* 57, IDS, Sussex

11 Sen, A (1981) *Poverty and Famines: an essay on Entitlement and Deprivation*, Clarendon Press, Oxford; Dreze, J and Sen, A (1989) *Hunger and Public Action*, Clarendon Press, Oxford

12 Keen, D (1994) *The Benefits of Famine: a Political Economy of Famine and Relief in South-Western Sudan, 1983–9*, Princeton University Press

13   Anderson, M (1994) *International Assistance and Conflict: an Exploration of Negative Impacts*, Collaborative for Development Action, Cambridge; Prendergast, J and Scott, C (1996) *Aid With Integrity: Avoiding the Potential of Humanitarian Aid to Sustain Conflict*, USAID, Washington DC; Anderson, M (1996) *Do No Harm: Supporting Local Capacities for Peace through Aid*, Collaborative for Development Action, Cambridge

14   Duffield, M (1994) 'An Account of Relief Operations in Bosnia', *Relief and Refugee Network*, Paper 3, Overseas Development Institute, p18

15   Duffield, M (1994) 'The Political Economy of Internal War: Asset Transfer, Complex Emergencies and International Aid', in Macrae, J and Zwi, A (eds) *War and Hunger: Rethinking International Responses to Complex Emergencies*, Zed Press, London, p61

16   de Waal, A (1989) *Famine That Kills*, Clarendon Press, Oxford

17   de Waal, A (1995) 'Compassion Fatigue', in *New Statesman*, 17 March

18   de Waal, A, op cit (note 10)

19   Macrae, J and Zwi, A, op cit (note 15)

20   Bush, K (1995) *Fitting the Pieces Together: Canadian Contributions to the Challenge of Re-building War-torn Societies*, IDRC, Ottawa

21   Miall, H (1992) *The Peacemakers: Peaceful Settlements of Disputes since 1945*, Macmillan, London

22   Storr, A (1991) *Human Destructiveness: the Roots of Genocide and Human Cruelty*, Routledge, London

23   Galtung, J (1996) *Peace by Peaceful Means*, Sage, London p132

24   de Waal, A, op cit (note 10) pxv

25   *The Economist*, 6 September 1997

26   Minear, L (1991) *Humanitarianism Under Siege: a Critical Review of Operation Lifeline Sudan*, Red Sea Press, Trenton

27   de Waal, A, op cit (note 10) p91

28   Minear, L (1997) 'Time to Pull the Plug on OLS?' *Crosslines* (March/April) pp59–60

29   Varnis, S (1990) *Reluctant Aid or Aiding the Reluctant? US Food Aid Policy and Ethiopian Famine Relief*, Transaction Publishers, New Brunswick

30   Duffield, M and Prendergast, J (1994) *Without Troops and Tanks*, Red Sea Press, Lawrenceville

31   *The Sunday Times*, 18 February 1996; Scott, C (1995) 'Humanitarian Action and Security in Liberia 1989-94', *Brown University: Thomas J.Watson Jr Institute for International Studies*, Occasional Paper 20; Avebury, E (1993) *Liberia: the Role of the United Nations*, Royal African Society, London

32   *The Economist*, 15 February 1997

33   Smillie, I, op cit (note 1); International Crisis Group (1996) *Report on Sierra Leone*, ICG, London

34   de Waal, A, op cit (note 10) p181

35   Slim, H and Visman, E (1995) 'Evaluation, Intervention and Retaliation: UN Humanitarian Operations in Somalia 1991-93', in Harriss, J (ed) *The Politics of Humanitarian Intervention*, Pinter, London; Luling, V (1997) 'Come Back Somalia? Questioning a Collapsed State', *Third World Quarterly* 18(2), pp287–302; Penrose, A (1995) *NGOs and Conflict Resolution*, Save the Children Fund, London

36   Gilkes, P (1995) *Acceptance is not Recognition: the Republic of Somaliland 1993–5*, Save the Children Fund, London; Abdillahi, M (1997) *Somaliland NGOs: Challenges and Opportunities*, CIIR, London

37   Sahnoun, M (1995) *Managing Conflict after the Cold War*, CIIR, London

38   Subsequent trials acquitted the Italians and Belgians for want of evidence; *The Guardian*, 12 April, 7 June and 3 July 1997

39   Sahnoun, M, op cit (note 37); Prendergast, J and Scott, C, op cit (note 13) p23

40   de Waal, A (1994) 'Humanitarianism Unbound', *Index on Censorship* (November/December)

41   Weiss, T (1995) 'Overcoming the Somalia Syndrome', *Global Governance* 1, pp171–87

42   Slim, H and Visman, E, op cit (note 35) p164

43   Destexhe, A (1994) 'The Third Genocide', *Foreign Policy* 97 (Winter), pp3–17

44   Melvern, L (1995) *The Ultimate Crime: Who Betrayed the UN and Why*, Allison and Busby, London, p11

45   de Waal, A, op cit (note 10) p196

46   African Rights (1994) *Rwanda: Death, Despair and Defiance*, African Rights, London

47   Ibid

48   Natsios, A, cited in Prendergast, J and Scott, C, op cit (note 13) p5

49   Eriksson, J (1996) *International Response to Conflict and Genocide: Lessons from the Rwanda Experience – Synthesis Report*, Joint Evaluation of Emergency Assistance to Rwanda, Overseas Development Institute, London

50   Seaman, J (1994) 'Relief, Rehabilitation and Development: are the Distinctions Useful?' *IDS Bulletin* 25(4), pp33–6

51   de Waal, A, op cit (note 10) p196

52   Ibid p210

53   Ibid

54   *The Guardian*, 17 September 1997; *The Economist*, 15 November 1997

55   de Waal, A, op cit (note 10) p212

56   Hodge, C and Grbin, M, op cit (note 2); Magas, B (1993) *The Destruction of Yugoslavia*, Verso, London; Woodward, S (1995) *Balkan Tragedy*, Brookings Institution, Washington DC; Silber, L and Little, A (1995) *The Death of Yugoslavia*, Penguin, Harmondsworth

57   Minear, L (1994) 'The International Relief System: A Critical Review', *Brown University: Humanitarianism and War Project*, mimeo

58   *The Guardian*, 15 September 1997

59   Mercier, M (1995) *Crimes Without Punishment: Humanitarian Action in the Former Yugoslavia*, Pluto Press, London

60   Weiss, T and Pasic (1997) 'Reinventing UNHCR: Enterprising Humanitarians in the Former Yugoslavia 1991–5', *Global Governance* 3, pp41–57

61   Mercier, M, op cit (note 59) p21

62   Hodge, C and Grbin, M, op cit (note 2) p86

63   Lind, M (1995) 'Twilight of the UN', *The New Republic*, 30 October

64   ICG (1996) *The Dayton Peace Accords: a Six-Month Review*, International Crisis Group,London
65   ICG (1996) *Elections in Bosnia and Herzegovina*, International Crisis Group, London
66   ICG (1997) *Media in Bosnia and Herzegovina: How International Support can be more Effective*, ICG, London
67   Holbrooke, R (1998) *To End a War*, Random House, New York
68   Hodge, C and Grbin, M, op cit (note 2) p5
69   Kumar, R (1997) 'The Troubled History of Partition', *Foreign Affairs* January/February, pp22–34
70   Galtung, J, op cit (note 23) p274
71   Evans, G (1994) 'Co-operative Security and Intra-State Conflict', *Foreign Policy* 96 Fall, pp3–20
72   Bush, K, op cit (note 20); Rupesinghe, K (1994) 'Advancing Diplomacy in a Post-Cold War Era', *Relief and Refugee Network Paper* 5, Overseas Development Institute, London
73   Henderson, M (1996) *The Forgiveness Factor: Stories of Hope in a World of Conflict*, Grosvenor Books, London; Johnston, D and Sampson, C (eds) (1994) *Religion: the Missing Dimension of Statecraft*, Oxford University Press, Oxford; Pearce, J (1997) 'Sustainable Peace-Building in the South', *Development in Practice* 7(4), pp438–55; Miall, H op cit (note 21)
74   Rupesinghe, K (ed) (1995) *Conflict Transformation*, Macmillan, London; Smillie, I, op cit (note 1)
75   Rupesinghe, K, op cit (note 74) p172
76   McDonald, G (1997) *Colombia: Peacebuilding from Below*, CIIR, London; Prado, T (1996) *Peace in the Making: Civil Groups in Guatemala*, CIIR, London
77   Sparks, A (1995) *Tomorrow is Another Country: the Inside Story of South Africa's Negotiated Revolution*, Heinemann, London
78   Miller, R (ed) (1992) *Aid as Peacemaker: Canadian Development Assistance and Third World Conflict*, Carleton University Press, Ottawa; Sahnoun, M, op cit (note 37)
79   Wilson, R (1997) *Civil Groups in the South African and Guatemalan Transitions*, CIIR, London
80   Herring, E (1995) *Danger and Opportunity: Exploring International Crisis Outcomes*, Manchester University Press
81   Slim, H, op cit (note 4)
82   *The Guardian*, 10 January, 1997
83   Herring, E, op cit (note 80)
84   Cranna, M (1994) *The True Cost of Conflict*, Earthscan, London
85   *The Guardian*, 10 January 1997
86   *The Economist*, 2 February 1997
87   Smillie, I, op cit (note 6, Chapter 4); Smillie, I (1996) *Service-Delivery or Civil Society? NGOs in Bosnia and Herzegovina*, CARE-Canada, Ottawa
88   Smillie, I, op cit (note 87) piv
89   Smillie, I, op cit (note 6, Chapter 4), p26
90   Anderson, M and Woodhouse,P (1993) *Rising from the Ashes: Development Strategies in Times of Disaster*, Westview, Boulder

91   *The Guardian*, 20 June 1997. Traders were also very active in rebuild-
     ing the economy across factional lines after the Biafran war
92   Christopolos, I (1997) *Local Service Institutions and the
     Humanitarian Imperative in Relief and Rehabilitation: a case study of
     the Angola Red Cross*, Swedish University of Agricultural Sciences,
     Stockholm, p5
93   Pottier, J (1996) 'Agricultural Rehabilitation and Food Insecurity in
     post-war Rwanda', *IDS Bulletin* 27(3), pp56–75
94   Cited in Kent, R (1987) *Anatomy of Disaster Relief; the International
     Network in Action*, Pinter, London, p33
95   Smillie, I, op cit (note 6, Chapter 4)
96   A phrase originally coined by Steve Commins of World Vision-USA
97   Harriss, J, op cit (note 35); de Waal, A, op cit (note 10)
98   *The Guardian*, 19 July 1997
99   Halliday, F (1994) 'Sleepwalking Through History? The New World
     and its Discontents', *Centre for the Study of Global Governance*,
     Discussion Paper, 4, London School of Economics
100 Slim, H and Visman, E, op cit (note 35)
101 de Waal, A, op cit (note 10) calls this a distinction between 'opera-
     tional neutrality' and 'neutrality of principle'
102 Anstee, M (1996) *Orphan of the Cold War: the Inside Story of the
     Angolan Peace Process 1992–3*, St Martin's Press, New York; *The
     Guardian*, 8 June 1996 (Victoria Brittain) and 28 August 1997
103 de Waal, A, op cit (note 10)
104 *The Guardian*, 17 September 1997
105 Donini, A (1995) 'The Bureaucracy and the Free Spirits: Stagnation
     and Innovation in the Relationship between the UN and NGOs',
     Third World Quarterly 16(3), pp421j–39
106 Roberts, A and Kingsbury, B, op cit (note 4); Rupesinghe, K, op cit
     (note 72)
107 Doyle, M (1995) *UN Peacekeeping in Cambodia: UNTAC's Civil
     Mandate*, Lynne Rienner, Boulder; BFWI, (1996) *The State of World
     Hunger*, Bread for the World Institute, Washington DC; Jonas, S
     (1996) 'Dangerous Liaisons: the US in Guatemala', *Foreign Policy* 103
     (Summer), pp144–60
108 Human Rights Watch (1993) *The Lost Agenda: Human Rights and
     UN Field Operations*, HRW, New York; Boyce, J (1997) 'External
     Assistance and the Peace Process in El Salvador', *World Development*
     23(12)
109 *The Guardian*, 19 July 1997
110 *The Guardian*, 21 June 1997; International Federation of Red Cross
     and Red Crescent Societies, op cit (note 6)
111 Weiss, T, op cit (note 7)
112 Slim, H (1996) *Doing the Right Thing: Relief Agencies, Moral
     Dilemmas and Moral Responsibility in Political Emergencies and War*,
     Nordic Africa Institute, Uppsala; Anderson, M op cit (note 13)
113 Weiss, T, op cit (note 41)
114 Higgins, R, cited in Minear, L, op cit (note 28)

CHAPTER 6

1   Helleiner, G et al (1995) *Report of the Independent Group of Advisers on Development Co-operation Issues between Tanzania and its Aid Donors*, DANIDA, Copenhagen
2   Cassen, R et al, op cit (note 62, Chapter 3)
3   Ibid; Riddell, R (1987) *Foreign Aid Reconsidered*, James Currey, London; Burnell, P, op cit (note 67, Chapter 2); Jepma, C (1995) *The Effectiveness of Development Aid*, Ministry of Foreign Affairs,The Hague
4   Institute of Social Studies (1996) *Evaluating Programme Aid*, 3 vols, ISS, The Hague; White, H (1966) 'Evaluating Programme Aid', *IDS Bulletin* 27(4)
5   Hook, S (1995) *National Interest and Foreign Aid*, Lynne Rienner, Boulder; White, H and McGillvray, M (1995) How well is aid allocated? *Development and Change* 26, pp163–83
6   Ensign, M (1992) *Doing Good or Doing Well? Japan's Foreign Aid Programme*, Columbia University Press; Rix, A (1993) *Japan's Foreign Aid Challenge*, Routledge, London; Steven, R (1990) *Japan's New Imperialism*, Macmillan, London
7   Clay, E and Stokke, O (eds) (1991) *Food Aid Reconsidered: Assessing the Impact on Third World Countries*, Frank Cass, London; Ruttan, V (1993) *Why Food Aid?* Johns Hopkins University Press
8   Cassen, R, et al, op cit (note 62, Chapter 3) p133
9   Clay, E et al (1996) *Joint Evaluation of European Union Programme Food Aid*, Overseas Development Institute, London
10 Berg, E (1993) *Rethinking Technical Co-operation: Reforms for Capacity-Building in Africa*, UNDP, New York; Fukuda-Parr, S (1995) 'Redefining Technical Co-operation: Challenges for the UN', *IDS Bulletin* 28(4), pp64–7; Moore, M (1994) *Institution-Building as a Development Assistance Method: a review of Literature and Ideas*, SIDA, Stockholm
11 World Bank (1998) *Assessing Aid: What Works, What Doesn't and Why*, Oxford University Press for the World Bank, Oxford; Burnell, P op cit (note 66, Chapter 2); Cassen, R et al, op cit (note 62, Chapter 3); White, H, op cit (note 4); Mosley, P, (1987) *Overseas Aid: Its Defence and Reform*, Wheatsheaf Books, Brighton; Mosley, P and Hudson, J (1995) *Aid Effectiveness: a study of the Effectiveness of Overseas Aid in the Main Countries Receiving ODA Assistance*, Department for International Development, London
12 Lipton, M and Toye, J (1990) *Does Aid Work in India?* Routledge, London
13 Ministry of Foreign Affairs (1995) *Aid in Progress: Development Co-operation and the review of Dutch Foreign Policy*, Government of the Netherlands, The Hague, p38
14 Griffin, K (1986) 'Doubts about Aid', *IDS Bulletin* 17(2), pp36–45; Griffin, K (1991) 'Foreign Aid after the Cold War', *Development and Change* 22(4), pp645–85; Snyder, D (1996) 'Foreign Aid and Private Investment in Developing Economies', *Journal of International Development* 8(6), pp735–45; White, H (1993) 'Is Development Aid Harmful to development?' *The Courier* 137 (Jan/Feb)

15   Sobhan, R (1982) *The Crisis of External Independence; the Political Economy of Foreign Aid to Bangladesh*, University Press, Dhaka, p226

16   Riddell, R, pers com

17   Burnside, C and Dollar, D (1997) 'Aid, Policies and Growth', Working Paper 1777, The World Bank, Washington DC; *The Economist*, 'Beyond Band Aids', 23 March 1996; Rondinelli, D (1995) 'American Foreign Aid Policy in the post-Cold War era', in Crotty, W (ed) *Post-Cold War Policy: the International Context*, Nelson-Hall, Chicago

18   Griffin, K (1991) op cit (note 14); IDS/IDR (1996) *An Evaluation of Development Co-operation between the EU and Ethiopia 1976–94*, DGVIII EU, Brussels

19   White, H (1996) 'How much Aid is used for Poverty-Reduction?' *IDS Bulletin* 27(1), pp83–99; Maxwell, S (1996) 'Apples, Pears and Poverty Reduction: an Assessment of British Bilateral Aid', *IDS Bulletin* 27(1), pp109–22; ACTIONAID/ICVA/EUROSTEP, *The Reality of Aid* (1995, 1996, 1997), ACTIONAID, London

20   US Senator Patrick Leahy, cited in Hewitt, A (ed) *Crisis or Transition in Foreign Aid*, Overseas Development Institute/Overseas Development Council/ North-South Institute London, p80

21   Griffin, K (1991), op cit (note 14) p678

22   Forward Studies Unit (1992) *Promoting Sustainable Social and Economic Development: the future of North-South relations*, European Commission, Brussels, pii

23   *The Courier*, no 155, November 1995, p1

24   ECDPM (1996) 'Beyond Lome IV: Exploring the Options for Future ACP-EU Co-operation', *Policy Management Report* 6, European Centre for Development Policy and Management, Maastricht, p55

25   Coghlan, N et al (1997) 'The EU and the Southern and Eastern Countries of the Mediterranean Basin: Patterns of Trade and Development', *EU/LDC News* 4(1), pp1–7; *The Economist*, 30 November 1996

26   Krueger, A (1993) *Economic Policies at Cross-Purposes*, Brookings Institution, Washington DC; Griffith-Jones, S et al (1994) 'Assessment of the IDB Lending Programme 1979–92', *Institute of Development Studies Research Report*, 25, Brighton

27   Hayter, T (1989) *Exploited Earth: Britain's Aid and the Environment*, Earthscan, London

28   A phrase coined by Edith Sizoo of Cultures and Development in Brussels

29   Fowler, A (1991) 'Building Partnerships between Northern and Southern NGOs', *Development in Practice* 1(1)

30   David Knox, ex-Vice President for Latin America

31   Mosley, P, Harrigan, J and Toye, J (1991) *Aid and Power: The World Bank and Policy-Based Lending*, 2 vols, Routledge, London; Stewart, F (1995) *Adjustment and Poverty: Options and Choices*, Routledge, London; Stewart, F, et al (1992) *Alternative Development Strategies in Sub-Saharan Africa*, Macmillan, London; Cornia, G, et al (1992) *Africa's Recovery in the 1990s: from Stagnation and Adjustment to Human Development*, Macmillan, London

32   There is a vast literature on the impact of adjustment. Particularly useful are the following: Mosley, P, et al, op cit (note 31); Stewart, F, op cit (note 31); Taylor, L (1988) *Varieties of Stabilisation Experience:*

Towards Sensible Macroeconomics in the Third World, Oxford
University Press, Oxford; Booth, D, et al, (1993) *Social, Economic
and Cultural Change in Contemporary Tanzania: a People-oriented
Focus*, SIDA, Stockholm; Killick, T (1995) 'Structural Adjustment
and Poverty-Alleviation: an Interpretative Survey', *Development and
Change* 26, pp305–31; White, H (1996) 'Adjustment in Africa: a
review article', *Development and Change* 27(4), pp785–815

33   Collier, P et al (1997) 'Re-designing Conditionality', *World
Development* 25(9), pp1399–1407

34   Stewart, F (1991) 'The Many Faces of Adjustment', *World
Development* 19(12), pp1847–64; Jamal, V and Weeks, J (1993)
*Africa Misunderstood or Whatever Happened to the Rural-Urban
Gap?* Macmillan, London; Mosley, P and Weeks, J (1993) 'Has
Recovery Begun? Africa's Adjustment in the 1980s Revisited', *World
Development* 21 (10), pp1583–1606; Mosley, P, et al (1995) 'Assessing
Adjustment in Africa', *World Development* 23(9), pp1459–74; Lewis,
P (1997) 'Shifting Fortunes: the Political Economy of Financial
Liberalization in Nigeria', *World Development* 25(1), pp5–22; Weeks, J
(1997) 'Analysis of the Demery and Squire "Adjustment and Poverty"
Evidence', *Journal of International Development* 9(6), pp827–36. For
the World Bank's view (World Bank, Washington DC) see Africa
Region (1995) *A Continent in Transition: Sub-Saharan Africa in the
mid-1990s*; Husain, I and Faruqee, R (1994) *Adjustment in Africa:
Lessons from Country Case Studies*; Operations Evaluation
Department (1995) *The Social Impact of Adjustment Operations*. Also
see Demery, L and Squire, L (1997) Adjustment and Poverty
Evidence: a response to Weeks', *Journal of International Development*
9(6), pp837–42

35   Sarris, A and Shams, H (1991) *Ghana under Structural Adjustment*,
New York University Press; Taylor, L (1996) 'Sustainable
Development: an Introduction', *World Development* 24(2), pp215–6;
ODI (1996) 'Adjustment in Africa: Lessons from Ghana', *Briefing
Paper*, 3, Overseas Development Institute, London

36   Taylor, L, op cit (note 32); Mosley, P (1995) 'The Failure of Aid and
Adjustment Policies in Sub-Saharan Africa', *Workshop on Sub-Saharan
Africa: Looking ahead*, University of Copenhagen; Mosley, P (1995)
'Development Economics and the Underdevelopment of Sub-Saharan
Africa', *Journal of International Development* 7(5), pp685–706

37   Cornia, G, Jolly, R and Stewart, F (1987) *Adjustment With a Human
Face*, Oxford University Press, Oxford; Woodward, D (1993) *Present
Pain, Future Hope?* 2 vols, Pinter, London

38   For evidence from rural areas see Booth, op cit (note 32); Booth, D et
al, (1996) *Coping with cost-recovery in Zambia*, SIDA, Stockholm;
Bourguignon, F et al (1991) 'Poverty and Income Distribution During
Adjustment', *World Development* 19(11), pp1485–1508; Duncan, A
and Howell, J (1992) *Structural Adjustment and the African Farmer*,
James Currey, London; Hewitt de Alcantara, C (1992) 'Markets in
Principle and Practice', *European Journal of Development Research*
4(2), pp11–16. For urban areas see Moser, C (1996) 'Confronting
Crisis: Household Responses to Poverty and Vulnerability in Four Poor
Urban Communities', *ESD Monograph* 7, World Bank, Washington

DC; Cohen, M (1990) 'Macro-Economic Adjustment and the City', *Cities* 7, pp49–60

39 Vivian, J (1995) 'How Safe are Social Safety-nets? Adjustment and Social-Sector Restructuring in Developing Countries', *Development and Change*, special issue

40 Stewart, F, op cit (note 31)

41 Colclough, C and Manor, J, op cit (note 7, Chapter 3); Berthelemy, J (ed) (1995) *Whither African Economies?* OECD Development Centre, Paris; Mosley, P, op cit (note 36); Bird, G (1996) 'Borrowing from the IMF: the Policy Implications of Recent Empirical Research', *World Development* 24(11), pp1753–60

42 Williamson, J (1994) *The Political Economy of Policy Reform*, Institute for International Economics, Washington DC

43 van der Hoeven, R (1991) 'Adjustment with a Human Face: still Relevant or Overtaken by Events?' *World Development* 19(12), pp1835–46; Lewis, P, op cit (note 34)

44 Greenaway, D and Morrissey, O (1992) 'Sequencing Lessons from Adjustment Lending Programmes', *CREDIT Research Paper* 92/11, University of Nottingham; Reed, D (1996) *Structural Adjustment, the Environment and Sustainable Development*, Earthscan, London; Booth, D, et al, op cit (note 38)

45 Taylor, L, op cit (note 35) p224

46 Stewart, F, op cit (note 84, Chapter 3); Killick, T, op cit (note 32)

47 Stewart, F, et al, op cit (note31); Cornia, G, et al, op cit (note 31); Parfitt, T (1993) 'Which African Agenda for the Nineties?' *Journal of International Development* 5(1), pp93–106; Ndulu, B (1995) Africa's Development Challenges in a Changing World Economy, *Workshop on Sub-Saharan Africa – Looking Ahead*, University of Copenhagen; Abugre, C (1995) *IDA Lending, Structural Adjustment and Participation: Towards an African NGO Position*, Third World Network, Accra

48 Parfitt, T, op cit (note 47); Clark, J (1991) *Democratizing Development*, Earthscan, London; Stoneman, C (1995) 'Beyond Structural Adjustment', *Development Studies Association Annual Conference*, Dublin

49 Hirschman, A (1971) *A Bias for Hope: Essays on Development and Latin America*, Yale University Press; Nelson, J (1992) 'Encouraging Democracy: What Role for Conditioned Aid?' *Policy Essay* 4, Overseas Development Council, Washington DC;

50 Gunning, J (1996) 'The Donors' Role in Africa: Reform of Aid and Trade Relationships', *Workshop on External Resources for Development*, Netherlands Economic Institute; Sandbrook, R (1996) 'Democratisation and the Implementation of Economic Reform in Africa', *Journal of International Development* 8(1), pp1–20

51 Burnell, P, op cit (note 67, Chapter 2); Nelson, J and Eglinton, S (1993) 'Global Goals: Contentious Means: Issues of Multiple Aid Conditionality', *Policy Essay* 10, Overseas Development Council, Washington DC; Riddell, R, op cit (note 3)

52 Robinson, M (1995) 'Towards Democratic Governance', *IDS Bulletin* 26(2); Stokke, O (ed) *Aid and Political Conditionality*, Frank Cass, London

53   Collier, P et al (1997) 'Redesigning Conditionality', *World Development* 25 (9), pp1399–1407
54   Sachs, J, op cit (note 85, Chapter 3)
55   Nelson, P (1996) 'Internationalizing Economic and Environmental Policy: Transnational NGO Networks and the World Bank's Expanding Influence', *Millennium* 25(3)
56   Crawford, G (1997) *Promoting Democracy, Human Rights and Good Governance through Development Aid*, Centre for Democratization Studies, University of Leeds
57   Mosley, P (1992) *Development Finance and Policy Reform: Essays in the Theory and Practice of Conditionality in Less Developed Countries*, Macmillan, London, p5
58   Archer, R (1993) *Conditionality: Aid, Penalties and Incentives*, Christian Aid, London; Haas, R (1997) 'Sanctioning Madness', *Foreign Affairs* 76(6), pp74–85; Cortright, D and Lopez, G (eds) *Economic Sanctions: Panacea or Peace-Building in a Post Cold-War World?* Westview, Boulder; Burnett, S (1992) *Investing in Security: Economic Aid for Non-economic Purposes*, Centre for Strategic and International Studies, Washington DC; Gunning, J, op cit (note 50); Prendergast, J and Scott, C, op cit (note 13 Chapter 5)
59   See the works cited earlier by Nelson, Nelson and Eglinton, and Stokke; Killick, T (1995) *A Principal-Agent Analysis of Conditionality: a Reader's Digest*, Overseas Development Institute, London
60   Fox, J (1997) *The World Bank and Mexico*, University of California at Santa Cruz
61   Baehr, P (1997) 'Problems of Aid Conditionality: the Netherlands and Indonesia', *Third World Quarterly* 18(2), pp363–76
62   ACFOA (1996) *Slave Labour in Burma*, Australian Council for Overseas Aid, Canberra
63   The IMF's decision to suspend US$220 million in loans in 1997 came as a surprise to President Moi, but didn't alter the political dynamics. See Gibbon, P (ed) (1995) *Markets, Civil Society and Democracy in Kenya*, Nordiska Afrikainstitutet, Uppsala; Bratton, M and van de Walle, N (1992) 'Toward Governance in Africa', in Hyden, G and Bratton, M (eds) *Governance and Politics in Africa*, Lynne Rienner, Boulder
64   Robinson, M, op cit (note 52)
65   Scott, J (1985) *Weapons of the Weak: Everyday forms of Peasant Resistance*, Yale University Press
66   Gillies, D (1996) 'Human Rights, Democracy and Good Governance: Stretching the World Bank's Policy Frontiers', in Griesgraber, J and Gurtner, B (eds) *The World Bank*, Pluto Press, London; Nelson, P, op cit (note 55); Nelson, P and Eglinton, S, op cit (note 51)
67   Crawford, G (1996) cited in a speech delivered to the Conference on the 'European Union and the Less Developed Countries', Overseas Development Institute, London
68   Killick, T, op cit (note 59)
69   Feinberg, R and Avakov, R (1991) *From Confrontation to Co-operation? US and Soviet Aid to Developing Countries*, Overseas Development Council, Washington DC

70   Crawford, G, op cit (note 56)
71   Denham, J (1990) *Pulling the other one: Alternative Conditionality,
      Accountability and the Debt Crisis*, Friends of the Earth, London;
      Forward Studies Unit (1996) *Partnership for Development:
      Conditionality and Coherence*, European Commission, Brussels;
      Abugre, C, op cit (note 47)
72   Mosley, P and Hudson, J, op cit (note 11)
73   Seers, D (1962) 'Why Visiting Economists Fail', *Journal of Political
      Economy* 70(4), pp325–38; Chambers, R (1983) *Rural Development:
      Putting the Last First*, Longman, London
74   Brand, S (1994) *How Buildings Learn*, Viking, London
75   Sizoo, E, pers com
76   Koulaimah, A (1997) *Who Said Coherence?* ECDPM, Maastricht
77   Toynbee, A (1952) *The World and the West*, Oxford University Press,
      Oxford, p28
78   *The Observer*, 20 October 1996; ACTIONAID (1996, 1997) *The
      Reality of Aid*, London
79   Lele, U and Goldsmith, A (1989) 'The Development of National
      Agricultural Research Capacity: India's Experience with the
      Rockefeller Foundation and its Significance for Africa' *Economic
      Development and Cultural Change* 37(2), pp305–44
80   Government of Canada (1995) *Canada in the World*, Ottawa
81   Krueger, A, op cit (note 26) p144
82   Bread for the World Institute (1995) 'At the Cross-roads: the Future
      of Foreign Aid', *Occasional Paper* 4, BFWI, Washington DC, p23
83   And also in the British Government's White Paper on international
      development, and the OECD's 'vision' for aid in the next century. See
      EUROSTEP (1996) *Partnership 2000*, EUROSTEP, Brussels; ODI
      (1995) *EU Aid post-Maastricht: 15 into 1?* Overseas Development
      Institute, London; Short, C (1997) 'The Role and Functions of the
      Department for International Development', *Speech to the School of
      Oriental and African Studies*, University of London (May)
84   Short, C (1997) 'Eliminating Poverty – a Challenge for the New
      Millennium', *Speech to the Commonwealth Institute* (June)
85   Chalker, L (1996) *Speech to the 'Conference on the European Union
      and the Less Developed Countries'*, Overseas Development Institute,
      London
86   Cassen, R et al, op cit (note 62, Chapter 3) p178
87   Emergency assistance is included in the portfolio of Commissioner
      Emma Bonino, along with fisheries policy and some aspects of
      consumer protection, such as the response to 'Mad Cow Disease'
      (BSE) from contaminated beef in the UK
88   Cited in Korten, D, op cit (note 15, Chapter 1) p168

CHAPTER 7

1   Jean-Bertrand Aristide, speaking to the annual conference of the
      Society for International Development, Santiago de Compostela,
      Spain, May 23 1997

2   Turner, M and Hulme, D (1997) *Making the State Work: Administration and Governance in Developing Countries*, Macmillan, London, p247

3   Micklethwait, J and Wooldridge, A, op cit (note 22, Chapter 1) p204

4   This concept has been used by a number of other authors, in various guises. See Hirschman, A (1967) *Development Projects Observed*, Brookings Institution, Washington DC; Seers, D (1983) *The Political Economy of Nationalism*, Oxford University Press, Oxford; Clay, E and Schaffer, B (eds) (1984) *Room for Manoeuvre: an Exploration of Public Policy in Agriculture and Rural Development*, Heinemann, London

5   Oman, C (1996) *The Policy Challenges of Globalisation and Regionalisation*, OECD, Paris; Mentz, J (1997) 'Personal and Institutional Factors in Capacity-Building', *ECDPM Working Paper* 14, Maastricht; Wood, A and Ridao-Cano, C (1996) 'Skill, Trade and International Inequality', *IDS Working Paper* 47, Brighton

6   *The Economist*, 17 August 1996

7   Sachs, J, cited in *The Guardian*, 22 June 1996

8   Riddell, R (1996) *Aid in the 21st Century*, UNDP Office of Development Studies, New York; Wood, A (1994) *North-South Trade, Employment and Inequality: Changing Fortunes in a Skill-Driven World*, Clarendon Press, Oxford; Hirschman, A (1958) *The Strategy of Economic Development*, Yale University Press

9   Mosley, P (1995) 'The Failure of Aid and Adjustment Policies in Sub-Saharan Africa: Counter Examples and Policy Proposals', *Conference on Sub-Saharan Africa: Looking Ahead*, Copenhagen; Cassen, R, et al op cit (note 62, Chapter 3); Griffith-Jones, S (1994) 'Assessment of the IDB Lending programme 1979-92', *IDS Research Report* 25, Brighton

10   *The Economist*, 25 October 1997

11   *The Economist*, 15 November 1997

12   Streeten, P (1997) 'An Introduction to a Primer for Reform-Minded Presidents or Prime Ministers', *World Development* 25(1), pp1–3

13   *The Guardian*, 31 October 1997

14   ACTIONAID (1997) *The Reality of Aid*, Earthscan, London, p243; *The Guardian*, 1 November 1997

15   Broad, R and Cavanagh, J (1996) 'Don't Neglect the Impoverished South', *Foreign Policy* 101, pp18–36

16   Elliot, L, writing in *The Guardian*, 7 September 1997

17   Sachs, J, op cit (note 7); World Bank (1994) *Reducing the Debt Burden of Poor Countries: a Framework for Action*, Washington DC

18   *The Guardian*, 17 January 1998 and 23 January 1998

19   *The Courier*, no 156, Brussels

20   Adamolekun, L, et al (1997) 'Political Transition, Economic Liberalisation and Civil Service Reform in Malawi', *Public Administration and Development* 17(2), pp209–22

21   Kasumba, G (1997) 'Decentralising Aid and its Management in Uganda: Lessons for Capacity-Building at the Local Level', *ECDPM Working Paper* 20, Maastricht

22   Kasumba, G, ibid

23   For the public sector see: Barzelay, M (1992) *Breaking Through
      Bureaucracy: a New Vision for Managing in Government*, University
      of California Press, Berkeley; Grindle, M (1997) 'Divergent Cultures?
      When Public Organisations Perform well in Developing Countries',
      World Development 25(4), pp481–95; Grindle, M and Hildebrand, M
      (1995) 'Building Sustainable Capacity in the Public Sector: What can
      be Done?' *Public Administration and Development* 15(5), pp441–64;
      Leonard, D (1991) *African Successes: Four Public managers of Kenyan
      Rural Development*, University of California Press, Berkeley; Esman,
      M (1991) *Management Dimensions of Development: Perspectives and
      Strategies*, Kumarian Press, West Hartford. For NGOs see: Fowler, A,
      op cit (note 4, Chapter4); Carroll, T (1992) *Intermediary NGOs: the
      Supporting Link in Grassroots Development*, Kumarian Press, West
      Hartford; Edwards, M and Hulme, D (eds), (1995) *Performance and
      Accountability: Beyond the Magic Bullet*, Earthscan, London;
      Bebbington, A, et al, (1993) *NGOs and the State in Latin America*,
      Routledge, London; Smith-Green, P (1995) *Accountability in
      Development Organisations*, Sage, New Delhi
24   Davey, K (1993) *Managing Growing Cities: Options for Urban
      Government*, Development Administration Group, Birmingham
25   Edwards, M and Hulme, D (1996) 'Too Close for Comfort? The
      impact of Official Aid on NGOs', *World Development* 24(6),
      pp961–74; Fowler, A, op cit (note 23)
26   Edwards, M (1997) 'Organisational Learning in NGOs: What have we
      Learned?' *Public Administration and Development* 17(2), pp235–50;
      Hudock, A (1995) 'Sustaining Southern NGOs in Resource-
      Dependent Environments', *Journal of International Development* 7(4),
      pp653–67
27   Grindle, M (1996) *Challenging the State: Crisis and Innovation in
      Latin America and Africa*, Cambridge University Press, Cambridge;
      World Bank (1997) *The State in a Changing World*, Washington DC
28   Gaebler, T and Osborne, D (1992) *Re-inventing Government*, Harvard
      University Press; Tendler, J (1997) *Good Government in the Tropics*,
      Johns Hopkins University Press Baltimore; Turner, M and Hulme, D
      op cit (note 2); Gilbert, R, et al (1996) *Making Cities Work: The Role
      of Local Authorities in the Urban Environment*, Earthscan, London
29   Klitgaard, R (1997) *Cleaning Up and Invigorating the Civil Service*,
      World Bank, Washington DC
30   Dia, M (1993) 'A Governance Approach to Civil Service Reform in
      Sub-Saharan Africa', *The World Bank Technical Paper* 225, Washington
      DC; Kiggundu, M (1997) 'Civil Service Reforms: Limping into the
      21st Century', *IDPM Conference on Public-Sector Management for the
      Next Century*, Manchester; Klitgaard, R, op cit (note 29)
31   Putnam, R, op cit (note 49, Chapter 1); Fisher, J (1997)
      *Nongovernments: NGOs and the Political Development of the Third
      World*, Kumarian Press, West Hartford
32   Bebbington, A and Riddell, R (1997) 'Heavy Hands, Hidden Hands,
      Holding Hands: Donors, Intermediary NGOs and Civil Society
      Organisations', in Hulme, D and Edwards, M (eds), (1997) *NGOs,
      States and Donors: Too Close for Comfort?* Macmillan, London;
      Fowler, A, op cit (note 4, Chapter 4)

33   Putnam, R, op cit (note 49, Chapter 1); Perez-Diaz, V (1993) *The Return of Civil Society*, Harvard University Press; Rau, Z (1991) *The Re-Emergence of Civil Society in Eastern Europe and the Soviet Union*, Westview Press, Boulder; Hulme, D and Edwards, M (eds) op cit (note 32)

34   Asia Foundation (1997) Bangladesh Programme Information Sheet, San Francisco, October; Other sensitive support strategies are described in: Brown, L and Ashman, D (1996) 'Participation, Social Capital and Inter-Sectoral Problem-Solving: African and Asian Cases', *World Development* 24(9), pp1467–79

35   World Bank (1996) *Review of Public Enterprise Reform and Privatisation Operations*, Washington DC; Cook, P and Nixson, F (1995) *The Move to the Market: Trade and Industry Reform in Transitional Economies*, Macmillan, London

36   Ryrie, W (1996) *First World, Third World*, Macmillan, London

37   Abbott, J (1996) *Sharing the City: Community Participation in Urban Management*, Earthscan, London

38   Harriss-White, B and White, G (1996) 'Corruption, Liberalisation and Democracy', *IDS Bulletin* 27(2), pp1–5

39   Wilks, A (1996) *The World Bank's Promotion of Privatisation and Private-Sector Development: Issues and Concerns*, Bretton Woods Project, London

40   Toye, J and Jackson, C (1996) 'Public Expenditure Policy and Poverty-Reduction: has the World Bank got it right?' *IDS Bulletin* 27(1), pp56–66

41   Blair, H (1997) 'Donors, Democratisation and Civil Society: Relating Theory to Practice', in Hulme and Edwards (eds) op cit (note 32)

42   Grindle, M, op cit (note 27); Williamson, J (1994) *The Political Economy of Policy Reform*, Institute for International Economics, Washington DC; van de Walle, N (1994) 'Political Liberation and Economic Policy Reform in Africa', *World Development* 22(4), pp483–500; Morrissey, O (1995) 'Politics and Economic Policy Reform: Trade Liberalisation in Sub-Saharan Africa', *Journal of International Development* 7(4), pp599–618

43   Milder, D (1996) 'Foreign Assistance: Catalyst for Domestic Coalition-Building', in Griesgraber, J and Gunter, B (eds) *The World Bank*, Pluto Press, London

44   Diamond, L and Plattner, M (1995) *Economic Reform and Democracy*, Johns Hopkins University Press

45   Rasheed, S (1995) 'The Democratisation Process and Popular Participation in Africa', *Development and Change* 26, p 351

46   Somavia, J (1997) 'The Humanitarian Principles of the UN Security Council', *Development in Practice* 7(4), pp353–62

47   Wedel, J (1996) 'Clique-run Organisations and US Economic Aid', *Journal of Post-Soviet Democratization*, vol 4(4)

48   Petesch, P (1996) 'National Programming for the New Global Development Agenda: What Role for Civil Society?' *Workshop on Managing Aid for National Development*, New York

49   Development Committee (1994) *Aid Effectiveness*, World Bank, Washington DC; DAC (1996) *Principles of Aid Effectiveness*, OECD, Paris; Helleiner, G, et al (1995) *Report of the Independent Group of*

Advisers on Development Co-operation Issues between Tanzania and its Aid Donors, DANIDA, Copenhagen

50 Meier, G and Seers, D (eds) (1984) *Pioneers in Development*, Oxford University Press, Oxford, p219; Hirschman, A (1971) *A Bias for Hope: Essays on Development and Latin America*, Yale University Press; Griffin, K and McKinley, T (1996) *New Approaches to Development Co-operation*, UNDP Office of Development Studies, New York; Forward Studies Unit (1996), *Partnership for Development, Conditionality and Coherence*, EU, Brussels; Forward Studies Unit (1997) *Towards a More Coherent Global Economic Order*, EU, Brussels; Sachs, J, op cit (note 7); UNDP (1996) *Human Development Report 1996*; New York; Hyden, G (1996) 'From Bargaining to Marketing: How to Reform Foreign Aid' in Stokke, O (ed) *Foreign Aid Towards the Year 2000: Experiences and Challenges*, Frank Cass, London; Hyden, G (1995) 'Toward a New Model of Managing Development Assistance', in Rasheed and Luke, D (eds) (1995); Hellinger, D, et al (1988) *Aid for Just Development*, Lynne Rienner, Boulder; Hewitt, A (ed), (1994) *Crisis or Transition in Foreign Aid*, ODI, London; Valderrama, M (1997) *New Directions in International Co-operation: a view from Latin America*, INTRAC, Oxford; DAC (1996) *Shaping the 21st Century: the Contribution of Development Co-operation*, OECD, Paris

51 Frankman, M (1996) 'International Taxation: the Trajectory of an Idea from Lorimer to Brandt', *World Development* 24(5), pp807–20

52 Griffin, K and McKinlay, T, op cit (note 50); ul Haq, M, Kaul, I and Grunberg, I (eds), (1996) *The Tobin Tax: Coping with Financial Volatility*, Oxford University Press, Oxford; ODI (1996) 'New Sources of Finance for Development', *ODI Briefing Paper* 1, London

53 Griffin and McKinley, ibid; Valderrama, M, op cit (note 50); Desai, M (1996) 'Private Finance and Development: Issues and Some Answers', *World Times Conference*, Boston

54 As the International Development Association does. See Sanford, J (1997) 'Alternative Ways to Fund the IDA', *World Development* 25(3), pp297–310; World Bank (1995) 'A New Threat to the World's Poor', *IDA 10 and 11*, Washington DC

55 Kaul, I, speaking at the Reality of Aid launch in London in October 1997

56 Helleiner, G et al, op cit (note 49); Banuri, T et al (1994) *Sustainable Human Development – from Concept to Operation*, UNDP, New York

57 Schelling, T (1997) 'The Costs of Combating Global Warming', *Foreign Affairs* 76(3), pp8–14

58 Burnell, P, op cit (note 67, Chapter 2)

59 Piccioto, R (1994) *Institutional Development and World Bank Operations: the New Project Cycle*, World Bank, Washington DC; Carroll, T, et al (1996) *Participation Through Intermediary NGOs*, The World Bank, Washington DC

60 Abugre, C (1995) *IDA Lending, Structural Adjustment and Participation: Towards an African NGO Position*, Third World Network, Accra; Archer, R (1993) *Conditionality: Aid, Penalties and Incentives*, Christian Aid, London

61 The Panel is one of a number of semi-independent complaints procedures that already exist; proposals have been made for a similar

system for international NGOs and their partners by Kamal Malhotra and Alan Fowler of Focus on the Global South in Bangkok

62   Edwards, M and Hulme, D (eds), op cit (note 23)

63   Rondinelli, D (1993) *Strategic and Results-Based Management in CIDA*, CIDA, Ottawa; Zadek, S and Gatward, M (1995) 'Social Auditing or Bust?' in Edwards, M and Hulme, D (eds), op cit (note 23)

64   Collier, P et al, 'Redesigning Conditionality', *World Development* 25(9), pp1399–1407; Gunning, J (1996) *The Donor's Role in Africa: Reform of Aid and Trade Relationships*, Netherlands Economic Institute; Fowler, A (1995) 'Assessing NGO Performance: Difficulties, Dilemmas and a Way ahead', in Edwards, M and Hulme, D (eds), op cit (note 23)

65   UN Press Release, 16 July 1997, New York: 'Secretary-General Pledges Quiet Revolution in United Nations'; *The Guardian*, 5 July 1997

66   There is also increasing co-ordination inside the UN via the 'UN System Conferences Action Plan' and UNDP's 'Aid Accountability Project'. See Development Assistance Committee and DAC, op cit (note 49); Short, C (1997) 'Democracy, Human Rights and Good Governance', *Speech to Manchester University*, June 30; Ministry of Foreign Affairs (1995) *Aid in Progress: Development Co-operation and the Review of the Dutch Foreign Policy*, The Hague; ECA (1996) *Report on the Economic and Social Situation for Africa in 1996*, Economic Commission for Africa, Addis-Ababa; World Bank, op cit (note 34); ACTIONAID, op cit (note 14)

67   World Bank (1998) Report of the Partnerships Review Group, Washington DC. See also James B Wolfensohn (1998) *Speech to the Annual Meetings of the World Bank and IMF*, Washington DC

68   Pers com, Sir Hans Singer

CHAPTER 8

1   From an official of the US-based Inner City Foundation, quoted on BBC Radio Four, August 13 1996

2   Bellerby, J (1931) *A Contributive Society*, Oxford Education Services, pix

3   Jordan's fee in 1993 was US$20 million, compared to wages of $1.75/day: Wiseman, J (1997) *Alternatives to Globalisation: an Asia-Pacific Perspective*, Community Aid Abroad, Melbourne, p39

4   ACFOA (1997) *Generating Power and Money: Australia and Thailand's Roles in Hydro Projects in Laos*, ACFOA, Canberra

5   Thurow, L, op cit (note 30, Chapter 1)

6   Cited in Brittan, S (1995) *Capitalism With a Human Face*, Edward Elgar, London, p50

7   Marquand, D (1997) *The New Reckoning: Capitalism, States and Citizens*, Polity Press, Cambridge; Soundings (1997) *The Next Ten Years: Key Issues for Blair's Britain*, special issue

8   Folbre, N (1994) *Who Pays for the Kids? Gender and the Structures of Constraint*, Routledge, London

9   Bellerby, J, op cit (note 2)
10   Harriss, J (1994) 'Between Economism and post-Modernism: Reflections on Research on Agrarian Change in India', in Booth, D (ed) *Redefining Social Development: Theory, Research and Practice*, Longman, London
11   Jazairy, I, et al (1992) *The State of World Rural Poverty*, IT Publications, London, pxviii; Lewis, D (1993) 'Going it Alone: Female-headed Households, Rights and Resources in Rural Bangladesh', *European Journal of Development Research* 5(2), pp23–42
12   Agarwal, B (1994) 'Gender and Command over Property: a Critical Gap in Economic Analysis and Policy in South Asia', *World Development* 22(10), pp1455–78
13   White, S (1992) *Arguing with the Crocodile: Gender and Class in Bangladesh*, Zed Press, London; Carter, M and Barham, B (1996) 'Level Playing Fields and Laissez-Faire: Post-Liberal Development Strategy in Inegalitarian Agrarian Economies', *World Development* 24(7), pp1133–50; Goldman, A and Smith, J (1995) 'Agricultural Transformations in India and Northern Nigeria: Exploring the Nature of Green Revolutions', *World Development* 23(2), pp243–63
14   Alauddin, M and Tisdell, C (1995) 'Labor Absorption and Agricultural Development: Bangladesh's Experience and Predicament', *World Development* 23(2), pp281–97
15   Villamora, L, et al (1992) 'Labour Demand for Organic Contour Farming', *ILEIA Newsletter* 8(4), pp6–8: Pretty, J (1995) *Regenerating Agriculture*, Earthscan, London
16   Moser, C (1998) 'The Asset Vulnerability Framework: Re-assessing Urban Poverty Reduction Strategies', *World Development* 26(1), pp1–20; Amis, P (1995) 'Making Sense of Urban Poverty', *Environment and Urbanisation* 7(1), pp145–57; Amis, P and Rakodi, C (1994) 'Urban Poverty: Issues for Research and Policy', *Journal of International Development* 6(5), pp627–34
17   Ahmad, A and El-Batthani, A (1995) 'Poverty in Khartoum', *Environment and Urbanisation* 7(2), pp195–206
18   Chomsky, N (1994) *World Orders, Old and New*, Pluto Press, London, p271; Mann, M (1986) *The Sources of Social Power*, 3 vols, Cambridge University Press, Cambridge
19   Mendes, C (1989) *Fight for the Forest*, Latin America Bureau, London; Vidal, J, in *The Guardian*, 26 April 1997; Taylor, R (1998) *New Statesman Trade Union Guide 1998*, p12
20   Coleridge, P (1993) *Disability, Liberation and Development*, Oxfam, Oxford, p13
21   Sen, G (1997) 'Empowerment as an Approach to Poverty', *Background paper for the 1997 Human Development Report*, UNDP, New York
22   Dasgupta, P (1993) *An Enquiry into Well-being and Destitution*, Clarendon Press, Oxford; Dreze, J and Sen, A (1991) 'Public Action for Social Security', in Ahmad, E, et al (eds) *Social Security in Developing Countries*, Clarendon Press, Oxford; SAARC (1992) *Meeting the Challenge: the report of the Independent South Asian Commission on Poverty Alleviation*, SAARC, Kathmandu; Kannan, K (1995) 'Public Intervention and Poverty Alleviation', *Development and Change* 26(4), pp701–27

23   Cited in Edwards, M (1997) book review of 'Popular Development and The Development Practitioner's Handbook', *Journal of Development Studies* 33(4), pp581–6

24   Moore, S, in *The Guardian*, 18 July 1996

25   Banuri, T, et al (1994) *Sustainable Human Development: from Concept to Operation*, UNDP Office of Development Studies, New York

26   Galbraith, J K (1992) *The Culture of Contentment*, Sinclair-Stevenson, London; Bellah, R (1985) *Habits of the Heart: Individualism and Commitment in American Life*, University of California Press, Berkeley; Putnam, R (1995) 'Bowling Alone: America's Declining Social Capital', *Journal of Democracy* 6(1), pp65–78.

27   Max-Neef, M (1990) 'Barefoot Economics', *Channel Four Television*

28   Marquand, D, op cit (note 7)

29   Korten, D, op cit (note 15, Chapter 1)

30   Rahman, M (1993) *People's Self-Development: Perspectives on Participatory Action Research*, Zed Press, London

31   Henderson, H (1996) 'Changing Paradigms and Indicators: Implementing Equitable, Sustainable and Participatory Development', in Griesgraber, J and Gunter, B (eds) *Development*, Pluto Press, London

32   Daly, H (1992) *Steady-State Economics*, Earthscan, London; Jacobs, M (1996) *The Politics of the Real World*, Earthscan, London; Giddens, A, op cit (note 52, Chapter 1)

33   Hewitt de Alcantara, C (1992) 'Markets in Principle and Practice', *European Journal of Development Research* 4(2), pp1–16; White, G (1993) 'The Political Analysis of Markets', *IDS Bulletin* 24(3); Sen, G (1996) 'Gender, Markets and States', *World Development* 24(5), pp821–9; Harriss-White, B (1996) 'Free-Market Romanticism in an Era of Deregulation', *Oxford Development Studies* 24(1), pp27–45

34   Nomani, F and Rahnema, A (1994) *Islamic Economic Systems*, Zed Press, London

35   Marquand, D, in *The Guardian*, 16 July 1997; Wiseman, J, op cit (note 3)

36   Inter-American Foundation (1996) 'Focus on Trade', *Grassroots Development* 20(2)

37   Reich, R, op cit (note 48, Chapter 1), p39

38   Cavanagh, J (1997) 'Rethinking Corporate Accountability', in Griesgraber, J and Gunter, B (eds) *World Trade*, Pluto Press, London; NEF/CIIR (1997) *Open Trading: Options for Effective Monitoring of Corporate Codes of Conduct*, NEF/CIIR, London; Stichele, M, et al (1996) *Making it our Business – European NGO Campaigns on Transnational Corporations*, CIIR, London; Zadek, C, et al (eds) (1997) *Building Corporate Accountability*, Earthscan, London

39   *The Guardian*, 7 November 1997

40   Harriss-White, B (1996) *Masters of the Countryside: a Political Economy of Agricultural Markets in South India*, Sage, New Delhi, p319

41   Mendes, C, op cit (note 19); Blauert, J and Zadek, S (1998) *Mediating Sustainability*, Kumarian Press, West Hartford

42   Inter-American Foundation (1996) *Grassroots Developments – Special Issue on Trade 20* (2), IAF, Washington DC

43 Stewart, F (1996) 'Groups for Good or Ill', *Oxford Development Studies* 24(1), pp9–25
44 Henderson, H, op cit (note 31) p112
45 *New Statesman*, 2 August 1997; *The Guardian*, 19 November 1997
46 Yunus, M (1994) 'Does the Capitalist System have to be the Handmaiden of the Rich?' *Grameen Dialogue* 20, pp1–4
47 *The Guardian*, 29 November 1997
48 *The Economist*, 21 June 1997
49 Healey, K (1996) 'La Kochalita's Export Saga', *Grassroots Development* 20(2), pp2–11; *The Observer*, 9 November 1997
50 Conroy, C and Litvinoff, M (eds) (1988) *The Greening of Aid*, Earthscan, London; Chambers, R (1993) *Challenging the Professions*, IT Publications, London
51 Dickson, J (1995) 'Culturally-Sustainable Rural Enterprise Development', *Small Enterprise Development* 6(1), pp43–9
52 Anderson, R (1997) 'Corporate-Indigenous Partnerships in Economic Development: the First Nations in Canada', *World Development* 25(4), pp1483–1503
53 Gilbert, R, et al (1996) *Making Cities Work*, Earthscan, London
54 Toye, J and Jackson, C (1996) 'Public Expenditure Policy and Poverty-Reduction', *IDS Bulletin* 27(1), pp56–66; Gaiha, R (1995) 'Does Agricultural Growth Matter in Poverty-Alleviation?' *Development and Change* 26, pp285–304; Cagatay, N, et al (1995) 'Gender, Adjustment and Macroeconomics', *World Development* 23(11), pp1827–38; Palmer, I (1995) 'Public Finance from a Gender Perspective', *World Development* 23(1), pp1981–86
55 White, B (1996) 'Globalization and the Child Labour Problem', *Journal of International Development* 8(6), pp829–37
56 *The Guardian*, 11 October 1997; see also Boyden, J and Myers, W (1995) *Exploring Alternative Approaches to Combating Child Labour*, UNICEF, Florence; Weiner, M and Noman, O (1995) *The Child and the State in India and Pakistan*, Oxford University Press
57 Hettige, H, et al (1996) 'Determinants of Pollution Abatement in Developing Countries', *World Development* 24(12), pp1891–1904
58 *The Guardian*, 23 September 1997
59 Henderson, H, op cit (note 31)
60 Folbre, N, op cit (note 8)
61 Edwards, M et al (1995) *Towards a Children's Agenda: New Challenges for Social Development*, Save the Children Fund, London; Edwards, M (1996) 'New Approaches to Children and Development', *Journal of International Development* 8(6), pp813–28
62 Elson, D (1995) *Male Bias in the Development Process*, Manchester University Press, Manchester
63 Cross, N and Baker, R (1991) *At the Desert's Edge: Oral Histories from the Sahel*, Panos Institute, London, p84 and p142
64 *New Statesman*, 26 September 1997
65 Platteau, J (1996) 'The Evolutionary Theory of Land Rights as Applied to Sub-Saharan Africa: a Critical Assessment', *Development and Change* 27(1), pp29–86; Gorman, M (1995) 'Older People and Development: the Last Minority?' *Development in Practice* 5(2), pp117–127; Ahmad, A and El-Batthani, A, op cit (note 17)

66   Pradervand, P (1989) *Listening to Africa – Developing Africa from the Grassroots*, Praeger, New York; Verhelst, T (1987) *No Life Without Roots: Culture and Development*, Zed Press, London

67   Ridley, M, op cit (note 1, Chapter 1) p237

68   Ibid, p58

69   Uphoff, N (1992) *Learning from Gal Oya: Possibilities for Participatory Development and Post-Newtonian Social Science*, Cornell University Press; Ostrom, E (1990) *Governing the Commons: the Evolution of Institutions for Collective Action*, Cambridge University Press

70   Jutte, R (1994) *Poverty and Deviance in Early-Modern Europe*, Cambridge University Press, p95

71   Schulz, M (1995) 'The Informal Sector and Structural Adjustment: Strengthening Collective Coping Mechanisms in Tanzania', *Small Enterprise Development* 6(1), pp4–14

72   Hawthorn, G (1993) 'Sub-Saharan Africa', in Held, D (ed) *Prospects for Democracy*, Polity Press, Cambridge

73   Edwards, M, et al, op cit (note 61)

74   Mulgan, G (1997) *Connexity: How to Live in a Connected World*, Chatto and Windus, London

75   Mundle, S (1998) 'Financing Human Resource Development in the Advanced Asian Economies', *World Development* 26(4)

76   Arenas de Mesa, A and Bertranou, F (1997) 'Learning from Social Security Reforms: Two Different Cases', *World Development* 25(3), pp329–48; Mesa-Largo, C (1997) 'Social Welfare Reform in the Context of Liberalisation', *World Development* 25(4), pp497–517; *The Guardian*, 14 July 1997

77   Colclough, C (1996) 'Education and the Market: Which Parts of the Neo-liberal Solution are Correct?' *World Development* 24(4), pp589–610

78   Bloom, G and Xingyuan, G (1997) 'Health Sector Reform in China', *IDS Bulletin* 28(1), pp1–11

79   Mernissi, F (1975) *Beyond the Veil: Male-Female Dynamics in a Modern Muslim Society*, John Wiley, London

80   Edwards, M, op cit (note 61); Hart, R (1997) *Children's Participation: the Theory and Practice of Involving Young Citizens in Community Development and Environmental Care*, Earthscan, London

81   Reding, A (1996) 'The Next Mexican Revolution', *World Policy Journal* XIII (3), pp61–70

82   Reilly, C (ed) (1995) *New Paths to Democratic Development in Latin America: the Rise of NGO-Municipal Collaboration*, Lynne Rienner, Boulder

83   Reilly, C, op cit (note 82); Smith Pyle, K (1997) 'NGOs in Recife: from Policy Advocate to Policy-maker', *Grassroots Development* 21(1), pp12–23

84   Rifkin, J, op cit (note 48, Chapter 1), p280

85   Scott Peck, M (1992) *The Different Drum*, Arrow, London, p17

86   Wainwright, H (1994) *Arguments for a New Left: Answering the Free-Market Right*, Blackwell, Oxford; Marquand, D, op cit (note 7); Dionne, E J (1996) *They Only Look Dead: Why Progressives Will Dominate the Next Political Era*, Simon and Schuster, New York; Marr, A (1996) *Ruling Britannia*, Chatto and Windus, London

87   Fowler, A, op cit (note 4, Chapter 4); Fox, J and Hernandez, L
     'Offsetting the Iron Law of Oligarchy', *Grassroots Development* 13(2),
     pp8–15
88   Putnam, R, op cit (note 26)
89   Rademacher, A and Tamang, D (1993) *Democracy, Development and
     NGOs*, SEARCH, Kathmandu
90   Cited in Reilly, C, op cit (note 82) p7
91   Putnam, R (1993) *Making Democracy Work: Civic Traditions in
     Modern Italy*, Princeton University Press. For earlier work on social
     capital, see Coleman, J (1990) *Foundations of Social Theory*, Harvard
     University Press. An alternative interpretation was elaborated by
     Gramsci: see Pearce, J, (1997) *Civil Society, Trick or Treat?* CIIR,
     London and Bratton, M, op cit (note 109, Chapter 3)
92   Putnam, R op cit (note 91)
93   Hall, J (1995) *Civil Society: Theory, History, Comparison*, Polity
     Press, Cambridge; Fierlbeck, K (1997) 'Civil Society', in Rai, S and
     Grant, W (eds) *Globalising Democracy: Power, Legitimacy and the
     Interpretation of Democratic Ideas*, Manchester University Press;
     Bratton, M (1994) *Civil Society and Political Transition in Africa*,
     Institute for Development Research, Boston
94   Salamon, L and Anheier, H (1997) *The Non-profit Sector in the
     Developing World*, Manchester University Press
95   Fowler, A, op cit (note 4, Chapter 4) p234
96   Pearce, J (1997) op cit (note 91) p105
97   Brittan, S, op cit (note 6); South Commission (1990) *The Challenge
     to the South*, Oxford University Press
98   Wainwright, H (1994) *Arguments for a New Left: Answering the Free-
     Market Right*, Blackwell, Oxford, p272
99   Mulgan, G, op cit (note 74); Altvater, E (1993) *The Future of the
     Market*, Verso, London; Mansbridge, J (ed) (1990) *Beyond Self-
     Interest*, University of Chicago Press
100 London Bench-Marking Group (1997) *Companies in Communities:
     Getting the Measure*, LBG, London, p4
101 Micklethwait, J and Wooldridge, A, op cit (note 22, Chapter 1)
102 Douthwaite, R (1992) *The Growth Illusion*, Green Books, Bideford,
     p301
103 Titmuss, R (1970) *The Gift Relationship: from Human Blood to Social
     Policy*, Allen and Unwin, London
104 Rose, H (1994) *Love, Power and Knowledge: Towards a Feminist
     Transformation of the Social Sciences*, Polity Press, Cambridge
105 Mulgan, G, op cit (note 74) p133
106 Ridley, M, op cit (note 1, Chapter 1) p265
107 Dahrendorf, R (1996) 'Economic Opportunity, Civil Society and
     Political Liberty', *Development and Change* 27(2), pp229–49
108 Bellerby, J, op cit (note 2)
109 Bellerby, J, ibid, p 47

CHAPTER 9

1   Davinder Lamba, Mazingira Institute, Nairobi, Kenya
2   Goulet, D (1995) *Development Ethics: a Guide to Theory and Practice*, Zed Press, London, p186
3   *The Guardian*, 7 January 1998
4   *The Economist*, 13 January 1998
5   Rosenau, J and Cziempiel, E (1992) *Governance Without Government: Order and Change in World Politics*, Cambridge University Press; Young, O (1994) *International Governance: Protecting the Environment in a Stateless Society*, Cornell University Press; Keohane, R and Ostrom, E (eds) (1995) *Local Commons and Global Interdependence*, Sage, London
6   Slaughter, A (1997) 'The Real New World Order', *Foreign Affairs* 73(5), pp183–7
7   Burnheim, J (1986) 'Democracy, Nation States and the World System', in Held, D and Pollitt, C (eds) *New Forms of Democracy*, Sage, London
8   Brack, D (1996) *International Trade and the Montreal Protocol*, Earthscan, London; Gosovic, B (1992) *The Quest for World Environmental Co-operation*, Routledge, London; Vogler, J and Imber, M (eds) (1996) *The Environment and International Relations*, Routledge, London
9   In the form of more efficient refrigeration and gas canister technology; Brack, D, op cit (note 8); *The Economist*, 13 September 1997
10 Agenda 21, the Rio Declaration, and the Forest Principles are non-binding; the Conventions on Climate Change, Biological Diversity and Desertification are binding but weak. See Brown, K (1997) 'The Road from Rio', *Journal of International Development* 9(3), pp383–9
11 Pimbert, M (1997) 'Issues Emerging in Implementing the Convention on Biological Diversity', *Journal of International Development*, 9(3), pp415–25
12 Brenton, T (1994) *The Greening of Machiavelli: the Evolution of Environmental Politics*, Earthscan, London; ITDG/NEF (1992) *The Gene Traders: Security or Profit in Food Production?* New Economics Foundation, London
13 Redclift, M (1997) 'Development and Global Environmental Change', *Journal of International Development*, 9(3), pp391–401
14 *The Guardian*, 10 and 11 December 1997
15 *The Economist*, 14 June and 6 December 1997
16 WorldWatch Institute (1996) *State of the World 1996*, Earthscan, London
17 Schelling, T (1997) 'The Cost of Combating Global Warming: Facing the Trade-offs', *Foreign Affairs* 76(3), pp8–14
18 One half of a 5.2 per cent reduction from emissions levels in 1990, by 2012; *The Economist*, 13 December 1997
19 Weizsacker, E, et al, op cit (note 44, Chapter 1)
20 Humphreys, D (1996) *Forest Politics: the Evolution of International Co-operation*, Earthscan, London, p164; Parikh, J, et al, (1997)

'Climate Change, North-South Co-operation, and Collective Decision-Making', *Journal of International Development* 9(3), pp403–13

21   Reich, R, op cit (note 48, Chapter 1) p313
22   Holdgate, M (1996) *From Care to Action: Making a Sustainable World*, Earthscan, London
23   de Mello Lemos, M (1998) 'The Politics of Pollution Control in Brazil', *World Development* 26(1), pp75–88
24   Roddick, J (1995) *Earth Summit North and South: Building a Safe House in the Winds of Change*, Centre for Development Studies, Leeds University
25   Humphreys, D, op cit (note 20)
26   Cited in Raghavan, C (1997) 'A New Trade Order in a World of Disorder?' in Griesgraber, J and Gunter, B (eds), *World Trade: Towards Fair and Free Trade in the 21st Century*, Pluto Press, London, p18
27   *The Economist*, 26 July 1997
28   Griffith-Jones, S (1996) 'The Mexican Peso Crisis', *IDS Discussion Paper* 354, Brighton; IDB (1995) *Overcoming Volatility: Economic and Social Progress in Latin America*, Inter-American Development Bank, Washington DC; *The Economist*, 27 September 1997
29   Over US$100 billion compared to US$53 billion for Mexico: *The Economist*, 8 November 1997; *The Guardian*, 4 and 8 December 1997
30   Fitzgerald, E (1995) 'The International Financial Institutions, the UN System and a Global Capital Market', *IDS Bulletin* 28(4), pp84–91; DAC (1996) *Development Co-operation Report 1996*, OECD, Paris; Streeten, P, op cit (note 12, Chapter 7)
31   Block, F (1996) 'Controlling Global Finance', (3), pp24–34; Taylor, L and Pieper, U (1996) 'Reconciling Economic Reform and Sustainable Human Development: Social Consequences of Neo-Liberalism', *UNDP Discussion Paper* 2, New York
32   15 October 1997
33   DAC, op cit (note 30) p49
34   Asaria, I (1995) *The World Bank – the next 50 years*, NGO Working Group on the World Bank, Washington DC; LeQuesne, C (1996) *Reforming World Trade: the Social and Environmental Priorities*, Oxfam, Oxford
35   ODI (1995) 'Developing Countries in the WTO', *Briefing Paper 3*, Overseas Development Institute, London
36   Dionne, E (1996) *They Only Look Dead: why Progressives will Dominate the Next Political Era*, Simon and Schuster, New York
37   Thomas, R (1997) 'The WTO and Trade Co-operation Between the ACP and the EU: Assessing the Options', *Working Paper 16*, ECDPM, Maastricht
38   Madden, P and Madeley, J (1993) *Winners and Losers: the Impact of the GATT Uruguay Round on Developing Countries*, Christian Aid, London
39   Atkinson, J (1995) *APEC – Winners and Losers*, ACFOA, Canberra
40   Khor, M (1996) 'The WTO and Foreign Investment: implications and Alternatives for Developing Countries', *Development in Practice* 6(4), pp304–14

41   Pimbert, M, op cit (note 11) p422; Griffin, K and McKinley, T
      (1996) 'New Approaches to Development Co-operation', *Discussion
      Paper 7*, UNDP, New York
42   Thomas, R, op cit (note 37) They are 'non-reciprocity', 'differentia-
      tion', and regional trade arrangements. In reality the rules and
      exemptions of regional agreements like the Lomé Convention are a
      great deal more complex than this. For a good summary, see Institute
      of Development Studies (1997) *Development Research Insights 24*,
      IDS, Brighton
43   ODI, op cit (note 35)
44   *The Economist*, 1 March 1997
45   The judgement gave the EU 15 months to comply; IDS, op cit (note
      42); *The Guardian*, 8 and 17 October 1997
46   Joseph, M (1997) 'Post-Lome Arrangements Must Mirror the
      Principles of Lome: a Perspective from the Banana Sectors of the
      Windward Islands', *Working Paper 18*, ECDPM, Maastricht
47   *The Guardian*, 8 October 1997
48   Griffin, K and McKinley, T, op cit (note 41)
49   By the International Treaty on Chemical Weapons ratified in 1997;
      The Guardian, 23 April 1997
50   *The Guardian*, 24 August 1996
51   *The Economist*, 23 August 1997; *The Guardian*, 11 October 1997
52   Melvern, L (1995) *The Ultimate Crime: Who Betrayed the UN and
      Why?* Allison and Busby, London, p354
53   As recommended by the Carnegie Commission on Preventing Deadly
      Conflict in 1998: *The Guardian*, 9 January 1998
54   *The Economist*, 22 January 1997; Imber, M (1996) *The
      Democratisation of the UN: a Sustainable Imperative?* Department of
      International Relations, University of Aberdeen
55   Mandelbaum, M (1995) cited in Weiss, T, 'Overcoming the Somalia
      Syndrome', *Global Governance* 1, pp171–87
56   Halliday, F (1994) *Sleepwalking Through History? The New World and
      its Discontents*, London School of Economics, Centre for the Study of
      Global Governance, London
57   As concluded by Lord Carrington's report for the USA United
      Nations Association in 1998: *The Guardian*, 9 January 1998. See also:
      Minear, L (1997) *Humanitarian Action and Peacekeeping Operations*,
      UNITAR, Singapore; Touval, S (1994) 'Why the UN Fails', *Foreign
      Affairs* 73(5), pp44–57
58   Haass, R (1997) 'Sanctioning Madness', *Foreign Affairs* 76(6),
      pp74–85; Somavia, J (1997) 'The Humanitarian Responsibilities of the
      UN Security Council', *Development in Practice* 7(4), pp353–62
59   Rupesinghe, K (ed) (1992) *Internal Conflict and Governance*,
      Macmillan, London; Slim, H (1997) 'Relief Agencies and Moral
      Standing in War', *Development in Practice* 7(4), pp342–52
60   *New Statesman*, 8 November 1996
61   *The Guardian*, 23 February 1998; Dilip Hiro in the *New Statesman*,
      13 February 1998
62   *The Economist*, 7 June 1997
63   Hoffman, S (1981) *Duties Beyond Borders: on the Limits and
      Possibilities of Ethical International Politics*, Syracuse University Press

64 Mernissi, F (1993) *Islam and Democracy: Fear of the Modern World*, Virago, London, p167
65 *The Guardian*, 5 and 16 April 1997
66 *The Guardian*, 3 September 1997; *The Economist*, 22 November 1997
67 Hausermann, J (1997) *What are Human rights and how are they Protected?* Rights and Humanity, London
68 Vincent, J (1986) *Human Rights and International Relations*, Cambridge University Press.
69 Higgins, R (1994) *International Law and How We Use It*, Clarendon Press, Oxford. Generally accepted principles of law are contained in the International Bill of Human Rights, and an expanding body of international law codified under the auspices of the International Court of Justice and the General Assembly, including the Genocide Convention (1948), the Declaration on Torture (1975), and the European and American Conventions on Human Rights (1950 and 1969)
70 Alston, P (ed) (1994) *The Best Interests of the Child; Reconciling Culture and Human Rights*, Clarendon Press, Oxford, p19. See also Etzioni, A (1997) *'The New Golden Rule: Community and Morality in a New Democratic Society*, Profile Books, London
71 Nussbaum, M and Glover, J (1995) *Women, Culture and Development: a Study of Human Capabilities*, Clarendon Press, Oxford; Gasper, D (1997) 'Culture and Development Ethics', *Development and Change* 27(4), pp627–61; Slim, H (1997) 'Relief Agencies and Moral Standing in War', *Development in Practice* 7(4), pp342–52
72 Halliday, F (1994) *Rethinking International Relations*, Macmillan, London
73 Mernissi, F, op cit (note 64)
74 Higgins, R, op cit (note 69) p185; Kaufman, J (1995) 'The UN at 50: Some Unsolved Problems', *IDS Bulletin* 28(4), pp68–73
75 Vincent, J, op cit (note 68) p54
76 Held, D, writing in the *New Statesman*, 29 August 1997; Archibugi, D and Held, D (eds) (1995) *Cosmopolitan Democracy: an Agenda for a new World Order*, Polity Press, Cambridge; Held, D (1995) *Democracy and the Global Order: from the Modern State to Cosmopolitan Governance*, Polity Press, Cambridge; Falk, R (1995) *On Humane Governance: Toward a new Global Politics*, Polity Press, Cambridge; Hirst, P (1994) *Associative Democracy: New Forms of Economic and Social Governance*, Polity Press, Cambridge; Giddens, A (1996) *Beyond Left and Right*, Polity Press, Cambridge; Zolo, D (1997) *Cosmopolis: Prospects for World Government*, Polity Press, Cambridge
77 Hirst, P and Thompson, G, op cit (note 17, Chapter 1)
78 Cited in Scott Peck, M (1992) *The Different Drum*, Arrow Books, London, p274
79 Sandel, M, op cit (note 47, Chapter 1)
80 Sandel, M, ibid
81 Streeten, P, op cit (note 12, Chapter 7); Seers, D, op cit (note 3, Chapter 3); Thurow, L, op cit (note 30, Chapter 1)
82 Interestingly, this option was supported during post-war negotiations by US President Franklin Roosevelt and British Prime Minister

Winston Churchill, who felt uncomfortable with the leap from nation state to the new United Nations: Lind, M (1995) 'Twilight of the UN', *New Republic* 30 October 1995

83   Knight, W (1996) 'Towards a Subsidiarity Model for Peacemaking and Preventive Diplomacy', *Third World Quarterly* 17(1), pp31–52

84   Young, O, op cit (note 5); Keohane, R and Ostrom, E, op cit (note 5)

85   Like the European Convention on Human Rights; Higgins, R, op cit (note 69); Hausermann, J, op cit (note 67)

86   Bergsten, F (1997) *The Asian Monetary Crisis: Proposed Remedies*, Institute for International Economics, Washington DC. See also: Stewart, F (1995) 'Biases in Global Markets: can the Forces of Inequality and Marginalisation be Modified?' in ul Haq, M, et al (eds) *The UN and the Bretton Woods Institutions: New Challenges for the 21st Century*, Macmillan, London; South Centre (1996) *UNCTAD: a New Lease of Life*, Geneva; South Centre (1996) *For a Strong and Democratic United Nations*, Geneva; South Centre (1996) *Enhancing South-South Trade*, Geneva

87   Stewart, F, ibid, p182; South Commission (1990) *The Challenge to the South*, Oxford University Press; South Centre (1993) *Facing the Challenge: Responses to the Report of the South Commission*, Zed Press, London

88   Mittelman, J (1995) 'Rethinking the International Division of Labour in the Context of Globalisation', *Third World Quarterly* 16(2), pp273–95; Dahrendorf, R (1996) 'Economic Opportunity, Civil Society and Political Liberty', *Development and Change* 27(2), pp229–49

89   *The Economist*, 18 October 1997

90   Lind, M,op cit (note 82)

91   Shaw, M (1994) *Global Society and International Relations*, Polity Press, Cambridge; Wapner, P (1995) 'Politics Beyond the State: Environmental Activism and World Civic Politics', *World Politics* 47, pp311–40; de Oliveira, M and Tandon, R (1994) *Citizens Strengthening Global Civil Society*, CIVICUS, Washington DC; Princen, T and Finger, M (1994) *Environmental NGOs in World Politics: Linking the Local and the Global*, Routledge, London

92   Slaughter, A, op cit (note 6)

93   Vogler, J (1995) *The Global Commons: A Regime Analysis*, John Wiley, Chichester

94   Cleary, S (1995) *In Whose Interest? NGO Advocacy Campaigns and the Poorest*, South Bank University, London; Nelson, P (1996) *Conflict, Legitimacy and Effectiveness: Who Speaks for Whom in Transnational NGO Networks*, ARNOVA, New York; van Rooy, A (1997) 'The Frontiers of Influence: NGO Lobbying at the World Food Conference, the Earth Summit and Beyond', *World Development* 25(1), pp93–114; Wilkinson, M (1996) 'Lobbying for Fair Trade: Northern NGOs, the European Community, and the GATT Uruguay Round', *Third World Quarterly* 17(2), pp251–67; CIIR/Christian Aid (1995) *NGO Campaigning on Trade Issues: Perspectives from Europe*, CIIR, London

95   Malhotra, K (1997) *A Southern Perspective on Partnership for Development*, IDRC, Ottawa; Gaventa, J (1998) 'Crossing the Great

Divide: Building Links between NGOs in North and South', in Lewis, D (ed) *Bridging the Chasm: International Perspectives on Voluntary Action*, Earthscan, London; Covey, J (1995) 'Accountability and Effectiveness in NGO Policy Alliances', in Edwards, M and Hulme, D (eds), op cit (note 23, Chapter 7)

96 Righter, R (1995) *Utopia Lost: the United Nations and World Order*, 20th Century Fund, New York

97 Worldwide, not just California. Imber, M, op.cit (note 54)

98 Winston Churchill, cited in Jolly, R (1995) 'UN Reform: Focus for Action', *IDS Bulletin* 26(4), pp8–14

99 Independent Working Group on the Future of the UN (1995) *The UN in its Second Half-Century*, IWG, Geneva

100 ODI (1997) 'The UN's Role in Grant-Financed Development', *Briefing Paper 2*, Overseas Development Institute, London

101 UN Press Release, New York, 16 July 1997

102 Ibid

103 *The Guardian*, 21 March 1997, *The Economist*, 8 November 1997

104 Burnheim, J, op cit (note 7)

105 Perraton, J (1997) 'The Global Economy', in Kelly, G, et al (eds) *Stakeholder Capitalism*, Macmillan, London

106 Development Committee (1996) *Serving a Changing World: report of the Task Force on the Multilateral Development Banks*, Development Committee, Washington DC

107 Caulfield, C (1997) *Masters of Illusion: the World Bank and the Poverty of Nations*, Macmillan, London

108 Rich, B (1994) *Mortgaging the Earth: the World Bank, Environmental Impoverishment and the Crisis of Development*, Earthscan, London; Caulfield, C, ibid

109 Blustein, P (1996) 'Loan Ranger', *Washington Post Magazine*, 10 November 1996

110 Pioneering work in these areas was carried out by UNICEF, UNDP, NGOs, and university economists, with extra pressure from Japan on the role of states

111 Abugre, C (1995) *IDA Lending, Structural Adjustment and Participation: Toward an African NGO Position*, Third World Network, Accra; Udall, L (1994) 'Grounds for Divorce: why IDA should De-link from the World Bank', in Cavanagh, J, et al, op cit (note 38, Chapter 8); Mosley, P (1997) 'The World Bank, Global Keynsianism and the Distribution of the Gains from Growth', *World Development* 25(11), pp1949–56

112 McRae, H, op cit (note 33, Chapter 1); Wood, A (1997) *The IMF's ESAF – what role for development?* Bretton Woods Project, London; Wood, A (1997) *The IMF's Final Frontier: Assessing Second-Generation Reforms*, Bretton Woods Project, London

113 *The Economist*, 13 December 1997

114 *The Guardian*, 5 January 1998

115 ul Haq, M (1995) 'An Economic Security Council', *IDS Bulletin* 26 (4), pp20–7

116 Cox, R, (ed) (1997) *The New Realism: Perspectives on Multilateralism and World Order*, Macmillan, London; Etzioni, A, op cit (note 70)

117   Rieff, D (1996) 'Whose Internationalism, Whose Isolationism?' *World Policy Journal* XIII (2), pp1–12
118   Cox, M (1995) *US Foreign Policy After the Cold War: Superpower Without a Mission?* Pinter, London; Walker, M (1997) 'Present at the Solution: Madeleine Albright's Ambitious Foreign Policy', *World Policy Journal* XIV (1), pp1–10

CHAPTER 10

1   *The Observer*, 30 November 1997
2   *Modern Times*, BBC2, October 1997
3   Sandel, M, op cit (note 47, Chapter 1), p343
4   UNRISD (1995) *After the Social Summit: Implementing the Programme of Action*, UNRISD, Geneva
5   Gellner, E (1983) *Nations and Nationalism*, Blackwell, Oxford; Goulet, D (1995) *Development Ethics: a Guide to Theory and Practice*, Zed Press, London
6   Goulet, D, ibid; Crocker, D (1997) 'Development Ethics', in Craig, E (ed) *Routledge Encyclopaedia of Philosophy*, Routledge, London
7   Following the philosophy of John Rawls: see Blocker, H and Smith, E (1990) *John Rawls' Theory of Social Justice: an Introduction*, Ohio University Press, Athens
8   Goulet, D, op cit (note 5); Goulet, D (1977) *The Cruel Choice: a New Concept in the Theory of Development*, Atheneum, New York; Qizilbash, M (1996) 'Ethical Development', *World Development* 24(7), pp1209–21; Kung, H and Kuschel, K (1993) *A Global Ethic: the Declaration of the Parliament of the World's Religions*, SCM Press, London; Kung, H (1991) *Global Responsibility: in Search of a New World Ethic*, SCM Press, London
9   FAO/FFHC (1987) 'The Golden Rule', *Ideas and Action* 174(3)
10   A view usually ascribed to the philosophy of Kant: see Scruton, R (1994) *Modern Philosophy: an Introduction and Survey*, Sinclair-Stevenson, London, p285
11   Evans, P (1993) 'Building an Integrative Approach to International and Domestic Politics: Reflections and Projections', in Evans, P, et al (eds), *Double-Edged Diplomacy*, University of California Press, Berkeley
12   Knight, B and Stokes, P (1996) *The Deficit in Civil Society in the UK*, Foundation for Civil Society, Birmingham
13   See Reich, R, op cit (note 48, Chapter 1)
14   Mohan Rao, J (1997) 'Ranking Foreign Donors: an Index Combining the Scale and Equity of Aid', *World Development* 25(6), pp947–61; Riddell, R (1996) *Trends in International Co-operation*, Aga Khan Foundation, Ottawa
15   Bread for the World (1995) *Causes of Hunger*, Washington DC
16   Galbraith, J K, op cit (note 26, Chapter 8); Bellah, R, op cit (note 26, Chapter 8)
17   Glyn-Jones, A (1997) *Holding up a Mirror: How Civilisations Decline*, Century, London
18   Elliot, C (1987) *Comfortable Compassion: Power, Poverty and the Church*, Hodder and Stoughton, London

19   Fromm, E (1976) *To Have or To Be?* Bantam, New York
20   Foy, C and Helmich, H (eds) (1996) *Public Support for International Development*, OECD, Paris; Action Aid et al (1997) *The Reality of Aid*, Action Aid, London
21   Singer, P (1993) *Practical Ethics*, Cambridge University Press, pp229–31.
22   Goulet, D, op cit (note 5); Engel, R and Engel, J (1990) *Ethics of Environment and Development: Global Challenge: International Response* (1990), Belhaven Press, London
23   Anand, S and Sen, A (1996) *Sustainable Human Development: Concepts and Priorities*, UNDP, New York
24   Summers, L, cited in *The Economist*, 18 October 1997
25   Singer, H (1984) 'The Ethics of Aid', *Discussion Paper 195*, Institute of Development Studies, Brighton
26   Cited in Dass, R and Gorman, P (1988) *How Can I Help?* Knopf, New York, p20
27   Waterman, P (1993) 'Internationalism is Dead: Long Live Global Solidarity', in Brecher, J, et al (eds) *Global Visions: Beyond the New World Order*, Black Rose Books, Montreal
28   *The Guardian*, 8 October 1997
29   Reich, R, op cit (note 48, Chapter 1); CCIC (1996) *From Donors to Global Citizens*, Canadian Council for International Co-operation, Ottawa
30   Opeskin, B (1996) 'The Moral Foundations of Foreign Aid', *World Development* 24(1), pp21–44
31   Hain, P (1996) *Ayes to the Left; a Future for Socialism*, Lawrence and Wishart, London
32   North, R (1990) *War, Peace and Survival*, Westview Press, Boulder, p251; Corbridge, S (1994) 'Post-Marxism and Post-Colonialism: the Needs and Rights of Distant Strangers', in Booth, D (ed) *Re-defining Social Development: Theory, Research and Practice*, Longman, London
33   NEXUS Internet Newsletter, 24 November 1997
34   OECD (1995) *Linkages: OECD and Major Developing Economies*, OECD, Paris, p85
35   Reich, R, op cit (note 48, Chapter 1) p311
36   Dower, N (1996) *Ethics, Global Stewardship and the Good Life*, Department of Philosophy, University of Aberdeen
37   Knight, B and Stokes, P, op cit (note 12) p12
38   Putnam, R (1995) 'Bowling Alone: America's Declining Social Capital', *Journal of Democracy* 6(1), pp65–78. Child sponsorship is a fund-raising technique whereby members of the public donate to charity in return for progress reports on a particular child.
39   Rose, C (1993) 'Beyond the Struggle for Proof: Factors Changing the Environmental Movement', *Environmental Values* 2, pp285–98
40   Brenton, T (1994) *The Greening of Machiavelli*, Earthscan, London
41   Holdgate, M (1996) *From Care to Action: Making a Sustainable World*, Earthscan, London
42   Luke, G (1997) *Australian Attitudes to Foreign Aid*, ACFOA, Canberra
43   *The Guardian*, 3 January 1998
44   *The Guardian*, 22 September 1997

45   Yankelovic, D (1996) 'Public Judgement on Development Aid', in Foy, C and Helmich, H (eds), op cit (note 20); Smillie, I (1996) 'Mixed Messages: Public Opinion and Development Assistance in the 1990s', in Foy and Nelmich, ibid; Young, O, op cit (note 5, Chapter 9)

46   Orr, D (1995) 'Educating for the Environment: Higher Education's Challenge for the Next Century', *Change* (May–June), pp43–6

47   Oxfam, Save the Children and Action Aid in the UK all made substantial cuts in 1995–6. These may be partially offset by higher government spending on development education announced in the White Paper on International Development in 1997; DFID (1997) '*Eliminating World Poverty: A Challenge for the 21st Century*', Department for International Development, London

48   Smillie, I (1995) *The Alms Bazaar: Altruism Under Fire*, IT Publications, London

49   Action Aid, ICVA/EUROSTEP (1997) *The Reality of Aid 1997*, Earthscan, London

50   This could be monitored and enforced in the UK by the Advertising Standards Authority, as I proposed to the Commission on the Future of the Voluntary Sector in 1996 (Edwards, M, *International Development NGOs: Legitimacy, Accountability, Regulation and Roles*, CFVS, London)

51   Cited in Edwards, M (ed) (1983) *Arriving Where We Started: 25 Years of Voluntary Service Overseas*, IT Publications, London

52   *The Guardian*, 17 July 1996

53   For example, reductions in carbon dioxide emissions (later agreed at Kyoto), a ban on landmines, and social chapters in all key trade agreements. See Ghazi, P, in the *New Statesman*, 29 November 1996 and Young, H, in *The Guardian*, 9 April 1996

54   Gaventa, J (1998) 'Crossing the Great Divide: Building Links between NGOs and CBOs in North and South', in Lewis, D (ed) *Voluntary Action in International Perspective*, Earthscan, London

55   Malhotra, K (1997) *Partnership: a View from the South*, IDRC, Ottawa. Oxfam has also supported some innovative alliances between Caribbean and European groups

56   Elliot, L, writing in *The Guardian*, 22 September 1997; Korten, D (1990) *Getting to the 21st Century: Voluntary Action and the Global Agenda*, Kumarian Press, West Hartford; Clark, J (1991) *Democratising Development: the Role of Voluntary Organisations*, Earthscan, London

57   Smillie, I (1996) 'Mixed Messages: Public Opinion and Development Assistance in the 1990s', in Foy, C and Helmich, H, (eds) op cit (note 20)

58   Research by the UK Home Office found that volunteering among those aged between 18 and 24 fell from 55 per cent in 1991 to 43 per cent in 1997; for the 18 to 22 year age group, the proportion of individuals making donations to charities fell from 17 per cent in 1971 to 6 per cent in 1994 (*The Guardian*, 21 January 1998)

59   These issues are explored in much greater detail in three books edited by Edwards, M and Hulme, D op cit (notes 65 and 67, Chapter 1)

60   Fowler, A, op cit (note 4, Chapter 4), using an analogy from Stephen Commins of World Vision International

61 Maren, M (1994) 'A Different Form of Child Abuse', *Penthouse*, December, p48
62 PLAN-UK mailshot, 1997
63 CCIC, op cit (note 29)
64 World Vision-UK (1997) *Supporting Transformational Development Through Child Sponsorship*, World Vision, Milton Keynes
65 Dass, R and Gorman, P, op cit (note 26)
66 Black, M (1992) *A Cause for our Times*, Oxfam, Oxford
67 Cited in Richards, M (1996) *Economics, Ethics and Deforestation*, Department of Philosophy, University of Aberdeen, p6

CHAPTER 11

1   Daly, H (1994) Farewell lecture to the World Bank, in Cavanagh, J, et al (eds) *Beyond Bretton Woods: Alternatives to the Global Economic Order*, Pluto Press, London, p111
2   Oxfam-UK field-worker in Zambia, (1987) pers com
3   Wildavsky, A (1979) *Speaking Truth to Power: the Art and Craft of Policy Analysis*, Little Brown, Boston; Chambers, R, *The Primacy of the Personal*, in Edwards, M and Hulme, D (eds) op cit (note 67, Chapter 1)
4   Dass, R and Gorman, P (1988) *How Can I Help? Stories and Reflections on Service*, Knopf, New York; Maxwell, N (1984) *From Knowledge to Wisdom*, Basil Blackwell, Oxford
5   Schumacher, E (1980) *Good Work*, Abacus, London
6   The title is taken from a well-known Australian film of the same name
7   Fowler, A (1995) 'Assessing NGO Performance: Difficulties, Dilemmas and a Way Ahead', in Edwards, M and Hulme, D (eds) op cit (note 67, Chapter 1)
8   Samoff, J (1996) 'Chaos and Certainty in Development', *World Development* 24(4), pp611–33; Guba, L (ed) *The Paradigm Dialogue*, Sage, London; Lincoln, Y and Guba, E (1985) *Naturalistic Enquiry*, Sage, London
9   Gleick, J (1987) *Chaos: an Emerging Science*, Pan, London, p24
10 Senge, P (1990) *The Fifth Discipline: the Art and Craft of the Learning Organisation*, Random House, London; Drucker, P (1990) *Managing the Non-Profit Organisation*, Harper Collins, New York; Peters, T (1994) *The Pursuit of WOW!* Macmillan, London; Handy, C (1993) *Understanding Organisations*, Penguin, Harmondsworth. For NGOs see: Edwards, M (1997) 'Organisational Learning in Non-Governmental Organisations: What have we Learned?', *Public Administration and Development* 17, pp235–50; Edwards, M (1994) 'NGOs in the Age of Information', *IDS Bulletin* 25, pp117–24
11 Argyris, C and Schon, D (1978) *Organisational Learning: a Theory of Action Perspective*, Addison Wesley, Menlo Park
12 Angelides, C and Caiden, G (1994) 'Adjusting Policy Thinking to Global Pragmatics and Future Problematics', *Public Administration and Development* 14(3), pp223–41
13 Cited in a book review by Bywater, M in the *New Statesman*, 9 January 1998

14   Roche, C (1996) *Institutional Learning in Oxfam – Some Thoughts*, Oxfam, Oxford
15   Edwards, M, op cit (note 10)
16   I have explored this theme in detail elsewhere: see Edwards, M (1989) 'The Irrelevance of Development Studies', *Third World Quarterly*, (January); Edwards, M (1994) 'New Directions in Social Development Research: the Search for Relevance', in Booth, D (ed) *Redefining Social Development: Theory, Research and Practice*, Longman, London; Edwards, M (1996) 'The Getting of Wisdom: Educating the Reflective Practitioner', in Hamdi, N (ed) (1996) *Educating for Real*, IT Publications, London; Edwards, M (1997) *Development Studies and Development Practice; Divorce, Unhappy Marriage or the Perfect Union?* Kimmage Manor, Dublin, Conference on the Academic-Practitioner Interface in Development.
17   Brown, D (1997) 'Social Learning in North-South Coalitions', in Lewis, D (ed) *International Perspectives on Voluntary Action*, London, Earthscan; Covey, J (1995) 'Accountability and Effectiveness in NGO Policy Alliances', in Edwards, M and Hulme, D (eds), op cit (note 67, Chapter 1)
18   Buchanan-Smith, M et al (1994), 'Food Security: Let Them Eat Information', *IDS Bulletin* 25, pp69–80
19   UNIDO (1996) *Reform at UNIDO 1993–96*, Vienna
20   Handy, C (1995) *Beyond Certainty: the Changing Worlds of Organisations*, Hutchinson, London
21   Mintzberg, H (1994) *The Rise and Fall of Strategic Planning*, Prentice-Hall, London
22   Handy, C, op cit (notes 10 and 20); Fowler, A, op cit (note 7)
23   Wierdsma, A and Swieringha, J (1992) *Becoming a Learning Organisation*, Addison-Wesley, London
24   Biggs, S and Sumberg, J (1994) *Rural Mechanisation and Collegiate Engineering*, Natural Resources Institute, Chatham
25   World Bank (1996) *Social Development and Results on the Ground*, Washington DC
26   For a good description see Righter, R (1995) *Utopia Lost: the United Nations and World Order*, 20th Century Fund, New York
27   Fowler, A, op cit (note 7)
28   Wildavsky, A, op cit (note 3) p12
29   Korten, D (1980) 'Community Organisation and Rural Development: a Learning Process Approach', *Public Administration Review* 40(5), pp480–511
30   'Companhero critico'; see Gosling, L and Edwards, M (1995) *Toolkits: a Practical Guide to Assessment, Monitoring, Review and Evaluation*, Save the Children, London
31   Cited in McAndless, H (1997) *Accountability in Development Organisations*, McAndrew Associates, Ottawa, p6
32   *The Observer*, 7 August 1997
33   Edwards, M and Hulme, D, op cit (note 3)
34   Smillie, I (1995) 'Painting Canadian Roses Red', in Edwards, M and Hulme, D, op cit (note 3); Piccioto, R (1994) *Institutional Development and Bank Operations: the New Project Cycle*, The World Bank, Washington DC

35   Rondinelli, D (1993) *Strategic and Results-Based Management in CIDA*, CIDA, Ottawa
36   Drucker, P, op cit (note 10)
37   Shah, P and Shah, M (1995) 'Participatory Methods for Increasing Accountability' in Edwards, M and Hulme, D, op cit (note 3); Fox, J (1996) 'Promoting Independent Assessments of MDB Poverty-Reduction Investments: Bringing Civil Society In', *Institute for Development Research Report* 12(5), Boston
38   Zadek, S and Gatward, M (1995) 'Social Auditing or Bust?' in Edwards, M and Hulme, D, op cit (note 3)
39   This is a common theme in aid agency evaluations; see World Bank (1993) *Portfolio Management: Next Steps* (the Wapenhans Report) and (1994) *Progress Report on Implementing Next Steps*, The World Bank, Washington DC
40   World Bank (1994) *The World Bank and Participation* and (1996) *Social Development and Results on the Ground*, The World Bank, Washington DC
41   Grindle, M (1997) 'Divergent Cultures: Why Public Organisations Perform well in Developing Countries', *World Development* 25(4), pp481–95
42   Gurstein, M and Klee, J (1996) 'Towards a Management Renewal of the UN', *Public Administration and Development* 16(1), pp43–56, and 16(2), pp111–22
43   Righter, R, op cit (note 26) p283
44   Interview with Dr N.Van der Walle, Overseas Development Council, Washington DC, 18 June 1996; Righter, R, op cit (note 26)
45   Gurstein, M and Klee, J, op cit (note 42)
46   Edwards, M (1993) 'Does the Doormat Influence the Boot? NGOs and International Advocacy', *Development in Practice* 3 (3), pp163–75; Chambers, R (1997) *Whose Reality Counts? Putting the Last First*, IT Publications, London; Kardam, N (1993) 'Development Approaches and the Role of Policy Advocacy', *World Development* 21(11), pp1773–86; Weiss, T (ed) 'NGOs, the UN and Global Governance', *Third World Quarterly* 16(3)
47   Kardam, N, ibid; Van Rooy, A (1997) 'The Frontiers of Influence: NGO Lobbying at the 1974 World Food Conference, the 1992 Earth Summit and Beyond', *World Development* 25(1), pp93–114. Fox, J and Brown, L D (eds) (1998) *The Struggle for Accountability: The World Bank, NGOs and Social Movements*, MIT Press, Cambridge, MA
48   Miller, A (1983) *For Your Own Good: the Roots of Violence in Child-rearing*, Virago, London, and (1991) *Banished Knowledge: Facing Childhood Injuries*, Virago, London
49   Chambers, R (1993) 'All Power Deceives', *IDS Bulletin*, Spring; Elliot, C (1987) *Comfortable Compassion*, Hodder and Stoughton, London
50   Guggenbuhl-Craig, A (1971) *Power in the Helping Professions*, Spring Publications, Dallas
51   Friere, P (1972) *Pedagogy of the Oppressed*, Penguin, Harmondsworth
52   de Bono, E (1994) *Parallel Thinking*, Viking, London
53   Suzuki-Roshi, cited in Dass, R and Gorman, P, op cit (note 4) p208
54   Guggenbuhl-Craig, A, op cit (note 50)

55   Kaplan, A (1997) *The Development Practitioner's Handbook*, Pluto Press, London
56   Chambers, R (1994) 'The Origins and Practice of PRA', *World Development* 22(7–10), pp953–69, 22 (9) 1253–68, 22 (10) 1437–54
57   Cooke, B (1998) 'Participation, Process and Management: Lessons for Development in the History of Organisational Development', *Journal of International Development* 10(1), pp35–54
58   Friere, P (1972) *Pedagogy of the Oppressed*, Harmondsworth, Penguin
59   Schon, D (1983) *The Reflective Practitioner*, Temple-Smith, London, p3; and (1987) *Educating the Reflective Practitioner*, Jossey-Bass, San Francisco
60   This definition comes from Chambers Dictionary
61   Edwards, M (1996) 'Development Practice and Development Studies: working together', *Development in Practice* 6(1), pp67–9
62   *The Economist*, 20 April 1997
63   Bauman, Z (1993) *Postmodern Ethics*, Blackwell, Oxford
64   Lewis, C S 'The Screwtape Letters' in Bloomsbury Dictionary of Quotations (1987) Bloomsbury, London
65   Dass, R and Gorman, P, op cit (note 4)
66   Ibid; Dass, R and Bush, M (1992) *Compassion in Action: Setting Out on the Path of Service*, Bell Tower, New York; Samuels, A (1993) *The Political Psyche*, Routledge, London; Seidler, V, op cit (note 7 Chapter 2)
67   Guggenbuhl-Craig, A, op cit (note 50)
68   Chambers, R (1997) 'Responsible Well-Being: a Personal Agenda for Development', *World Development* 25(11), pp1743–54
69   Rose, H op cit (note 104, Chapter 8)
70   Skynner, R and Cleese, J (1993) *Life and How to Survive It*, Methuen, London, p412
71   Guggenbuhl-Craig, A, op cit (note 50) p155
72   Edwards, M, op cit (1989) (note 16), p135
73   Dass, R and Bush, M, op cit (note 66) p261

CHAPTER 12

1   Gurumayi, C (1999) *Courage and Contentment*, SYDA Foundation, South Fallsburg, New York, p130
2   *Bhagavadgita*, Chapter 17, verse 20
3   Hutton, W, in *The Observer*, 1 February 1998
4   *The Guardian*, 2 February 1998
5   Fukuyama, F (1994) *The End of History and the Last Man*, Penguin, Harmondsworth
6   This was a quotation used by television commentators on the day of Princess Diana's funeral in London in 1997
7   Thurow, L, op cit (note 30, Chapter 1)
8   Scott Peck, M (1992) *The Different Drum*, Arrow, London, p95
9   Cited in Orr, D (1995) 'Educating for the Environment', *Change* (May/June), pp43–6
10   Tagore, R (1993) cited in Coleridge, P, *Disability, Liberation and Development*, Oxfam, Oxford

11   Dass, R and Bush, M (1992) *Compassion in Action: Setting Out on the Path of Service*, Bell Tower, New York, p5
12   Cited in Scoones, I and Thompson, J (eds) *Beyond Farmer First*, IT Publications, London, p264
13   Cited in Curle, A (1990) *Tools for Transformation: a Personal Study*, Hawthorn Press, Stroud, p3
14   Gurumayi Chidvilasananda, op cit (note 1)

Index